THIS WAS HARLEM

"Harlem is distinctly an American community, a replica of which could not be found anywhere on earth except in this country. . . . it is what it is because of American customs, habits, environment, prejudices, and conditions."

—The New York *Age* (April 9, 1932)

THIS WAS HARLEM

HARLEM

A CULTURAL PORTRAIT, 1900-1950

Jervis Anderson

FARRAR STRAUS GIROUX · NEW YORK

The excerpt from "I Know What the Caged Bird Feels" (p. 34) from *The Complete Poems of Paul Laurence Dunbar* is reprinted by permission of Dodd, Mead & Co. Excerpt from *Music on My Mind* (pp. 154–57) by Willie Smith and George Hoefer, copyright © 1964 by Willie Smith and George Hoefer; reprinted by permission of Doubleday & Company, Inc. Selections from Claude McKay's "Harlem Dancer" (p. 195) and "If We Must Die" (p. 196) from *Selected Poems of Claude McKay*, © 1953, reprinted with the permission of Twayne Publishers, a division of G. K. Hall & Co., Boston. Excerpt from "The Weary Blues" (p. 204) from *Selected Poems of Langston Hughes*, copyright 1926, renewed 1954 by Langston Hughes; reprinted by permission of Alfred A. Knopf, Inc. First stanza from "To John Keats, Poet at Spring Time" (p. 206) in *On These I Stand* by Countee Cullen, copyright 1925 by Harper & Row, Publishers, Inc.; copyright 1952 by Ida M. Cullen; reprinted by permission of the publisher. Excerpt from "There's a Boat Dat's Leavin' Soon for New York" (p. 141) by George and Ira Gershwin, copyright © 1935 by Gershwin Publishing Corporation; copyright renewed, assigned to Chappell & Co., Inc.; international copyright secured; ALL RIGHTS RESERVED; used by permission. Excerpt from "Gimme a Pigfoot" (p. 157), words and music by Wesley Wilson, copyright © 1962 by Northern Music Co., New York, N.Y.; rights administered by MCA Music, a division of MCA, Inc., New York; used by permission; all rights reserved. Excerpt from "Harlem at Its Best" (p. 185), copyright © 1935; renewed 1963, Metro-Goldwyn-Mayer, Inc.; all rights administered and controlled by Robbins Music Corporation; all rights reserved; used by permission.

Acknowledgment is made to the Collection of American Literature, Beinecke Rare Book and Manuscript Library, Yale University, for permission to reprint correspondence from the James Weldon Johnson Memorial Collection of Negro Arts and Letters

Library of Congress Cataloging in Publication Data
Anderson, Jervis. This was Harlem.
    Includes index.
    (N.Y.)—History. I. Title.
F128.68.H3A65   974.7′1   81-17474   AACR2

For William Shawn

Contents

Part Four / Life and Letters

Part Five / Hard Times

Part Six / Style, Class, and Beyond

Illustrations

ILLUSTRATIONS

PART ONE

The Road Uptown

"Forgotten Streets"

IN ONE of the early months of 1914, St. James Presbyterian, a black church then occupying premises on West Fifty-first Street, in Manhattan, decided to move farther uptown, to Harlem. Blacks had been moving to Harlem ever since 1900, abandoning the West Side between the Twenties and the low Sixties, where they had lived for decades. Life on the congested and hostile middle West Side, with its over-crowded tenements and its increasing eruptions of anti-Negro feeling, had grown harder and harder for them, and in Harlem more and more houses were becoming available that were superior to any they had ever occupied elsewhere in Manhattan. Though by 1914 most blacks were moving to Harlem because they had nowhere else to go—not even to Brooklyn, where only those of a higher income could afford to live—more than a few were going there only because the district was becoming the fashionable place for Negroes to be. When St. James Presbyterian decided to join the migration, however, it was not following fashion but yielding to necessity. After observing the exodus from the West Side for more than ten years, during which other black churches had left for Harlem, St. James had judged the movement to be irreversible: Harlem was clearly replacing the West Side as the main black settlement in Manhattan, and to survive and remain useful the church, too, would have to move—to the place where a sizable number of its members were already living.

Until 1900, Harlem had been a virtually all-white neighborhood, and the blacks who began settling there at that time did not see themselves as the advance guard of a larger community. They en-countered enough hostility and resistance from white Harlemites—though not from their new landlords, whose surplus of apartments they were filling—to discourage any such view. They were satisfied just to have found themselves a refuge, away from the violence and the horrid tenement conditions of the West Side. The higher rents in

Harlem and the hostility of its white residents were prices worth paying for the chance to live in a quiet and attractive neighborhood and in apartments as nice as the ones to be found up there. However, if any of them were uneasy about being a part of a small and isolated black colony in white Harlem, it must have delighted them to notice that as the months passed their numbers were being augmented by other Negro refugees from the West Side, and that the churches, too, were joining the migration. To them, the latter development was probably the most heartening of all. Most blacks knew how accurately their churches could read the momentum of Negro migration. From what had occurred in the past when blacks had moved from one neighborhood to another, they could be sure that the churches would not be moving now unless their leaders had concluded that Harlem would be a future center of Manhattan's black population.

Most white Harlemites did not readily realize this; as they watched the early stages of black migration into their district, few of them imagined what the arrival of the churches signified. If some whites were already selling their homes and taking flight, it was not because they thought that Harlem would one day become predominantly black. They simply did not wish to share their community with people whose color they disliked, whose social and racial position they considered inferior to their own, whose cultural habits they deplored, and whose future effect upon property values they could well predict. The majority stayed behind—for a while, at least—and they did what they could to resist the Negro "invasion," as they called it; for they did not see a black takeover of their neighborhood as inevitable.

By 1900, blacks had been living in Manhattan for nearly three hundred years—since 1626, when eleven Africans were brought to the Dutch settlement of New Amsterdam to work under conditions resembling indentured servitude. Others were brought in after 1664, when—the Dutch having surrendered to the English—New Amsterdam had become New York and the indentured servants had become slaves. Some of these Africans worked in the village of Harlem, and from then on a handful of their descendants lived in the community —few enough to be ignored by most whites except the families they served. The majority of Manhattan's early black population worked first on the Dutch and later on the English holdings near the island's southern tip, and they remained in that area until after 1827, when slavery was abolished in New York. Their numbers had grown, of course. In 1830, the census reported that there were 13,976 blacks in Manhattan, most having been born in New York.

Early in the nineteenth century, this population began leaving the lower section of Manhattan. Moving steadily northward, they settled here and there on the island, a few along the East Side, the majority along the West Side. In a sense, they were not just on the move but on the run. They stayed in certain neighborhoods for as long as they were able to and abandoned them when one circumstance or another —pressure from incoming white groups, the expansion of commerce and industry, or their own desire for better housing—propelled them into new territory. Their churches sprang up along the way and then followed them wherever they went, or wherever it seemed that they would be settling for a while. By the eighteen-nineties, the majority of the blacks were to be found on the West Side from the Twenties up through the low Sixties. Their churches were there, too—including St. James Presbyterian.

The New York Presbytery, the governing body of the denomination in the city, was not wholly in favor of the St. James decision to move to Harlem. Those members of the Presbytery who supported the decision were opposed by a faction from the Church of the Puritans, a white congregation in Harlem, which included some owners of property in the district. At a meeting of the Presbytery in June of 1914, when a delegation from St. James requested a contribution of $40,000 toward the cost ($83,000) of putting up a church building on West 137th Street, delegates from the Church of the Puritans raised three objections. First, they asked, "Why give all that money to Negroes when white churches need it?" Second, they said that it would be unwise to invest $83,000 in a new building in Harlem, where, because of the Negroes who had already moved into the district, property values were going down. And, third, they pointed out that there were "already seven colored churches" in Harlem, serving "28,000 Negroes." In effect, the Church of the Puritans was resisting any further Negro migration to Harlem.

John M. Royall, a member of the St. James delegation, replied in behalf of his church. As a real-estate man of much experience and considerable success, he was qualified to address the question of property values, and as an officer of St. James he knew the circumstances that had influenced its decision to move to Harlem. First of all, Royall told the Presbytery, incoming Negroes were not the cause of declining property values in the district. The cause, he said, was a great building boom that had occurred in Harlem a few years earlier. This boom had produced so many apartments that there were not enough white tenants to occupy them. As a result, landlords had lowered their rents in the hope of attracting white tenants, and when that policy failed they had had to let their apartments to Negroes— at much higher rents than they had asked of whites. Royall also noted that in sections of the West Side where blacks were charged steep rents property values had risen. Turning to the reason his church felt it necessary to move uptown, Royall said, "St. James is needed in Harlem to help absorb [its] kindred people, and to assist in the readjustment of their living to suit the new condition. Churches of every description, except of the Presbyterian faith, have found a home in Harlem. And St. James, being in West Fifty-first Street, is too far removed from her people and members to keep pace." The opposition failed. St. James moved to West 137th Street late in 1914, and remained there until 1927, when it moved to its present home, on West 141st Street.

In the years before 1914, and for many years thereafter, the members of St. James Presbyterian would not have referred to themselves as "black"—"black" being a term that was not as acceptable then as it has since become. Theirs was not a mass church—members of which might not have objected to being called black—but one of several upper-class non-white congregations of Manhattan. Many of its communicants were in the professions, in small but profitable businesses, or in humble but respectable trades. A few, like John Royall, were men of means, though not by the white standards of that or any other day. Some belonged to what there was of Manhattan's non-white elite. And the majority of its important members were light-skinned. All this was true in even larger measure of people who worshipped at St. Philip's Protestant Episcopal, the wealthiest non-white church in the city. In 1911, when St. Philip's bought property in Harlem, John G. Taylor, a leader of the white homeowning community uptown, used certain racial epithets to describe the Negroes who were behind the deal. This brought a reply from Hutchens C. Bishop, rector of St. Philip's, who *was* behind the deal, and who himself looked so white that only Negroes knew he was not. "Mr. Taylor," Bishop said, "did not know enough of the real progressive element among the colored people to talk seriously about them. We are willing to be judged by the testimony of Seth Low, Robert C. Ogden, John J. Delany, George R. Sheldon, Joseph H. Choate, and Jacob Schiff [all upper-class white New Yorkers], who know something of us." A Negro businessman added, "The trouble is that our white neighbors, many of them newcomers in the country, don't know anything about us, and have determined not to learn anything about us. They insist on taking the worst element in the race as examples of our progress, while insisting that only the best in all other races shall be used as examples of decency and progress." Such speakers, including most of those who were not light-skinned, preferred to describe themselves as "colored." Some, perhaps the more racially aware, leaned toward "Afro-American." And hardly anyone really objected to "Negro"—only to the fact that most white Americans were still writing the word with a small "n." But almost none of them—representing the elite of their race in the city—would have thought of calling themselves "black."

Regardless of their shadings of color or their differences in social and economic position, however, most non-whites in Manhattan were trapped in a common predicament. A few upper-class white New Yorkers—the Lows, the Ogdens, the Schiffs—may have recognized a "progressive element" in the colored population, but ordinary whites made no distinctions whatever among people of Negro background. Even if they had wished to differentiate socially and intellectually among blacks, it would have been hard for them to do so—for almost all the blacks in Manhattan were herded together in squalid tenements on the West Side. In a city like Washington, D.C., Negroes of means and cultural distinction lived apart from the masses, in attractive residential enclaves of their own. In Manhattan, Negroes of all classes lived together in the tenement ghettos. Almost every contemporary observer remarked upon this fact. Mary Rankin Cranston, a white native of Georgia who was employed by the League for Social

Service, in Manhattan, wrote in 1902 that "there is no good and no bad Negro section . . . all are crowded together indiscriminately, the good with the bad, the moral with the immoral." Mary White Ovington, an upper-middle-class white Brooklynite and a social worker among black families on the West Side, said in 1905 that "their difficulty in procuring a place to live compels the colored people to dwell good and bad together." And G. L. Collin, a white reporter, observed in 1906 that "college graduates and cutthroats are huddled in the same tenements."

The blacks living on the middle West Side in the eighteen-nineties had moved up there from Greenwich Village—from the blocks of Canal, Mulberry, Thompson, Wooster, Sullivan, Spring, Gay, Jones, Bleecker, Macdougal, West Third, and West Tenth Streets. By 1900, only a few Negro households remained on these streets. "The ambitious Negro has moved uptown, leaving this section [the Village] largely to widowed and deserted women and degenerates," Miss Ovington wrote around that time. "Here alone in New York I have found . . . men and women who, unsuccessful in their struggle with city life, have been left behind in these old forgotten streets." Ambition was not the only reason that blacks had left the Village. Many had been forced out by white immigrant groups—especially the Italians. A section of the Village that had once been called Little Africa later became Little Italy. Bayrd Still was to write, in his *Mirror for Gotham*, that "the red would be seen overrunning the old Africa of Thompson Street, pushing the black of the negro rapidly uptown, against querulous but unavailing protests, occupying his home, his church, his trade and all, with merciless impartiality."

It was then that black neighborhoods sprang up in the Tenderloin district, from the Twenties to the Fifties west of Sixth Avenue, and by 1900 the areas of greatest concentration extended as far north as Sixty-fourth Street west of Broadway. The section known as Columbus Hill, from Sixtieth to Sixty-fourth Street, came to be called San Juan Hill, since many black veterans of the Spanish-American War lived there and since racial battles were always breaking out in its streets. In the nineties, when a surprisingly large number of the faces to be seen on Seventh Avenue were black, the avenue from the Twenties to the Forties came to be called the African Broadway, and the newspapers reported that it was the main artery of Manhattan's new Negro quarter. One such report appeared in the *Tribune* in October of 1895:

> It is the southwestern corner of the old Tenderloin that the negroes have marked out for their own, and have already pretty completely settled. On both sides of Seventh ave., chiefly on Twenty-seventh, Twenty-eighth, Twenty-ninth, and Thirtieth sts. . . . they have taken up their abodes. . . . Nearly 10,000 of them are already there. . . .
>
> Always and invariably on "dress parade" is the new quarter. How the most of the men support their wives and families is a mystery, for they seem to do nothing but lounge about street corners. . . . The younger women, arrayed in gowns that are wonderfully good imitations of the fashions, though heaven knows how they can afford them, walk in pairs and trios up and down Seventh Ave. . . .
>
> All the business of the quarter is in the hands of others. There is hardly a negro who has even the tiniest shop or store. Germans sell them their provisions, Jews . . . sell them their clothes. The genius of trade does not seem to have taken possession of a single inhabitant of this quarter. Even the most industrious get no further than odd jobs. . . . There is . . . a colored "Four Hundred" in New York, made up of men who have not a little property. But these are not the negroes of Seventh Ave. The people . . . are poor, with only a dollar or two standing between them and starvation most of the time, every cent going as fast as it comes in. . . .
>
> [There is a] daily promenade of gayly dressed girls and sprig young colored men. Yellow is the prime tint of the young colored girls' clothes. The favorite dress of the young men "in style" is a glossy silk hat, patent leathers, a black suit with a sack coat of remarkable shortness, and a figured waistcoat. Paste diamonds are *de rigueur*.
>
> And as the procession of young colored people passes and repasses along on the east side [of Seventh Avenue] the Hebrews across the street stand out in front of their shops and impress the "sheapness" of their goods upon everybody within earshot. The panorama never stops unrolling from eight . . . to close upon midnight.

Referring to the black precincts of the West Side, *Harper's Weekly* said in January of 1897, "Amid scenes of indescribable squalor and tawdry finery, dwell the negroes, leading their lighthearted lives of pleasure, confusion, music, noise, and fierce fights that make them a terror to white neighbors and landlords alike."

Many black residents of the Tenderloin—employed and unemployed, criminals and law-abiding, those who were "in style" and those who were not—were fairly recent migrants from the South. W. E. B. Du Bois, the black scholar and intellectual leader, described them in 1901 as "country bred." Five years later, a black clergyman said that the majority of the newcomers from the South "were once the field or plantation hands, whence they progressed to gangs at sawmills, then to small towns for higher wages, and thence North, herded together, untouched by the civilization either of the whites or of the educated blacks." He added, "They bring straight to the evils and temptations of New York the ignorance of the backwoods of the South." To such migrants, the idea of New York had been irresistible. According to Paul Laurence Dunbar's novel *The Sport of the Gods*, published in 1902, which deals with Negro life in New York in the eighteen-nineties, they "had heard of New York as a place vague and far away, a city that, like Heaven, to them had existed by faith alone. All the days of their lives they had heard about it, and it seemed to them the center of all the glory, all the wealth, and all the freedom of the world." New York continued to excite the imagination of black migrants for many years to come.

Among the wage earners, most black women in New York were domestic workers, dressmakers, beauticians, nurses, and midwives; unskilled men worked as elevator operators, cooks, porters, doormen, housemen, hallboys, messengers, coachmen, hostlers, draymen, hackmen, housecleaners, waiters, janitors, furnacemen, and day laborers; and a smaller group of skilled workers included carpenters, masons, bricklayers, woodturners, tailors, blacksmiths, barbers, railroad firemen, plasterers, plumbers, steam fitters, shoemakers, upholsterers, goldsmiths, coopers, and harnessmakers. Among the professionals and businessmen were teachers, physicians, lawyers, preachers, musicians, actors, caterers, undertakers, restaurateurs, saloonkeepers, and small hoteliers. So it was not quite true, as the *Tribune* reported in 1895, that "there is hardly a negro who has even the tiniest shop or store." Writing for the *Times* in November of 1901, Du Bois said that five and a half per cent of the city's black population was in businesses of various kinds. "The Negroes have something over a million and a half dollars invested in small business enterprises," he continued. "In the sixty-nine leading establishments $800,000 is invested. . . . Five leading caterers have $30,000, seven undertakers have $32,000, two saloons have over $50,000, and four small machine shops have $27,500 invested."

In the hostility that blacks encountered and in the rents they were charged, they paid dearly for the refuge they had found in the Tenderloin and other parts of the West Side. The hostility came chiefly from the Irish, who viewed sections of the West Side as their turf, and who had—as *Harper's Weekly* said in 1900—a "natural antipathy to the negroes." This is not to say that other ethnic groupings were exempt from the antagonism of the Irish. "Negro, Italian, and Jew [bit] the dust with many a bruised head under the Hibernian's stalwart fist," Jacob Riis wrote in *The Battle with the Slum*, one of his studies of New York tenement life in the early years of this century.

On the West Side, for the most part, Negroes had their blocks and whites had theirs. The groups did coexist uneasily on a few blocks, but seldom did they share a tenement dwelling. And, however poor was the condition of the houses, blacks generally paid higher rents than any other ethnic group. In 1899, a graduate student at Columbia found that blacks occupied the worst houses in the Tenderloin and San Juan Hill districts and that they paid up to five dollars more than whites did "for the same class of rooms." *Harper's Weekly* made similar findings in December of 1900:

> Property is not rented to negroes in New York until white people will no longer have it. Then rents are put up from thirty to fifty per cent, and negroes are permitted to take a street or sometimes a neighborhood. There are really not many negro sections, and all that exist are fearfully crowded. . . .
>
> They [the landlords] charge enormous rentals for very inferior houses and tenements, which yield more when the negroes have taken possession than they did in time of seemingly greater prosperity. . . . Moreover, they make no repairs, and the property usually goes to rack and ruin. . . . As a rule . . . negroes in New York are not beholden to the property owners for anything except discomfort and extortion. . . . Housed as they are, it is

wonderful that they should be as good as they are; it is wonderful that they are not all entirely worthless.

It was also surprising that in some of those wretched tenement rooms an air of graciousness managed to reign. A white visitor to one of these places found that although it was poor, bare, and squalid, it had "a certain style" and was pervaded by "an atmosphere of refinement." According to Riis, in *How the Other Half Lives*, his most famous study of the New York tenements, "The poorest negro housekeeper's room in New York is bright with gaily colored prints of his beloved 'Abe Linkum,' General Grant, President Garfield, Mrs. Cleveland, and other national celebrities, and cheery with flowers and singing birds." And Mary White Ovington found that some of the rooms she visited were "sadly cluttered" but not "bare and ugly." Breakfast and dinner were served with "the air of a social function." No doubt, such tenants understood the humanizing and dignifying uses of style—or, at any rate, the necessity of putting the best foot forward.

Black Bohemia

SECTIONS OF the black Tenderloin that harbored vice and offered various forms of entertainment were known as Negro Bohemia. Here one found the saloons, wine cellars, and poolrooms; night clubs, honky-tonks, and dance halls; herb doctors, mediums, and voodoo men; brothels and gambling dens; pimps, prostitutes, and assorted hustlers. Some of what went on in the streets and behind the doors of Negro Bohemia was a milder version of what went on in parts of the white Tenderloin. And life in much of the white Tenderloin was merely a reflection of the illicit, lighthearted, fun-loving side of Manhattan in the late nineteenth and early twentieth centuries. Samuel Hopkins Adams' historical novel *Tenderloin*, based on the life of those decades, describes the New York of the eighteen-nineties as "a city of crime and gaiety," a place that "gambled and whored blithely." Its residents "paid uncomplaining tribute to a political overlord, who, holding no office, ruled the city by a loose tyranny of extortion and blackmail through the agency of Tammany Hall and the organized corruption of the Police Department, selling dispensations to lawbreakers who ranged from the highest to the lowest, from the powerful presidents of railway and shipping lines down to the dope-joint proprietors of Mott Street."

On the morning of February 14, 1892, a Sunday, Charles H. Parkhurst, minister of the Madison Square Presbyterian Church, preached one of the more indignant sermons ever heard in Manhattan. In remarks that were later printed in the newspapers, Parkhurst denounced the leaders of Tammany Hall as "polluted harpies that, under the pretense of governing this city, are feeding day and night on its quivering vitals." They were, Parkhurst said, "a lying, perjured, rum-soaked, and libidinous lot." Continuing, he accused them of protecting the brothels and gambling dens, which, he said, flourished like the "roses in Sharon." In official quarters of the city, Parkhurst's remarks were not well received. Much of the response suggested that the sermon had gone beyond the call of religious duty. However that might be, Parkhurst was denounced by the police, and prominent citizens of Manhattan called for his head. The *World* accused him of bearing false witness. Charles Dana, of the *Sun*—described by contemporaries as a friend of Tammany—declared that he should be driven from his pulpit. Most serious of all, a number of clergymen quickly dissociated themselves from Parkhurst's remarks—possibly because certain churches owned property in the Tenderloin and collected munificent rents from the vice lords of the district.

But Parkhurst had certainly not invented his material. Much of it, and worse, was echoed in the novel *Tenderloin*:

> Saloons kept open, morning, noon, night, and Sundays. Professional faro and roulette games were conducted behind uncurtained windows at street-level in the West Thirties. Two-dollar harlots paraded Sixth and Seventh Avenues. Peep shows flourished in Fourteenth Street. Pestilential tenements and profitable brothels paid their ground rentals to fashionable churches.

Herbert Asbury's *The Gangs of New York*, a book published in 1928, had this to say:

> Many of the worst dives with which New York was infested during these days of iniquity, and which were utilized as rendezvous by the gangs of criminals and the hordes of fallen women, were in the area between Twenty-fourth and Fortieth Streets and Fifth and Seventh Avenues, a region of such utter depravity that horrified reformers referred to it as Satan's Circus. As late as 1885, it was estimated that at least half of the buildings in the district were devoted to some form of wickedness, while Sixth Avenue, then the wildest and gayest thoroughfare in the city, was lined with brothels, saloons and all-night dance halls, and was constantly thronged by a motley crowd seeking diversion and dissipation. This area . . . was the original Tenderloin, so named by Captain, later Inspector, Alexander S. Williams. After long and unrewarded toil in outlying districts, Captain Williams was transferred to the command of the Twenty-ninth [police precinct] in 1876. A few days later a friend, meeting him on Broadway and noting his expansive smile, asked the cause of his merriment.

"Well," said Williams, "I've been transferred. I've had nothing but chuck steak for a long time, and now I'm going to get a little of the tenderloin."

That, then, was the world of which Negro Bohemia was a part. On the whole, however, black memoirists have not had much to say about vice and corruption in the black Tenderloin—about its dealings with Tammany Hall and the police. They have spoken mostly about the clubs, saloons, and other places of entertainment that abounded in the area. A number of the saloons were owned by leading black prizefighters of the eighteen-nineties and the early nineteen-hundreds: George Dixon's, on Sixth Avenue between Twenty-seventh and Twenty-eighth Streets; Joe Walcott's, on Thirty-third Street, on part of the site now occupied by Gimbels; and Joe Gans' Little Egypt, on West Thirty-third Street. These spots were frequented by such other well-known black pugilists as Joe Jeannette, Sam Langford, Sam McVey, and Jack Johnson, and by such contemporary black jockeys as Isaac Murphy, Pike Barnes, Jimmie Winkfield, Willie Simms, Soup Perkins, Johnny Stoval, Spider Anderson, Linc Jones, and Monk Overton.

John B. Nail's saloon, on Sixth Avenue near Twenty-eighth Street, was considered a place for gentlemen. The *Sun* reported in 1903 that it was "conducted with the quietness and manners of a high-class Broadway bar and billiard room." Many of its customers came there from Brooklyn, where most of New York's Negro elite, including Nail himself, lived. Nail, a light-skinned native of Baltimore, had migrated to New York in 1863. He was the father of John E. Nail, who became a major real-estate broker—one of the rental agents who helped transform Harlem into a black community. The senior Nail was also the father-in-law of James Weldon Johnson, who at different points in his career was a teacher, a songwriter, a poet, a novelist, a diplomat, an editorial writer for the New York *Age*, and a leader of the National Association for the Advancement of Colored People.

Edmond's, on West Twenty-eighth Street, was owned by Edmond Johnson, a man whose speech and manners were as crass as some of the worst in the Tenderloin. Eubie Blake played one of his early New York dates at Edmond's—in 1905, when he was twenty-two years old. Decades later, when Blake was approaching his nineties, he remembered Edmond's as "a cabaret over a stable." Edmond's moved to Harlem in 1910, and it was there that Ethel Waters made one of her earliest appearances in New York, as a singer and dancer.

Barron Wilkins' café—another that moved to Harlem in later years —was called Little Savoy, and was situated on West Thirty-fifth Street. The black musician Noble Sissle said of it in the nineteen-forties:

> From the stories the boys tell me, Barron Wilkins' place up to about 1908 was the most important spot where Negro musicians got acquainted with the wealthy New York clientele, who became the first patrons of their music. Barron, a big, jovial personality with a heart as large as his rotund figure, was one of the greatest benefactors the Negro musician had in New York. He had a great love and respect for talented artists. Although the exclusive clientele, coming to his café to hear the Negroes sing and play, at first came on slumming expeditions, soon they found themselves regular patrons of the interesting entertainment that his unique array of talent afforded, not only by Barron's regular entertainers but by the new Southland Troubadours who came daily to New York from all over America. . . . Barron's became so popular because this wise operator kept his floor an open floor. Anyone who had anything to offer worth while could always get up and do a number. . . . There was no dancing by the guests. The entertainers worked the tables. Sometimes they sang twenty choruses to a song. . . . It was his fabulous spot that sparked off the renaissance of the Negro musician in New York City.

In *The Sport of the Gods*, Paul Laurence Dunbar describes the "Banner Club," a popular night spot in Negro Bohemia:

> It drew its pupils from every class of people and from every part of the country. . . . Parasites came there to find victims, politicians for votes, reporters for news, and artists of all kinds for color and inspiration. . . .
>
> The Banner was only one of a kind. It stood to the stranger and the man and woman without connections for the whole social life. It was a substitute . . . to many youths for the home life which is so lacking among certain classes in New York. . . .
>
> Here the rounders congregated, or came and spent the hours until it was time to go forth to bout or assignation. Here too came sometimes the curious who wanted to see something of the other side of life. . . .

Of course, the place was a social cesspool, generating a poisonous miasma and reeking with the stench of decayed and rotten moralities.

Cooper and Ransom's wine and billiard saloon, on Sixth Avenue, admitted only blacks of "the better class." When it opened, in February of 1883, the *Globe*, then the leading Negro journal of the city (it was later renamed the *Age*), reported, "The 'spread' was truly fine . . . bountiful and artistic in the extreme. . . . The first floor is the saloon proper and is devoted to the dispensation of liquid refreshments and the amusements of the knights of the cue. . . . The second floor is a reading and card room, besides two private rooms for small parties of gentlemen. All the rooms on this floor are elegantly frescoed and richly papered, the floors being covered with rich Brussels."

Perhaps the best-known of all the clubs in Negro Bohemia was Ike Hines', on West Twenty-seventh Street. James Weldon Johnson's novel *The Autobiography of an Ex-Colored Man*, published in 1912, contains this description of the club:

The floor of the parlor was carpeted . . . the windows were draped with lace curtains, and the walls were literally covered with photographs or lithographs of every colored man in America who had ever "done anything." There were pictures of Frederick Douglass and of Peter Jackson [one of the better black heavyweight boxers of the time], of all the lesser lights of the prizefighting ring, of all the famous jockeys and the stage celebrities, down to the newest song and dance team. . . . In the back room there was a piano, and tables were placed round the wall. The floor was bare and the center was left vacant for singers, dancers and others who entertained the patrons. . . . There was no open bar because the place had no liquor license. . . . The front room on the next floor was a sort of private party room; a back room . . . was devoted to the use of new and ambitious performers. In this room song and dance teams practiced their steps, acrobatic teams practiced their tumbles, and many other kinds of "acts" rehearsed their "turns." . . .

No gambling was allowed, and the conduct of the place was surprisingly orderly. It was, in short, a center of colored Bohemians and sports. Here the great prizefighters were wont to come, the famous jockeys, the noted minstrels, whose names and faces were familiar on every bill-board in the country; and these drew a multitude of those who love to dwell in the shadow of greatness. . . . There was at the place almost every night one or two parties of white people, men and women, who were out sightseeing, or slumming. They generally came in cabs; some of them would stay . . . until morning. There was also another set of white people who came frequently; it was made up of variety performers and others who delineated "darky characters;" they came to get their imitations first-hand from the Negro entertainers they saw there.

It was at Ike Hines' that many blacks first heard ragtime piano music, which was, according to James Weldon Johnson, "just growing to be a rage" in New York. The main character of Johnson's novel (who narrates some of the author's own early experiences in Manhattan) recalls hearing his first ragtime pianist at Hines' place:

> The stout man at the piano began to run his fingers up and down the keyboard. This he did in a manner which indicated that he was master of a good deal of technique. Then he began to play; and such playing! I stopped talking to listen. It was music of a kind I had never heard before. It was music that demanded physical response, patting of the feet, drumming of the fingers, or nodding of the head in time with the beat. The barbaric harmonies, the audacious resolutions, often consisting of an abrupt jump from one key to another, the intricate rhythms in which the accents fell in the most unexpected places, but in which the beat was never lost, produced a most curious effect. And, too, the player—the dexterity of his left hand in making rapid octave runs and jumps was little short of marvellous; and with his right hand he frequently swept half the keyboard with clean-cut chromatics which he fitted in so nicely as never to fail to arouse in his listeners a sort of pleasant surprise at the accomplishment of the feat.

Ragtime music, Johnson's novel goes on to say, was "originated in the questionable resorts about Memphis and St. Louis by Negro piano-players who knew no more of the theory of music than they did of the theory of the universe, but were guided by natural musical instinct and talent." Continuing its account of early ragtime, the book also says, "It made its way to Chicago, where it was popular some time before it reached New York. These players often improvised crude and, at times, vulgar words to fit the melodies. This was the beginning of the rag-time song." But for some time—until the more sophisticated compositions of men like James Scott and Scott Joplin began to be published—most respectable families, black and white, abhorred ragtime music. "Take that ragtime out of my house," Eubie Blake's mother, a devout member of a church in Baltimore, once ordered her young son when she heard him playing his piano lessons in syncopated rhythm. If some families regarded ragtime as obscene, it was because of its origins in brothels and because of its crude and vulgar lyrics. John Stark, who was a music publisher in the early nineteen-hundreds—and probably the most important promoter of classic ragtime music—once used these words to describe some of the cruder compositions: "Many of them are unfit to be seen on your piano or to be sung to your friends."

White reformers and clergymen described the dives and fleshpots of the Tenderloin as Satan's Circus. Black preachers may not have used that term in condemning the worst features of Negro Bohemia, but they could hardly have thought it inappropriate. One of them later said that when he looked at the black Tenderloin he saw "human derelicts," "moral shipwreck," "degeneracy and vice," "ravening wolves," and "spiritual decay," and that, as a result, he felt called by "the command of Jesus Christ to set a light in a dark place, make an oasis in a desert, and to let a stream of living water flow through this valley of Baca." The speaker was Reverdy C. Ransom, pastor of the Bethal African Methodist Episcopal congregation, on West Twenty-fifth Street. Part of what Ransom felt called upon to do was to launch a campaign against prostitution—a campaign that is reminiscent in some respects of a personal crusade that William Gladstone once conducted in Victorian London. In the evenings, after Parliament adjourned, the Prime Minister (when he was not the leader of the Opposition) often took to the streets, detaining prostitutes and urging them to forsake their occupation. Those who seemed at all responsive to his entreaties were invited home for tea with Mrs. Gladstone. "Nevertheless," writes the English historian J. H. Plumb, "what was at work was Gladstone's powerful sexual nature: through these quaint methods of sublimation . . . he was able to take his lust and live his life of dedicated respectability . . . a respectable Dr. Jekyll and a sexy Mr. Hyde." Despite what is commonly rumored about preachers, there is no evidence to suggest that

Ransom cultivated a similar duality of moral and personal style, yet there is something subtly or playfully erotic in an account he later gave of a meeting with one of the prostitutes he wished to save:

> En route to the Mission one night I saw approaching me a comely young colored woman, spoke to her pleasantly, as I did to all. She returned the greeting. I extended my hand, she took it and said, "Anything doing tonight?" I said, "Do you know who I am?" She said, "No." I said, "I am pastor Ransom . . ." she started to withdraw her hand, I told her "No, I want to tell you something. I am acquainted with many of you girls, I know how sickness and trouble often overtake you; now, if you ever get sick or in trouble and do not know what to do, or where to go, either come or send for me and then there will be something doing."

Prostitution in Negro Bohemia was one of the first problems that confronted Adam Clayton Powell, Sr., when, in 1908, he arrived in Manhattan to assume the ministry of the Abyssinian Baptist Church, which was then on Fortieth Street between Seventh and Eighth Avenues. Powell, who had recently resigned the pastorate of a church in New Haven, later reported how shocked he was to find that his new church was situated in "the most notorious red-light district in New York City." When services ended on Sunday evenings, prostitutes standing across the street "in unbuttoned Mother Hubbards" brazenly solicited worshippers as they streamed out of the Abyssinian church. Enlisting the aid of the police, Powell launched a "gospel bombardment" in the vicinity of his church—a campaign that made his path among the unrepentant sinners exceedingly perilous. "My son Adam was a little chap, and I often kept him at my side as a mascot," Powell wrote later in his autobiography, *Against the Tide.* "This proved very unfair to him. When the crusade was at its height and both men and women were being sent to jail, I was leading my mascot along the sidewalk. One of the women had filled a paper flour bag with waste . . . and, standing on the roof, she aimed it at our heads. It missed its mark but struck the sidewalk near Adam's feet and ruined his little white suit." Powell's church remained on West Fortieth Street until the early nineteen-twenties, when, somewhat later than most, it joined the black migration to Harlem. By then, much of the black Tenderloin, including the activities of Negro Bohemia, had moved uptown as well.

Social Leadership

IN 1899, one observer describing aspects of Negro church life in Manhattan took note of "the Southern type of revival meetings" and worshippers who "groan, shout, perspire, and encourage the preacher to do his worst." This was clearly a reference to the storefront churches. There were not so many of them on the West Side, however —not nearly as many as were later to spring up in Harlem. The majority of the black churches on the West Side were of the traditional sort. As Miss Ovington wrote, in reference to such congregations, "Strangers who visit colored churches to be amused by the vociferations of the preacher and the responses of the congregation will be disappointed in New York. Others, however, who attend desiring to understand the religious teaching of the thoughtful Negro find much of interest. They hear sermons marked by great eloquence."

One of the most eloquent of these preachers was Reverdy Ransom, of the Bethel church. A man with fair skin, reddish hair, and a face that was often as stern as a schoolmaster's, Ransom was both a minister and one of the radical Negro activists of his time. He was born in Ohio during the Civil War and educated at Wilberforce University, in Ohio; in 1924 he became a bishop of the African Methodist Episcopal Church, which was once regarded as the most racially militant of all black religious organizations in America. In the pulpit and on secular platforms, Ransom displayed the militant traditions of his church as well as the extemporaneous power and fluency of nineteenth-century oratory. Part of a speech he once delivered in praise of the abolitionist William Lloyd Garrison has been widely quoted as an example of his eloquence and fierce advocacy of Negro rights:

> What kind of Negroes do the American people want? Do they want a voteless Negro in a republic founded upon universal suffrage? Do they want a Negro who shall not be permitted to participate in the government which he must support with his

treasure and defend with his blood? Do they want a Negro who shall consent to be set apart as forming a distinct industrial class, permitted to rise no higher than the level of serfs or peasants? Do they want a Negro who shall accept an inferior social position, not as a degradation, but as the just operation of the laws of caste based on color? What kind of Negro do the American people want? Taught by the Declaration of Independence, sustained by the Constitution of the United States, this nation can no more resist the advancing tread of the hosts of the oncoming blacks than it can bind the stars or halt the resistless motion of the tide.

In May of 1899, when news arrived of a recent lynching in the Deep South, Ransom delivered one of his aggressive sermons at the St. John's A.M.E. Church in Cleveland. His "utterances were sensational in the extreme," a correspondent for the New York *Tribune* wired his paper. Ransom, the reporter said, "advised the negroes to become skilled in the handling of dynamite and use it when attacked, for the protection of their homes and lives." It is hardly surprising that in 1905 Ransom was one of the progressive Negro Americans who joined W. E. B. Du Bois in forming the Niagara Movement, the nucleus of the National Association for the Advancement of Colored People, which was founded four years later.

Perhaps the only aspect of Ransom's ministry that his fellow-clergymen deplored was his insistence upon serving as friend and spiritual adviser to black actors and musicians, for in the eyes of the respectable Negro clergy of those days there was no more immoral style of life than that of the musical stage. But, as Ransom explained, it troubled him that no effort was made to welcome the actors and musicians to the church, especially since "most of these people came from Christian homes, many of them were even the children of clergymen, most of them had been brought up in the atmosphere of the Negro churches in the communities from which they came."

Adam Clayton Powell, Sr., who would have had little trouble passing for white and was tall, well built, and handsome, made a most impressive appearance—especially in a cutaway coat, which, from photographs, he seems to have favored on Sundays. He was born in 1865, in Franklin County, Virginia, and he spent part of his boyhood in Kanawha County, West Virginia, and part of his early twenties in

Rendville, Ohio. He subsequently moved to Washington, D.C., intending to study law at Howard University—an ambition that did not last. He soon entered the Wayland Theological Seminary (now part of Virginia Union University), in Washington; studied later at the Yale Divinity School; and was ordained by Wayland in 1892. After ministering to congregations in Philadelphia and New Haven, he arrived in New York in 1908 to become pastor of the Abyssinian Baptist Church. The congregation had been founded a hundred years earlier on Worth Street (then called Anthony Street), in downtown Manhattan. Subsequently, keeping pace with the northward passage of the black population, it had moved to Thompson Street and Waverly Place before settling on West Fortieth. Under Powell's leadership—first on West Fortieth Street and then on West 138th Street, in Harlem—Abyssinian Baptist became the largest and richest Negro Baptist congregation in the world. And after 1937, when Powell resigned in favor of his son and namesake, the Abyssinian pulpit became the most politically outspoken in America.

As rector of St. Philip's Protestant Episcopal Church from 1886 to 1933, Hutchens C. Bishop led what was generally claimed—especially by its own members—to be the richest and most prominent of all black congregations. St. Philip's was organized in 1818 as an offshoot of Trinity Church, in downtown Manhattan, and more Negroes of means and education worshipped there than at any other church in the city. St. Philip's "drew some of the most outstanding persons of the race to its membership," one of its publications noted. "In the early days on Mulberry Street and again on Twenty-fifth Street [where it was situated until 1910, when it moved to Harlem], some of the most eminent men of New York were to be found on the Vestry. . . . These men . . . were the 'big wigs' of New York. They were brilliant men too. . . . Eyewitnesses tell us that it was not unusual on a Sunday morning, during the reading of the Lessons, to see members of the Vestry seated in the front pews with their Greek Testaments in their hands." Bishop was a native of Baltimore and a graduate of the General Theological Seminary of New York. He was bald, light-skinned, and mild-mannered, and he is remembered in a journal of the church for his "wisdom and administrative genius."

In appearance and style, George Sims, the pastor of Union Baptist Church, on West Sixty-third Street, was a rough diamond compared with the more refined and prominent ministers on the West Side. Unlike them, he had not inherited the church he led but had founded it himself. A tall, rugged-looking man who could not be mistaken for anything but a black, Sims resembled one of those tough, brawling heavyweight prizefighters of bareknuckle days. If his knuckles were not callused, his palms must have been, for, born in Cumberland, Virginia, in 1871, he had spent a number of his early years working on farms and railroads. But he had been brought up in a religious home, and upon coming to New York he studied informally for the ministry. He was ordained in 1898, and later that year he organized the Union Baptist Church. Although it eventually became one of the major Negro churches in Manhattan, its first services were held in one of the little storefronts in the San Juan Hill district; its early members were recent migrants from the South; and Sims' first sermons were about as blunt as he himself looked. Miss Ovington wrote of Sims' preaching: "When he talked of Christ from his pulpit, Jesus became alive, a workman, a carpenter who took off his apron and went out to answer the call to preach. . . . There was much shouting, much noisy getting of religion."

Other major black churches on the West Side in the first decade of this century included Mother A. M. E. Zion, on West Eighty-ninth Street; St. Cyprian's Episcopal (with a large West Indian membership), in the San Juan Hill district; and Mount Olivet Baptist, St. Benedict the Moor (Catholic and interracial), and St. Mark's Methodist Episcopal, all on West Fifty-third Street. Before Powell and Ransom arrived in New York, William H. Brooks, the pastor of St. Mark's, had been the city's most politically active black minister. In 1906, *The Colored American*, a leading Negro magazine of the time, described Brooks as "the most influential . . . the ablest, of the Afro-American clergy of New York City."

The elite among the black clergymen and professionals lived or led their social lives mostly in the environs of Fifty-third Street between Sixth and Eighth Avenues. Ransom called this area "the principal place of resort of our group." Of the black settlements in Manhattan, the West Fifty-third Street district was the most attractive and most culturally stylish. The tenements there were not as crowded or as unsightly as those farther down in the Tenderloin. Moreover, quite a few blacks lived in private dwellings of their own. The Y.M.C.A., the Y.W.C.A., and some of the major churches were in the area. It was where the more successful actors and musicians lived or gathered. Its social and political clubs were dominated by blacks of old New York family backgrounds or by the more educated migrants from other sections of the country. And its small boarding houses, hotels, and restaurants were more respectable than those in other parts of the Tenderloin. James Weldon Johnson, who lived on West Fifty-third Street in the early years of the century, wrote that before some of these places opened "there was scarcely a decent restaurant in New York in which Negroes could eat," and that "the sight offered at these hotels, of crowds of well-dressed colored men and women lounging and chatting in the parlors, loitering over their coffee and cigarettes while they talked or listened to the music, was unprecedented." Fifty-third Street, the *Evening Telegram* said in 1906, "is to the Negro colonies what Fifth Avenue is to white society."

Among the culturally distinguished blacks who frequented the better parlors and dining rooms of West Fifty-third Street was Theodore Drury, founder and director of Manhattan's only Negro opera company. A black contemporary described Drury as "picturesque" and as cultivating "a foreign air." Each year, Drury's company presented a one-night season of grand opera, usually at the Lexington Opera House, on East Fifty-eighth Street, and of one performance, in May of 1906, the *Times* said, "A good part of the audience was colored, too, and the boxes were filled by the leaders of New York's colored society." One of these leaders said later, however, that although the operas were great social events and financial successes, "none of us . . . took them too seriously."

Harry Burleigh, a prominent singer, composer, and arranger of Negro spirituals, was another member of the cultivated set that lounged and chatted in the clubs and hotel restaurants of West Fifty-third Street. A graduate of the National Conservatory, in New York City, where he had studied under Antonín Dvořák, Burleigh was one of the few Negro musicians on the West Side with classical training. And he was the only black in the choirs of Manhattan's Temple Emanu-El and St. George's Episcopal Church.

The blacks on Fifty-third Street dressed much as whites on Fifth Avenue. The men wore frock coats, vests, and wide-bottom trousers.

Their shirts, fastened with studs, had detachable stiff collars and cuffs, made of linen, celluloid, cotton, or paper. Heavy watch chains dangled across their vests. Straw hats were commonly worn in summer, and derbies (or "high dicers") in winter. They carried walking sticks and wore high boots polished with Bixby's Best Blacking. The women were turned out in heavy-bosomed box blouses and full skirts that covered their ankles. They almost never smoked—at least in public. The older men preferred pipes and cigars, while the younger ones liked cigarettes, and smoked such popular brands as Virginia Brights, Sweet Caporal, and Richmond Straight Cut. Those who kept up with serious periodicals would have read such white journals as *The North American Review*, *The Atlantic Monthly*, *Harper's Weekly*, *The National Police Gazette*, *Town Topics*, and *Leslie's Weekly*, and such black ones as *The Colored American*, *The Christian Recorder*, and *The Voice of the Negro*.

The Society of the Sons of New York, which had its clubhouse on West Fifty-third Street, was a resort of the black upper crust. The *Tribune* noted in 1892 that it was "the ambition of every respectable colored man in this city" to belong to the Society. But to become a member a colored man not only had to be respectable, and more, but also had to have been born and bred in New York. (If, occasionally, a non-New Yorker was considered for associate membership, it was because he could furnish proof that he was "a citizen in good standing in the United States.") The black New Yorkers who formed the Society were probably uniting socially against newcomers to the city, especially those from the South—a group whose public influence and importance had been steadily growing. By 1900, most Negro preachers, businessmen, actors, musicians, lawyers, doctors, and political figures in New York had been born either in the South or in other parts of the country, and it rankled native New Yorkers to find themselves steadily being overshadowed or outshone by a group they had once regarded as cultural inferiors. Miss Ovington wrote in 1911, "The taint of slavery was far removed from these people, who looked with scorn upon arrivals from the South. . . . These old New York colored families, sometimes bearing historic Dutch and English names, have diminished in size and importance. . . . And into the city has come a continual stream of Southerners and more recently West Indians, some among them educated, ambitious men and women, full of the energy and determination of the immigrant who means to attain to prominence in his new home. These newcomers occupy many of the pulpits, are admitted to the bar, practice medicine, and become leaders in politics, and their wives are quite ready to take a prominent part in the social world."

The Society's founders were related historically to the earliest group of New York's black well-to-do, the majority of whose survivors were living in Brooklyn at the end of the eighteen-hundreds and during the early years of the nineteen-hundreds. Speaking mainly of this group, the *Times* said, in July of 1895, "It will be news to many white persons to learn that many negro men own and occupy brownstone dwellings in fashionable neighborhoods, employ white servants, and ride in their own carriages behind horses driven by liveried coachmen. Some not only own the houses they live in but also houses tenanted by rich white families, and there are negro men in New York whose wealth is well along toward the million-dollar mark. . . . In selecting servants, negro people seem to prefer Swedes and Poles though some hire Southerners of their own race."

In February of 1903, the *Tribune* told the story of a white woman, brought up in the South, who "found it necessary to call upon a colored woman on a matter of business." When she rang and "an uncommonly good-looking white girl came to the door," an exchange took place:

> "I must have the wrong number," the caller said. "I wanted to see Mrs. So-and-So, and she's a colored woman."
> "This is where she lives," the girl said. "Won't you come in?"
> "But how do you happen to be here?"
> "I'm her maid."
> "But you are a white person, are you not?"
> "Of course, but what has that got to do with it?"

The *Tribune* went on to say, "The girl knew nothing of the color line; she was the daughter of German parents; she had to work. If a colored woman paid her good wages and treated her well, what possible reason could there be for not keeping the position?"

Socially, however, members of this old Negro upper class kept virtually to themselves—ignored by whites of similar position and cut off from less exalted members of their own race. The saloonkeeper John B. Nail, who had a "wide acquaintance among colored men of wealth and of high social position," gave this account to the *Sun* in January of 1903:

> You must remember that the object of the wealthy and educated colored man is to be as inconspicuous as possible, so far as white people are concerned. He doesn't want to spend his hours in being reminded of the fact that the great mass of his fellow-citizens despise him on account of his color. He wants to forget that as much as he can.
>
> When he seeks society he cannot do it as a white man with the same income. There are no restaurants like Delmonico's or Sherry's for him. . . . There are not enough wealthy colored families to keep such a place going on the scale they would demand. So they do their entertaining at home. They spend more money on their home life, their dinners, and their parties than white men of the same income would, because they have no place to spend it outside.
>
> You must remember that in this generation all the sons of wealthy colored men go to college and there are hundreds of college graduates among them. Some send their sons to the English universities where, of course, there is no prejudice against the negro at all. That isn't always a healthy experiment because it unfits a young man for his life here and makes home miserable for him.
>
> A great many go to Howard University at Washington. Quite a number go to Oberlin, and there is a scattering . . . at Harvard and Yale.
>
> The girls go to any of the Northern women's colleges. They come back here with the same social desires and tastes that you find in white young folks of similar training. But they are barred. They are classed with the most degraded and brutal element of their race.
>
> The result is the only one that . . . could be expected. Colored families of high class keep their family and social affairs out of sight of the rest of the world, white and black, as much as they can. They visit one another and keep a very strict and careful line drawn about themselves and try to make their standards as high as they can.
>
> White servants? Why, of course. They are obliged to have white servants. Negro servants in a high-class colored family are practically an impossibility.

If there is one thing the negro of the servant class doesn't know it is that the color of his skin doesn't make him the equal of his master. You know what a fresh colored servant is in a white family? Just imagine the hell that would be raised by a fresh colored servant in a colored family. . . . The thing is impossible. So they get foreigners, who have not the prejudices against our race existing here.

If the male members of such families spent an occasional social evening in Manhattan, it was to visit Nail's saloon, or to fraternize with their own kind in the clubhouse of the Society of the Sons of New York. They were less impressed by the rest of society on and around West Fifty-third Street.

Music and Comedy

WEST Fifty-third street was predominantly a social and residential center for Negro stage personalities, including musicians, and what the solid old families of Brooklyn would have called cultural parvenus. There seem to have been two classes of actors and musicians: those who worked mainly in rathskellers and cheap vaudeville houses, and those connected with the more highly regarded forms of Negro musical comedy. However, the *Sun* made no distinction between the groups when, in 1903, it said about the West Fifty-third Street district: "The neighborhood is full of theatrical boarding houses . . . with their scandals, their romances, and their literary discussions. . . . In no other quarter of New York can there be found such elaboration of manners and of the picturesque combination of colors in dress as are to be found in the boarding house parlors." Nor was any distinction made by a contemporary Negro observer who, in commenting on aspects of manners on West Fifty-third Street, stated that "hordes of the newly rich had heard that good eating was a mark of civilized living, and they interpreted good eating in terms of bulk, and packed away enormous feeds washed down with amazing quantities of champagne and fine liquors."

At any rate, the successful and talented from the world of music and the stage gathered frequently in the restaurants of the Maceo and Marshall Hotels, converted brownstones on West Fifty-third, though fewer of them went to the Maceo, which advertised itself as the "headquarters of clergy and businessmen." It was the Marshall that was the headquarters of the actors and the musicians. Its restaurant and private dining rooms were noted for Creole sauces and Maryland fried chicken. There were also other special Southern dishes, probably for the Negro railroad men who stayed at the Marshall when they stopped over in New York. On Sunday evenings, when an orchestra played, dinner in the Marshall's restaurant was by reservation only. Some of the actors and musicians lived at the hotel, and others had rooms nearby, but the Marshall was where they all gathered to eat, drink, talk, and try out ideas for their work. One of them later recalled that they spent many hours there discussing "the manner and means of raising the status of the Negro as a writer, composer, and performer in the New York theatre and world of music." The Marshall, he said, was "the radiant point of the forces that cleared the way for the Negro on the New York stage."

It may therefore be said that the Marshall helped shape the Negro musical theatre that developed and flourished in Manhattan during the late eighteen-nineties and early nineteen-hundreds. This was a transitional theatre, blending some of the less primitive styles of Negro comedy with certain aspects of the Broadway musical. Some of its leading creators were products of the old minstrel stage, known for its grotesque and ludicrous portrayals of "darky" characters. Up to the early eighteen-nineties, almost all Negro entertainers had been minstrels. Although the mode of comedy that was shaped in Manhattan represented a break with the minstrel tradition, the break was not a clean one—perhaps it could not have been—and some of the worst habits of the minstrel past were clearly observable in the new black theatre. Here, from George Walker, one of the reformed comedians and later a member, with Bert Williams, of the comedy team of Williams and Walker, is an account of what had happened to the black minstrels: "Black-faced white comedians used to make themselves look as ridiculous as they could when portraying a 'darky' character. In their make-up they always had tremendously big red lips, and their costumes were frightfully exaggerated. The one fatal result of this to the colored performers was that they imitated the white performers in their make-up as 'darkies.' Nothing seemed more absurd than to see a colored man making himself ridiculous in order to portray himself."

It was men like Walker who, not wanting to look so ridiculous, began, especially in Manhattan, to introduce a new quality into Negro comedy. This was not immediately or consistently noticeable, however. Many of the black comedians, including Walker, still looked and sounded almost as silly as they had in the past. A few still relied heavily on the grotesque minstrel grins that were so pleasing to whites. And words like "coon"—a mainstay of the minstrel idiom

—still cropped up in their songs and skits. But this continuation of minstrel mannerisms was, for the most part, superficial, and served chiefly as a protective convenience. It was necessary to the economics of black comic acting, for whites, who made up the bulk of the audiences, were not ready to accept any sudden break with the gestures of Negro comedy they had become accustomed to. Behind the protective façade of what these new comedians were doing, however, a quiet revolution was going on. The entertainers had started to be themselves rather than the darkies invented by whites. They had begun to impose their own interpretation on Negro material, to portray characters and situations in which blacks could recognize their own conduct and folkways—and at which most of them (though certainly not the Negro middle class) could laugh without undue embarrassment. Whether or not whites were aware of this subtle change in the work of black comedians, they were now laughing more honestly than in the past, for they were enjoying material that blacks themselves found genuinely amusing.

The gradual emergence of a post-minstrel style in Negro comedy coincided with a new development in theatre—the arrival on the New York stage of musical-comedy revues that were written, produced, acted, and directed by all-black companies. These were among the most popular shows in Manhattan in the eighteen-nineties and early nineteen-hundreds, and the stars of the Negro musical stage were among the celebrated personalities of New York's theatrical life. A black journalist wrote in 1903, "At no time have colored stage folk been accorded such consideration and loyal support from show managers, the press, and the general public."

One of the older comedy stars was a Kentuckian named Ernest Hogan. A brilliant performer, Hogan was best known for his role in *The Oyster Man*, a musical revue. He had been a minstrel for most of his career, however, and found it more difficult than his slightly younger colleagues in Manhattan to sever his attachment to the past. In the late eighteen-nineties, he wrote a song entitled "All Coons Look Alike to Me," which managed to offend even those blacks who were laughing wildly at the work of the post-minstrel comedians. Hogan seemed unable to understand the unfavorable reaction to his composition until it was explained to him that his song was im-

mensely popular among whites only because its title confirmed a
view they commonly expressed about blacks. Hogan was shocked by
this, and is said to have spent the remaining years of his life regret-
ting his most successful attempt at songwriting.

Bob Cole and the Johnson brothers—James Weldon and J. Rosamond—led an all-black ensemble, the Cole and Johnson company,
but were more widely known as one of the best song-writing teams of
that period. As a lyricist, playwright, actor, director, stage manager,
and dancer, Cole was the most versatile member of the partnership;
James Weldon Johnson, a graduate of Atlanta University, was the best
educated; and J. Rosamond, who had studied at the New England
Conservatory, had the soundest musical training. In the sphere of
song-writing, these men pushed the movement away from minstrelsy
a step farther. They wrote romantic numbers mostly, refuting one of
the popular notions of the time—that Negro artists and performers
were deficient in the "finer" sentiments. "We want to clean up the
caricature," J. Rosamond Johnson explained to a Broadway music
publisher. And Jack Burton, a historian of Tin Pan Alley, wrote,
"Rosamond Johnson's songs set a new pattern for syncopated Negro
music. His whimsical comedy numbers made no reference to crap-
shooting, chicken-stealing, and razor-wielding, the favorite themes of
most Negro tunesmiths at the turn of the century. In his romantic
songs, he presented dark-skinned but blue-blooded Romeos and
Juliets in a tropical setting far removed from the Mississippi River
backdrop against which kinky-haired wenches and shiftless roust-
abouts had danced for years in the afterpiece of innumerable minstrel
shows." Among such songs were "My Castle on the Nile," "Since
You Went Away," "Come Out Dinah on the Green," "The Congo
Love Song," "The Maiden with the Dreamy Eyes," "Tell Me,
Dusky Maiden," and—perhaps the most popular—"Under the Bamboo Tree." Some of these compositions enjoyed a vogue beyond
the world of Negro theatre. They became popular hits on Broadway,
where they were sung by such stars as May Irwin, Lillian Russell,
Anna Held, Fay Templeton, and Marie Cahill. In New York and
London, "Under the Bamboo Tree" was one of the best-known tunes
of the early years of the century.

Will Marion Cook, whose "Rain Song" enjoyed moderate popularity around that time, was not the song-writing success or the

Broadway celebrity that Cole and the Johnson brothers were. He was brusque, insulting, and short-tempered, and resented the fact that race prejudice confined him to the world of Negro music. He could never have got along smoothly with the publishers of Tin Pan Alley. But then songwriting was not his main occupation. He was primarily a composer-arranger and a conductor—"the most original genius among all the Negro musicians," James Weldon Johnson called him. Cook, who came from Washington, D.C.—his father was a lawyer and his mother was a college teacher—had been trained as a classical musician. After attending the conservatory at Oberlin College, he had gone to Berlin, where he studied the violin under Joseph Joachim and music theory at the Hochschule. He then came to New York, with ambitions for a career on the concert stage, only to discover that the city was not yet ready for classical musicians of his color. Turning his back on the classical tradition, Cook later became something of a chauvinist in the matter of Negro music. By the time James Weldon Johnson made his acquaintance, around 1900, Cook "had thrown all these [classical] standards over," Johnson recalled. "He believed that the Negro in music and on the stage ought to be a Negro, a genuine Negro; he declared that the Negro should eschew 'white' patterns, and not employ his efforts in doing what 'the white artist could always do as well, generally better.' "

Cook did not confine himself entirely to popular music, however. He was somewhat like "the caged bird" of which a contemporary Negro poet had written:

> I know why the caged bird beats his wing
> Till its blood is red on the cruel bars;
> For he must fly back to his perch and cling
> When he fain would be on the bough a-swing.

Cook would do what circumstances had obliged him to do, but he would not let it be forgotten that it was to the strains of another, "higher" form of music that he had been trained to fly. After listening to an evening of Cook's popular compositions, a white New Yorker wrote, "I am told that Mr. Cook declares that the next score he writes shall begin with ten minutes of serious music. If the audience doesn't like it, they can come in late, but for ten minutes he will do something worthy of his genius."

The poet who knew "why the caged bird beats his wing"—and also, in a later line, why he "sings"—was Paul Laurence Dunbar, the sweetest singer among the black poets of his generation, and, as it happened, a friend and colleague of Cook's. In 1898, they had collaborated—music by Cook and lyrics by Dunbar—on *Clorindy, The Origin of the Cake-Walk*, one of the musical-comedy hits of the period. Dunbar often shared the company of the actors and musicians at the Marshall Hotel, and he enjoyed contributing the lyrics for some of their shows. He was not, however, one of the professionals of the Negro stage. Around 1900, he was the most highly regarded black writer in America—less for his novels and short stories than for his poems. His position as a poet had been established in 1896, when his book *Lyrics of Lowly Life* appeared, with an introduction by William Dean Howells. "What struck me in reading Mr. Dunbar's poetry," Howells wrote, "was what had already struck his friends . . . here was the first instance of an American negro who had evinced innate distinction in literature. . . . Dunbar was the only man of pure African blood and of American civilization to feel the negro life aesthetically and express it lyrically . . . his brilliant and unique achievement was to have studied the American negro objectively, and to have represented him as he found him to be, with humor, with sympathy, and yet with what the reader must instinctively feel to be entire truthfulness."

Dunbar was not a resident of New York. He lived in Washington, D.C., but since the life of Manhattan seems to have fascinated him—and since his publishers were there—he made frequent and prolonged visits to the city. He liked dropping in on the night spots of Negro Bohemia and mingling with the stage folk who gathered at the Marshall Hotel. His popularity is captured in a description by a friend who had watched Dunbar's arrival at a social affair on the West Side in 1899. Acquaintances rushed up to greet him, strangers looked on and exchanged "awed whispers," but "it did not appear that celebrity had puffed him up; he did not meet the homage that was being shown him with anything but friendly and hearty response." There was certainly reason for Dunbar to be lionized in the social and cultural circles of the West Side. Manhattan's black community was full of religious leaders, theatre personalities, musicians and composers, and businessmen and other professionals, but it possessed no poet or novelist of distinction. Dunbar was all that it could claim, even if he did not belong to the city. James Weldon Johnson later became a notable poet and novelist, but up to the early nineteen-hundreds he had published almost nothing of merit, unless it was the few songs he had written as a member of the Cole and Johnson partnership. What literary life went on in the black community of Manhattan was a life not of writing but of reading—of discussing the authors of the day, with special attention to those who were deemed "morally elevating." These discussions were to be heard at Y.M.C.A. and Y.W.C.A. gatherings, in parlors and clubs, and in the forums and lyceums of the major churches. It seems odd that no serious black writing had yet emerged in a city that gave such an impetus to black theatrical and musical expression and was already well on the way to becoming one of the main Northern arenas for progressive black intellectuals.

Two of Dunbar's acquaintances on the West Side were Bert Williams and George Walker, who were stage partners. As actors and entertainers, Williams and Walker were probably the principal leaders of the movement away from minstrelsy and toward a more acceptable form of Negro comedy. They had met and teamed up in San Francisco and had moved to New York in 1896, advertising themselves as the "Two Real Coons." To be sure, this—especially to sensitive blacks—was an unfortunate description. Yet it contained a measure of historical accuracy, racial dissent, and theatrical opportunism, as Walker explained in an article he wrote for *The Theatre Magazine* in 1906:

> In those days [just before he and Williams came to New York] black-faced white comedians were numerous and very popular. They billed themselves "coons." Bert and I watched the white "coons," and were often much amused at seeing white men with black cork on their faces trying to imitate black folks. Nothing about these white men's actions was natural, and therefore nothing was as interesting as if black performers had been dancing and singing their own songs in their own way. . . .
> We thought that as there seemed to be a great demand for black faces on the stage, we would do all we could to get what we felt belonged to us by the laws of nature. . . . As white men

with black faces were billing themselves "coons," Williams and Walker would do well to bill themselves the "Two Real Coons," and so we did. . . . As the "Two Real Coons," we made our first hit in New York, while playing at Koster and Bial's.

They went on to produce and act in their own musical revues, and New Yorkers of all races flocked to such of their shows as *Sons of Ham, In Dahomey, Bandana Land,* and *In Abyssinia*—productions that made Williams and Walker the most acclaimed Negro comic actors of the day.

Even as comic partnerships go, Bert Williams and George Walker were a most dissimilar couple, seeming to have nothing in common but their racial background and a love for the work they did together. Walker was an American, born in Lawrence, Kansas, in 1873, and Williams a West Indian, born in Antigua in 1874. Walker was black-skinned and of medium height and build, and—to judge from his photographs—seemed always to be grinning. He was not handsome, but his face had an expression of mischievous charm and energy that women must have found appealing. Williams was light-skinned, tall, broad-shouldered, and handsome. His face, even when he smiled, had a controlled, introspective quality. Offstage, his manners and bearing were correct and elegant. He seems to have read widely. One source states that Mark Twain was his favorite author, and that his library contained works by Darwin, Paine, Wilde, Schopenhauer, Voltaire, Kant, and Goethe. Walker, of whose literary interests there is no record, was an agile dancer and an effervescent performer, who always appeared in the role of the clever and intelligent partner. Williams played the slovenly, lazy, dull-witted, and slow-footed half of the team. Most of his movements onstage, in walking or in dancing, suggested a character who was severely deficient in intelligence and had seldom encountered anything in life but failure. And most of the sounds he made, talking or singing, were droll, melancholy, and wistful, expressing a yearning for the good fortune that seemed to attend every household but his own. Walker, who wore expensive, custom-made clothes, onstage and off, was called "dapper," and is said to have dressed "always a point or two above the height of fashion." According to Ann Charters, who has written a biography of Williams, Walker "greatly preferred that his suits, shirts, and cravats were the only ones of their kind, and he began to get a reputation as a dandy both on and off the stage." She adds:

> As a friend said, he was a "man just born for clothes." He spent more hours with his tailor than he spent with his wife. Suits were made for him by the dozen, and he always had four or five fittings before he was satisfied with the way they looked. He bought the latest style and nothing but the best of everything, particularly addicted to light colored suits, big soft handkerchiefs . . . in his jacket pocket, high white collars, large silk patterned ties, and bright roses or carnations pinned carefully in his buttonhole. He dressed to please himself and impress the public—and help him win the favors of pretty young showgirls.

Offstage, Williams dressed conservatively and carried himself with an understated Edwardian dignity. James Weldon Johnson saw him as "highly intelligent and with a certain reserve which at times exhibited itself as downright snobbishness." Williams' wife, Lottie, was a pretty and demure-looking Chicago showgirl, who retired from the stage after their wedding. Walker's wife, Ada Overton, was a native New Yorker and a singer and dancer in the Williams and Walker company. She had a statuesque figure, dressed as fashionably as her husband, danced almost as well, and was the brightest black female star of the period.

In Dahomey, which opened at the New York Theatre in February of 1903, was one of the first Negro comedy revues to appear on Broadway. The show introduced Williams and Walker to the largest and most critical audience that the two had yet entertained. "The way we've aimed for Broadway and just missed it in the past seven years would make you cry," Williams said when *In Dahomey* opened. "I used to be tempted to beg for a fifteen-dollar job in a chorus just for one week so as to be able to say I'd been on Broadway once." Now they had finally made it, and, as the critic for the *Tribune* said, had "vindicated their right to appear on Broadway." Touching on a quality in Williams' work that had already made him a star in the cheaper houses, the critic wrote, "Williams is the . . . butt, the abused one. He manifests . . . a pathetic knowledge that something is wrong somewhere with the eternal scheme of things. He sang a song with the sad refrain 'I'm a good, substantial, full-fledged, real first-class Jonah Man,' which was re-demanded a dozen times; and those who had come to scoff were loudest in their applause."

Of Williams' songs, the one that he made most famous—and that contributed heavily to his own fame—was "Nobody." But none of his songs was more expressive of the character he frequently portrayed, or of the sombre and plaintive style of his work, than "I'm a Jonah Man":

> My hard luck started when I was born
> Leas' so the old folks say.
> Dat same hard luck been my bes' fren'
> Up to dis very day.
> When I was young my mamma's fren's—
> to find a name they tried.
> They named me after papa and the same day papa died.
> For I'm a Jonah, I'm a Jonah man.
> My family for many years would look on me
> And then shed tears.
> Why am I dis Jonah
> I sho' can't understand
> But I'm a good substantial full-fledged
> Real first-class Jonah man.

"He was very melancholy about it," the *Tribune's* critic said. "He was totally unaware why anybody should laugh. His very dance at the end was the angular illustration of woe."

Williams once said that nearly all his songs were based on the idea that he was getting the worst of it. So were many of the stories he told—like the one Lawrence W. Levine gives in his book *Black Culture and Black Consciousness*:

> He would tell his audiences a story in the first person of a young black boy who supported his family by catching and selling fish. One day he took his catch up a mountain lined with houses of white people. Rebuffed again and again, he finally made his way to the top, where he found a small white man standing in the doorway of a house. "I walks up to him and I bows low to him, ver' polite, and I sez to him, I sez: 'Mister, does you want some fresh feesh?' And he sez to me, he sez: 'No, we don't want no fish today.'" Making his way down the mountain the boy is overtaken by a landslide which carried him painfully to its foot. Digging his way out, he looked up and saw at the top the little man beckoning him. "So I sez to myself: 'Praise God, that w'te

man done changed his mind.' So I climbs back again up the mountain, seven thousand feet high, till I comes to the plum top and w'en I gits there the little white man is still standin' there waitin' for me. He waits till I'm right close to him before he speaks. Then he clears his throat and sez to me, he sez: 'And we don't want none tomorrow neither.' "

Williams and Walker made the cakewalk—an ebullient strut—one of the most popular dances in Manhattan. At the height of its fashion, it was danced with enthusiasm throughout the city, and with no more enthusiasm than in white New York society, where one of its leading exponents was William K. Vanderbilt. Cakewalk contests were held regularly at Madison Square Garden, and the winners received grand pianos, gold and silver watches, gold-headed canes, and some more modest prizes. In 1895, when Billy Farrell and his wife, both blacks, won the world's cakewalk championship at the Garden, a hundred and eight couples competed, and the judges were Vanderbilt, Mayor William L. Strong, and James J. Corbett. "There were a lot of theatrical people in the walk as well as those colored society cakewalkers," Farrell recalled almost forty years later. "The first time around, these society walkers made us look pretty small. But the second time around we did a lot of new stuff, like me kneeling and tying my wife's shoelace without missing a beat. We walked from ten until four the next morning." The prizes, delivered the following day, were three sets of furniture, four pianos, two dozen silk hats, and "miles of stockings."

Though people had been strutting the cakewalk in New York before Williams and Walker arrived in the city, the dance became the rage it did only after the two men began including it in their musical shows. For this development, most of the credit must surely belong to George Walker and his wife, Ada. George was the great dancer of the team, and Ada was only slightly less accomplished. She once said that "there was sunshine in the hearts" of those who danced the cakewalk, and that the dancers had to show they were "interested and happy." In the Williams and Walker company, only George and Ada—nimble of foot and bubbly of spirit—were qualified to meet those demands. A man like Williams could scarcely have contributed much, or anything, to the popularity of the cakewalk—Bert of the lugubrious face and the slow, awkward, and woeful dancing feet. If he had any sunshine in his heart, only his friends and family saw any evidence of it. Onstage, it seldom broke through the overcast of his face, the melancholy of his voice, and the other inclemencies of his style.

The Williams and Walker partnership ended in 1909, when Walker, suffering from what was then an incurable illness—syphilis —retired from the stage. In 1910, Williams joined the Ziegfeld Follies. And there, over the next nine years (he died in 1922), he became even more celebrated than he had been before, and confirmed his position as one of the great comic performers in the history of the American stage. W. C. Fields, who appeared regularly with the Follies, said later that Williams was "the funniest man I ever saw and the saddest man I ever knew."

Departures and Arrivals

BY 1910, when Bert Williams joined the Ziegfeld Follies, Negroes had been moving to Harlem for about a decade, and the district was well on the way to becoming the new center of Manhattan's black population. During that decade, industrial development and racial violence began forcing many blacks to abandon their dwellings on the West Side, and the first of these two circumstances was described in the *Herald* in 1903:

> With the advent of the Pennsylvania's big station and tunnel in the heart of the old Tenderloin, that famous landmark of vice and blackmail passes into history. "Killed by a railroad" should be its epitaph. . . . Dives disappear before derrick and stone masons. Politicians and boodlers vanish before the headlight of the railroad. . . . In March, 1900, the directors of the Pennsylvania road authorized an increase of $100,000,000 of stock. . . . No hint of the company's real purpose was then disclosed—to acquire the Long Island Railroad, to tunnel under the two rivers and the big city and to erect a monumental station near Herald Square. In December of the following year the Pennsylvania purchased several parcels of property in Thirty-third Street between Seventh and Eighth Avenues. That was the beginning of the mad rush for property in the neighborhood. Next came the final struggle for all the real estate left, which ended early this spring in the complete acquisition by the company of the valuable territory between Seventh and Eighth Avenues, Thirty-first and Thirty-third Streets.

During this mad rush for industrial property, many tenements occupied by blacks were bought up and later demolished.

In the summer of 1900, there occurred the second major event that contributed to the exodus of blacks from the middle West Side. On the night of August 15th, long-simmering racial tensions erupted into the most violent attack on Negroes that New York had seen since the draft riots of 1863—when scores of black families had fled Manhattan and taken up residence in Brooklyn. In the early years of the nineteenth century, Hell's Kitchen, where the rioting broke out in 1900, had been one of the more tranquil neighborhoods of the city. Dutch settlers had called it Bloemendael, the Vale of Flowers. But this changed drastically, as Richard O'Connor has written in his book *Hell's Kitchen*:

> With the coming of the Civil War, with vast migrations from Europe and rapid industrialization, the countrified charm of the section vanished forever, and its streets were invaded by jerry-built rows of tenements, grog-shops, slaughterhouses, railroad yards, warehouses, gas reservoirs. Gangs of hoodlums battled police for supremacy in its streets. Riots and disorders were fomented along its noisome thoroughfares.

By 1900, Hell's Kitchen had become probably the most warlike area in all of Manhattan, and from most accounts it was the police who led that year's attack on the blacks. One account, *Story of the Riot*, was written by Frank Moss:

> On August 12 . . . a Negro named Arthur Harris was with his wife at 41st Street and 8th Avenue. He says that he left her to buy a cigar, and when he returned he found her in the grasp of a man in citizen's dress. This man was a police officer named Robert J. Thorpe, who had arrested her, as he claimed, for "soliciting." Harris says that he did not know Thorpe was an officer, and that he attempted to rescue his wife. The policeman struck Harris with his club, and Harris retaliated with his penknife, inflicting a mortal wound and then ran away. Thorpe was attached to the 20th precinct and was much liked by his comrades. Policemen thronged his home; and his funeral . . . was attended by Chief Devery, Inspector Thompson and other officials. . . .
>
> During the day of the funeral there were rumors of coming trouble . . . those colored people who have illicit dealings with the police . . . seeing the signs of coming trouble, closed their places and kept off the streets. . . . Several officers told informants of mine that they were going to punish the Negroes that night. There are numerous gangs of rowdies in the district who are hostile to Negroes and friendly with the unofficial powers that are now potent in police affairs. There was an understanding

· 43 ·

between the forces that night that resulted in the holding of the streets for hours by crowds of roughs who raced up and down Broadway, 7th, and 8th Avenues, and the side streets from 34th to 42nd streets—in pursuit of Negroes, and were not attacked by the police except in one or two cases where they invaded Broadway hotels hunting for colored men.

The unanimous testimony of the newspaper reports was that the mob could have been broken and destroyed immediately and with little difficulty . . . policemen stood by and made no effort to protect the Negroes who were assailed. They ran with the crowds in pursuit of their prey; they took defenseless men who ran to them for protection and threw them to the rioters, and in many cases they beat and clubbed men and women more brutally than the mob did. They were absolutely unrestrained by their superior officers. It was the night sticks of the police that sent a stream of bleeding colored men to the hospital. . . . Men who were taken to the station house . . . were beaten by policemen without mercy.

White reaction to the event was mixed. The *Tribune*, expressing an opinion that was shared by most newspapers in Manhattan—though not all—said, "These assaults . . . on negroes in our streets were utterly inexcusable and outrageous. . . . The police of Southern cities have seldom if ever behaved worse than the police of New York behaved. . . . The universal feeling of respectable society is that the city has been disgraced." Yet a writer for *Harper's Weekly* commented, "I heard many native Americans, even New Englanders, say after the riot that they would have been glad if many of the negroes had been killed." In the wake of the riot, most Negroes, knowing themselves to be outnumbered and endangered, and fearing a recurrence of the attacks, maintained a self-protective silence. Some began looking for homes elsewhere, and others began to arm themselves. One woman declared, "Let every Negro get a permit to carry a revolver. . . . Don't you get caught again. Have your houses made ready to afford protection from the fury of the mob." This view was not shared by the city's recognized black leaders, most of whom counselled calm. By calling, professional position, and cultural attitude, these were not the sort of men to demand militant retaliation. They were successful businessmen, ministers, lawyers, and doctors, and they leaned to milder forms of civic protest. A few days after the riot, the Reverend William H. Brooks, pastor of St. Mark's, on West Fifty-third Street, addressed his congregation, "This is a conservative church and the pastor is a conservative man. Neither church nor pastor wishes any notoriety, and we hate sensationalism next to sin. . . . Not one finger must be raised in retaliation. . . . We must fight by due process of law." In what he said, Brooks may have been encouraged by some of the favorable newspaper comments he had read, for he went on to point out that the New York press had "stood for law against lawlessness, humanity as opposed to inhumanity, justice as opposed to injustice, and right as opposed to might." In a letter to Mayor Robert Van Wyck, Brooks therefore said, "We ask for no money consideration. . . . The rights of citizenship we value above money. We ask for the conviction and removal from the force of those officers whom we are able to prove guilty. . . . We feel keenly our position, and again appeal to you for common justice."

But on this occasion Brooks' faith in due process was badly misplaced. James Weldon Johnson later reported: "An investigation was held in which colored citizens who testified to having been beaten by the police were themselves treated as persons accused of crime. . . . The investigation turned out to be a sham and a whitewash." By 1905, when a race riot broke out in the San Juan Hill district, blacks were fleeing the West Side in increasing numbers. Now, as one eyewitness reported, "every day was moving day." A few of the families were finding places to live in the West Nineties, but most of them—their belongings packed in horse-drawn vans and wagons— were making their way to Harlem.

The Harlem that the blacks were entering had a white working-class population—people of various European nationalities. But, especially west of Lenox Avenue, Harlem was one of the chief upper-middle-class districts of Manhattan. Streets and avenues were lined with fine brownstones and splendid apartment houses. Here and there stood a luxurious mansion. Frederic Birmingham, who grew up in white Harlem during the nineteen-twenties, recalled in a 1960 memoir that poorer residents often found themselves "tiptoeing up some of the shaded streets and looking with wide eyes on the mansion of some merchant prince or beer baron, its handsome lawns covered with sportive cast-iron animals, its own stables right on the property and possibly a 'gazebo' made out of cedar logs and covered with wisteria and honeysuckle." Of pre-black Harlem, Gilbert Osofsky, a historian of the community, added:

> The people attracted to this "residential heaven" were . . . older and wealthier New Yorkers—"people of taste and wealth." Few neighborhoods in the entire city at the turn of the century had so disproportionate a number of native Americans or immigrants from Great Britain, Ireland and Germany, including German Jews, living in it. . . . Many late-nineteenth-century Harlemites were born in downtown Manhattan or immigrated to America in the years 1830–1850, and subsequently moved to the community after 1870. . . . The homes of municipal and federal judges, mayors, local politicos . . . prominent businessmen and state politicians . . . were scattered throughout Harlem. Their children attended Grammar School 68, "referred to as the 'Silk Stocking School' of the City" because its "pupils were practically all from American families, and . . . more or less prosperous people." . . . A young Jewish boy moved to Harlem from the Lower East Side in the first decade of the twentieth century and recalled seeing rich German Jews, "Uptown Jews," strutting down Seventh Avenue in top hats, black coats and canes.

And Lloyd Morris, in his *Incredible New York*, gives this sketch of life in the "impeccably respectable, conservative, and prosperous" Harlem of the late nineteenth century:

> On pleasant summer evenings, you saw families sitting out on their stoops, and children playing in streets seldom disturbed by traffic. You surmised that the aroma of well-cooked meals saturated the low brownstone dwellings. You could be sure that every parlor displayed an aspidistra, a "suite" of mahogany-stained furniture upholstered in velveteen, an upright piano and gilt-framed chromos and engravings on the walls. Upstairs, the principal bedroom would have a gleaming, knobby brass double bed, with cover and "pillow-shams" of crochet lace over a lining of pink or blue sateen. In these homes, pinochle was played and pyrography cultivated as a genteel art. As you walked past them you heard the strumming of mandolins and banjos, the tinkle of a piano and youthful voices singing. . . . Harlem, once a village, rejoiced in its "small-town" atmosphere. Like Brooklyn, it proudly exalted the

domestic virtues, the pieties of religion, the authority of convention. It went to see sultry actresses like Fanny Davenport and Olga Nethersole when they brought French plays to the Harlem Opera House—an occasional shock was pleasant. . . . But in real life Harlem wanted nothing to do with loose morals. It distrusted . . . flamboyance . . . ostentatious luxury.

Seventh Avenue, with its theatres and other showplaces, was already a boulevard of high style and fashion—though in later years blacks were to heighten the style and bring something of their own bravura to the fashion. But the main thoroughfare of business and entertainment was West 125th Street. Here one found the Harlem Opera House, Hurtig & Seamon's Music Hall (where Sophie Tucker and Fanny Brice sometimes appeared), the New Orpheum Theatre, and cinema houses like Proctor's, the Victoria, and the Orient. Here, too, were the big department stores, the banks, insurance companies, jewelry stores, bakeries, beaneries, and hash houses. The wealthier families dined out at Pabst's Restaurant. And the intersection of Seventh Avenue and 125th Street—white Harlem's equivalent of Union Square—was where the stepladder suffragettes, Socialists, and Henry George single-taxers made the more radical speeches of the day.

Though white Harlem "wanted nothing to do with loose morals," it had been unable to keep out gambling dens, saloons, poolrooms, beer gardens, burlesque houses, and dance halls. And in 1911 the *Harlem Home News*, quoting a prominent white member of the community, called attention to some "degrading" dances that had made their appearance uptown:

> I wonder . . . if the parents know that the "nigger" dance is a sort of double "hootchie kootchie" in which hugging and squeezing and suggestive motions play a prominent part?
> The "turkey trot" or "shivver" . . . is a kind of hopping dance in which the bodies are kept shivering in a senseless manner.
> The "grizzly bear" is a shuffle in which the dancers allow their limbs to come in contact with each other in a way that shocks respectable women and makes decent men's blood boil with rage.

Worse, the young white people in Harlem were to be seen dancing these steps not only on weeknights but on Sunday evenings as well. The *Home News* did not say where these dances had originated or how the white sons and daughters of Harlem had come to be doing them but such dances had probably made their way up from the Negro West Side, because by 1911 blacks from that part of Manhattan had been settling—and therefore dancing—in Harlem for more than ten years.

A Struggle for Harlem

IN DECEMBER of 1905, the *Herald* took note of an "untoward circumstance" that had been "injected into the private-dwelling market in the vicinity of 133rd and 134th Streets." Flats "that were occupied entirely by white folks have been captured for occupancy by a Negro population." There were still a few white residents on 133rd Street between Lenox Avenue and Seventh Avenue, but nearly all of 134th between those avenues had been taken over by blacks. Further, real-estate brokers were predicting that it was "only a matter of time" before the blocks between Seventh and Eighth Avenues became "a stronghold of the Negro population." The cause of this "colored influx," the *Herald* said, "is inexplicable."

There were at least two causes, and neither was inexplicable, at least to the Negro refugees who were virtually being driven out of the middle West Side, and to the white landlords of Harlem who saw them as a godsend—who were welcoming them with vacant apartments, if not exactly with open arms. Perhaps it was the landlords' side of the story that the *Herald* did not know. Up until the late eighteen-nineties, not all the blocks in the vicinity of Lenox Avenue above 125th Street had been fully built up. As a result, white tenants may have found that section of Harlem less desirable than the area farther to the west, in the direction of Seventh and Eighth Avenues. Besides, while the blocks in that area were within easy walking distance of the Eighth Avenue Elevated train, the Lenox Avenue neighborhood offered no similar transportation facilities. This circumstance began to change around 1900, when it was announced that a subway tunnel was about to be built along Lenox Avenue. What followed has been explained by Gilbert Osofsky: "Speculators who intended to make astronomic profits when the subway was completed bought the marshes, garbage dumps, and lots left unimproved or undeveloped in the 1870's and 1880's. Between 1898 and 1904, the year that the Lenox Avenue line opened at One Hundred and Forty-fifth Street, 'practically all the vacant land in Harlem' was 'built over.'" And more houses were built in the environs of Lenox Avenue than there were white tenants to occupy them.

In addressing the New York Presbytery in 1914, John M. Royall, the black realty man and officer of St. James Presbyterian Church, had given a lengthier and more colorful account of how the Lenox Avenue subway affected the future of housing and land values in Harlem:

> The great subway proposition . . . filled the people's minds and permeated the air. Real-estate operators and speculators conjured with imagination of becoming millionaires, bought freely in the west Harlem district, in and about the proposed subway stations. . . .
>
> Men bought property on thirty- and sixty-days contracts, and sold their contracts, not their property, for they never owned it, and made substantial profits. I have known buyers to pay $38,000 and $75,000 for tenements which showed a gross income of only $2,600 and $5,000 per year. On they went; buying, buying; giving no heed to the fact that old staid Knickerbocker property owners were standing still looking on, not investing, but puzzled to their very souls as to what the final results would be.
>
> This unhealthy speculative condition continued until owners commenced to figure the income from these newly acquired properties, when, lo! they began to realize all that glittered was not gold. Straightaway, these new owners, one and all, commenced saying to their brokers, who up to this time had been like Moses leading buyers into Canaan, "I don't mind buying if you can get Esau under contract to purchase before the deal is closed." With the brokers thus cornered, the market awoke from a drugged and drunken stupor, struck amidships like the famous Titanic, reeled, tottered, and solemnly settled beneath a sea of depreciated values. . . .
>
> Shrewd real-estate operators and cunning lawyers brought into existence many reckless bond and mortgage companies, which really loaned more money on property than the entire value of same. . . .
>
> Is there any wonder, then, that this day of reckoning between assets and liabilities haunts the west Harlem district owners like a spectre, and fills [their] midnight dreams with terror? . . .

Facing financial destruction, the new property owners commenced to consult Moses (their brokers) and their cunning lawyers for help out of the difficulty. These two gentlemen (the broker and the lawyer) soon struck upon the bright idea of capitalizing race prejudice, and enticed the new owners, whose only alternative was to sell, to enter an alliance—a conspiracy to put colored tenants in their property, and thereby force their wealthier neighbors to buy from them. And, on the other hand, a certain class of buyers, whose only conscience was money, were urged into the use of the same methods, placing colored people in property so that they might buy other parcels adjoining. . . .

Innocently enough, the colored tenants, looking for better accommodations, flocked to Harlem and filled houses as fast as they were opened to them. This worked decidedly to the advantage of the property owners, enabling a great number of them either to dispose of their property or to get a healthier and more lucrative return from rents paid by colored tenants. . . .

Do you know that tenements in the west Harlem district are showing a much larger return to owners than they formerly brought when occupied by white tenants? Do you know the property is more fully rented? Do you know that there is not today three per cent of vacancies in all the tenement properties occupied by colored people in Harlem?

Royall knew. By 1914, he was one of several Negro brokers who had induced white landlords "to put colored tenants in their property." The first and most prominent of these black brokers was Philip A. Payton, Jr.—the pioneer among Negro realty men in Manhattan, and, as he came to be called, the father of black Harlem. Payton, born in Westfield, Massachusetts, in 1876, came to New York in 1899—to what he saw as "the city of cities." For some time, however, he did not find New York to be the city he had imagined—what poor blacks from the South had seen, in the words of Paul Laurence Dunbar, as "the center of all the glory, all the wealth, and all the freedom of the world." Though Payton was a college-educated man—a graduate of Livingston College, in North Carolina—the only jobs he was able to find in Manhattan were as a barber, a slot-machine attendant in a department store, and a porter in an apartment building. Around 1900, Payton's job as a porter—in which he probably saw some of the worst sides of Negro tenement life in Manhattan—gave him an idea that changed his life. Since there seemed to be no black real-estate agents in the city, why shouldn't he become an agent himself and help blacks to find better housing? His thought happened to occur at a time when blacks on the West Side were under pressure—when they were beginning to feel a desperate need for new living space, and when, because of overbuilding in Harlem, this space was becoming available uptown. Payton's first few attempts to establish and maintain a real-estate agency—in the Tenderloin and in downtown Manhattan—were failures. His offices closed down almost as soon as he had opened them. "The hardships I suffered and the funny experiences I underwent while establishing myself as a real-estate man in New York would fill a book in which a reader could shed a few tears and secure many a good laugh," he said later. "Besides being dispossessed three times and once evicted for non-payment of rent, I have walked from Nassau Street to Harlem on more than one occasion for want of a nickel." It might have been at the end of a long walk to Harlem that Payton approached one of the hard-pressed white landlords and offered himself as a broker for Negro tenants. As he recalled later, a dispute had broken out between two landlords of adjoining houses, and "to get even, one of them turned his house over to me to fill with colored tenants." He went on, "I was successful in renting and managing this house and after a time I was able to induce other landlords to . . . give me their houses to manage."

In 1903, Payton, along with several other Negroes of means and position, organized the Afro-American Realty Company, with headquarters in downtown Manhattan—probably the largest enterprise of its kind that has ever been owned and run by blacks in New York. A year after it was founded, the *Tribune* carried this report:

> With offices rivalling in richness of decoration those of many Wall Street bankers, and with $500,000 capitalization, the Afro-American Realty Company yesterday began business as a corporation. . . . It will lease, buy and build flats and apartments for rental to negroes in the boroughs of Manhattan, the Bronx, and Brooklyn, and its avowed object is to make it possible for a negro to live anywhere he desires, if he has the money to pay the rent.
>
> The corporation got its start about a year ago in the attempt of one of the well known realty companies of this city to oust the negro tenants of One-hundred-and-thirty-fifth st. between Fifth

and Lenox Avenues, the object being to make it a "white" street and raise rentals. Wealthy negroes who were interested in real estate resented this attempt, got together, and after vainly trying to get leaseholds on property in that street, bought outright two flat houses tenanted by whites, dispossessed them and rented the flats to negroes who had been put out of the other houses.

For about five years, the Afro-American Realty Company, under Payton's management, helped to swell the influx of blacks into Harlem. In 1908, the company failed, and thereafter Payton returned to his own real-estate business on West 134th Street.

Inspired by Payton's example (his income, too, no doubt), other Negro real-estate men—John M. Royall, Watt Terry, John E. Nail, and Henry C. Parker—opened firms of their own. The firm of Nail & Parker became the most successful in the history of black Harlem, obtaining more houses for Negroes and therefore contributing more heavily to the black movement into the district than any of the other real-estate enterprises. James Weldon Johnson has left this account of how white Harlemites reacted to the growing black migration into their community:

> In the eyes of the whites who were antagonistic, the whole movement took on the aspect of an "invasion"—an invasion of both their economic and their social rights. They felt that Negroes as neighbors not only lowered the values of their property, but also lowered their social status. . . . Their conduct could be compared to that of a community in the Middle Ages fleeing before an epidemic of the black plague. . . . The presence of a single colored family in a block, regardless of the fact that they might be well-bred people, with sufficient means to buy their new home, was a signal for precipitate flight. The stampeded whites actually deserted house after house and block after block.

But not all whites were ready to abandon their old district. "The Negro invasion . . . must be vigilantly fought, fought until it is permanently checked, or the invaders will slowly but surely drive the whites out of Harlem," said the *Harlem Home News* in July of 1911. "We now warn owners of property . . . that the invaders are clamoring for admission right at their doors and that they must wake up and get busy before it is too late to repel the black hordes that stand ready to destroy the homes and scatter the fortunes of the whites living and doing business in the very heart of Harlem. . . . The negro must have some place to live, but why must he always drive the white man out of his home in order to find a home for himself? Isn't there any other way of providing homes for the colored man?"

In the view of John G. Taylor, the president of the Harlem Property Owners' Protective Association, there *was* another way. He had suggested some months earlier that Negroes "should buy large tracts of unimproved land near the city and there build up colonies of their own," for "that would be better for all concerned, and movements of that kind would be given unlimited financial support." Of course, no one seriously believed that any such movement would ever come about. White Harlem was stuck with the black migration, and—short of establishing separate black "homelands"—the community would have to find a way either to live with the newcomers or to keep more of them from coming in.

The latter course was the one favored by property owners, block associations, civic committees, churches, newspapers, and business organizations. Plans were made to evict black tenants from buildings they already occupied. Certain groups looked into the possibility of passing laws to prevent blacks from owning or renting property in Harlem. Banks were petitioned to cut off loans to black homeowners and to white speculators who sold or rented to Negroes. Taylor urged the white tenants and homeowners on 136th Street to build a "dead line" between themselves and the black newcomers—in other words, to erect "a twenty-four-foot fence in the backyards." This was to be more than a screen protecting the eyes of unfriendly neighbors from one another. It was also to be a white boundary, beyond which the black invaders were not to pass. According to one newspaper, white homeowners "signed an agreement not to sell to Negroes for the next fifteen years," and "The document . . . even limits the number of colored servants each signer should have."

Though the lines of resistance could hardly have been more carefully and firmly drawn, there were white property owners and speculators who had no desire to join or honor such lines. They were not stirred by appeals to racial solidarity and civic unity. Their feelings were chiefly monetary, and since it was customary for Negroes to be charged higher rents and purchase prices, they knew that big profits were to be made from the inflow of blacks. When Caroline Morolath, the owner of a house on West 137th Street, rented to blacks, she was sued by Rafael Greenbaum, who owned a house next door. Greenbaum asked ten thousand dollars in damages, on the ground that Mrs. Morolath, by renting to blacks, had made it impossible for him to rent or sell to whites.

Taylor called people like Mrs. Morolath "white renegades," but they were not shamed or intimidated by the description. They intended to proceed by their own lights, according to their own interests. They went right on selling and renting to blacks, and, as a result, in helping their own pockets, they also helped to make housing conditions for Negroes in New York more decent and livable than at any time in the past.

But, though it may not have seemed so at the time, the back of the resistance had been virtually broken in March of 1911. Whites apparently did not realize it, for they went on fighting for several years after. But blacks must surely have sensed it. Some of their churches had already followed them into Harlem, and it was in March of 1911 that St. Philip's Protestant Episcopal, the richest and best-known of all their churches, decisively entered the lists. A year earlier, it had moved into a new building on West 133rd Street, and now it bought, for more than a million dollars, a row of apartment buildings on the north side of West 135th Street, occupying almost the entire block from Lenox Avenue to Seventh. As the emergence of the year's first crocus announces that spring is on its way, so did the arrival of so important a church as St. Philip's signify that Harlem was sure to be the next major settlement of blacks in Manhattan. When St. Philip's bought the row of apartment houses on 135th Street, the *Age* said, "The deal pulled off by this progressive pair [the real-estate agents Nail and Parker] . . . involving the huge sum of $1,000,070, not only puts the firm at the very front, but influences the life of the colored people of New York as nothing of the kind has done in many a long year. It puts on the books of St. Philip's Church, the wealthiest colored church corporation in the country, the best property owned by colored people in Manhattan or in any other borough, and it opens up to colored tenantry the best houses that they have ever had to live in."

Taylor did not believe that the St. Philip's deal would seriously affect the fuure of white residence in Harlem. The chances were, he said, that the Negroes would "not stay long in the new apartments." He and others did not see "how colored people can possibly afford to pay the rents the new owners will have to charge to make the investment pay." Besides, he added, "we understand there is $400,000 in mortgages on the property, $160,000 of which will be due in the next eight months, and if the program to keep colored people in the apartments is carried out, we fail to see where the church is going to borrow the money." Nor was Taylor alone in feeling that the black migration into Harlem could still be checked, or, at any rate, that it should be. In 1912, a letter to the *Times*—probably from a white Harlem resident—said, "Can nothing be done to put a restriction on the invasion of the Negro into Harlem? At one time it was a comfort and a pleasure to ride on the Sixth and Ninth Avenue elevated, but that is a thing of the past. Now you invariably have a colored person sitting either beside you or in front of you. . . . There is an enormous colony of them around 135th Street and Lenox Avenue, and they are coming closer all the time. . . . Why cannot we have Jim Crow cars for these people?"

But John Royall was one of the blacks who knew in 1911 that the battle for Harlem was virtually over. That is why he could say so confidently to the New York Presbytery in 1914, "Are you aware of the fact that Negroes are buying property in Harlem? Has anyone told you that the colored people have purchased about ten per cent of the tenements in which they live? And . . . about forty per cent of all the private houses occupied by them? . . . The colored people are in Harlem to stay."

PART TWO

Shaping a Black Metropolis

"The Promised Land"

WHEN SOME nineteenth-century New Yorkers said "Harlem," they meant almost all of Manhattan above Eighty-sixth Street. Toward the end of the century, however, a group of citizens in upper Manhattan—wanting, perhaps, to shape a closer and more precise sense of community—designated a section that *they* wished to have known as Harlem. The chosen area was to be bordered on the north by 155th Street, on the south by 110th Street, on the west by Morningside Drive and St. Nicholas Avenue, and on the east by the East River. This was the Harlem to which blacks were moving in the first decades of the new century as they left their old tenements and settlements on the middle and lower blocks of the West Side.

By 1930, most of Harlem's white population had fled, and blacks inhabited virtually the entire district. "The old Harlem was dead," a former white resident lamented in the mid-twenties. "I lived there all my life until not long ago, when I was squeezed out by the Negro population invading the old section. All the *Gemütlichkeit* of it is gone. Gone are the comfortable *Weinstuben* where one could smoke his pipe and peacefully drink his glass of Rhine wine. Gone is the old *Liedertafel* and the hundred-and-one social organizations, and the *Turnvereine* and the singing clubs where one could pass the evening peacefully. They have all moved elsewhere, and the new places do not have the atmosphere of the old ones. . . . It used to be so pleasant to pass a Harlem street on a summer evening. The young ladies were accompanying their Lieder with the twanging of the soft zither, and the stirring robust melodies from the Lutheran churches used to fill the air on a Sunday. It is all gone now." And in a 1929 issue of *The New Yorker* Arthur Gerald Goldberg, an old resident of Harlem, wrote of his childhood in the district:

> I can remember, back in the fabulous golden nineties, when Harlem was neither Negro nor Italian. . . .

Harlem had a social life all its own. Our parents, I suppose, used to go downtown occasionally, but my recollection is that there was a self-sufficiency to our life up there that made us somewhat independent of the rest of the city. When my mother went shopping she used to go to Koch's in 125th Street, Harlem's main business thoroughfare. When we went to the theatre we would go to Hammerstein's Columbus Theatre in 125th Street near Park Avenue, or to the magnificent Harlem Opera House.

I still believe that the Harlem Opera House was the handsomest theatre in New York City. It had a large gilded foyer, the like of which is not seen nowadays, in which the Harlem élite would stroll between the acts. Harlemites used to subscribe for Monday night seats much as their more aristocratic neighbors downtown did for the opera. I saw everything there: Irving in "The Bells," Joseph Jefferson in "Rip Van Winkle," Stuart Robson in "A Comedy of Errors," Mansfield in "Dr. Jekyll and Mr. Hyde" and "Beau Brummel"—"San Toy," "The Geisha," "The Runaway Girl," the Bostonians in "Robin Hood"—those were the days!

After the show we would go over to the Harlem Casino and watch our parents drink genuine Pilsner beer while we were allowed the luxury of lemonade or ginger ale. These places are dim, almost forgotten names to me now, the Harlem Casino, Hollanders', and, years later, Pabst's.

On Sunday morning my father took me driving up Seventh Avenue, past farms and rocky shanty-covered cliffs, across Macomb's Dam Bridge to Jerome Avenue, where we would watch the trotting races. Then we would drop in to Huber's Road House. . . .

That was Harlem—the vanished Harlem of the pleasant, placid nineties.

As the community became predominantly black, the very word "Harlem" seemed to lose its old meaning. At times, it was easy to forget that "Harlem" was originally the Dutch name "Haarlem"; that the community it described had been founded by people from Holland; and that for most of its three centuries—it was first settled in the sixteen-hundreds—it had been occupied by white New Yorkers. "Harlem" became synonymous with black life and black style in Manhattan. Blacks living there used the word as though they had coined it themselves—not only to designate *their* area of residence but to express their sense of the various qualities of its life and atmosphere. As the years passed, "Harlem" assumed an even larger meaning. In the words of Adam Clayton Powell, Sr., the pastor of the Abyssinian Baptist Church, Harlem "became the symbol of liberty and the Promised Land to Negroes everywhere." In August of 1925, a writer for *The Saturday Evening Post* reported, "Harlem . . . draws immigrants from every country in the world that has a colored population, either large or small. . . . Ambitious and talented colored youth on every continent look forward to reaching Harlem. It is the Mecca for all those who seek Opportunity with a capital O." The sight of Harlem, said a black novelist in the nineteen-twenties, "gives any Negro security." And in 1930 Eslanda Goode Robeson wrote, in a biography of her husband, Paul Robeson, "Only Negroes *belong* in Harlem . . . it is a place they can call home."

A "Promised Land to Negroes everywhere" was bound, in time, to become overcrowded; and this squeeze occurred during the nineteen-thirties, when it seemed as though blacks from every part of the country and every part of the globe were living there. "The most populous city block in the United States and probably in the world is bounded by Seventh and Lenox Avenues and 142nd and 143rd Streets," A. J. Liebling wrote in 1937. "For number of human beings to the cubic foot, the block in Harlem is without a serious rival." As the black population spilled across one or two of the borders that had been defined by those former white residents—as it extended west, across Morningside Drive and St. Nicholas Avenue, and north, toward Washington Heights—people began to say that Harlem was spreading. This only meant, of course, that blacks were moving into areas that were previously all white, and into sections of Washington Heights, west of Amsterdam Avenue, that were not formally regarded as being parts of Harlem. As a black businessman said in 1920, "the natural boundaries of Harlem will be the limits of Negro property expansion." In other words, Harlem would be almost any place uptown, above 110th Street, where there were noticeable concentrations of blacks. This remained true as late as 1966. That year, the novelist Ralph Ellison—a native of Oklahoma who moved to Manhattan in 1936—appeared before a congressional committee, and he began his testimony by saying, "I live in New York City, on Riverside Drive at 150th Street. It isn't exactly Harlem, but Harlem has a way of expanding. It goes where Negroes go, or where we go in certain numbers. So some of us think of it as Harlem, though it is really Washington Heights."

In 1911, Harlem was still a good way from being all black. Negroes then lived in a relatively small section—on various blocks from 130th to 140th Streets between Fifth and Seventh Avenues. Much of the area east of Fifth, and as far south as 110th Street, was called East Harlem, and was occupied mostly by Italian and Jewish immigrants. Years later, it became one of the main centers of Manhattan's Hispanic community. The small black section in central Harlem shortly before the First World War was generally described as the black belt—especially by whites who still hoped that it could be kept from expanding. They hoped in vain.

The success of men like John M. Royall, John E. Nail, Philip A. Payton, Jr., and Henry C. Parker—black real-estate brokers who prospered from having opened the gates of Harlem to blacks—fathered a host of black real-estate agents, who exploited and accelerated the movement uptown. Between 1911 and 1922, almost all the major black churches moved to Harlem. So did social and theatrical clubs; college fraternities and sororities; the black Y.M.C.A. and Y.W.C.A.; black Democratic and Republican politicians and their clubhouses; and black branches of such fraternal organizations as the Masons, the Elks, the Pythians, and the Oddfellows. Migrants from the South and other parts of America streamed in, as did thousands from the West Indies, Africa, and Latin America. The National Association for the Advancement of Colored People, the National Urban League, and Socialist and black-nationalist organizations opened offices in Harlem. Major black newspapers—notably the *Age* and the *Amsterdam News*—moved their plants and editorial offices to the district. Along with them came such leading black journalists as Fred R. Moore, Jerome B. Petersen, George Harris, T. Thomas Fortune, James Weldon Johnson, Lester Walton, and William Melvin Kelly, Sr. Musicians, actors, popular entertainers of all sorts, lawyers, doctors, preachers, and businessmen moved uptown to live and work.

As whites surrendered to the "invasion" and gradually abandoned Harlem for areas more to their liking, the black belt broadened further. In 1914, according to the historian Gilbert Osofsky, "Negroes lived in some 1,100 houses within a twenty-three-block area of Harlem." He was using figures from a National Urban League survey, which estimated the black population to be nearly fifty thousand. That year, the magazine *The Outlook*, in an article titled "A Negro City in New York," carried this report:

> In one district in New York City a Negro population equal in numbers to the inhabitants of Dallas, Texas, or Springfield, Massachusetts, lives, works, and pursues its ideals almost as a separate entity from the great surrounding metropolis. Here Negro merchants ply their trade; Negro professional men follow their various vocations; their children are educated; the poor, sick, and orphan of the race are cared for; churches, newspapers, and banks flourish heedless of those, outside this Negro community, who resent its presence in a white city. . . .
>
> If one stands at the corner of One Hundred and Thirty-fifth Street and Fifth Avenue, in four directions can be seen rows of apartments or flat houses all inhabited by Negroes. This is virtually the center of the community. The houses are in good repair; windows, entrances, halls, sidewalks, and streets are clean, and the houses comfortable and respectable inside to a degree not often found in a workingman's locality. The ground floor of the buildings in every case is occupied by a store or business office. Here and there one sees the name of some Nationally known firm whose agent, always a Negro, has opened a branch business among the people of his own race.

The *Age* was then one of the oldest and certainly the largest of the black newspapers in New York City. (Founded as the *Rumor*, it had later been renamed the *Globe* and then the *Freeman* before becoming the *Age*.) Possibly, it was the largest journal of its kind in the country, for it called itself "The National Negro Weekly." It was also one of the main forces behind the growth of a black community in Harlem. In 1914, the *Age* had not yet moved uptown—it did so in 1919—but from its offices, at 247 West Forty-sixth Street, in the Tenderloin district, it had been calling Negro attention to the new frontier of Harlem, running almost all the real-estate advertising aimed at blacks, lecturing them on the advantages of building a fine neighborhood of their own, and training a severe eye on all forms of conduct that it deemed harmful to the kind of community it wished to see develop. When the *Age* urged its readers to look to the wonderful opportunities that Harlem presented, it was not addressing the common people. It spoke to ordinary blacks only when it was displeased or embarrassed by aspects of their conduct—as when, in June of 1910, the paper declared itself "mortified" by the news that immoral people were moving into apartments and tenements in Harlem. They "should be driven out by whatever means necessary," the paper said, and it went on to denounce the amount of loitering, loud and vulgar talk, and "skylarking and other disgusting amateur athletics" that took place on street corners. Such behavior, the *Age* said, "hurts the race."

The *Age* appears to have been written chiefly for those blacks who were being "hurt" by the conduct it criticized—the people it liked to call "the better element of the race." These were the professionals, the businessmen, the conspicuous achievers, and others of exemplary social, moral, and religious background. One of its readers wrote to the editor in October of 1912, "The New York *Age* . . . finds men of value in the great heaps scattered all about us; it recognizes ability; it crowns merit; it contends that only the highest and the best in our civilization shall be given prominence, and never falters to do honor to the men who can do things honorably." It was mainly to such people that the *Age* was speaking when it encouraged blacks to migrate to Harlem—when it promoted Harlem as a sedate community of homes and "a gold mine" for enterprising black professionals and businessmen. As such, the paper represented one of the prevailing tendencies in the black cultural and political leadership of that era. The *Age*, conservative and Republican, was one of the major Northern advocates of Booker T. Washington's practical programs for black self-reliance and economic progress—or "uplift," a term that was then commonly used. Washington, who until 1915, the year of his death, was the nation's most powerful black Republican, was a shareholder in the *Age*—although Fred R. Moore, its editor, did not wish the fact to be publicly known. The paper made no attempt, however, to conceal its enthusiasm for Washington and his policies. "The *Age*," it said of itself in 1923, "has always believed with Booker T. Washington that the future development of the race is in large measure dependent upon economic development of the individual, and for this reason has given much space in its news and editorial columns to the need of business development within the race. . . . It has never been a sensational paper, and believes in cleanliness and accuracy. . . . It numbers among its subscribers and readers the better element of the race."

Moore, a self-made man, was a good example of the old-style newspaper editor, full of fight, right-mindedness, and stern Victorian sermons. But he was primarily a businessman, excited by dividends and other results of efficient management. Light-skinned, and of medium height and build, he was born in Virginia in 1857 and grew up in Washington, D.C., where, as a young man, he worked as a messenger in the Treasury Department. On moving to New York around 1888, he worked as a messenger in the Western National Bank and then as a delivery clerk for the New York Clearing House. In 1893, he turned to real estate, and founded the Afro-American Investment & Building Company. In this position, he displayed abilities that caught the eye of Booker T. Washington, who appointed him an organizer of the National Negro Business League, which Washington formed in 1900 to encourage commercial enterprise among blacks. Moore, who had been a student of Washington's philosophy for some time, could hardly have been better suited to his new job. Blacks must "learn to value money and study thoroughly the plan of investment," he told a convention of the Business League in 1904. Three years later, in partnership with Washington, Moore acquired control of the *Age* from T. Thomas Fortune, its founding editor.

Moore and the *Age* were not alone in advocating business enterprise among blacks in Harlem. Clergymen—and Moore might so easily have been one—also preached the gospel of investment and profit. In October of 1912, Adam Clayton Powell, Sr., urged members of his Abyssinian Baptist congregation to "go into business on a larger scale in Harlem." Powell "produced figures showing that $4,500,000 is spent in the Harlem district for food, clothes, and shoes alone, twenty per cent of which . . . is profit," the *Age* said. "Dr. Powell stated that no race can ever become rich by saving its money." To some degree, the appeals to Negro business enterprise were successful. In 1914, as *The Outlook* reported that year, several black professionals and entrepreneurs were operating in Harlem. On West 135th Street, George Harris, who was a graduate of Harvard, and later became the first black alderman elected from Harlem, edited the *News*, a weekly paper he had founded. Its staff of twelve included graduates of Dartmouth and the University of Chicago. There were twenty physicians, fifteen lawyers, eight dentists, twenty-five regis-tered nurses, four pharmacists, and two architects in the black com-munity. "From the juncture of One Hundred and Thirty-fifth Street and Fifth Avenue can be seen the business signs of Negroes and Negro firms whose holdings and interests reach an aggregate of four million dollars," the magazine said. But there was less to the picture than met the eye. A number of the "business signs of Negroes and Negro firms" were just signs, for though such businesses may have been run by blacks, they were in fact owned by whites. In 1916, the *Age* reported, there were 145 businesses on the Negro stretch of Lenox Avenue, only twenty-three per cent of them owned and oper-ated by blacks. The percentage increased gradually, however, and in 1921 the *Age* was able to report that "about eighty per cent" of the businesses on 135th Street between Lenox and Seventh Avenues were owned by blacks. Though the early black-owned businesses were small in size and number, never before had so many of them sprung up in any one section of Manhattan. Along 135th Street (from Fifth to Seventh Avenues) and Lenox Avenue (from 130th to 140th Streets), there were grocery stores, meat markets, restaurants, bakeries, and candy and cigar stores; barber shops, beauty parlors, dress and shoe shops, tailor shops, drugstores, and real-estate and employment agencies; furniture movers, ice-coal-and-wood dealers, small hotels, laundries, and whitewashing and calcimining outfits. In 1920, three of the larger businesses were the Verbena Perfumery Company, on Lenox Avenue, which exported to Central America and the West Indies; the Lafayette Dress Company, on Seventh Avenue; and Thomas & Thomas, on 135th Street, which imported cocoa, nut-meg, cinnamon, sarsaparilla bark, and other spices from the West Indies.

The leaders of the church and the press who had urged blacks to open businesses in Harlem, as a means of advancing themselves and the cause of the race generally, had neglected to appeal to black customers for their support. That was a mistake. Several black busi-nesses offered services that could not be obtained elsewhere in Har-lem. But wherever black customers had a choice a considerable number of them turned to white establishments, even when—as was often the case—such establishments did not welcome their patronage. A Harlem newspaper reported at one stage, "Many of the white businessmen boast of the fact that Negroes will support their businesses whether they are discriminated against or not, and although some of the drygoods merchants on 7th and 8th Avenues receive the bulk of their business from the colored customers, they often tell advertising solicitors from the colored papers that they are not interested in colored trade and want no more of it than they now have." One black resident noted in 1914 that every nationality was "making money out of Negroes in Harlem—except Negroes."

Various reasons were given for this circumstance. "One great handicap is that our people have never been accustomed to trading with Negro merchants," the president of the Colored Men's Business Association said in 1916. "That has created a prejudice which it is hard to overcome. There are many loyal and truehearted race men and women who would give their custom to Negro merchants, but it never occurs to them that a race merchant can supply their needs." But black customers had reasons of their own for dealing with white businessmen. "In patronizing the Negro merchant," one of them said, "we often have to accept an article different from the kind wanted . . . his stock is not complete, and in most cases we are simply informed that the article wanted is not in stock and no effort is made to cater to the prospective customer by securing it." Another customer felt that "the Negro merchant does not appreciate our trade," and explained, "He seems to think that simply because he is a Negro all Negroes must trade with him, and he becomes rude and insulting if you are not satisfied with his attitude." A third said, "I am willing to patronize Negro merchants, even to the extent of paying a few cents more than the same article would cost elsewhere; but he has no conception of the courtesy due customers, and in most cases he is absolutely unreliable in fulfilling his promises, especially of delivery."

The Harlem that black clergymen and editorial writers envisioned—a sedate, industrious, and morally upright community of businesses and homes—was not wholly the one that took shape. Along with businessmen, professionals, and other "better" elements of the race, there migrated to Harlem much of the vice and crime from the

Tenderloin and San Juan Hill districts downtown, where the majority of blacks had been living. In April of 1911, when the "unwelcome" elements in Harlem were increasing, the *Age* devoted two editorials to the subject, both titled "Clean 'Em Out." The first said:

> Street-walking women and the animals that live upon their dirty money and boldly loaf in the path of good people must go. And decent people who harbor low characters and sustain their crimes, they must go. . . .
>
> Take Harlem. What could be made the ideal city of law-abiding, frugal, industrious, decent Negroes, is infested by the dance-hall harlot and the diamond-decked lover. . . .
>
> Information reaches us that one of the notorious sporting-house keepers in this city, whose houses are already places of shame, seeks to lease a beautiful private house in a recently acquired block in Harlem for "hotel" purposes. . . .
>
> We seek no unnecessary struggle. We seek no fame. We seek no title of reformer, but we do set our sign against the effrontery of vice and the insolence of crime.

The second editorial, a week later, said:

> The princes of shame . . . boldly unfurled their banner . . . marching in triumph from the deserted Tenderloin to Harlem, there to parade, unafraid, in the highways.
>
> Our seeming deeper concern for Harlem is due to a desire to check the spread of evil in that section. . . . Harlem must be saved, because Harlem, an important section of it, is to be always the center of the colored population of our city. Our churches will someday be planted there. The home-owners are already there, and thousands of good people have taken apartments there. . . . The children are there, the business houses are there. The social workers are there. Therefore, Harlem is worth fighting for. It deserves the jealous protection of all good men.

A month earlier, the *Harlem Home News*, a white publication, observed that "Harlem is evidently the burglar's as well as the holdup man's 'meal ticket.'" The paper did not disclose the racial identity of any specific offenders, but there may have been a clue in what it quoted a white resident as saying: "I favor lynching the scamps." An investigator employed by the National League for the Protection of Colored Women found in 1911 that black street gangs were springing up in Harlem—"organized for the defense of the colored boys against similar gangs of poor white boys." These gangs went by names like the Harlem Rats, the Harlem Black Devils, the Broad Shoulders and Caps, and the Harlem Hoboes.

It was also in 1911 that one of the earliest outbreaks of racial violence took place in Harlem—the result of what had started out as a meeting in friendly rivalry. The meeting was a baseball game that was played at Olympic Field, then at 136th Street and Fifth Avenue; and the contestants were the Moon Athletic Club, a black team, and the Silver Stars, who were billed as Harlem's "hope of the white race."

For the first three innings, the contest had proceeded smoothly, though the white Silver Stars had found it virtually impossible to hit a ball through that portion of the infield patrolled by Harry Lyons, the black shortstop. Lyons had snagged every ball within his reach and even some which, under ordinary circumstances, would have been beyond his reach. What looked like sure base hits were converted into easy outs. The Silver Stars soon noticed that Lyons' extraordinary feats at shortstop were due to something more than his agility. According to the *Harlem Home News*, which covered the event, Lyons was wearing "the largest baseball player's glove ever seen . . . fully as large and plump as a good old-fashioned feather pillow." Before coming to bat in the fourth inning, the Silver Stars called this matter to the attention of the umpires—protested the use of a glove which, if it was not illegal, was surely irregular. Ruling in favor of the Silver Stars, the umpires ordered the black shortstop to remove his glove. Lyons refused. He could not wear a smaller mitt, he said, as he had "powerful big hands."

During the ensuing discussion, tempers flared. Both benches emptied, and spectators rushed onto the field to join the fray. Fists flew, bottles and other missiles were hurled, and baseball bats were wielded. During the melee, Harry Lyons was seen to toss away his glove, run from the field, and return with a razor.

When order was restored, more than a dozen of the combatants required medical attention. One of them was Lyons, who had been carried off the field, unconscious. That was not the worst or the end of his troubles, however. When Lyons came to in the hospital, he was placed under arrest and charged with felonious assault. Such a charge was clearly for whatever damage he had done with his razor, though it could just as easily have been for the havoc he had wreaked with his glove.

Saloons were among the "unwelcome" elements that accompanied the migration from the black Tenderloin to Harlem. Though Harlem had always had some saloons, they multiplied when the black "invasion" began. Blacks were opening saloons of their own, and, to exploit the growing black trade, more whites than before were entering the saloon business. In 1914, the *Age* noted that Harlem was "infested" with saloons and that they prospered by catering chiefly to blacks. A year later, Eugene Kinckle Jones, a leading official of the National Urban League, estimated that there were ninety-eight saloons and liquor stores in Harlem. It was bad enough that there were so many of them—doing business even on Sundays—but they also served women, and this, in the minds of community leaders, was the worst aspect of the liquor trade.

Black saloonkeepers had more than moral censure to worry about: their drinking places were not doing nearly as well as the white-owned ones, for, as the white saloonkeepers and other white businessmen discovered, many black customers preferred to spend their money in white establishments. One of the few black saloons that did well among black patrons was Barron Wilkins' Astoria Café, on 134th Street at Seventh Avenue. John W. Connor, who ran an ailing business at the Royal Café, on West 135th Street, was heard to complain, "If those who drink liquor would only visit colored saloons in large numbers as they do white saloons, the colored saloon men would soon be in a position to compete with any bar in New York. They say we do not carry this brand or that brand; neither did some of the white saloons in the beginning. But colored people, in buying from their own people, do not seem to be as lenient and patient as with the white tradesmen. . . . Today I can show you saloon after saloon in Harlem where colored men congregate in large numbers all day, and only a few years ago the Negro's money was not wanted under any circumstances. But as soon as the proprietors of these places found it would be necessary to cater to the colored people to make money . . . Negroes forgot all about past discriminations. . . . The colored barbershops are loyally supported, but I should hate to see Italians open barbershops for colored in Harlem. You would find them crowded with Negroes." To stimulate business, black saloonkeepers began offering nonalcoholic inducements to potential customers. Reorganizing their establishments, they set aside special rooms where groups were invited to gather for small social affairs, sip light beverages, and listen to music—an innovation that evolved gradually into the great Harlem cabarets of later years. In 1914, Connor announced that in the afternoons and evenings, from two to eight, his Royal Café would be serving tea and cocoa, and patrons would be entertained with ragtime music. These affairs were called afternoon teas, and were so successful that other saloons began presenting them as well. The Harlem branch of the Women's Christian Temperance Union was said to be jubilant at this sober turn of events.

Not long after Connor introduced his afternoon teas, Barron Wilkins took the experiment a step further. At his Astoria Café, he began presenting tango teas, which were livelier than the afternoon teas. Guests were free to sip, chat, and listen to music, if that was all they cared to do, but if they were inclined to try more active forms of enjoyment they were welcome to take a turn on the dance floor, where professionals had been hired to demonstrate and teach one of the latest dances, the tango. Although the beverages remained non-alcoholic, the ladies of the Temperance Union cannot have been pleased with the new arrangement; they must surely have felt that wherever popular dancing appeared liquor was not far behind. In fact, considering where the tango teas were being held—in the side rooms of saloons and cafés—liquor was virtually there already.

Tango teas, which spread to other drinking places, gave employment to a number of up-and-coming black performers. In 1914, the young Goldie Cisco—who in 1921 danced in the chorus line of Eubie Blake and Noble Sissle's all-black Broadway musical *Shuffle Along*—was one of those who demonstrated the tango at Barron Wilkins' café. At Leroy's Café—which was on West 135th Street, and was owned by Leroy Wilkins (a brother of Barron Wilkins)—Mamie Sharp, a popular song stylist of the period, was to be heard singing "I'm Crazy About My Tango Man." And on other tango evenings, in other cafés, other vocalists were to be heard in renditions of "That's Why I'm Loving Someone Else Today," "When You Play in the Game of Love," "Back to the Carolina You Love," and "Every Girl Is My Girl."

Style in Ragtime

TANGO TEAS were only one of the symptoms of Harlem's infatuation with the tango. Dance fans were flocking to the Palace Casino, at 135th Street just off Fifth Avenue, and the Manhattan Casino (later renamed the Rockland Palace), at 155th Street and Eighth Avenue, to attend tango picnics, tango contests, and tango balls. New York, in a heady prewar fling, was embracing what were called "modern" dances. Especially among white socialites downtown, these dances were replacing the old polka, schottische, and cakewalk. And what was true of white socialites downtown was true of black ones uptown as well. But among the masses of Harlem the tango was more of a fad —a fashionable diversion, or classy respite, from such animated and risqué rhythms of the popular dance floor as the black bottom, the grizzly bear, the eagle rock, the turkey trot, the bunny hug, the Texas Tommy, scratchin' the gravel, and ballin' the jack. It was to these that the decorous white citizens of Harlem were referring when they used the term "nigger" dances. Willie (the Lion) Smith, one of the pioneering jazz pianists of Harlem, recalled several years later, "Some of these dances were pretty wild. They called them 'hug me close,' 'the shiver,' 'hump-back rag' . . . 'the lovers' walk.' These were just some of the frantic dances that were beginning to replace the dignified cakewalking struts." The masses of Harlem took to the tango partly because it was new, partly because they liked its association with high society, partly because they realized that black musicians had contributed something to its development and popularity, and partly, no doubt, because they wished to show that they, too, were capable of meeting its demand for controlled and elegant movement at a quick tempo.

Today, the dance steps that the masses once preferred may be as extinct as the cakewalk, the polka, and the schottische. They survive mainly in the heads of people, now quite old, who used to dance them or in the history books of popular dancing. In one of these books—*Jazz Dance*, by Marshall and Jean Stearns—the turkey trot is described as "a fast, marching one-step, arms pumping at the side, with occasional arm flappings emulating a crazed turkey." Of the Texas Tommy, another book—*Dancing and Dancers of Today*, by Caroline and Charles Caffin—says, "Dancers are perhaps more acrobatic than eccentric . . . the whirl which spins his partner towards the footlights with such momentum that without aid she must assuredly fly across them, must be nicely adjusted so that in neither force nor direction shall she escape the restraining grasp of his hand outstretched just at the right moment to arrest her." (From this description, the Texas Tommy seems to have prefigured the Lindy Hop, which was invented in Harlem in the late nineteen-twenties, and was one of the most famous dance steps associated with the history of the community. In fact, according to Ethel Williams, a black performer who did both dances, the Texas Tommy "*was* like the Lindy.")

A number of the vernacular steps that the black masses favored were also popular in the clubs and cabarets of downtown Manhattan, where the prewar "modern" dances enjoyed their strongest vogue. The meeting of these cultural styles and their impact on the social conventions of the period are described by Lloyd Morris in his book *Incredible New York*:

> In a cabaret, little tables were massed around a large central space, where a show was put on by singers and teams of professional dancers, and where the patrons also danced. No matter where you went, you saw couples leaving their tables, their food and champagne to push onto the dance floor. There, locked in a tight embrace, they moved through the startling figures of the Texas Tommy, the bunny hug, the grizzly bear, the turkey trot, the one-step, or the tango. Never before had well-bred people seen— much less performed—such flagrantly salacious contortions. Yet, as a popular song declared, "everybody's doing it. . . ."
>
> The cabarets and the scandalous "modern dances" set off a hurricane of protest. Outraged conservatives, clergymen, educators, social workers, editors of newspapers joined in a massive attack. They were stirred to wrath by "vice," by "immorality," openly condoned and participated in by New York's "best people." . . . Few of these enraged protesters foresaw that the new night life and the new dances were to help bring about a revolution in morals, manners, fashions in clothes, social customs. . . . At all the cabarets you saw lines of men and women, in full evening

attire, held back by a velvet rope and a stern head waiter who was busily checking their names against his list of advance reservations. . . . You heard "Alexander's Ragtime Band" wherever you went, and its snappy rhythm made you want to shake your shoulders and your feet.

Negro syncopation—the music as well as the men who played it—had no small influence on the evolution of styles that was taking place in prewar Manhattan, or on the early development of Irving Berlin, the composer of "Alexander's Ragtime Band." It was from black stage shows that some of the lively dance steps had found their way into white cabarets. One of these shows was *Darktown Follies*, which opened at the Lafayette Theatre in Harlem in 1913. The production, James Weldon Johnson wrote some time later, "drew space, headlines, and cartoons in the New York papers; and consequently it became the vogue to go to Harlem to see it . . . the beginning of the nightly migration to Harlem in search of entertainment." One of those who went up to Harlem to see *Darktown Follies* was Florenz Ziegfeld, and, impressed by the production, he bought the rights to part of the show in order to use it in his downtown Follies. What chiefly captured Ziegfeld's fancy was a number titled "At the Ball," in which the entire cast appeared and danced a rousing version of ballin' the jack. Ethel Williams, one of the stars, said later, "I'd 'ball the jack' on the end of the line every way you could think of—and when the curtain came down I'd put my hand out from behind the curtain and 'ball the jack' with my fingers."

The moral spokesmen for the black community were as severely outraged by the dance craze as were those in the rest of Manhattan. "The Negro race is dancing itself to death," Adam Clayton Powell, Sr., said in 1914. "You can see the effect of the tango, the Chicago, the turkey trot, the Texas Tommy, and ragtime music not only in their conversations but in the movement of their bodies about the home and on the street. Grace and modesty are becoming rare virtues." These virtues were very much on the mind of the *Age* two years later, when it commented on women entertainers who were "extremely careless about their attitudes and actions in dancing" and men who were "equally careless as to the character and nature of the songs they sang."

The leaders of the "modern"-dance movement in Manhattan—especially among the ballroom and parlor set—were a white couple, Vernon and Irene Castle. As the Texas Tommy prefigured the Lindy Hop, so the Castles, especially Irene, foreshadowed the gaiety and social mutinies of the jazz age. According to Lloyd Morris, the Castles "transformed the dance craze from a transient mania into a permanent element of American civilization." In *Incredible New York* the author continues:

> The Castles were not only national idols, but national arbiters of etiquette. You went to study them at their small, smart supper room, Sans Souci, or at Castles in the Air, a cabaret where they danced once every evening. . . . The cult of joy was a serious matter, and it involved the elderly and middle-aged as well as the young. . . . Meanwhile, dainty Irene Castle was setting sartorial fashion. Because Castle dances were mildly acrobatic, she had bobbed her hair, replaced unyielding corsets by an elastic girdle, substituted silk bloomers and a slip for petticoats, adopted short, light, flowing frocks. Imitated on Fifth and Park Avenues, these radical innovations soon produced a nationwide revolution in feminine attire. The final collapse of a whaleboned morality was signalized by "the new lingerie, in which everything is combined in one garment, easily slipped on." And—as the wild younger generation soon discovered—just as easily slipped off.

The orchestra of James Reese Europe, the best-known of the black bands in New York, was almost the only one that the Castles danced to—at Harlem's Manhattan Casino, in the clubs and cabarets downtown, at society balls, or on extended tours of the United States. The partnership was mutually profitable: the Castles attracted as much attention to Europe's orchestra as they gained from dancing to it. Europe not only played the Castles' favorite music, he also wrote much of it—compositions like the innovation trot, the lame-duck waltz, the half and half, the Castle-house rag, the Castle walk, and the foxtrot (the last arranged from a composition by W. C. Handy). Europe's music, Irene Castle said near the end of her career, "was the only music that completely made me forget the effort of the dance."

The orchestra was then called the Tempo Club, an offshoot of the Clef Club, which Europe founded in 1910. Noble Sissle, who joined the group in 1916, once said that James Europe was "the Duke Ellington of his time." In March of 1914, the *Evening Post* called him "one of the most remarkable men, not only of his race, but in the music world of this country." Though Europe was not the handsome and urbane figure that Ellington was, he was striking in appearance. He was strongly built, often sported a white suit and white shoes, and, wearing small, round, wire-framed glasses, had the look of a starchy rural schoolmaster—grave, studious, businesslike, and censorious. Irene Castle thought he was "a very commanding figure when he faced his men."

Like many of the successful and influential blacks then living in Manhattan, Europe was not a native New Yorker. He was born in Mobile, Alabama, in 1881, and grew up in Washington, D.C. He studied the violin under Enrico Hurlei, an assistant director of the United States Marine Band, and in 1904 he moved to New York and settled on the West Side. There he played and conducted for some of the popular black musical comedies of the time and was a member of a black vaudeville elite that gathered at the Marshall Hotel, on West Fifty-third Street.

On West Fifty-third, in a building opposite the Marshall, Europe formed the Clef Club, an organization of New York musicians. (Noble Sissle, who knew a number of the original Clef Club men, said they "were wonderful musicians and singers, but very few of them read music." A writer in Harlem was to wonder why Europe had given the name Clef Club to "a musical association of colored men who could not read notes.") In 1910, when Europe founded the club, he wanted merely to provide a central hiring place for the black musicians of the city. They were then badly disorganized and were poorly paid by the ballrooms, hotels, restaurants, clubs, and private families that hired them from time to time. Calls for their services would be sent in to various barbershops, saloons, and poolrooms of the Tenderloin, where their names were well known. The Clef Club not only served as a main booking office for these musicians but also fixed the contractual terms of their work.

From among those who registered, Europe picked the men who made up his Clef Club Orchestra, a pioneering big band and the most remarkable group of its kind that New York had yet seen. Of its first public performance, at Harlem's Manhattan Casino, in 1910, the *Age's* theatre critic wrote, "Never has such a large and efficient body of colored musicians appeared together in New York City in a concert . . . nearly one hundred in all." A flyer advertising another concert, also at the Manhattan Casino, listed almost a hundred and fifty instruments. They included fifty mandolins, thirty harp guitars, ten banjos, twenty violins, a saxophone, ten cellos, five clarinets, five flutes, five bass violins, three timpani and drums, two organs, and ten pianos. In 1913, in a concert that brought ragtime to Carnegie Hall, the Clef Club drew these raves from the magazine *The Craftsman*:

> Few white people had ever heard of the orchestra . . . a band of a hundred and twenty-five members . . . this concert really formed an epoch in the musical life of the Negro and also in the development of Negro music. . . .
>
> It was an astonishing sight . . . that filled the entire stage with banjos . . . eloquent in syncopation. . . . As one looked through the audience, one saw heads swaying and feet tapping in time to the . . . rhythm, and when the march neared the end and the whole band burst out singing as well as playing, the novelty of this climax . . . brought a very storm of tumultuous applause.

In 1914, when certain conflicts developed among the Clef Club's membership, Europe resigned as leader and organized a smaller orchestra, which he called the Tempo Club. This was the group to which the Castles danced, and which entertained some of New York's and America's richest families.

Recalling the early years of the Clef Club and the Tempo Club, Noble Sissle later said: "After the turn of the century, the rage was the Viennese Waltz—lots of gypsy bands playing violins, mandolins, cellos, and things. The gypsy bands used to serenade around people eating, and, after that, they played dances like the Blue Danube. There was no common American dance music. About 1910, James Europe formed the Clef Club. They played a lively kind of music— none of this one-two-three stuff, with no in-between steps. Well, the white people heard about them and came to listen, and before you could turn around they were hiring the Clef Club to come and play. The Clef Club used to go on after the gypsy band finished playing, and whatever was the last waltz the gypsy band played, the Clef Club would start off by playing it in ragtime. All of a sudden, people commenced getting up and trying to dance it. And this was the beginning of the Negro taking over New York music and establishing our rhythms.

"Later, when Europe formed the Tempo Club, we played in parlors, drawing rooms, yachts, private railroad cars, exclusive millionaires' clubs, swanky hotels, and fashionable resorts. We played everywhere—from the Everglades (in Palm Beach) to the Green Brier Hotel (in White Sulphur Springs) to the Metropolitan Club (in New York) to Newport's finest. I think we boys who came to New York and were in the music profession at that time lived through the happiest and most interesting time in the development of American music. We were snatched from all walks of life, from all environments, and suddenly found ourselves playing and singing at the homes of the Vanderbilts, the Goulds, the Wanamakers. One day we would be in Pittsburgh, playing for the Stotesburgs; next day we would be in Washington, playing for Mrs. Evelyn McLean; another day we would be playing on the private yacht of the Astors. We were the only musicians who could play jazz music to satisfy society people. It was our music, and the wealthy people would not take a substitute when they could buy the original."

Just as Duke Ellington later hesitated to describe his music as jazz, James Reese Europe had an aversion to the term "ragtime." He preferred to say he played "syncopated rhythms" or "the music of the American Negro." In 1909, when the *Age* quoted John Philip Sousa as saying that ragtime was dead, Europe replied that "there never was any such music as ragtime." That term, he said, was "merely a nickname or a fun-name given to Negro rhythm by our Caucasian brother musicians many years ago." Whether this was so or not, Europe was among the few black musicians of his time who shunned the word "ragtime." His dislike for it may have been influenced by his background. He came from a household of classically trained musicians and from a section of the black middle class that strove to gain the highest standing for black cultural endeavors. To such people, .the word "ragtime" was low-life in sound and meaning, and tended to relegate the music it described to an inferior status. They also felt that blacks who consented to the use of such a word were, however unwittingly, lending support to the view, widely held among whites, that no art form springing from black life was worthy of critical esteem.

As far as is known, Scott Joplin, the greatest of all ragtime artists, did not object to the use of the term. What he did object to were the lyrics of most ragtime songs. Joplin thought of them as vulgar, as preventing serious and respectable audiences from appreciating the true merits of the music itself. Some of his own classic compositions —"Maple Leaf Rag," "Pineapple Rag," "The Entertainer," and "Euphonic Sounds"—had, along with compositions by James Scott and Joseph Lamb, helped to raise ragtime music in public esteem, though not high enough, apparently. Joplin, who is generally said to have been born in Texarkana, Texas, in 1868 (other sources give his birthplace as either Texarkana, Arkansas, or Marshall, Texas), moved to Manhattan during the first decade of the century. He then settled on the West Side, near the music-publishing district. A number of his famous pieces were released by John Stark, one of the leading promoters of ragtime music, whose publishing house was in the area. In 1915, Joplin joined the migration to Harlem, where he lived on West 131st Street. Two years earlier, speaking to a reporter from the *Age*, he had deplored the crudely worded ragtime songs that were still being written:

> I have often sat in theatres and listened to beautiful ragtime melodies set to almost vulgar words . . . and I have wondered why some composers will continue to make people hate ragtime because the melodies are set to such bad words.
>
> I have often heard people say, after they had heard a ragtime song, "I like the music but I don't like the words." . . .
>
> If someone were to put vulgar words to a strain of one of Beethoven's beautiful symphonies, people would begin saying, "I don't like Beethoven's symphonies." So it is the unwholesome words and not the ragtime melodies that many people hate.
>
> Ragtime rhythm is a syncopation original with the colored people, though many of them are ashamed of it. But the other races throughout the world are learning to write and make use of ragtime melodies. It is the rage in England today. When composers put decent words to ragtime there will be very little kicking from the public about ragtime.

Joplin had an especially urgent reason for praising the finer possibilities of ragtime. He had recently completed the most ambitious work of his life—*Treemonisha*, a folk opera (Joplin insisted it was grand opera) in syncopated rhythm. *Treemonisha* contained a number of lovely melodies, with some of the most "decent words" that had yet been set to syncopated music, and Joplin did not wish his opera to be associated with the worst connotations of the word "ragtime." "I am a composer of ragtime music," he told a journalist in Harlem, "but I want it thoroughly understood that my opera 'Treemonisha' is not ragtime . . . the score complete is grand opera."

But *Treemonisha* was already being hurt by the prejudices he feared. Even before he settled in Harlem—where his wife, Lottie, ran a boarding house to help support the family—Joplin had been trying to attract serious public attention to his opera. The public, however—or, at any rate, the entrepreneurs of music and theatre— had dismissed it as a work of no serious merit. No music house cared to publish it, and no producer wanted to stage it. All of those who heard about it may have shared the feeling of a black journalist who—upon hearing, in 1908, that Joplin was composing grand opera —said, "From ragtime to grand opera is certainly a big jump." But Joplin's faith in *Treemonisha* remained unshaken, and in 1911 he published the score at his own expense. The public's response was hardly more encouraging than it had been earlier. About the only magazine that took note of the published score was *The American Musician*, whose reviewer wrote that Joplin had "created an entirely new phase of musical art and has produced a thoroughly American opera." No financial backers came forward, however.

In 1915, Joplin decided to stage the work himself—no doubt as a means of revealing its dramatic possibilities to any major producer who happened to attend. Rudi Blesh and Harriet Janis, the authors of *They All Played Ragtime*, record the outcome:

> A single performance . . . took place in a hall in Harlem in 1915. The performance was by full cast, but without scenery or orchestra. Joplin played the orchestral parts in the piano. The musical drama made virtually no impression. Without scenery, costumes, lighting, or orchestral backing, the drama seemed thin and unconvincing, little better than a rehearsal, and its special quality in any event would have been lost on the typical Harlem audience that attended. The listeners were sophisticated enough to reject their folk past, but not sufficiently to relish a return to it.

Not only was the performance a disaster but it also appears to have broken Joplin's spirit. His health, which had been failing, worsened rapidly, and less than two years later he was dead, at the age of forty-eight. As Blesh and Janis put it, Joplin did not recover "from the blow that completely crushed the hopes of a lifetime." The future would be kinder to him and to the work on which he had staked his life. In the nineteen-seventies—during a furious revival of interest in ragtime music and a joyous reappraisal of Joplin's genius—his opera achieved something of the status he had believed it to deserve. His shorter compositions became popular again, and in 1975 *Treemonisha* was produced by the Houston Grand Opera and had a reasonably successful run on Broadway. Vera Brodsky Lawrence, a musicologist, who had labored indefatigably to bring Joplin's neglected opera to modern attention, wrote in 1975 that *Treemonisha* was a work "of as great quality as Joplin had believed it to be." She added, "But perhaps most significant amid this universal furor of recognition is the vindication, at long last, of Joplin's unquenchable belief in his beautiful opera. Exactly sixty years after the shattering fiasco at that Harlem rehearsal hall, 'Treemonisha' is finally receiving the rapturous acclaim that Scott Joplin so passionately desired for it but that he was destined never to realize."

ABOVE, LEFT: Mary White Ovingt
was a writer, a social work
among black families in the ear
nineteen-hundreds, and a foundir
member of the N.A.A.C.P.

ABOVE, RIGHT: Philip A. Payton, Jr

LEFT: Sheet-music cover for one
Bert Williams's favorite songs. "I'
a Jonah Man" was the theme sor
of In Dahomey, the Williams ar
Walker musical comedy hit
1903-4

ᴀʙᴏᴠᴇ: "The Frogs," a social club of leading black theatre professionals that was founded in Manhattan in 1908. Back row, left to right: Bob Cole (performer and writer), Lester A. Walton (critic), Sam Corker (writer), Bert Williams (comedian), James Reese Europe (conductor and composer), and Alec Rogers (song writer). Front row, left to right: Tom Brown (dancer), J. Rosamond Johnson (composer), George Walker (dancer), Jesse A. Shipp (song writer), and R. C. McPherson (song writer)

ʀɪɢʜᴛ: Ada Overton Walker (wife of George Walker), who was the leading female performer of the Williams and Walker theatrical company

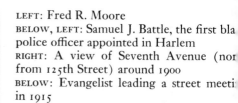

LEFT: Fred R. Moore
BELOW, LEFT: Samuel J. Battle, the first bla[ck]
police officer appointed in Harlem
RIGHT: A view of Seventh Avenue (nor[th]
from 125th Street) around 1900
BELOW: Evangelist leading a street meeti[ng]
in 1915

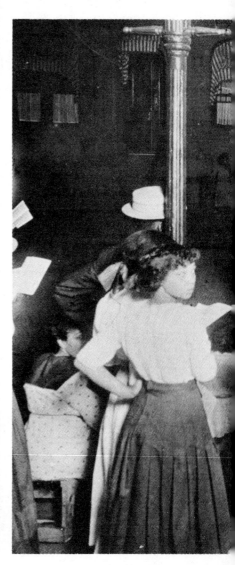

ABOVE: Apartment of a Harlem working-cla[ss]
family in 1910
LEFT: Charles S. Gilpin

LEFT AND BELOW: Madame C. J. Walker and her mansion, Villa Lewaro
BOTTOM: Salon of Villa Lewaro

ABOVE: The "Harlem Hellfighters" return from France in 1919. They are marching up Fifth Avenue, on their way to Harlem
RIGHT: The "Silent Parade" of 1917, when thousands from Harlem marched down Fifth Avenue to protest the race riots in St. Louis

The Beauty Business

WATCHDOGS of morality in prewar Harlem kept a sharp eye on "the better class" of women, observing whether and how they were adapting to the changing social fashions of the city. The vigil was not always rewarding or reassuring. In 1910, these guardians were appalled to hear what certain women in Harlem were doing at their wine parties and soirées—smoking cigarettes. Some of them were even prominent church members. From his pulpit at the Abyssinian Baptist Church, Adam Clayton Powell, Sr., let it be known that he had heard what was going on—"our best women" sitting with their feet up on chairs, smoking cigarettes. "What a spectacle!" the preacher declared. "What a defilement of pure womanhood. What a desecration of sacred motherhood. What a damnation of childhood!" Reverdy C. Ransom, from *his* pulpit at the Bethel African Methodist Episcopal Church, was equally reproving. He could only conclude, he said, that black society women were trying to copy what white society women on Fifth Avenue were doing.

By 1914, black society women, like their white counterparts, were also doing the tango and other "modern" Castle dances. But there is no evidence that they descended to the likes of the turkey trot, the grizzly bear, the Texas Tommy, and all the other vernacular steps that were done to the funkier versions of ragtime music.

During this period, and for some time afterward, the pages of black newspapers were crowded with the advertisements of beauty culturists and manufacturers of beauty products. Black-No-More was a cream for "bleaching and beautifying" the complexion. Fair-Plex Ointment made the "skin of women and men . . . bright, soft and smooth." The makers of Cocotone Skin Whitener advised, "Don't envy a clear complexion, use Cocotone . . . and have one." And—as if replying to Cocotone's claim—an ad for Golden Brown Ointment declared, "Don't be fooled by so-called 'skin-whiteners.' But you can easily enhance your beauty, lighten and brighten your dark or sallow skin by applying Golden Brown. . . . It won't whiten your skin—as that can't be done." Though there was a brisk trade in these creams and ointments, it was chiefly light-skinned Harlemites—constituting almost a distinct social class—who bought them. Of course, a few dark-skinned Negroes used these "lighteners" as well, in the hope of gaining social acceptance among their fair-skinned brethren, but most of them ridiculed the promise of the ointments. Besides, they feared one of the worst accusations which could be made against them—that they were ashamed of their color.

The *Age* had been advertising skin-lighteners since at least 1909. But as a leading black publication it seemed to have doubted the wisdom of its policy in encouraging the use of such mixtures. The paper betrayed a tone of defensiveness when it said, in January of 1909, "Prominent white women of New York have always used cold cream for the face, but since Complexion Wonder Creme [which the *Age* advertised] was discovered, colored people use it as much as white people."

Eight months later, the *Times* reflected the views of people who were not impressed by the *Age's* argument:

> In the columns of our contemporary which professes to be devoted to the best interests of the negro race appears a large advertisement inviting its readers to buy seven cosmetic preparations by the use of which colored men may obtain "better situations in banks, clubs, and business houses" and colored women may "occupy higher positions socially and commercially, marry better, get along better." One of the preparations purports to be a cream that makes "dark skin lighter colored. . . ." The advertisement implies that negroes should be ashamed of their own features and should by all means mask them into some resemblance to the Caucasian race. . . .
>
> But whether genuine or not its admission to the columns of the organ of negro uplift affords a revelation of racial psychology that is both curious and saddening. The exhortation to stand proudly upon nature's endowments—to be a man, or a mouse, or a long-tailed rat—is not needed by most races. While the negro disesteems himself and seeks to be something else will he be respected as he is?

Complexion Wonder Creme was manufactured by the Chemical Wonder Company, among whose other products, which the *Age* also advertised, was Wonder Uncurl, a pomade that "tends to keep the hair straight and pliable so that it will dress well." Another product was a "magnetic-metallic comb which helps straighten the hair." These were early signs of the great hair-beautifying industry that developed in Harlem. As had happened with skin-lighteners, the advertising columns of black newspapers were loaded with information about anti-kink ointments, hair-growing preparations, special soaps and shampoos, combs, wigs, beauty parlors, and competing hairdressing schools and systems.

Although the hairdressing industry catered chiefly to women, it gratified aspirations of certain men as well. In 1911, one newspaper, reporting on "the latest fad," said:

> "Have you had your hair straightened yet?" This question can be heard many times during the day up in Harlem where the colored population is large. . . . Up around 135th Street and Lenox Avenue . . . colored men can be seen in large numbers who are wont to take off their hats repeatedly, even on the street when the temperature is far from freezing, and stroke their glossy hair with their hand in an affectionate manner.

This may have been the beginning of a practice that came to be known as conking. Recalling the early years of the practice, James P. Johnson, one of the originators of Harlem jazz piano, once said, "Up on 153rd Street there was a former barber named Hart who had invented a hair preparation named Kink-No-More, called Conk for short. His preparation was used by all musicians. . . . You'd get your hair washed, dyed and straightened then trimmed. It would last about a month."

Among the persons of wealth and social influence in Harlem were the community's great beauticians. Mme J. L. Crawford, who moved from the middle West Side to Harlem in 1911, was probably the first of them to settle there. She was followed by, among others, Mme Anna Malone, who introduced the Poro Beauty System; Mme Estella, the founder of the Nu-Life School of Beauty Culture; and Mme Sarah Spencer Washington, who originated the Apex Beauty System. The greatest, wealthiest, and most influential of them all was Mme C. J. Walker, the creator of the Walker System. This system claimed two unique distinctions: it used "no curling irons or straightening tongs," according to one of the Walker advertisements in the black press, and, unlike other systems, which emphasized hair-straightening and hairdressing, it emphasized hair-growing, thanks to a formula whose ingredients were known only to the founder.

When Mme Walker settled in New York, in 1914, she was already a woman of considerable wealth—nearly a millionaire. Her Walker Manufacturing Company, in Indianapolis, had been producing her hair-growing mixture for several years and distributing it exclusively among a chain of beauty parlors she had set up across the United States and in parts of Central America and the West Indies. Mme Walker's beauty headquarters in Harlem—managed by her only child, a daughter named A'Lelia—occupied two adjoining brownstones on 136th Street between Lenox and Seventh Avenues. The buildings accommodated not only beauty parlors but also the Walker College of Hair Culture and private apartments that were splendidly furnished. No beautician in New York was qualified or authorized to practice the Walker System unless she had received a diploma from the college—"a passport to prosperity," the Walker people claimed. Mme Walker's enterprise, the black novelist and poet Claude McKay later said, "became essential to Negro society." McKay went on, "Her schools of beauty attracted students from the most cultivated Negro families. Around her gathered some of the most arresting types of Negro beauty."

Mme Walker shared a residence with her daughter on West 136th Street. Before arriving in Manhattan, she had bought a house in Flushing, Queens, but she appears never to have lived there. Perhaps she preferred to stay in Harlem while awaiting the completion of a mansion that was being built for her in the Westchester village of Irvington, overlooking the Hudson. Harlemites were fascinated by Mme Walker, a woman who had risen from nothing to become one of the richest blacks anyone had ever heard about. They knew the means by which she had amassed her wealth, and that was fascinating enough. But everyone wondered what she might be worth and what the size of her annual income might be. "Well," she said in 1916—replying to one of many inquiries on the subject—"until recently it gave me great pleasure to tell . . . the amount of money I made yearly, thinking it would inspire my hearers. But I found that for so doing some looked upon me as a boastful person who wanted to blow my own horn. And then again I received so many requests for money that I concluded it was best to keep mum on that score. I will say, however, that my business last year yielded me an annual income which runs into six figures and I'm going to try to eclipse my 1915 record this year." A year later, she replied to another inquiry, "I am not a millionaire, but I hope to be someday."

In one respect, at least, Mme Walker's appearance did not reflect her great wealth and success: her face, wide and roundish, with an open and kindly expression, gave her the look of a retiring and matronly sort whose main enjoyments were children, the church, and passing pleasant afternoons playing cards with friends. In other respects, however, she both looked and acted as important and rich as she was. She was built along grand lines—about six feet tall, and generously proportioned—and in some of the roomy and heavy-bosomed dresses of the day she had the appearance of a formidable queen mother. She owned expensive cars, supported charities generously, gave scholarships to needy black young men and women, contributed to the Tuskegee Institute—whose founder, Booker T. Washington, she admired—and lived in splendid surroundings.

Still, it was not until 1917, when her mansion at Irvington was completed, that Mme Walker could be seen in all her magnificence. When the mansion was receiving its finishing touches, a reporter from the *Times* looked the place over and wrote this description of it:

> The structure is a three-story and basement affair with roof of red tile, in the Italian Renaissance style of architecture, and was designed by V. W. Tandy, a negro architect. It is 113 feet long and 30 feet wide and stands in the centre of a four-and-a-half-acre plot. It is fireproof, of structural tile, with an outer covering of cream-colored stucco, and has 34 rooms. In the basement are a gymnasium, bath and shower, kitchen and pantry, servants' dining room, power room for an organ, and storage vaults for valuables.
>
> The visitor enters a marble room, whence a marble stairway leads to the floor above. On the first floor are the library and conservatory, a living room 21 x 32 feet, and a dining room with a hand-painted ceiling. Adjoining the two drawing rooms is a

chamber for an $8,000 organ. . . . Mme. Walker likes music. When the organ is played, sounding pipes will carry the strains to different parts of the house.

The second floor contains bedrooms, bathrooms, showers, dressing rooms, sewing rooms, and two sleeping porches. On the third floor are servants quarters. The owner employs eight servants, including a butler, sub-butler, chef, and maids of all work. In addition, she has a social secretary and a nurse. On the third floor are also bathrooms, a billiard room and a children's nursery. Mme. Walker loves children. They are frequent guests at her house. . . .

Plans for finishing the house call for a degree of elegance and extravagance that a princess might envy. There are to be bronze and silver statuary, sparkling cut-glass candelabra, paintings, rich tapestries, and countless other things which will make the place a wonder house.

Villa Lewaro, as the house was called, became a center for grand entertainments. Blacks of high standing—professors, lawyers, doctors, journalists, businessmen, clergymen, and what were then called race leaders—vied for invitations to her receptions, dinner parties, and balls. Passing such stylish evenings in her mansion, how could they not have been impressed by her wealth and acquired position? Few among them, however, would have exchanged *their* origins for those from which she sprang.

The hair-growing formula on which Mme Walker built her fortune had come to her, she said, in a dream one night after a day of toiling over her washtub. Born Sarah Breedlove in Louisiana in the mid-eighteen-sixties, she married when she was fourteen and was widowed at twenty, at which point, in order to support herself and her young daughter, she became a washerwoman. She later gave at least two accounts of what occurred then. "I was at my tub one morning with a heavy wash before me," she said in the first of these. "As I bent over the washboard, and looked at my arms buried in soapsuds, I said to myself, 'What are you going to do when you grow old and your back gets stiff? Who's going to take care of your little girl?' This set me to thinking, but with all of my thinking I couldn't see how I, a poor washerwoman, was going to better my condition. . . . One night I had a dream, and something told me to start in the business in which I'm now engaged. This I did. I went to Denver, Colorado, and began my business with a capital of $1.25." In the second account, she said that in 1903, when her hair began falling out, she prayed "to the Lord" for a cure. "He answered my prayer, for one night I had a dream, and in that dream a big black man appeared to me and told me what to mix up for my hair. Some of the remedy was grown in Africa, but I sent for it, mixed it, put it on my scalp, and in a few weeks my hair was coming in faster than it had ever fallen out. I tried it on my friends; it helped them. I made up my mind I would begin to sell it." Reflecting, in 1917, on what she had subsequently made of herself, she added, "Perseverance is my motto. It laid the Atlantic Cable; it gave us the telegraph, telephone, and wireless. It gave to the world an Abraham Lincoln, and to a race freedom. It gave to the Negro Booker T. Washington and Tuskegee Institute. It made Frederick Douglass the great orator he was, and it gave to the world Paul Laurence Dunbar, and to poetry a new song."

Harlem at Sixteen

IN 1916, Charles Martin, a minister of the African Methodist Episcopal denomination, wrote an article titled "The Harlem Negro," which appeared in one of the publications of his church. It was in part a typical clergyman's piece—preachy and morally querulous in much of its tone, and biassed and selective in its presentation of the desirable and undesirable features of life in Harlem. But, despite these quirks, the article renders a reasonably representative portrait of what Harlem had become in the first sixteen years of its development as a black community.

Blacks in Harlem, the preacher said, loved "good things, plenty to eat, often too much to drink," and were "blessed or cursed with a wonderful optimism." They were "caught and held in the flightiness and gay life," and they seemed reluctant to patronize their "own." There were too many saloons, too many gamblers, too many pickpockets, pocketbook snatchers, burglars, and spurious diamond dealers—some feeding on "the credulity and superstition of the hardworking Harlemite." Certain blacks liked nothing better than to gather on sidewalks and around street-corner lampposts. "To stand aside and look at the laughing, hilarious crowds that the theatres belch forth, you would think that there is never a care in Harlem." But that was not true. The "foppishly dressed young man," the "gayly dressed young woman," the "well-groomed gentleman," and the "tastily gowned lady" did not mean that all Harlemites were "a thoughtless people, living only for the day, eating, drinking, and dressing."

Harlem, he went on, was full of preachers who claimed to be Doctors of Divinity, but only they themselves seemed to know how they had come by their degrees. The preacher you addressed in the morning as the Reverend Mr. So-and-So could very well be the Reverend Dr. So-and-So by nightfall: "No spot like Harlem for conferring titles." Harlem was also full of beautiful churches, large and small. Although there were various "fads and fallacies in religion," Harlemites "turning out for . . . religious exercise on Sunday" were "a beautiful sight." Sunday schools were well attended, but some of the children were "wise beyond their years," and this "presented a serious problem." For example: "A teacher in one of the Sunday Schools . . . was questioning his class on love, I Corinthians 13 being the lesson. He asked for a definition of love, expecting that Paul's description [concerning charity] would be given as an answer. What was his surprise when the boy said, 'Love is a fire without insurance.' "

In 1916, orators of a radical and "socialistic" bent were beginning to appear on the street corners of Harlem, Martin wrote. The West Indians were increasing in numbers, and were forming societies "to cement old friendships and retain local traditions." Harlem was "lodge mad and procession wild"—encouraged partly by the many fraternal societies that had sprung up there. Mourners in Harlem seemed to emphasize the funeral parade over the funeral ceremony: "The grand funeral is the rage today, and our undertakers, artists in their line, cannot be expected to counsel economy." Harlemites loved "expensive house weddings," which probably had something to do with "the frequency of divorce." The "most skillful physicians of the race" were living and practicing uptown. There were now black policemen on the streets (the first was Samuel Battle, who later rose to the position of lieutenant), and newspapers and printing presses were becoming "plentiful." A few blacks sold tickets in the subway, though it appeared that their "real job" was cleaning the station. "Formerly, it was said that the colored man and oftener the woman frequented white bookstores for Bibles and dream books, and more dream books than Bibles; but now we boast a Negro bookstore. . . . We love flowers, we have our own florists. . . . There are banks but no colored clerks as yet. . . . We also own a few private houses. . . . We have our composers and musicians of no mean order. Tennis, cricket, baseball, football, basketball, athletics in general . . . and it is reported that [the black Harlemite] has even invaded the golf links. Some of our ladies own and drive their own automobiles. . . . Private libraries are on the increase and there are fine collections on racial lines. . . . A colored regiment has lately been organized in Harlem and the colored man is marching under the flag that often fails to protect him when alive but honors him when dead."

Democracy and the Flag

IN MATTERS of the flag, 1916 could well be called the end of one era in Harlem, and 1917 the beginning of another. The "colored regiment" that Martin, the A.M.E. clergyman, referred to in his review of Harlem life was the 15th Regiment of the New York National Guard, formed in 1916, which was to become one of the most famous regiments in black American history. All its commissioned officers—Colonel William Hayward and his top command—were white and all its rank and file black. A number of the black troops had been recruited from the West Side of Manhattan, but the majority came from Harlem, which was the regiment's headquarters. Many Harlemites could not have been prouder that their community had been chosen as the base for the first black military unit ever recognized in New York State; indeed, they thought of it as Harlem's own regiment, and saw it as a sign of the district's growing importance and prestige as a black community. Other Harlemites saw the regiment as a sign of something troubling. A war was being fought in Europe, and there was a general feeling in this country, shared in Harlem, that it was only a matter of time before the United States intervened. If that happened, there was every likelihood that the New York 15th would be sent overseas to fight. Those who applauded the existence of a black regiment in Harlem were in no way disturbed by the prospect of its soldiers' being sent to Europe. Their feeling was that it could only be helpful to the Negro cause for blacks to serve with the armed forces of their country —to demonstrate their loyalty and patriotism during what was called the world crisis. Those who were troubled by what the regiment signified argued that blacks owed no such obligation to a country that denied them their full rights as citizens. It would not be the first time, they said, that blacks had borne arms on the side of their country. Look at how well they had fought in the Spanish-American War.

And what difference had that made in the way their country treated them?

After the New York 15th had had a year or so of training, crowds were coming out on weekends to watch its crisp march-pasts and to listen to the lively syncopated airs of its musicians—led by James Reese Europe, who, at Colonel Hayward's invitation, had given up his society orchestra to organize a regimental band. In one of the parades uptown, a group of Harlem's "best people"—ministers, newspaper editors, civil-rights spokesmen, businessmen—strutted proudly along. They were showing the pride that one section of the Harlem community took in its regiment. But a report in the *Age* about a later parade showed how the other side felt. The soldiers made a "splendid showing," the report said. "The sight of these colored men marching with the easy swing of veteran soldiers to the music of their magnificent band, while the national and regional colors fluttered above them in the bright sunlight of a perfect spring morning, was indeed thrilling. The spell, however, was broken by a young man standing on the sidewalk who said, 'They'll not take me out to make a target of me and bring me back to Jim Crow me.' "

The regiment's "splendid showing" in the spring of 1917 bore witness to a remarkable transformation. Months earlier—when it was newly organized, and its first recruits were striving to look and act like the real soldiers they weren't—most onlookers had found it merely amusing. Many of the early recruits were Pullman porters, hotel waiters, railroad redcaps, apartment-house and theatre doormen. Owing, no doubt, to the habits of their previous occupations, such men took more readily to saluting than to almost any other form of military conduct. One of their white leaders said later that the men "would walk out of their way to approach officers so as to find an excuse to salute." And, recalling an early parade of the regiment, a Harlem businessman said, "It was amusing to see a group of colored soldiers marching through 134th Street with broomsticks on their shoulders and responding to the sharp commands of their superior officers." Late in 1916, the regiment had staged a march down Fifth Avenue. At its head was Bert Williams, the great black comedian, astride a magnificent white horse. Surveying the scene—Williams on his horse and the men following in mismatched uniforms and with their broomsticks on their shoulders—bystanders on Fifth Avenue could not help snickering at "these darkies playing soldiers," according to one report. They returned three years later, however—and their reception then was of a quite different sort.

In July of 1917, three months after the United States entered the war, the men from Harlem were mustered into the regular Army. They sailed for France that November, leaving behind—in Harlem and in black communities throughout America—the fiercely debated question of black participation in the war. Such a debate might have been triggered by almost any war—for nothing attracts more attention to the contradictions of black American citizenship than the call to military service. In 1917, however, the discussion seemed less avoidable than at any other time. It was President Woodrow Wilson who had described American intervention as necessary to the survival of democracy abroad, and had reminded Americans that they were the "champions of the right of mankind." Such a description fell strangely on the ears of many black citizens, for they had come to regard Wilson—despite his admirable qualities of mind and spirit—as one of the more racist Presidents to occupy the White House. Among these blacks there was a feeling that Wilson could hardly have been more insensitive to their struggle for equal citizenship. During his Presidency, even the token gains they had made under previous Republican Administrations were being revoked. Prominent blacks who had been appointed to important federal positions—especially during the Administration of Theodore Roosevelt—were being thrown out of office. Of the Wilson Administration's "generally indifferent, even hostile, regard for blacks," David M. Kennedy writes in his *Over Here: The First World War and American Society:*

> The South, Woodrow Wilson once remarked, was the only place he felt really at home, the only place where nothing had to be explained to him—including the traditional Southern race system. He had screened the film "The Birth of a Nation" in the White House, and had endorsed its pro-Ku Klux Klan interpretation of post-Civil War Reconstruction as "history written with lightning." The President had raised no objection when Postmaster General Albert S. Burleson had in 1913 widened the practice of segregation among federal employees. When a delegation of black leaders called at the White House to protest

Burleson's policy, they were brusquely dismissed because Wilson found their language "insulting." In the election of 1916, Wilson had personally helped to stir racial hatreds in East St. Louis. . . . In the face of such attitudes at the highest political level, it took a truly vaulting leap of faith for Afro-American leaders to persist in the belief that the war could somehow be made to serve the advancement of their race.

How, then, were they to answer or applaud Wilson's call to defend democracy elsewhere? They surely believed it was necessary to defend "the right of mankind." But how were they to defend that right abroad when some of the few rights they enjoyed at home were being annulled under a President who scarcely lifted a finger in their behalf? "One colored man came into a Harlem barbershop where a spirited discussion of the war was going on," James Weldon Johnson later wrote. "When asked if he wasn't going to join the Army and fight the Germans, he replied amidst roars of laughter: 'The Germans ain't done nothin' to me, and if they have, I forgive 'em.'"

Among those in Harlem who held the opposite view—that blacks would have to bear arms, regardless of their treatment in America— were a number of the black clergymen. As ministers, they doubtless felt that it was part of their calling to invoke faith wherever the grounds of belief were uncertain; and as guides to civic conduct they must have considered it their duty, especially in times of crisis, to assert the preeminence of national interest. Thus, on a Sunday morning in March of 1917, F. M. Hyden, minister of the St. James Presbyterian Church, in Harlem, read from Genesis 15:14, "And also that nation, whom they shall serve, will I judge: and afterward shall they come out with great substance." Basing his sermon on that passage, Hyden said, "The future historian when he comes to set down the facts in connection with the world war should have before him the fact that colored men went to war not as an endorsement of the President, but as a measure of national defense. . . . Volunteered service in such a time as this constitutes . . . the strongest argument and the noblest appeal for political and economic rights which colored men could present to the nation after the war is over."

Not all the black ministers agreed, however. Adam Clayton Powell, Sr., for example, appears to have interpreted his calling and his duty in more defiant terms. Despite his collar and robe, he was a restless secular moralist, always champing at his religious bit—especially when burning public issues arose. On such occasions, he tended to speak his mind rather than yield to the temperate commands of the Gospels. Also preaching on a Sunday in March of 1917, Powell told his Abyssinian Baptist congregation, "This is the proper time for us to make a special request for our constitutional rights as American citizens. The ten million colored people in this country were never so badly needed as now. . . . As a race we ought to let our government know that if it wants us to fight foreign powers we must be given some assurance first of better treatment at home. . . . Why should not the colored Americans make a bloodless demand at this time for the rights we have been making futile efforts to secure [from a] government that has persistently stood by with folded arms while we were oppressed and murdered?"

In 1917, blacks were victims of more than Wilson's neglect. In parts of the country, hundreds were being beaten to death, lynched, or murdered in other ways by whites—many of whom were probably encouraged by the silence of the White House. This was during an early stage of the great migration from the rural South to the munitions centers of the Southwest, the Middle West, and the North, where blacks were seeking wartime employment. One writer said, "The cup overflowed with the East St. Louis massacre of July 2, 1917, in which four hundred thousand dollars' worth of property was destroyed, nearly six thousand Negroes driven from their homes, and hundreds murdered, a number of them burned alive in houses set afire over their heads."

A few weeks later, some eight thousand blacks, mostly from Harlem—organized by churchmen and other civic leaders of the district—staged a silent march down Fifth Avenue, to protest the violent events in East St. Louis. Carrying picket signs, and dressed as finely as Harlemites then did, they strode to the sound of muffled drums while thousands of white New Yorkers looked on from the sidewalks. But despite the misgivings that the East St. Louis events aroused, established black leaders continued to argue that it was the Negro's patriotic duty to serve his country during wartime. One such leader was W. E. B. Du Bois, the editor of *The Crisis*—the organ of the N.A.A.C.P. As a founder of the modern protest movement, Du Bois's credentials as an aggressive spokesman for black rights were unchallengeable, yet he sounded very much like the Reverend Mr. Hyden when, in a *Crisis* editorial, he argued, "Let us not hesitate. Let us, while this war lasts, forget our special grievances and close our ranks shoulder to shoulder with our own white fellow-citizens and the allied nations that are fighting for democracy. We make no ordinary sacrifice, but we make it gladly and willingly with our eyes lifted to the hills."

Much tougher arguments—more like Powell's—were being made from Harlem soapboxes and stepladders, most often and most strongly at the corner of Lenox Avenue and 135th Street. This intersection looked much like a small-town square, with people sauntering and lingering to see and hear what was going on—but it was also one of the major radical forums of black America. It was chiefly here that the political and race radicals—young firebrands like Hubert Harrison, Wilfred A. Domingo, Chandler Owen, and A. Philip Randolph—made their speeches. No black citizen, they declared, should think of bearing arms in France, and certainly not as a condition to gaining his rights at home. Freedom, they said, was unconditional. And there were socialists among them who posed this question to their listeners: What business do Negroes have fighting a "capitalist" and "imperialist" war? These men later founded and edited magazines to promote their views on socialism and the world conflict, and the relevance of both to the black struggle in America. To Du Bois's call for unity and the postponement of "special grievances," Harrison replied in his magazine, *The Voice*, "America cannot use the Negroes to any good effect unless they have life, liberty, and manhood assured and guaranteed to them . . . the so-called leaders . . . have already established an unsavory reputation by advocating this same surrender of life, liberty, and manhood, masking their cowardice behind the pillars of wartime sacrifice." In *The Messenger*, the magazine Randolph and Owen edited, they asked, "Since when has the subject race come out of a war with its rights and privileges accorded for such a participation? . . . Did not the Negro fight in the Revolutionary War, with Crispus Attucks dying first . . . and come out to be a miserable chattel slave in this country for nearly 100 years?"

These young agitators, who migrated to Harlem from the South and the West Indies (Randolph from Florida; Owen from North Carolina; Harrison from the Virgin Islands; Domingo from Jamaica), typified Harlem's first generation of radical political thinkers. Calling themselves "New Crowd Negroes," they consigned almost all their more conservative elders to "the Old Crowd." These elders not only considered the younger men brash and impudent—an "affliction"—but pointed out that they were also relatively unschooled. None of them had graduated from a university. The *Age*, an organ of the older leadership, described them as "loud-lunged orators, with more voice than brains." Loud-mouthed they were, but they certainly did not lack brains. Even without college degrees, they were about the brightest intellectuals in Harlem—with the possible exceptions of James Weldon Johnson and Du Bois himself, when he was living in the community. In night schools and in private study, they had trained themselves in literature, history, economics, philosophy, and political theory—all of which they spouted with a natural gift of oratory and, it seemed, a natural talent for pamphleteering. In one capacity or another, they exerted a significant influence on aspects of the racial and political militancy that later evolved in Harlem.

When the regiment from Harlem arrived in France, in December, it was renamed the 369th Infantry and was assigned to the 161st Division of the French Army. It may seem odd that these men were not placed with the armed forces of their own country, but what is perhaps even more odd is that, considering the segregation and the racial hostility within the American Army then, they had escaped into a freedom that few other black soldiers enjoyed. Serving with the French Army, they were able to fight in the front lines instead of working as stevedores on piers and supply ships—the role that was assigned to most black units of the American Army. In May of 1918, a month after the 369th Infantry went into action, Captain Hamilton Fish, Jr., one of its white officers, wrote home to his father:

> Our regiment is the most envied American regiment in France, and has the greatest opportunity to make a wonderful record. We are with the French Army and have the incomparable advantage of the instructions and experience of the French. We are, to all intents and purposes, a part of the French Army, and supplied by them with all of our rifles, bayonets, helmets, gas masks, knapsacks, food, and ammunition. The men looked splendid in the American khaki uniforms and French leather equipment and

brown helmets. I wonder what the Germans will think when they take one of our boys prisoner and find that he cannot speak French and comes from Harlem. I am a great believer in the fighting quality of the educated American Negro. . . . I believe (if the censorship regulations were abolished) the 15th New York (now the 369th U.S. Infantry) would be as well known as the Rough Riders were in the Spanish-American War.

Still, in such a campaign no thoughtful black soldier could fail to reflect on the contradictions of his position as an American fighting man. In November of 1918, during one of the climactic battles of the war, a soldier from Harlem wrote in his diary, "I seem to feel that the Germans (who have done so much to destroy the high ideals for which we have fought so hard and were willing to sacrifice so much), after the coming of peace, will enjoy more privileges and will have the door of opportunity opened to [them] more heartily than to the American Negro, whose patriotism is above question, and who has given his life's blood on every field of honor, in order to keep the flag which stands for such noble ideals from touching the ground."

When the war ended, the 369th Infantry (now nicknamed the Harlem Hellfighters) had indeed made "a wonderful record." For its part in the Battle of Meuse-Argonne, its regimental colors and more than a hundred and fifty of its men were decorated with the Croix de Guerre. In New York, the *Age*, proud of how well the boys from Harlem were doing, had printed almost every available detail of their activities in battle—and very little about the doings of other black regiments. A black soldier wrote to the *Age*:

I have seen many of your papers since I have been in France. But every time I look at it, I do not see anything about any outfit but the 15th of New York. Did you know that there were more colored troops in France? . . . it looks as if you all should put a little in about the poor old stevedores who have been over here going on 13 months, and struggle to and from these docks singing and rejoicing because they think they are playing their part. When it is raining and snowing, they go on just the same with their smile. So when one picks up a paper and sees nothing about the stevedores it makes one feel like they are overlooked. If it was not for the work the stevedores did behind the lines the boys with the guns could not have whipped the Germans as they did.

The *Age* acknowledged its error. But, it added, its partisanship was understandable, in view of "the peculiar fact" that the 369th was "made up of the men from New York." The regiment's "record of achievement and endurance," the *Age* said on a later occasion, "has not only won fame for the organization, but reflects everlasting credit on the race with which it is identified and the city whence it came."

Toward a Black Theatre

UNTIL ABOUT 1914, the theatres of Seventh Avenue and 125th Street were off limits to blacks. *Their* theatres were the Lincoln and the Crescent, on 135th Street between Lenox and Fifth Avenues. This was Harlem's "Off Broadway." Harlem's "Broadway" was Seventh Avenue and 125th Street, and, in its own fashion, it was a great white way. Only patrons of that color were admitted to the Lafayette and the Alhambra (on Seventh Avenue), and to such places as the Harlem Opera House, Hurtig & Seamon's Music Hall, and Proctor's (on 125th Street). But as the black belt spread west to Seventh Avenue, and beyond, and south toward 125th Street, the major theatres found it increasingly difficult to maintain their all-white policy. In place of exclusion they instituted segregation. Blacks were now welcome, but only to the balcony (or, as it came to be called, "nigger heaven")—an arrangement that lasted for some time. Recalling his days in Harlem just after the First World War, the journalist George S. Schuyler wrote, "Aside from the Lincoln and Lafayette theatres, none of the considerable number of theatres welcomed Negro patrons in their orchestra sections. [A. Philip] Randolph and I would stroll south on Seventh Avenue to catch the vaudeville show at the Alhambra. . . . Entering the lobby, he would flatten himself against the wall near the ticket window, toss in the money, and ask for two orchestra seats. Sometimes the deception worked, but when it didn't, we would be sold tickets for the back balcony."

The Lafayette, at Seventh Avenue and 132nd Street, was the first of the major theatres to desegregate, partly because it fell sooner than the others within the widening perimeter of the black community. In November of 1912, soon after the Lafayette was built, Lester Walton, who was the theatre critic of the *Age*—and a son-in-law of its editor, Fred Moore—inquired of the owners what their policy toward "colored patrons" would be. The policy, he was told, would be "white." The Lafayette would consider seating "highly respectable colored people" in the orchestra, but all others would be sent to the balcony. The trouble was that those colored people who considered themselves highly respectable were not respectable enough, according to the Lafayette's standard. Hence they, too, were being directed to the balcony. A week after Walton's interview with the management, the *Age* reported that "prominent Negroes" were being barred from the orchestra section of the Lafayette. One such Negro was employed in a white bank downtown—a distinction that in those days ought surely to have qualified him for a place among the "respectable." Another of the "prominent Negroes" turned away was Edward E. Lee, a leading Tammany politician (an official of the United Colored Democracy, the black arm of the Democratic Party organization in Manhattan) and a deputy sheriff of New York—but then the Lafayette may have found it hard to believe that anyone respectable could have belonged to the notorious Tammany Hall machine. The Lafayette appears to have overestimated its potential white support. Its orchestra section was hardly ever full, and the owners soon disposed of the theatre as a losing enterprise. In 1914, when the theatre passed into new hands, Lester Walton was appointed manager—a sign that the policy of segregation would be abolished—and it was at this point that the Lafayette became what it would remain for several years: the most stylish black showplace in Harlem. Under Walton's management, the Lafayette stirred the revival of black musical-comedy productions—shows that had gone out of fashion since the great Williams and Walker entertainments of the eighteen-nineties and early nineteen-hundreds. In October of 1915, when *Darkydom*—the black musical-comedy hit of that year— opened at the Lafayette, a Harlem writer called it "the biggest and best colored attraction since Williams and Walker's 'Bandana Land,' " and saw it as an indication that "the colored musical show is once more on the ascendancy."

The Lafayette helped to nurture an even more important development in the realm of drama. In 1916, black Harlem's first legitimate-theatre group was organized there. Charles Gilpin, a native of Richmond, Virginia, was then considered one of the most gifted actors on the American stage, but since there were virtually no serious parts for blacks, he had been reduced to playing vaudeville and touring with small black road companies. When one of these companies, called the Negro Players, disbanded, in 1913, soon after making an appearance at the Lafayette, Gilpin remained in Harlem and founded the Lafayette Players. Though it was a black company, it did not present black plays, for there were almost no such plays at the time. It presented Shakespeare and revivals of such popular Broadway productions as *Madame X, The Servant in the House, On Trial, Within the Law, Very Good Eddie,* and *The Divorce Question.*

The subject matter of these plays was connected only remotely, if at all, with black American experience, and the Lafayette Players were often criticized by Harlem intellectuals for staging them before all-black audiences. Yet the plays filled a gap both in the lives of those who performed them and in the cultural experience of those who came out to see them. They gave the performers the only chance they then had of appearing on the legitimate stage, and they enabled Harlem audiences to see black actors and actresses in something other than the usual song-and-dance routines. According to George S. Schuyler, "This was a boon to the Negro public which was not available elsewhere in colored America. These Lafayette Players were tops and I spent many pleasant evenings watching them play to packed houses." For the players, there was this additional advantage, described by James Weldon Johnson:

> The Negro performer in New York, who had always been playing to white or predominantly white audiences, found himself in an entirely different psychological atmosphere. He found himself freed from a great many restraints and taboos that had cramped him for forty years. . . . One of the well-known taboos was that there should never be any romantic love-making in a Negro play. . . . So, with the establishment of the Negro theatre in Harlem, coloured performers in New York experienced for the first time release from the restraining fears of what a white audience would stand for; for the first time they felt free to do on the stage whatever they were able to do.

Among the intellectuals who criticized the Lafayette Players for reviving and producing defunct Broadway shows was Theophilus Lewis, who wrote theatre reviews for A. Philip Randolph's radical *Messenger.* In his book *No Crystal Stair,* Theodore Kornweibel, Jr., a young scholar, sums up Lewis's feelings about the Lafayette Players and their relationship to black theatre:

> Noticing that . . . Gilpin, probably the finest black actor then playing, had transformed his part into a thing of beauty, Lewis despaired that Gilpin was condemned to perform in such trash. Blacks simply would not write enough good theatre to keep a fine artist like Gilpin well employed. . . .
>
> Lewis went to the heart of the matter when he noted that one of the fundamental causes of weakness in the black theatre was its unwritten philosophy that the only "legitimate" theatre was the white stage, particularly Broadway. The black theatre had wrongly tried to excel at the things Broadway did, even though the white stage usually portrayed blacks only in caricature. The Lafayette Players, the only permanent company of adult performers in Harlem, took their cues from Broadway and performed ten-year-old castoff plays. . . . Lewis asked, why not produce black drama on the black stage for black audiences?

What Lewis overlooked was that there were no such dramas then. Moreover, when plays using black life and experience as their subject matter did come into being, they were neither written by blacks and produced by blacks nor performed before predominantly black audiences. Such dramas first appeared in the spring of 1917, when three one-acters—*Granny Maumee*, *The Rider of Dreams*, and *Simon the Cyrenian*—were staged at the Garden Theatre, on Broadway. They were written by Ridgely Torrence, a white poet and playwright from Xenia, Ohio, and produced by Emilie Hapgood. The casts, however, were predominantly black, and Broadway critics praised the event, calling it one of the most important developments in the history of American theatre. According to the *Globe*, "at certain moments" the program "reached depths of vivid, full-blooded drama that Broadway at its best but feebly imitates," adding that "it opened up that sadly neglected storehouse of dramatic material, the life of the American Negro." The *Evening Post* said, "Here at last, we have the beginnings of something like a folk theatre, entirely domestic if not altogether national." And *The New Republic* welcomed "the emergence of an artistic Cinderella into the palace where she belongs."

Though one publication called Torrence's plays the first steps toward the building of a national black theatre, there were not soon to be further steps—not until the production of Eugene O'Neill's *The Emperor Jones*, in 1920, and *All God's Chillun Got Wings*, in 1924. (Earlier, O'Neill had written *The Dreamy Kid*, a one-acter, based on the life of a black fugitive from the law. Louis Sheaffer, O'Neill's biographer, calls it the playwright's "apprentice work for *The Emperor Jones* and *All God's Chillun Got Wings*.") Once again, progress in the building of a black theatre had been made through the efforts of a white playwright. O'Neill's plays made another vital contribution as well: they brought to national attention two of the finest black actors to have yet appeared on the American stage— Charles Gilpin (in the first of the two plays) and Paul Robeson (in both).

In 1920, there was hardly an actor more deserving of national exposure than Gilpin, who had gone virtually unrecognized while appearing in roles that were either inappropriate or inferior to his gifts. Gilpin was rescued from obscurity when the Provincetown Players, in casting Brutus Jones, the lead role in *The Emperor Jones*, decided, after some debate, to use a black actor rather than a white actor in blackface. Gilpin, who still lived in Harlem, was not unemployed when the call came from the Provincetown Players, but, all the same, he may be said to have been out of work. According to Louis Sheaffer, Gilpin was "tracked down to Macy's," where he was found running an elevator, and where this dialogue took place:

> "Are you Charles Gilpin?" a deputized Provincetowner in-quired as he got on the elevator. "Yes. Corsets, ladies' underthings —second floor." "Are you an experienced actor?" "Yes. Glass-ware, silverware, household furnishings." "We have a good part for you in a play by Eugene O'Neill." "How good? Draperies, upholsteries, linens." "The leading part. Would you like to act again?" "Yes, what's the pay? Furniture, bed clothing, bathroom supplies—fifth floor." "The best we can pay is fifty dollars." "It's a deal. Going down. Where do I go?"

On opening night, Sheaffer writes, "the place rang with cheers for Gilpin—the audience refused to leave." Heywood Broun, of the *Tribune*, wrote, "Gilpin is great. It is a performance of heroic stat-ure." A year later, *The New Republic* said, "It has remained for Charles Gilpin in *The Emperor Jones* to be ranked with the greatest artists of the American stage." If Gilpin had "not been a Negro," Moss

Hart later said in his autobiography, "he would have been one of the great actors of his time." And a few years before O'Neill died he remarked to a friend, "I can honestly say there was only one actor who carried out every notion of a character I had in mind. That actor was Charles Gilpin." But while Gilpin was carrying out every one of O'Neill's notions about Brutus Jones, he was injecting others of his own; he was also tampering with the playwright's lines—often substituting words for some in the script that he considered racially offensive. And on certain nights it was clear that Gilpin had had too much to drink—though he had so mastered the role that his drinking did not seriously affect his performance. O'Neill eventually lost patience with him, however, and before the play opened in London he replaced Gilpin in the leading part. "I'd be afraid to risk him in London," O'Neill said to an acquaintance. "So I've corralled another Negro to do it over there . . . a young fellow with considerable experience, wonderful presence and voice, full of ambition and a damn fine man personally with real brains."

O'Neill was referring to Paul Robeson. Like Gilpin, Robeson lived in Harlem. He had settled there in 1919, when, after graduating from Rutgers, he entered Columbia Law School. Harlem had taken quickly to the young Robeson, as his wife, Eslanda, wrote in her biography of him:

> He soon became Harlem's special favorite . . . everyone knew and admired and liked him. . . . No matter how great his achievements then or later, his easy good-natured simplicity kept him from being regarded with awe. . . . When Paul Robeson walks down Seventh Avenue he reminds one of his father walking down the main street of Somerville [New Jersey]: it takes him hours to negotiate the ten blocks from One Hundred and Forty-Third Street to One Hundred and Thirty-Third Street; at every step of the way he is stopped by some acquaintance or friend who wants a few words with him. And always Paul has time for those few words. In 1919, Paul strolled the "Avenue," and soon became one of its landmarks; he was often to be seen on the corner of One Hundred and Thirty-Fifth or One Hundred and Thirty-Seventh Street, the centre of a group. He could talk to anyone about anything. He had spent so much time with his father and in the Church that he had sympathy and understanding for the elderly, old-fashioned Negro. . . . He could talk fascinatingly about games

by the hour. He had a gorgeous bass voice, and could always be counted upon to carry the low voice part in harmonizations when "the fellows" got together at parties, or even on street corners.

When Robeson took over the title role in *The Emperor Jones*, in a 1924 revival of the play, he was praised almost as highly as Charles Gilpin had been. George Jean Nathan, in the *American Mercury*, called him "one of the most thoroughly eloquent, impressive, and convincing actors that I have looked at and listened to in almost twenty years of professional theatre-going." Laurence Stallings wrote in the *World*, "A great many competent judges have said that he rose to a power and dignity overshadowing Gilpin's." In January of 1925, O'Neill wrote in *The Messenger*, "My experiences as author with actor have never been so fortunate as in the cases of Mr. Gilpin and Mr. Robeson. . . . I would say that the Negro artist on the stage is ideal from an author's standpoint." It was a wonderful tribute, and augured well for the future of the black theatre. But, as O'Neill went on to say, an important ingredient of black theatre was still missing: "Where are your playwrights?" No plays of any consequence had yet appeared, or, at least, none had yet been produced.

"Here Comes My Daddy Now"

In 1919, "Harlem had a complete life of its own," Paul Robeson's wife wrote. "There were young and old Negro physicians and dentists, with much larger practices than they could comfortably look after themselves; Negroes owned beautiful houses and modern apartments; there were many fine churches; . . . there were Negro graduates from the finest white universities in America; there were Negroes in every conceivable profession, business, and trade." George S. Schuyler recalled in 1966, "The Harlem of 1919 was a small community amid a sea of whites. It extended from 130th Street to 143rd Street, from Seventh to Madison Avenue, with some blocks extending to Eighth Avenue. Lenox Avenue was much more attractive than it is now, with more trees and fewer people. There were more private houses and fewer storefront churches, less loitering and more decorum, and the people were well-dressed in contrast to the shabbiness one sees today." And A. Philip Randolph said some years later, "There was a certain standard, social standard, in the life of Negroes in Harlem then, different from today. You had a little gloss. There was a greater sense of respectability within the Negro group. They were trying to do things, trying to achieve status for the race. You had the underworld, to be sure, but you had some good types of people. They set the tone of the community. . . . A lot of these people were in the churches, and you saw them in the so-called better-class restaurants that Negroes would go to. All of these churches had great preachers, great spiritual strength."

Harlem may still have been a "small" community in 1919, but during the war its population had grown by several thousand. It had received its share of wartime migration from the South, the Caribbean, and parts of colonial Africa. Some of the new arrivals merely lived in Harlem: it was *New York* they had come to, looking for jobs and for all the other legendary opportunities of life in the city. To others who migrated to Harlem, New York was merely the city in which they found themselves: Harlem was exactly where they wished to be. The Harlem of 1919 was certainly a livelier and more populous district than the one that the men of the 369th Infantry had left in November of 1917, when they sailed to fight in France.

On the morning of February 17, 1919, when the Hellfighters, laden with military decorations, returned from France, some two thousand of them received a rousing welcome from New Yorkers as they marched up Fifth Avenue on their way to Harlem—no longer darkies playing soldiers. The *Times* reported, "The negro soldiers were astonished at the hundreds of thousands who turned out to greet them, and New Yorkers, in their turn, were mightily impressed with the magnificent appearance of these fighting men, which looked the part of a regiment that had been cited as a whole for bravery. . . . They marched with the careless, natural precision of men who had long ago mastered the technique of their profession." They were stepping smartly to the tempos of James Europe's ragtime military band. Major Arthur Little, a white officer, who marched in the front ranks of the parade, later recalled:

> The multitude of fellow citizens who greeted us that day— the tens of thousands who cheered, the women who wept—the men who cried "God bless you, boys!"—all were united to drown the music of Jim Europe's Band. They did not give us their welcome because ours was a regiment of colored soldiers—they did not give us their welcome in spite of ours being a regiment of colored soldiers. They greeted us that day from hearts filled with gratitude and with pride and with love, *because ours was a regiment of men, who had done the work of men.*

After marching past the reviewing stand, at Sixtieth Street—where Governor Al Smith, former Governor Charles Whitman, Acting Mayor Robert L. Moran, and William Randolph Hearst took the salute—the regiment continued up Fifth Avenue, turned west on 110th Street, and proceeded north up Lenox Avenue. As they took the turn onto Lenox, one of Harlem's main boulevards, Europe's band swung into "Here Comes My Daddy Now." The "multitude went wild with joy," the *Times* said. The *Age* noted, "The Hellfighters marched between two howling walls of humanity. . . . from the rooftops thousands stood and whooped things up. . . . so frantic did many become that they threw pennants and even hats away." And, according to Major Little, "Mothers, and wives, and sisters, and sweethearts recognized their boys and their men; and they rushed right out through the ranks to embrace them. For the final mile or more of our parade about every fourth soldier . . . had a girl upon his arm—and we marched through Harlem singing and laughing."

It had been a splendid day in New York. "We wonder how many people who are opposed to giving the Negro his full citizenship rights could watch the Fifteenth on its march up the Avenue and not feel either shame or alarm," James Weldon Johnson wrote later in the *Age*. "And we wonder how many who are not opposed to the Negro receiving his full rights could watch these men and not feel determined to aid them in their endeavor to obtain these rights." On such a day, there could not have been many. The march, one eyewitness said, had taken place "under a canopy of blue, with not a cloud in the sky. . . . the February sun, usually cold and unfriendly, beamed down . . . with springtime cordiality."

The "springtime cordiality" ended that summer. "Eight months after the armistice, with black men back fresh from the front, came the Red Summer of 1919, and the mingled emotions of the race were bitterness, despair, and anger," one black historian wrote. "There developed an attitude of cynicism that was a characteristic foreign to the Negro. There developed also a spirit of defiance born of desperation." More than twenty race riots broke out that year, in which hundreds of blacks, including soldiers who had recently returned from France, were shot, lynched, or beaten to death. In Europe, as Arthur Schlesinger, Jr., has written, "The experience of victory now suggested that men had within them the resources for salvation." In America, among the black masses, the end of the war brought not only violence and despair but also the further debasement of a civilization. Which faction in Harlem had been right in 1917? Was it the established leadership, who had hoped or believed that black participation in the war would result in full citizenship rights at home? Or was it the obstreperous young radicals, one of whom had asked, "Since when has the subject race come out of a war with its rights and privileges accorded for such a participation?"

Nowhere in America was there a stronger black reaction to the postwar developments than in Harlem. The little magazines that the street-corner radicals had founded during the war became more bellicose and irreverent in tone than at any time earlier. *The Crusader*, edited by Cyril Briggs, a former writer for the *Amsterdam News*, announced that now it feared "only God." Hubert Harrison's *The Voice* called itself the "journal of the new dispensation." *The Challenge*, edited by William Bridges, was just that—a debunker of almost every conventional attitude and idea in America. Wilfred Domingo's *The Emancipator* declared that it had come "to preach deliverance to the slaves." And Randolph and Owen's *The Messenger* was cited by the Justice Department in 1919 as "by long odds the most dangerous of all the Negro publications."

Garvey: "Poet and Romancer"

No POLITICAL organization thrived more on the postwar disillusionment and despair than Marcus Garvey's Universal Negro Improvement Association—the largest and most dramatic black mass movement ever to exist in America. Most of its original adherents in Harlem—where it was founded, in 1917—had been the Southerners and West Indians who streamed into the community during the war. Many of them had joined the U.N.I.A. while the war was still going on. But it was in 1919—when, as one Harlemite put it, there "recurred the feeling on the part of some Negroes that there was no future in the United States for them"—that the majority began pouring into Garvey's movement. This was as much because of their sense of their plight as because Garvey, who was one of the most brilliant speakers in Harlem, played enchantingly on the postwar discontent. From the U.N.I.A.'s platform in Liberty Hall—the movement's auditorium, on West 138th Street—and in its weekly newspaper, *Negro World*, he exhorted blacks to be proud of their color, to build social and economic institutions of their own, and to look to Africa as their once and future homeland. Tens of thousands, not only in Harlem but in other parts of America and the world, found instant solace in his black-nationalist message. In America, writes his biographer, David Cronon, blacks were "ready for any program that would tend to restore even a measure of their lost dignity and self-respect." When the U.N.I.A. held its first annual convention, in the summer of 1920, Garvey claimed an international following of two million, and though this figure was probably inflated, it does not seem beyond the bounds of possibility.

Garvey was himself a wartime migrant to Harlem. A native of Jamaica, he arrived in Harlem in 1916, at the age of twenty-eight, bringing with him the rudiments of the racial program for which he became famous. In his homeland, he had been an admirer of Booker T. Washington's philosophy of black self-improvement and had formed the Jamaica Improvement Association. In America, however, his ideas veered in the direction of black nationalism—or, as his critics put it, black racism. He became what was then described as a race radical, while other protégés of Washington, like the *Age's* Fred Moore, remained what can best be described as conservative progressives. Among Garvey's early acquaintances in Harlem were other radicals of his age group—men born in the eighteen-eighties— who preached on the street corners. They were not strictly race radicals, however, but socialist and antiwar ideologues. On occasion, these soapboxers were willing to yield a few minutes of their speaking time to any member of the audience who wished to present his own program for black progress—though, irrepressible polemicists that they were, they often set to work to demolish his arguments as soon as they reclaimed their platform. This was the sort of reception they accorded Garvey, the West Indian newcomer. Many years later, A. Philip Randolph recalled, "I was on a soapbox speaking on socialism when someone pulled my coat and said, 'There's a young man here from Jamaica who wants to be presented to this group.' I said, 'What does he want to talk about?' He said, 'He wants to talk about a movement to develop a Back-to-Africa sentiment in America.' I said, 'Yes, I'll be glad to present him.' " Being Socialists, men like Randolph were not taken with Garvey's doctrine; and, being an emergent black nationalist, he was not impressed by theirs. Drifting away from their gatherings, Garvey went fishing for disciples of his own. He had poor success, however, for, according to his biographer, "skeptical Harlemites paid scant attention to him," dismissing him as "just another West Indian carpetbagger."

Garvey's fortunes began to improve in June of 1917, when Hubert Harrison, the eldest and most learned of the radical group, invited him to share a platform at the Bethel A.M.E. Church, on West 132nd Street. Harrison, having become unhappy with the Socialist Party, had renounced some of his former beliefs and was translating the remainder into his own version of black militancy. No longer as certain as he had once been that socialism contained the answer to the race problem, Harrison, in his magazine, addressed the Socialist Party: "The roots of Class-Consciousness inhere in a temporary economic order; whereas the roots of Race-Consciousness must of necessity survive any and all changes in the economic order." Thus,

Harrison said—expressing a view that would be especially appealing to a man like Garvey—black socialist radicals should sever their ties to the party, thereby freeing themselves to pursue their own racial strategies and programs. Harrison was the senior radical in Harlem; and as he had been an inspiration to younger men like Randolph who took up socialism, so he now became a theoretician of the black-nationalist strategies to which Garvey was inclined. To pursue his program, Harrison had founded an organization called the Liberty League; and, because he was familiar with Garvey's views, he had invited the Jamaican to speak at his inaugural meeting. Bringing his "magnetic personality, torrential eloquence, and intuitive knowledge of crowd psychology" into play, Garvey, according to one observer, "swept the audience." He endorsed Harrison's movement and pledged to support it. "But," this observer added, "Garvey was not of the kidney to support anybody's movement."

Not long after his performance on Harrison's platform, Garvey launched his Universal Negro Improvement Association, and by the middle of 1919, when, because of race riots all over the country, blacks turned to his organization in droves, it had become the largest movement of its kind in the United States. In August of the following year, Garvey, addressing the first convention of the U.N.I.A., declared:

> We are striking homeward toward Africa to make her the big black republic. And in the making of Africa the big black republic, what is the barrier? The barrier is the white man; and we say to the white man who dominates Africa that it is to his interest to clear out now, because we are coming, not as in the time of Father Abraham, 200,000 strong, but we are coming 400,000,000 strong, and we mean to retake every square inch of the 12,000,000 square miles of African territory belonging to us by right Divine.

Partly because of his West Indian origin, the popularity of his movement, the nature of his program, and his attacks on the indigenous black protest organizations, Garvey was resented, even hated, by almost all the protest leaders and a major segment of the black middle class. J. A. Rogers, a Jamaican-born journalist and historian who was then a resident of Harlem, wrote, "Such opponents held that the Back-to-Africa program was diverting attention from the fight for justice here in America and disrupting its course. [Garvey] opposed the joining of white trade unions by Negroes and those organizations fighting for rights here at home. As for the Negro church, he practically rejected it and had his own rituals and Sunday services." For these reasons, as well as Garvey's homely physical appearance and what some called his arrogance, his critics were unsparing in the epithets they used to describe him—"jackass," "ignoramus," "pig," "buffoon," and, of course, "ugly."

One of the less mocking sketches of him was written by Lucien White, of the *Age*—although its conservative and middle-class editors were no admirers of Garvey. "The massive head and big-boned torso serve to mislead one as to the man's actual physical development, for they are of almost giant proportions, judging from the photographs," White wrote. "Close personal contact reveals that he is only of medium height, sturdy of lower limb . . . but possessing the physical development indicated by photos of the upper body . . . small feet, slightly built legs, large trunk . . . topped with head that has ample room for developed brain. Small, rather close-set eyes sparkle as he chats, but become grim and icy when he is not pleased." Another portrait devoid of invective was written by Herbert Seligman, for the *World*. Garvey, Seligman said, "might, to judge by his appearance, be a politician or a professional man." He continued, "Of medium height, his head set close down upon broad shoulders, his slender, longish arms terminating in narrow hands, he presents a sedentary, almost studious type. . . . His manner is easy and his voice agreeable, with a slightly English intonation that falls strangely upon the ears of Americans unaccustomed to natives of the British West Indies. Nor is there anything bizarre in Marcus Garvey's talk. It is fluent, even compelling if one does not stop to check him up." Garvey's imagination, Seligman said, was "capacious." To walk into his business offices—on 135th Street between Lenox and Fifth Avenues —was to enter "a fantastic realm in which cash sales of shares and the imminence of destiny strangely commingle." The reference was to shares in the Black Star Shipping Line, the centerpiece of Garvey's several business enterprises and perhaps the most ambitious of his conceptions. He had founded the Black Star Line to show that blacks were capable of owning and managing major business ventures and to give substance to his idea that blacks should one day return to

Africa—preferably in ships of their own. The Black Star Line, Garvey's biographer writes, was "a supremely audacious move that aroused the greatest excitement in the colored world." He adds, "Here was an enterprise belonging to Negroes, operated by and for them, that gave even the poorest black the chance to become a stockholder in a big business enterprise."

Garvey's imagination was not only capacious but romantic as well. The higher ranks of his U.N.I.A. comprised various levels of African "nobility"—"knights," "dukes," and "duchesses"—all created by Garvey, who named himself "the Provisional President of Africa." African kings and queens there were, just as there were English ones; but no one had ever heard of African knights, dukes, and duchesses. Well, everyone would hear of them now. Garvey's royal investitures were held at the U.N.I.A's Liberty Hall, on West 138th Street, described as a "low-roofed, hot, zinc-covered building that held 6000 persons." The *Age* carried this account of one of his induction ceremonies:

> . . . upon the arrival of His Excellency the Provisional President, the band played the [U.N.I.A.'s] national anthem of Africa— then His Excellency, whose garb was topped by a towering red plume, ascended the kingly dais, followed by a procession of subjects passing in review, led by the Chaplin General and other officials.
> . . . Deputies and a number of delegates, men and women, were presented to His Excellency, and each one was required to kneel in humble submission at the foot of the throne.
> The individuals chosen for special high honors were announced as having been recommended by His Excellency the President. . . . The honors dispensed included . . . "Duke of Uganda," "Duke of the Niger," Knight Commander, Order of the Nile," and "Knight Commander, Distinguished Service Order of Ethiopia." . . .
> The subjects honored were brought to the foot of the throne, where each kneeled and received his accolade from the sword wielded by His Excellency. . . .

"Though he was opposing British imperialism, he imitated its forms," wrote J. A. Rogers, who had known Garvey when they both lived in

Jamaica. "Apparently, he had never been able to throw off the impression British folderol and glitter had made on him in his childhood." Also, it all illustrated Garvey's gifts for organization and for inspirational propaganda. By surrounding himself with the trappings of royalty and aristocracy, by offering his followers a vision or a fantasy of racial and social grandeur, he attracted a larger and more rapturous allegiance than he might have otherwise.

Harlem, as Garvey knew, loved grand parades and street ceremony, and no parades were grander than the ones he staged as highlights of the U.N.I.A.'s annual conventions. On these occasions, thousands of delegates—from all over the United States, the Caribbean, Central America, and Africa—marched up and down the broad avenues of Harlem, their banners inscribed with tributes to Africa and to great black figures of the past. The rank and file were preceded by various paramilitary units of the U.N.I.A.—the marching band, the African Legion, the African Motor Corps, and the Black Star Nurses. All except the nurses, who were dressed in white, had on uniforms in brilliant combinations of black, red, green, and blue. Large convertibles gaily decorated with bunting carried the V.I.P.s of the movement—all colorfully robed, braided, and beribboned. Riding at the head of this spectacle, in the most impressive of the limousines, was the Provisional President of Africa himself, attired—as Rogers saw him—"in raiment that outdid Solomon in all his glory."

Within nine years of his arrival in Harlem, Garvey built the largest black mass movement in the nation's history and became perhaps the most celebrated and controversial black figure of his time. All of this began to unravel in 1925, when—after being convicted on a charge of using the mails to defraud while selling shares in his Black Star Line—he was jailed in the Atlanta federal penitentiary and later deported from the United States. Among his followers—and among thousands of blacks who were not—his major accomplishment was that of arousing a previously dormant sense of racial pride and of nurturing in them an awareness of Africa as their ancestral homeland. Though he hardly needed to have added to so important an achievement, the fact is that he failed in almost all other aspects of his program. Some of his failures resulted from his own mistakes in administration and leadership, including his misreading of black American middle-class society, some from the bitter opposition of his enemies, some from traits of personal character, such as his extraordinary vanity. He was not, however, a crook, not the dishonest man that many of his critics accused him of being. He was, as Rogers wrote, "a poet and a romancer." His dreams were too large, his conceptions too impractical—at least for the times in which he lived.

From Ragtime to Jazz

DURING the war, some of the early black saloons and cafés of Harlem continued their evolution into full-fledged cabarets. John W. Connor's Royal Café had begun catering to what Ethel Waters (who had lately come to Harlem from Chester, Pennsylvania, her home town, to try her luck as a singer) called "the sophisticates, bowed down . . . with culture and ennui." Barron Wilkins' Astoria Café drew its usual high-spending interracial crowd from the worlds of sport and show business. But Leroy's Café seems to have become the best of the night spots. Ethel Waters thought that the proprietor, Leroy Wilkins, was a stickler for good manners and conduct. On weekends, tuxedos were required. Miss Waters was much less impressed by Edmond Johnson, the owner of Edmond's Cellar, at 132nd Street and Fifth Avenue—where she worked, during and after the war. Johnson, nicknamed the Mule, was a brawling, coarse-mouthed man who had run a similar establishment down in the Tenderloin. Many years after Miss Waters had escaped from Edmond's Cellar and risen to national stardom, she said of it, "After you worked there, there was no place to go except into domestic service. Edmond's drew the sporting men, the hookers, and other assorted underworld characters." It was, she added, "the last stop on the way down in show business."

In clubs like Leroy's, Edmond's, and the Astoria Café, between 1914 and 1920, one of the transitional modes of the jazz piano reached its full development. This keyboard style, bridging the idioms of classic ragtime and jazz, was known as stride, or Harlem stride, piano, and among its major exponents were James P. Johnson, Willie (the Lion) Smith, and Luckey Roberts. Before settling in Harlem, these men—Johnson was from New Brunswick, New Jersey; Smith from Goshen, New York; and Roberts from Philadelphia—had played in many of the rougher clubs and barrooms of San Juan Hill and the Tenderloin, where pianists of their style were called ticklers.

According to James Lincoln Collier, a jazz historian, the stride-piano style "was created simply by the players jazzing or swinging the rags, or pseudoragtime music, they had grown up on—that is, pulling the melody away from the ground beat." George Hoefer, another jazz commentator, says, "New York pianists tried to get an orchestralike effect with their instruments. They assimilated some of the harmonies, chords, and techniques of the European concert pianists. . . . New York striders were, unlike the jazz and ragtime pianists from other parts of the country, steadily in the aura of big-city sophistication and closer to the rhythms of Broadway." Hoefer also quotes Johnson: "The difference between stride and traditional piano ragtime was in the structure and the precise bass played in a rag style by the left hand, while the characteristic strides were performed by the right hand."

These stride innovators played to full houses but for small paychecks—as Smith recalled in later years:

To the Harlem cabaret owners, to all night-club bosses, the money was on a one-way chute—everything coming in, nothing going out.

. . . It was your job to draw in the customers. All the owner had to do was count the money.

For all this, they paid you off in uppercuts. That was a saying we got up in those days; it meant you were allowed to keep your tips, but you got no salary. Sometimes they would give us a small weekly amount—like twenty dollars. That was known as a left hook.

When I started at Leroy's he acted as though he was doing me a big favor by letting me sit at the piano. After I'd been at the club for a couple of weeks I noticed the place was packed. It was time for me to have a little talk with Mr. Leroy. So one night I took time out and sent for an order of southern-fried chicken, the speciality of the house. . . . Instead of the chicken I got Leroy hollering, "What the hell you think you're doin' now, Lion? Ain't you got any food at home? You tryin' to take advantage?"

I looked calmly around the crowded room. "I want a small left hook, man, or else I'm movin' on." It was common practice for a piano player to keep on the go because you weren't considered too good if you stayed at the same place too long a time. It signified you were not in hot demand.

Smith went on, "I wound up with a salary of eighteen dollars a week plus tips. Old man Wilkins could see which side of the bread had the butter."

The start of the nineteen-twenties may be seen as the end of the ragtime era and the opening of what came to be called the jazz age. The transition was as inevitable as the passage from one generation to another. Politically, the ragtime years witnessed some of the more radical developments in American life—socialist and antiwar agitation and the beginning of black-nationalist ferment. Musically and socially, however, the ragtime period was relatively circumspect in its mannerisms; it seems now (though it surely did not seem so then) to have been just a livelier extension of the Victorian constraints it wished to escape. For all its syncopated rhythms, its innovations in "modern" dance and female attire—even the vulgar wording of some of its songs—it did not wander far from the scored melodies of the recent past, the authority of traditional forms and opinion. After all, some of the early ragtime music (to which middle-class and upper-class people danced the two-step, the tango, and the foxtrot) was just a syncopated version of the waltz and the march—except, of course, when sections of the black masses were using ragtime music to do the erotic Texas Tommy, the grizzly bear, and the bunny hug.

At all events, the jazz age would be far more irreverent—and in matters like drinking downright illegal. Making use of some of the assertions that had characterized the ragtime era, and reflecting some of the psychological aftermaths of the war, the jazz age ventured into improvisation and spontaneity—pursuing the unwritten variation in melody, decorating the written statement, capturing new styles on the wing, and expressing what was irrepressibly genial in the spirit of the twenties.

Four musical styles appear to have met in Harlem by 1920 and to have influenced the emergence of jazz in the community: ragtime, stride piano, blues, and some of the early Dixieland sounds of New Orleans. But until about 1922 the dominant forces in Harlem music were the blues singers and the stride pianists (most of whose styles reflected the clear influence of the progressive or classic ragtime piano). Ethel Waters, who worked with a number of these stride pianists while singing in Harlem during and after the war, later paid them this tribute:

I was learning a lot in Harlem about music and the men up there who played it best. All the licks you hear, now as then, originated with musicians like James P. Johnson. And I mean *all* of the hot licks that ever came out of Fats Waller and the rest of the hot piano boys. They are just faithful followers and protégés of that great man, Jimmy Johnson. Men like him, Willie (the Lion) Smith, and Charlie Johnson, could make you sing until your tonsils fell out. Because you wanted to sing. They stirred you into joy and wild ecstasy. They could make you cry. And you'd do anything and work until you dropped for such musicians. The master of them all, though, was Luckey Roberts.

Duke Ellington described Willie Smith—whom he met soon after he arrived in New York, in the early nineteen-twenties—as "the greatest influence on most of the great piano players" who were exposed to the "luxury" of "his fire, his harmonic lavishness, his stride." Ellington's list of such piano players included himself, Fats Waller, James P. Johnson, Count Basie, Donald Lambert, Joe Turner, Sam Ervis, and Art Tatum.

After the war, Mamie Smith was regarded in New York as the first lady of the blues, although it was Lucille Hegamin who was then called Harlem's favorite. Miss Smith, a native of Cincinnati, had, according to one description, a heavy voice, heavy hips, a light complexion, and wavy brown hair. In 1920, after appearing occasionally at the Lincoln Theatre and at one or two of the cabarets in Harlem, she made what has been called the first recording of an "actual blues performance by a Negro artist with a Negro accompaniment." The recording was "Crazy Blues," on the Okeh label, and was backed up by a five-piece band, with Willie (the Lion) Smith on piano. "Crazy Blues," originally titled "Harlem Blues," was written by Perry Bradford, an ebullient, cigar-smoking pianist-composer, who also wrote "That Thing Called Love" and "You Can't Keep a Good Man Down." The recording of "Crazy Blues," which sold tens of thousands of copies in Harlem and elsewhere, helped make the gorgeous Mamie Smith the highest-paid blues singer in New York. According to Samuel Charters and Leonard Kunstadt, historians of the New York jazz scene, Mamie Smith "made so much money she never really counted it." They also tell us:

> It is estimated that she made nearly $100,000 in recording royalties alone. She was making between $1000 and $1500 a week in the

large theatres in New York and Chicago and making nearly as much in the smaller theatres. . . . She bought large houses on 130th Street, St. Nicholas Place, and Long Island. Visitors at 130th Street remember lavish furnishings with an electric player piano in every room. The closets were stuffed with player-piano rolls. She bought ermine robes, silver gowns, gowns of gold cloth. For an engagement at the Bal Tabarin in Atlantic City she spent $3000 for a cape of ostrich plumes. Standing in a spotlight on a darkened stage, the silver gown shimmering, the ostrich plumes gently swaying, the diamonds on her fingers and around her neck glittering, Mamie was a breathtaking sight. She didn't even have to sing. She just walked grandly across the stage and there were storms of applause.

In 1918, the Pace & Handy Music Company, formerly of Memphis, moved to New York and opened offices on Broadway, downtown—one of a few black publishing houses in that part of the city. The partners were Harry Pace and W. C. Handy, the latter popularly known as the father of the blues. Just before leaving Memphis, their company had published one of the hit songs of that year, "A Good Man Is Hard to Find." The song, written by Eddie Green, had been introduced by Alberta Hunter at the Dreamland Cabaret, in Chicago, where Miss Hunter had previously introduced Handy's "Loveless Love" and "Beale Street Blues." Though relatively unknown at the time, she was later to become one of the brighter night-club stars of black Harlem and white Manhattan. "A Good Man Is Hard to Find" was an even greater hit in New York after Sophie Tucker—who had heard Alberta Hunter's version in Chicago—sang it on Broadway, and it was the success of this number that helped to establish the Pace & Handy Company in New York.

In 1921, when Harry Pace learned that Mamie Smith's "Crazy Blues" was being played in almost every household of Harlem that owned a Victrola, he set out to exploit its popularity, and founded a recording company of his own—Black Swan Records, with headquarters on Seventh Avenue near 135th Street. Its first successful recording was of Ethel Waters singing "Down Home Blues," for which she demanded a payment of a hundred dollars. At first, Harry Pace could not see himself meeting so brazen a demand. His company was losing money, for its first few records had failed, and Miss

Waters was not then an artist of any stature. At Edmond's Cellar, where she worked—the bottom of the cabaret heap—she drew little more than thirty-five dollars a week, and she had recently been turned down for a part in *Shuffle Along*, the brilliant black musical of 1921, by a casting director who regarded her as just a cheap honky-tonk singer. Harry Pace relented, however, as Miss Waters later wrote:

> Mr. Pace paid me the one hundred dollars, and that first Black Swan record I made had "Down Home Blues" on one side, "Oh, Daddy" on the other. It proved a great success and a best seller among both white and colored, and it got Black Swan out of the red. In those days you sang down into little horns just like the one you see in those ads of His Master's Voice. My second Black Swan record had "There'll Be Some Changes Made" on one side and "One Man Nan" on the other. . . . Pace and Handy then suggested that I go out on tour with Fletcher Henderson's Black Swan Jazz Masters, with Fletcher as my accompanist.

Miss Waters' records not only helped to get Harry Pace's company out of the red but also helped her to climb out of Edmond's Cellar.

In 1919, when the ragtime Army bands returned from France, they began billing themselves as jazz orchestras. Tim Brymm called his group, which had served with the 350th Artillery, the Overseas Jazz Sensation, and James Europe's Harlem Hellfighters band set out on a tour of major American cities, playing what were advertised as jazz concerts. There were other signs as well that the jazz age was dawning. "By 1919," one commentator has written, "the growing number of Harlem cabarets, sprouting up like dandelions in the spring, had begun to use four-, five-, and six-piece jazz bands. . . . These jazz bands, featuring improvised blues, were to help usher in a new era in Harlem—the Harlem the world heard about during the Prohibition days."

PART THREE

High and Handsome

"What a City!"

HARLEM has never been more high-spirited and engaging than it was during the nineteen-twenties. Blacks from all over America and the Caribbean were pouring in, reviving the migration that had abated toward the end of the war—word having reached them about the "city," in the heart of Manhattan, that blacks were making their own. It was chiefly the earlier migrants to Harlem who were spreading the word. They were "pleased with the conditions" they had found—as *The Saturday Evening Post* reported in August of 1925—and were writing "letters back to their former homes describing in glowing terms their great adventures." Because such adventures were chiefly the kind they wrote about—they omitted "the unfavorable features of their transplanting"—their letters, which were read "in churches, lodges, and at other gatherings," set off the new wave of migration, which "reached flood tide during 1923."

As Harlem's population continued to grow and spread, its social and religious institutions multiplied. The intraracial discords that had developed as various class and regional groupings encountered one another were aggravated: Northern-born blacks looked down on the speech and manners of those who had recently arrived from the rural South; an upper class, consisting mainly of light-skinned professionals, fought to be recognized as Harlem's most representative social grouping; West Indians and black Americans often glared xenophobically at one another across borders of accent and cultural style. Black nationalism and other radical ideologies reached and fell from the zenith of their fashion and appeal. There sprang up a lively movement in literature and art, invigorated as much by the meeting —even clash—of regional and class groupings as by the literary life and atmosphere of Manhattan itself. It was to this movement that the literary critic John Chamberlain was referring when, at the end of the decade, he wrote of the "pullulation of energy" in the "Negro town of Harlem" that had "flowed into the novel, into poetry, into the short story." The energy flowed into entertainment as well, and into other forms of popular culture. Harlem came to set the standard for what was modish in black urban life. Floyd Snelson, a Harlem journalist, was to write, "Men and women dressed in the height of fashion. . . . Luxurious imported furs, the rarest 'birds of paradise' and precious egrette fancy feathers adorned the hats of milady. . . . Some gals had twenty-five pounds of beguiling beads sewed into a single gown. Evening shoes were bedecked with rhinestone heels and attachments . . . gay Lotharios were bedecked in full dress suit, tails, English walking suit, and silk hat and cane, and sometimes a modest sack coat tuxedo. Everyone . . . wore their 'black cloth' to a 'swell function' almost every night. . . . Everybody of the day wore as many diamond carats as they could obtain . . . the ladies wore several rings on each finger. . . . Many gals wore six diamonds, from the rings of as many suitors. Hundred-dollar and five-hundred-dollar dresses were ordinary hangers in clothes closets. Hand-made, lace-trimmed under-things of costly fabrics were casual luxuries, and hats made to cost hundreds of dollars were not quite such a foolish thing. Everybody lived like a millionaire . . . everybody went for higher-priced cars. Jack Johnson was burning up his high-powered Lincoln, and other big shots parked Packards, Cadillacs, Stutzes, Locomobiles, Wintons, Hudsons, etc."

In its finer residential features, Harlem was almost unique among black urban communities—barring, of course, those strongholds of the black bourgeoisie that were to be found in cities like Atlanta, Washington, D.C., and Durham, North Carolina. Many Harlemites lived more spaciously, confidently, and comfortably than did others of their race in the black precincts of most large cities. Such people felt that there was not a better place than Harlem anywhere—no place they would rather have been. This feeling was shared even by some in the community who did not live as well. They were proud just to think that they, too, were citizens of so splendid a "metropo-lis," teeming with black institutions and organizations of all kinds; marked by quiet side streets, broad boulevards, elegant Victorian brownstones, exclusive apartment houses; and accommodating the elite of black Manhattan.

There were, to be sure, Harlemites who did not take so bracing a view of the place or of their lives in it. Some—like the more aggrieved followers of Marcus Garvey, the founder of the Universal Negro Improvement Association—dismissed the gloss and frills of Harlem living as mere window dressing, concealing the harder and shabbier facts of black life. Many Garveyites would just as soon have taken their chances elsewhere—preferably in unknown parts of Africa, which their leader preached so enchantingly about. Other Harlemites, the poorest ones, thought of little besides their struggle to make ends meet. They lived on the toughest blocks and in the worst tenements; worked at the lowest jobs, when they worked at all; and suffered the most frequently and severely from crime and disease. If *they* bothered to write letters back home, they can scarcely have omitted "the unfavorable features of their transplanting." What else —beyond the obligatory diversions of church, saloon, and dance hall —was there for them to write home about?

In the twenties, most visitors—unless they were reporters sent up by the major metropolitan dailies—did not see the less attractive sides of life in Harlem. Or, if they did, what they saw was not allowed to spoil the impression they had already formed from what they had heard of the area—that it was Manhattan's capital of gaiety and amusement. In any event, that impression, as far as it went, was correct. In the years that followed the ratification of the Eighteenth Amendment, there was no livelier place in all of New York City, especially after dark. Nightly, thousands of white visitors—most from downtown, some from other parts of the country, a few from cities abroad—made their way to Harlem. There they enjoyed its "hot" and "barbaric" jazz, the risqué lyrics and "junglelike" dancing of its cabaret floor shows, and all its other "wicked" delights. "And we'll get drunker and drunker," says a character in *Parties*, one of Carl Van Vechten's novels of the twenties, "and drift about night clubs so drunk that we won't know where we are, and then we'll go to Harlem and stay up all night and go to bed late tomorrow morning and wake up and begin it all over again." Harlemites did indeed own Pierce-Arrows, Lincolns, Cadillacs, Wintons, Hudsons, Stutzes, Packards, and Duesenbergs, but not nearly as many as were to be seen uptown from around midnight till just before sunrise.

In his book *Incredible New York*, Lloyd Morris writes:

> The swarming, prosperous crowds bent on nocturnal diversion found Harlem exotic and colorful. To them it seemed a citadel

of jazz and laughter where gaiety began after midnight. From then onward, you saw throngs on Lenox and Seventh Avenues, ceaselessly moving from one pleasure resort to another. Long after the cascading lights of Times Square had flickered out, these boulevards were ablaze. Lines of taxis and private cars kept driving up to the glaring entrances of the night clubs. Until nearly dawn the subway kiosks poured crowds onto the sidewalks. The legend of Harlem by night—exhilarating and sensuous, throbbing to the beating of drums and the wailing of saxophones, cosmopolitan in its peculiar sophistications—crossed the continent and the ocean.

In November of 1927, *The American Mercury*, commenting on a visit by the Mexican artist and caricaturist Miguel Covarrubias, said, "It is noteworthy that, immediately after his arrival in New York, Covarrubias almost automatically found his way to Harlem, the scene which has afforded the widest scope for the exercise of his peculiar powers. He was immediately captivated by the color, the rhythm, the incomparable vitality of Negro life, especially as it exists in the theatres, on the streets, in the cabarets." Stanley Walker, city editor of the *Herald Tribune* in the nineteen-thirties, recalled that white crowds "began going to the hot spots of Harlem . . . after the discovery that Negro rhythm, Negro songs, even though they might be astoundingly vulgar, were high art because of their naturalness." For anyone who loved staying out late, Walker said, Harlem was "like no other spot in America." There were no late-night speakeasies more thrilling than the classier ones in Harlem. Some years after Prohibition ended, a journalist up there wrote:

> One could visit these places and partake of as much liquor as his carcass could hold, realizing that it was against the law. It afforded a thrill in visiting these places to ring a bell, a small peek-hole to be opened, a man who would look out through the opening in the door to recognize your face or take the password, to whisper a few words, mention a few names, and finally enter. What a thrill that was.
>
> Young college parties who had never tasted liquor had flasks in their pockets. In most of these places one would not get the best of liquor. Prices were exorbitant, but who cared; they were defying the law, showing their resentment to the Prohibition Amendment.

The American Mercury might well have been thinking of Harlem when it said, in 1927, "Ten years ago, gin was drunk only by what were then called darkeys; no virtuous white woman in all this Christian realm had ever tasted it. But now it is the common beverage of American youth, and the daughters of the white *noblesse* carry it to parties as they used to carry smelling salts."

But no set of people was more enchanted by nineteen-twenties Harlem than the blacks who were still strangers to it—those who were just arriving there, and those in distant places who were then getting ready to leave for New York. Most came to Harlem to enjoy a wider freedom and a better life. But more than a few were thinking chiefly of the good times they would be having, of the high Harlem style they had heard and read about. There is no better example of the latter than Sportin' Life, the devilish character in *Porgy and Bess* (adapted from a novel written in the twenties), who sings sweetly to the attractive and hesitant Bess:

> There's a boat dat's leavin' soon for New York.
> Come wid me, dat's where we belong, sister.
> You an' me kin live dat high life in New York.
> Come wid me, dere you can't go wrong, sister.
> I'll buy you de swellest mansion
> Up on upper Fifth Avenue
> An' through Harlem we'll go struttin' . . .
> Come along wid me, dat's de place . . .
> Dat's where we belong!

On the streets of Harlem, it was often easy to spot those who had just arrived, whether they had come in search of the better life or the sweet one. In 1927, the *Times* gave this description of a typical Harlem newcomer: "He is a seedy, collarless, slouching fellow, wearing a battered old soft hat. Slow in motion, he is constantly buffeted by the swift black tides of the avenue that sweep past him. . . . A product of the plantations, he shakes his head in puzzled fashion as he surveys the hurrying throngs and endless rows of brick and mortar. . . . He has come here as to a promised land. . . . As he strolls jauntily along the avenue, swinging a cane, with his head erect, his most intimate friends of the plantation would not recognize him." But after he had been in Harlem for a while it was not so easy to tell him apart from others on the avenue—as the *Times* also observed:

> Strutting the streets of the "Black Belt" are Negroes of enviable physique, with slim waists and straight broad shoulders. Many of these have found jobs on the piers as stevedores. They receive good pay and can afford to wear good clothes. Some of them dress conservatively. . . . Others like to dress up and appear the glass of fashion and the mold of form. . . . Silk shirts, bright ties and gay spats and form-fitting garments of every mode may be seen on a Sunday afternoon on Lenox and Seventh Avenues north of 125th Street. . . . When the many churches disgorge their large congregations, men and women appear in the latest and newest creations of the tailor's and dressmaker's art.

To almost all the newcomers, educated or not, Harlem seemed at first even more dazzling than they had dreamed it would be. Arna Bontemps, a young man arriving from California in 1924, was to describe his first few days in Harlem as "a foretaste of paradise." He said:

> A blue haze descended at night and with it strings of fairy lights on the broad avenues. From the window of a small room in an apartment on Fifth and 129th Street I looked over the rooftops of Negrodom and tried to believe my eyes. What a city! What a world! And what a year for a colored boy to be leaving home the first time! Twenty-one, sixteen months out of college, full of golden hopes and romantic dreams, I had come all the way from Los Angeles to find the job I wanted, to hear the music of my taste, to see serious plays and, God willing, to become a writer. The first danger I recognized that fall, however, was that Harlem would be too wonderful for words. Unless I was careful, I would be thrilled into silence.

When the great bandleader Cab Calloway, who grew up in Rochester and Baltimore, first saw Harlem, in 1929, he was, he said, "awestruck by the whole scene." Never had he beheld "so many Negroes in one place," or a street as glamorous as Seventh Avenue. "It was beautiful," he added. "Just beautiful . . . night clubs all over, night clubs whose names were legendary to me." The young Duke Ellington—a native of Washington, D.C.—is said to have remarked on first seeing Harlem, in the early twenties, "Why, it is just like the Arabian Nights."

In some of the books they later produced, the young men who went to Harlem to become writers were to set down their early impressions of the place. "Oh, to be in Harlem again after two years away," says the main character in a novel by Claude McKay. "The deep-eyed color, the thickness, the closeness of it. The noises of Harlem. The sugared laughter. The honey-talk on its streets. And all night long, ragtime and 'blues' playing somewhere . . . singing somewhere, dancing somewhere! Oh, the contagious fever of Harlem." In a short story by Rudolph Fisher, an elderly woman from the South arrives in Harlem. She has been driven uptown by a grandson, who met her at the railroad station, and as they begin the ride up Harlem's Seventh Avenue he announces proudly:

> "This is it. . . . Get a good eyeful. Here's One Hundred and Twenty-fifth Street—regular little Broadway. And here's the Alhambra, and up ahead we'll pass the Lafayette."
> "What's them?"
> "Theatres."
> "Theatres? Theatres. Humph! Look, David—is that a colored folks church?" They were passing a fine gray-stone edifice.
> "That? Oh. Sure it is. So's this one on this side."
> "No! Well, ain' that fine? Splendid big church like that for colored folks."
> Taking his cue from this, her first tribute to the city, he said, "You ain't seen nothing yet. Wait a minute."
> They swung left through a side-street and turned right on a boulevard. "What do you think o' that?" And he pointed to the quarter-million-dollar St. Mark's.
> "That a colored church, too?"
> " 'Tain' no white one. And they built it themselves. . . ."
> She heaved a great, happy sigh. . . .
> They circled a square and slipped into a quiet narrow street overlooking a park, stopping before the tallest of the apartment-houses in the single commanding row.
> Alighting, Miss Cynthie gave this imposing structure one side-wise, upward glance, and said, "Y'all live like bees in a hive, don't y'?—I boun' the women does all the work, too." A moment later, "So this is a elevator? Feel like I'm glory-bound sho' nuff."

As time passed, and Harlem revealed more of itself to the new-comers, some were not to find the place so dazzling, after all. Miss Cynthie would probably have been less disillusioned than most, for she had said to a porter at the railroad station, "Reckon places is pretty much alike after people been in 'em awhile." Exploring beyond the nicer streets and avenues, a newcomer was bound, in time, to come upon scenes like one described by another of the writers who were living in Harlem during the twenties:

> Fifth Avenue begins prosperously at 125th Street, becomes a slum district above 131st Street, and finally slithers off into a warehouse-lined, dingy alleyway above 139th Street. The people seen on Fifth Avenue are either sad or nasty looking. The women seem to be drudges or drunkards, the men pugnacious and loud —petty thieves and vicious parasites. The children are pitiful specimens of ugliness and dirt. The tenement houses in this vicinity are darkened dungheaps, festering with poverty-stricken and crime-ridden step-children of nature. This is the edge of Harlem's slum district; Fifth Avenue is its board-walk. Push carts line the curbstone, dirty push carts manned by dirtier hucksters, selling fly-specked vegetables and other cheap commodities. Evil faces leer at you from doorways and windows. Brutish men elbow you out of their way, dreary looking women scowl at and curse children playing on the sidewalk. That is Harlem's Fifth Avenue.

That was also a part of the Harlem that tourists seldom saw, and a part that Sportin' Life could not have read or heard about when he dreamed of buying the swellest mansion on upper Fifth Avenue.

"There Won't Be Any More Liquor"

THE NIGHT IN 1920 that the Eighteenth Amendment went into effect, an important New York politician was among a number of drinkers who were having a few—or more—in a downtown saloon. Though the refreshments flowed freely, they failed to brighten the spirit of the gathering—so depressing was the shadow that the new law cast over the house. The bartender, the most sorrowful member of the wake, addressed the man of politics, who was in a position to know about such things.

"Christy," he said, "are they really going to enforce it?" Yes, Christy replied. "There won't be any more liquor." As events were to prove, Christy was wrong. There *would* be more liquor. Citizens would simply invent their own. And, since almost anyone could make gin and whiskey—almost anyone who had the will and the formula—there was probably more liquor during Prohibition than before it was outlawed.

In Harlem—as elsewhere in New York—Prohibition not only induced orgies of illegal drinking but encouraged other forms of carefree behavior as well. Though moviegoing cannot have been so wild or so new a thing to do in 1927, black clergymen condemned it as a form of pleasure. Perhaps it was because more people were going to movies in the twenties than at any time in the past. In February of 1927, M. C. Strachan, speaking to his Seventh-Day Adventist congregation, on West 127th Street, denounced movie houses as "nurseries of vice and seminaries of crime" and proposed the expulsion of any church member seen entering or leaving a moving-picture theatre. Some of the movies playing in Harlem at the time were *We're in the Navy Now*, with Wallace Beery; *Broken Hearts of Hollywood*, with Douglas Fairbanks, Jr.; *The Great Gatsby*, with Warner Baxter; *Blonde or Brunette*, with Adolphe Menjou; and *Hotel Imperial*, with Pola Negri. They hardly seem now to have had much to do with vice and crime.

HIGH AND HANDSOME

In November of 1921, James W. Brown, pastor of the Mother Zion African Methodist Episcopal Church, on West 136th Street, was moved to address his congregation on the subject of desecration of the Sabbath—"Harlem's greatest danger," he called it. Enumerating the sins that were committed against the Lord's Day, Brown mentioned gambling, pool-playing, "improper" dancing, moviegoing, and the selling of alcohol. The last, he said, was by far the most shocking, and he urged a ban on all Sunday commerce in liquids—except the selling of milk to the poor.

The *Age*, which applauded the clergyman's lecture, calling it a "powerful sermon," had itself been appalled by the increasing signs of moral laxity in a community it had helped to build and whose character it wished to continue influencing for the better. Nothing was more important to the post-Victorian moralists who edited the paper than that black Harlem should be and remain predominantly a "community of homes." And no aspect of life in the community had become more alarming to them than the flood of booze that Prohibition had let loose in the district. As part of its crusade against this spate of hooch, the *Age* called upon churchgoers to set an example by shunning the trade in whiskey, and thus to help preserve Harlem as a place of "decency and respectability." When, as a result, it was accused of trying to turn Harlem into a Sunday school, the paper replied that "if stamping out hooch joints and closing up some of the undesirable cabarets" is making a Sunday school out of Harlem, "we plead guilty." Harlem was "a wide-open town" for illegal whiskey, the *Age* charged on another occasion; and immunity from police interference was "widespread." There was enough evidence to support the paper's claim. Few, if any, of the saloons had closed down when Prohibition began. In fact, new ones had opened up, and all were flourishing—despite occasional perfunctory raids by the police.

Along Lenox Avenue, liquor was to be obtained in the most unlikely places—delicatessens, shoe shops, newsstands, stationery stores, soda fountains, cigar stores, and drugstores. They were really cheap speakeasies, stocking large amounts of moonshine behind a thin camouflage of legitimate merchandise. Only the drugstores could have done without protective cover. Under Prohibition, physicians remained free to prescribe alcohol for their patients, and drugstores were allowed to dispense it—though not *all* the "drugstores" that suddenly sprang up in Harlem, and not to as many "patients" as suddenly showed up with prescriptions. It was estimated that the number of Harlem drugstores more than doubled during the first three years of Prohibition.

Though the bootleg stuff along Lenox Avenue was about the worst in Harlem, it did not fail to deliver what many of the drinkers wanted—the kick of a Georgia mule, as they put it. For some, however, this kick turned out to be much more powerful than they had expected. A few of them recovered later in Harlem Hospital; others did not. This was hardly surprising, for much of what they swallowed might have been deadly even to a Georgia mule. If one Harlem journal was not exaggerating in behalf of its crusade against liquor, the ingredients of the hooch being sold on Lenox Avenue were: wood alcohol, benzine, kerosene, pyridine, camphor, nicotine, benzol, formaldehyde, iodine, sulphuric acid, soap, and glycerin.

At one point, Fred R. Moore, the editor of the *Age*—in pressing the paper's campaign against the "hooch hounds"—invited the preachers of Harlem to join him at a public meeting "for the purpose of arousing the people to the real peril confronting them." The conditions are "hurtful," Moore said, in an open letter, "and our people are being degraded and debauched" by bad whiskey. "Should we stand for this?" he asked. The response was neither loud nor unanimous. No public meeting resulted from his call. A few churches passed resolutions deploring the conditions he had outlined, and Adam Clayton Powell, Sr., the pastor of the Abyssinian Baptist Church, on West 138th Street, pledged his "hearty cooperation." But nothing was heard from other ministers, and—like drugstores and cabarets—there were more preachers in Harlem than in any other community of its size in Manhattan. Although Moore was on friendly terms with most of the clergymen, he did not hesitate to embarrass the ones who had remained silent. Naming no names, he took to printing certain rumors in his paper. Was there a minister who had accepted "contributions" from bootleggers to keep his mouth shut? Had another received "a check for a substantial sum" when he made the plight of his church known to a hooch seller? The published rumors brought at least one minister forward. While he denied taking money from anyone in the liquor business, he confessed that his son did indeed work for a bootlegger. But this, he added, was a circumstance over which he had no control, for, at twenty-one, the boy was old enough to choose his own path.

The time came, apparently, when the bootleggers of Harlem grew tired of Moore's campaign against them. A letter that Moore claimed to have received in the morning mail, and published in his paper in 1924, contained this threat:

> I note with precarious interest your front-page spread concerning the bootleg traffic in Harlem. Now this has got to be stopped, as it brings about many losses to white people in the section who have invested large sums of money in bootleg, and they are not about to lose without a bitter fight. . . . So it is up to you, Mr. Editor, to desist from attacking us and giving the matter publicity . . . if not, the bootlegger's ring in Harlem will get rid of you through foul means.

Concerning the authorship of this note, a degree of skepticism is permissible. Moore was a fierce and resourceful crusader, and one may wonder whether, to arouse public indignation, he had not sat down and written himself a letter. In any event, his campaign against whiskey was no more successful than the Eighteenth Amendment. Bootleggers continued to flourish. And a resident of Harlem was to say some time later, "Washtubs, bathtubs, and basements became breweries. In almost any block, in any apartment house, one could buy his liquor at a reasonable price. Harlemites who brewed their own . . . found it a paying proposition, and decided that doing porter work wasn't in their line any longer." Yes, there *would* be more liquor, and, in Harlem, there was little that the law, the church, or the press could do about it.

Streets of Dreams

IT WAS often said during Prohibition that you could buy or sell almost anything on the streets of Harlem: diplomas, "hot" goods, quick cures, "power" over enemies and loved ones, "stocks" in Texas oil wells—anything that looked too good to be true or that held the promise of a miracle. "Harlem's grafters alone would supply the material for a volume," *The Saturday Evening Post* said in 1925. "They include at least a dozen varieties of doctors, proclaiming schools of medicine that probably do not exist anywhere else on earth. . . . Fortune tellers abound, also dealers in good luck." *Survey Graphic* added, also in 1925, "Black art flourishes in Harlem—and elsewhere in New York. . . . Feats of witchcraft are done daily. A towel for turban and a smart manner are enough to transform any Harlem colored man into a dispenser of magic to his profit. . . . Stop in front of a well-known drug store on Lenox Avenue. Here roots, herbs, and barks are displayed in the window. . . . In curled forms, in powders, in spirally bunches, in thick little knots, they lie there; they are sold as cures for various forms of illness. . . . No one can tell whether these plants are really what they are represented to be or not. Their sale is under no supervision; they may be roots of saplings dug in the Bronx, or bark from cherry trees disguised." But nothing sold more readily than bets on the numbers, Harlem's great game of chance, in which the odds against winning were a thousand to one. To play, you wagered anything from a penny upward on a three-digit number. Before noon, your number and the amount of your bet were collected by a "runner," who made rounds daily for the "banker." You won, or "hit," when certain Wall Street figures—published in the afternoon papers —contained your three digits in a certain order. On the winning bet of a penny, you were paid six dollars; on that of a dollar, six hundred dollars; and so on. You were free, of course, to bet any amount above a dollar, but there was an additional risk in doing this: the odds were already steep, and in the event that you hit, the odds against your collecting were even higher. The larger the amount you won, the more likely it was that your banker would disappear or welsh on paying—and since the game was illegal, there was no point in your going to the police. The banker usually claimed that, because there had been too many big winners that day, his bank was broken. This was hardly ever true. There were seldom many big winners on any one day; and the bankers nearly always collected far more in bets than they could conceivably need to pay off the winners. It is no wonder that they were among the big shots of Harlem, or that the *Age* once denounced them as "plutocrats," living "high," drinking "deep," and riding "easy" in expensive automobiles, driven by "liveried chauffeurs."

Poorer Harlemites did not much care how well the plutocrats lived as long as bets were paid, for hitting was about the only chance they had at a real payday. Win or lose, they met their runners every morning—on street corners, at coffee counters, in tenement lobbies, saloons, and barbershops—and put their pennies, nickels, dimes, quarters, or dollars on the numbers of their choice. A number was not just chosen at random; it had to be one that the player had invested with significance—a number that had occurred in a dream; a number that cropped up in a casual conversation and remained in memory as though it held a latent message; the number on the cap of a new mailman or on the license plate of a new automobile; the number of a street or building that had recently been in the news. Players looked everywhere for a number that appealed to the imagination.

Churchgoers took numbers from the Bible, from hymnals, and even from the mouths of their preachers. Most preachers in Harlem abhorred numbers playing. A few realized, however, that certain members of their congregation depended on the game for an income and for what contributions they made to church revenue. In the course of a Sunday service, such preachers would discreetly suggest to the congregation numbers that might be worth playing. They did this by placing a subtle stress on the number of a hymn they were announcing or on the number of a chapter and verse they were about to read from the Bible. Now and then, a minister would break entirely with discretion—as one did in 1926, when he declared to his members, "Now, here is a number that might come out, so you had better put it down and play it for the church." Even ministers who deplored the numbers game were sometimes obliged to soften their objections in order to meet the needs of the church's treasury. On a Sunday in 1924, as the collection plate was about to be passed around, one clergyman appealed to his congregation for a minimum contribution of two hundred dollars but made it very clear that he wanted no numbers money to be put in the plate. Members obeyed his wish, and when the plate was returned to the pulpit it held eight honest dollars. Well, as the preacher could plainly see, this was ridiculously short of the announced target. And, as any student of the Bible knows, there is no law that altereth not, save that of the Medes and the Persians. Hence, after revoking his earlier edict, the preacher directed that the plate be passed around once more. This time when it was returned to him, it bore a harvest of four hundred dollars.

The Saturday Night Function

DURING the twenties—and later as well—there were certain home entertainments in Harlem at which all and sundry were cordially welcome. Invitations were handed out in the streets, in bars, in barbershops, and in beauty parlors, or were left in mailboxes or in apartment-house elevators. These were little cards printed with promises of a joyful time:

> Hey! Hey!
> Come on boys and girls let's shake that
> thing
> Where?
> At
> Hot Poppa Sam's
> West 134th Street, three flights up
> Jelly Roll Smith at the piano
> Saturday night. . . .
> Hey! Hey!

> Fall in line, and watch your step,
> For there'll be Lots of Browns with
> plenty of Pep At
> a *Social Whist Party*. . . .
> Refreshments just it. Music won't quit.

> Shake it in the morning. Shake it at night
> at a SOCIAL MATINEE PARTY. . . .
> Music too tight. Refreshments just right.

These affairs—also called parlor socials—were commonly known as rent parties. Admission ranged from ten cents to a dollar, and the guests were usually truck drivers, tradesmen, housemaids, laundry workers, seamstresses, porters, elevator operators, and shoeshine boys, though certain writers and artists also enjoyed them. Many of

the guests were lonesome or unattached; some could not afford—
and, in any event, would not have been let into—the classier Harlem
night spots; others had recently come up from the South, and had no
other entrée into the festivities of a Harlem Saturday night. Recalling
such parties, a journalist from the community wrote in the forties,
"Saturday night was gay time in Harlem then, and music streamed
out of the windows of small overcrowded apartments. There was
always an upright piano of some uncertain vintage, a guitar, and
sometimes a trumpet and even a snare drum, tugged in by somebody
just for kicks."

The rent-party tradition did not originate in Harlem—though
rents there were so high that Harlem would surely have had to invent the tradition if it had not already existed. Ira Reid, a black
sociologist, wrote in the nineteen-twenties:

> For many years it has been the custom of certain portions of the
> Negro group living in Southern cities to give some form of party
> when money was needed to supplement the family income. The
> purpose for giving such a party was never stated, but who cared
> whether the increment was used to pay the next installment on
> the "Steinway" piano, or the weekly rent? . . . These parties
> were the life of many families of a low economic status who
> sought to confine their troubles with a little joy. . . .
>
> No social standing was necessary to promote these affairs.
> Neither was one forced to have a long list of friends. All that the
> prospective host required to "throw" such an affair would be a
> good piano player and a few girls. Of course you paid an admis-
> sion fee—usually ten cents. . . . The music invited you, and the
> female of the species urged that you remain. The neighborhood
> girls came unescorted, but seldom left without an escort.

In Harlem, Reid added, the rent party underwent an evolution in
"éclat." Possibly, no one down South had thought of printing up
invitations to these proletarian shindigs or of calling them parlor
socials, social matinées, or social whist parties. Such terms would
have promised something finer than the hosts of a working-class Saturday night were in a position to offer. But in Harlem, one of the
great centers of black style, plain reality often put on the attractive
clothes of imagination; by a miraculous act of the mind, shadow
was often transformed into substance. And, especially during Prohi-

bition, camouflage had a way of heightening the allure of whatever it concealed. Behind the front door of a social whist or matinée party, the lights—red or blue—were soft and low. Drinks were bathtub gin and whiskey. Food was fried fish, chicken, corn bread, rice and beans, chitterlings, potato salad, pigs' feet. "Whist" games were actually poker and dice. Music, in the parlance of the day, was "gut bucket," played by some of the masters and students of Harlem stride piano. Dancing—the Charleston, the black bottom, the monkey hunch, the mess around, the shimmy, the bo-hog, the camel, the skate, and the buzzard—went on till the break of day. Willie (the Lion) Smith, one of the piano players who entertained at these affairs, recalls in his autobiography:

> They would crowd a hundred or more people into a seven-room railroad flat and the walls would bulge—some of the parties spread to the halls and all over the building. All the furniture was stashed in another apartment except the chairs and beds. . . .
>
> The rent party was the place to go to pick up on all the latest jokes, jive, and uptown news. You would see all kinds of people making the party scene. . . . The parties were recommended to newly arrived single gals as the place to go to get acquainted. . . .
>
> Of course, there were also parties where there was such a racket all night long that the neighbors called the cops to quiet the joint down, and these would usually end with the law having a ball for themselves.

You were not regarded as much of a jazz pianist unless, wherever else you appeared, you played the rent-party circuit. You earned your spurs not only by sending the dancers into flights of ecstasy but also by "cutting," or outperforming, rival piano players. Maurice Waller, a son of Fats Waller, has described these pianists—one of whom was his father—as "garish extroverts who led the revolution in black music." At one Saturday-night function or another, there would be Smith, Eubie Blake, Corky Williams, Abba Labba, Lippy Boyette, Claude Hopkins, James P. Johnson, Luckey Roberts, Duke Ellington (new in town then), and—the youngest of the group— Fats Waller. None was more of an extrovert than Fats—a portly, jocose youngster whose talent was large and ebullient and whose appetite for food, drink, and pleasure became as immense as his talent. He was then mastering not only the piano but the organ as well. When he was not entertaining at rent parties, he could be heard at the Lincoln Theatre, on West 135th Street, playing organ accompaniments to silent movies or vaudeville shows. After once hearing Waller at the Lincoln, the equally young Bill Basie (not yet known as the Count) became "a daily customer, hanging on to his every note, sitting behind him all the time, enthralled by the ease with which his hands pounded the keys and [his feet] manipulated the pedals." Fats was the youngest son of an assistant preacher at the Abyssinian Baptist Church, and old man Waller had hoped to raise the boy for a career in the ministry. To Fats, however, music was a higher, more joyous calling. He had learned the piano in various Harlem homes, including James P. Johnson's, whose wife later said, "Right after James P. heard Fats Waller playing the pipe organ, he came home and told me, 'I know I can teach that boy.' Well, from then on, it was one big headache for me. Fats was seventeen, and we lived on 140th Street, and Fats would bang on our piano till all hours of the night. . . . I would say to him, 'Now go on home, or haven't you got a home?' But he'd come every day and my husband would teach. Of course, you know the organ doesn't give you a left hand, and that's what James P. had to teach him."

Duke Ellington, five years older than Fats Waller, was also a student and admirer of the Harlem piano masters. Before coming to New York in 1923 as a member of Elmer Snowden's band, the Washingtonians, Ellington had met James P. Johnson when Johnson made an appearance in Washington, D.C. Johnson's most popular composition at the time was "Carolina Shout," and Ellington, fascinated by the work, had spent hours at the piano trying to capture and reproduce the Johnson style. When he arrived in New York, his own playing showed clear signs of Johnson's influence.

Perhaps none of the early Harlem pianists have left a more detailed and captivating account of the rent-party scene than Willie (the Lion) Smith, whose autobiography contains these recollections:

> Piano players called these affairs jumps or shouts and we would get substitutes to play our regular [night-club] jobs for us. It wasn't always easy to do this because a lot of the shouts were on a Saturday night and the bosses frowned on us getting off. We made a lot of them after our regular jobs were over for the night. . . .

It got so we never stopped and we were up and down Fifth,
Seventh, and Lenox all night long hitting the keys. We even had
a booking agent—old Lippy. He'd say, "You boys wanna jump
for ten or twenty?" This meant he had a couple of parties paying
from ten to a double sawbuck each. On a single Saturday he'd
book as many as three parties for us and we'd alternate between
them. . . .

There were, of course, some of the chitterling struts where a
bunch of pianists would be in competition. Lippy was a great
promoter and was always trying to steam up the guests to argue
about who was the best. It sometimes got annoying, especially
when you had your eyes on a good-looking chick, or wanted to
take time out to get in the games they always had going in one
or two of the back bedrooms. But you had to stay by the keyboard to hold your own reputation for being a fast pianist.

Sometimes we got carving [that is, cutting] battles going that
would last for four or five hours. Here's how these bashes worked:
the Lion would pound the keys for a mess of choruses and then
shout to the next in line, "Well, all right, take it from there,"
and each tickler would take his turn, trying to improve on a
melody. . . .

Hard cash was bet on the outcome and more than once [the
listeners would] get ready to fight between them as to who had
won.

We would embroider the melodies with our own original ideas
and try to develop patterns that had more originality than those
played before us. Sometimes it was just a question as to who
could think up the most patterns within a given tune. It was pure
improvisation. . . .

The best time of all at these parties came early in the morning.
Then we'd play in a slow-drag style with the drummer muffling
his hides and stroking the snare lightly and politely with the
brushes. Sometimes we would doctor the piano by placing newspapers behind the hammers and put tin on the felts in order to
get an old-fashioned player-piano effect. This also gave us a
guitar sound.

During these early hours close to dawn the dancers would
grab each other tightly and do the monkey hunch or bo-hog.
Their shuffling feet would give everything a weird rhythmic
atmosphere. The lights would be dimmed down and the people
would call out to the piano player, "Play it, oh, play it," or

"Break it down," or "Get in the gully and give us the everlovin' stomp."

Those were happy days.

Bessie Smith, who appeared regularly in Harlem during the twenties, often sang these lyrics:

> Up in Harlem ev'ry Saturday night
> When the high brows git together it's just too tight.
> They all congregates at an all-night strut
> And what they do is tut-tut-tut.
> Old Hannah Brown from 'cross town
> Gets full of corn and starts breakin' 'em down.
> Just at the break of day
> You can hear old Hannah say—
> "Gimme a pig foot and a bottle of beer
> Send me, gate, I don't care."

And Bessie seldom sang of what she herself had not seen or experienced.

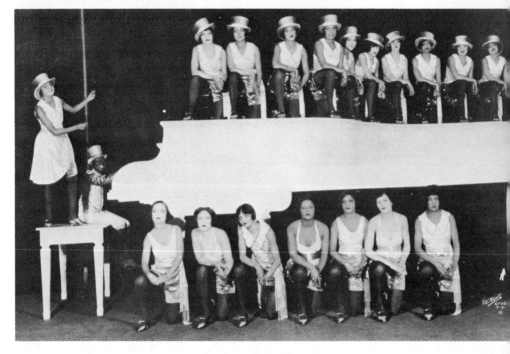

TOP, LEFT: Countee Cullen, in 1920, as a student at DeWitt Clinton
High School
TOP, RIGHT: Claude McKay, in the early nineteen-twenties
LEFT: Florence Mills, starring in *From Dixie to Broadway*, in 1924
ABOVE: Langston Hughes, around 1927

LEFT: Carl Van Vechten and Ethel Waters
TOP, LEFT: James Weldon Johnson
TOP, RIGHT: Aaron Douglas, the painter most closely linked to the
Harlem Renaissance
ABOVE: Zora Neale Hurston

THE CRISIS

Reg. U. S. Pat. Off.

A Record of The Darker Races

1929   1909

NAACP

15c THE COPY   **MAY 1929** $1.50 THE YEAR

LEFT: Lenox Avenue at 134th Street, in the early nineteen-twenties
BOTTOM, LEFT: William Stanley Braithwaite
BELOW: Reading room of the Schomburg Collection (later the Schomburg Center for Research in Black History) in the nineteen-twenties

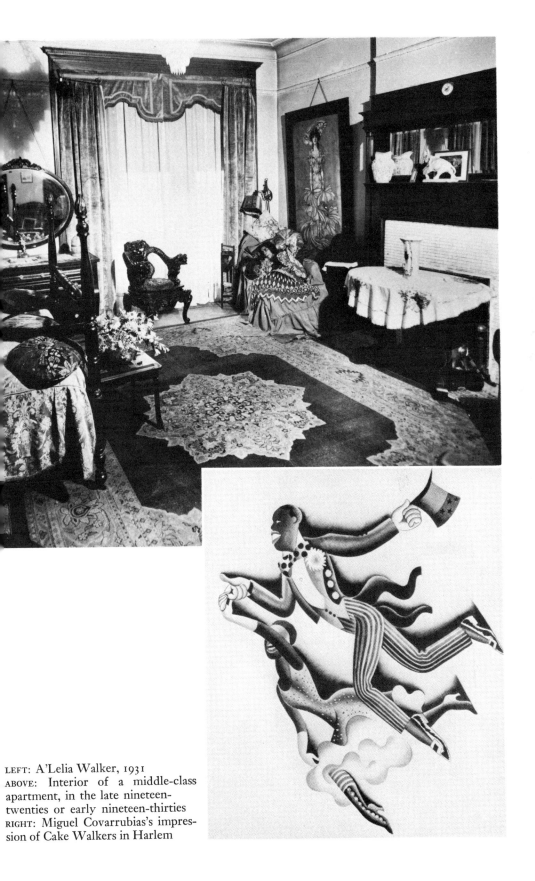

LEFT: A'Lelia Walker, 1931
ABOVE: Interior of a middle-class apartment, in the late nineteen-twenties or early nineteen-thirties
RIGHT: Miguel Covarrubias's impression of Cake Walkers in Harlem

Around Midnight

IN 1926, according to *Vanity Fair*, the Negro was "in the ascendancy." Almost everyone was dancing the Charleston or singing spirituals and the blues. As *Vanity Fair* added, "mulatto maids of white actresses" were hired "with an eye to their dexterity at dancing the Charleston"; and "coloured men" taught the Charleston to "the smart folk of Park Avenue." New York's theatregoers and music lovers were acclaiming the performances of Paul Robeson, Roland Hayes, Jules Bledsoe, Abbie Mitchell, Bessie Smith, Taylor Gordon, Florence Mills, Ethel Waters, and Bill (Bojangles) Robinson. Jazz artists like Fletcher Henderson, Don Redman, Duke Ellington, Coleman Hawkins, Edith Wilson, Louis Armstrong, and Fats Waller had begun to assert their influence on the musical idiom in which they worked. And, as *Vanity Fair* also reported, Harlem cabarets were "more popular than ever."

These cabarets and night clubs were also more numerous than ever. They had been increasing since the war, but during the early years of Prohibition, when they sprang up in astonishing profusion, Harlem came to be known as the night-club capital of the city—and of the nation. And nowhere was the entertainment livelier and more infectious than it was in Harlem. A white visitor from downtown Manhattan recorded these responses to a Harlem floor show:

> First, there is the impulse to look at your neighbor and see how he reacts. The big bass drum boom, booms. Enthusiastic wails writhe from the cornet—another flash from two dozen tawny, brown legs, whip-snapping, now hip-twisting, and watch 'em strut! Boom, boom-de-boom, boom. Well, to hell with your neighbor. If he doesn't like it, he ought to stay home.
>
> Precisely from that decision, one will enjoy watching a Negro show in Harlem. One by one, our cherished biases are taken off like arctic overcoats. It becomes natural to laugh and shout in the consciousness of an emotional holiday. Then, when the last am-

biguously worded song is done, one puts on again one's hat, coat, and niceties, and once again is staid, proper, and a community pillar.

Among the well-known night spots was the Lenox Club, at Lenox Avenue and 143rd Street, where the post-midnight set often stayed for breakfast. The *News* described its atmosphere in the Prohibition era: "Here the crowd is usually about 90 per cent colored, and the 7 o'clock whistles that call the faithful back to work on Monday morning find the boys and girls of both races drinking briskly, with an hour or two yet to go. . . . You will not enjoy the Lenox if you object to dancing shoulder to shoulder with colored couples. . . . You will not enjoy it if you blush at the dancing in the revue that suggests the end to which dancing originally was dedicated."

The Bamboo Inn, on Seventh Avenue, was—as one Harlemite wrote in 1928—"*the* place to see 'high Harlem' . . . well-dressed men escorting expensively garbed women and girls; models from *Vanity Fair*, with brown, yellow, and black skins," and "doctors and lawyers, Babbitts and their ladies with fine manners."

On West 133rd Street between Lenox and Seventh Avenues—a block with so many night clubs that it was known as Jungle Alley— were the Clam House, Tillie's Chicken Shack, Pod's & Jerry's, and Mexico's. The Clam House drew more white visitors than its neighbors did. There, "Gladys Bentley," accompanying herself at the piano, sang some of the naughtier lyrics of the decade. Bentley "used to draw the celebrities like flies," a Harlem journalist said, adding, "Those were the days of double entendre songs with much *ennui*, and if ever there was a gal who could take a popular ditty and put her own naughty version to it, La Bentley could do it." The artist Romare Bearden, who was then growing up in Harlem, recalls that " 'Gladys Bentley' was a woman dressed as a man. You also had a male performer who called himself 'Gloria Swanson.' So Harlem was like Berlin, where they had such things going on in cabarets at the time."

Tillie's Chicken Shack served some of the tastier late-night meals uptown—fried chicken and sweet-potato pie were its specialties. Its regular patrons—whites from Sutton Place and blacks from Seventh Avenue—gathered there around midnight as much to dine as to hear Elmira, the torch singer, in her suggestive rendition of "Stop It, Joe."

At Pod's & Jerry's, a lair of Willie (the Lion) Smith, one heard the best in Harlem stride piano. According to Smith, "the customers . . . varied from tush hogs up to the biggest names on Broadway"—Bix Beiderbecke, Paul Whiteman, Hoagy Carmichael, Artie Shaw, Jack Teagarden, Benny Goodman, Texas Guinan, Mae West, Tallulah Bankhead, Helen Morgan, Joan Crawford, Beatrice Lillie, William Powell, Jack Dempsey, and Gene Tunney.

Mexico's bore the nickname of its owner, who had been a mercenary south of the border. Duke Ellington, who frequented Mexico's, said that its proprietor "ran the hottest gin mill on 133rd Street, and you were always seeing cats walking along the streets, tubas on their shoulders, making their way over to his 'cutting contests.' " Ellington went on, "We used to hang out at his place, drinking up his booze. We called it 'a ninety-nine per cent,' one more degree . . . would bust your top." Milton (Mezz) Mezzrow, a white clarinettist and saxophonist from Chicago, who played in Harlem, later described the after-hours cutting contests that were held in places like Mexico's:

> The contests generally happened in the early morning, after the musicians came uptown from their various jobs. There was always some small private club or speakeasy that had a piano in it, and when some new musician came to town he was obliged to come up with his instrument and get off for the other musicians. If he didn't show, that proved he wasn't sure of himself in the fast company around Harlem. The one that rated best on his particular instrument was told, "Hey man, So-and-So's in town and he was looking for you at Such-and-Such's this morning." All the contenders for the title were worked up that way, each being told the others were looking for him because they wanted to cut him down. . . . Things really got stirred up that way, and before the night was over all the cats were in some smoky room, really blowing up a breeze. If it was a close call—say, for instance, Lester Young and Ben Webster and Don Byas were all blowing their saxes, and the people couldn't come to much decision about who was best—then somebody would sneak out and get Coleman Hawkins, and when he unwrapped his horn it settled all arguments and sent the boys back to practice some more. These contests taught the musicians never to rest on their laurels.

Smalls' Paradise, at Seventh Avenue and 135th Street, was one of the top four night clubs of Harlem—Barron Wilkins' Exclusive Club,

Connie's Inn, and the Cotton Club were the others. Of the four, Smalls' was the most accessible to ordinary Harlemites. Not many of them could afford its prices, but those who could were more welcome there than they were at the other top places. Smalls' was known for its big-band jam sessions, its colorful floor shows, and its waiters, who danced the Charleston while balancing full trays on their fingertips. It had a special appeal to visitors from downtown—especially the ones who felt that black music and entertainment were bound to be livelier in places where black customers formed a substantial portion of the audience. On weekends, the club was packed (tables were by reservation only), as were most of the other clubs. But on weeknights, when business was slower, Ed Smalls sometimes turned to the boys in the band. "There ain't enough cars upstairs," he once said to them. "I want cars outside to make this place really look like something." His musicians were unlikely to ignore such a request, for his cabaret paid as well and as promptly as any other uptown. (Because he was respectful of the churches, he was the most highly regarded cabaret owner in Harlem even by those clergymen who denounced night clubs as places of sin.) At Smalls' urging, the boys called up every acquaintance who owned a handsome automobile, and the following night—as one of them later said—"people couldn't get in for the cars sitting around outside."

Barron Wilkins' club, at Seventh Avenue and 134th Street, was one of the oldest cabarets in the community. It had moved uptown from the Tenderloin district in the first decade of the century and had been known as the Little Savoy, the Astoria Café, and Barron's Executive Club before it was named the Exclusive Club. Almost every important black pianist in New York had been hired by Wilkins at one time or another. Duke Ellington was virtually unknown when he and his Washingtonians (then led by Elmer Snowden) played there in 1923. Wilkins' club, Ellington wrote later, was then Harlem's "*top spot*"—the place "where they catered to big spenders, gamblers, sportsmen, and women, all at the peak of their various professions." Wilkins had hired Ellington and his friends on the recommendation of Ada (Bricktop) Smith, one of the leading blues singers of the day, who was then performing at the club—some years before she left for Paris, where she became one of the jazz celebrities of Europe. "People would come in who would ask for change for a C-note in half-dollar pieces," Ellington recalled. "At the end of a song, they would toss the two hundred four-bit pieces up in the air, so that they would fall on the dance floor."

In the twenties, Konrad Bercovici, a white journalist and novelist, described the Exclusive Club:

> Only members are admitted. It opens on week-days at about eleven o'clock p.m., officially, but the place really never gets started before one o'clock at night. It is frequented by white men, with only a sprinkling of negroes, although it is known as a colored man's cabaret. *Bons viveurs* from all the strata of society, financiers, lawyers, and theatrical people, with their women or in search of them, are dancing to the negro jazz band, while expensive food and drinks are being served at the tables, and the thick smoke of cigars and perfumed cigarettes hovers low over the white-haired heads of the males and the wavy hair of the females.
>
> Between the dances a professional singer or dancer is doing his or her stunt, and as the entertainers are always negroes the art is generally a very special one, fit only for the sophisticates of Barron Wilkins' club. One must have his purse well garnished when visiting the place. A hundred-dollar bill will not go very far and is not intended to do much service in this luxuriously fitted-out cabaret. But what charm! What exoticism! One easily forgets that all Harlem is not like it! Harlem, the Harlem of the poor, overcrowded, underfed, with children crippled with rickets and scurvy. . . .
>
> In its present form Wilkins' is the rich man's black and white cabaret. Southern gentlemen coming to the city, who cannot very well get on without negro society, are the first to look it up; and they learn to know after an experience or two that they must be on their guard. No affront or insult to the colored race would be suffered by any one of Wilkins' associates.

Wilkins was tall and sturdily built, like some of the athletes he befriended and supported. He sponsored Negro baseball teams; he had helped to finance Jack Johnson's pursuit of the heavyweight championship in 1908; and he donated generously to Sam Langford, a former black heavyweight challenger, when, in the early twenties, Langford became blind and destitute. Wilkins had, in Bercovici's words, "a tender, loving gaze," and many Harlemites sought him out in times of financial need. His generosity bought him much of the political clout he wielded in the community. According to the *Times*, he was "a power" in Harlem, especially at election time. But, the paper added, Wilkins swung between Republicans and Democrats "as the mood suited, or as his private interests dictated." Among his private interests during Prohibition was that of remaining in the good graces of the police. This he succeeded in doing, for his influence with the police was said to be greater than that of any other black in Manhattan. There was about Wilkins a faint aroma of the solid citizen who deals secretly in contraband; and, as a result, there was a feeling in Harlem that he paid heavily for his privileged standing with the law. But Wilkins, as the *Times* said, "always denied that he paid graft to the police." The occasion for that remark was Wilkins' death, in May of 1924. He was murdered one evening on Seventh Avenue, a short distance from his Exclusive Club. The assailant, a gunman and gambler called Yellow Charleston, claimed at his trial that he had been a business acquaintance of Wilkins', having regularly supplied the cabaret owner with stolen whiskey.

Connie's Inn, at Seventh Avenue and 131st Street, presented some of the finest cabaret revues in the city. Among them were *Keep Shufflin'* and *Hot Chocolates*, both with music by Fats Waller and lyrics by Andy Razaf. These revues, which also ran as theatre productions on Broadway, introduced such popular songs as "Ain't Misbehavin' " and "What Did I Do to Be So Black and Blue." The crowd at Connie's was usually all white. "No, you can't go to Connie's Inn with your colored friends," Nancy Cunard, a visiting Englishwoman, had occasion to say. "The place is for *whites*." Blacks were admitted only as waiters or entertainers. The *Age*, which already had an intense dislike for the owners of Connie's Inn—the brothers George and Connie Immerman, who, the paper charged, operated some of the worst hooch-selling shops on Lenox Avenue— was outraged by the club's policy of barring even Harlem's best blacks while admitting all the " 'slummers,' sports, 'coke addicts,' and high rollers of the white race who came to Harlem to indulge in illicit and illegal recreations."

Connie's patrons did not in fact fit that description. According to a report in the *News*, regulars at the club included "the piquant Lenore Ulric, blonde Hilda Ferguson . . . Michael Arlen, suave and smiling, rap-tap-tapping on his table in appreciation of a spine-rippling dance . . . Jack Pickford . . . Mark Hellinger . . . Gertrude

Vanderbilt . . . Harry K. Thaw, without whose name no roster of night club customers would be complete." Jimmy Durante, in his book *Night Clubs* (written with Jack Kofoed), called Connie's Inn the "swankiest of all the Harlem places." He went on, "They even have a red canopy outside—and, my God, you know that's the real top of the limit! It costs dough to play Connie's. . . . Smalls' Paradise, which is another one of the class joints, is easier on the pocket-book, principally because there's no cover-charge and ginger ale isn't rated in the same class with champagne."

When Durante called Connie's the "swankiest" of the Harlem night spots, he must have forgotten the times he had spent at the Cotton Club, over on Lenox Avenue at 142nd Street. It was the Cotton Club, after all, that was called "the aristocrat of Harlem"—and, however blacks may have felt about the term, there was some truth to it. The songwriter Harold Arlen, who helped to write some of the brilliant floor shows at the Cotton Club, called it "the hangout for the Mink Set, escaping Park Avenue for the earthier realities of Harlem." Lady Mountbatten, the wife of the English nobleman who later became First Lord of the Admiralty, was sometimes seen there along with the Park Avenue set. The financier Otto Kahn was "fascinated" by the place, according to Arlen. So, apparently, was Mayor Jimmy Walker, who often unwound there after a day at City Hall. The Duke Ellington orchestra began its rise to national and international fame when it opened at the Cotton Club, in December of 1927. It then included Bubber Miley and Louis Metcalf (trumpet); Joe Nanton (trombone); Otto Hardwicke (alto saxophone); Harry Carney (clarinet, alto, and baritone sax); Fred Guy (banjo and guitar); Sonny Greer (drums); Wellman Braud (bass); Rudy Jackson (clarinet and tenor sax); and Ellsworth Reynolds (violin). The elegant air of the Cotton Club agreed with Ellington's personal style. "Duke loved the highest of societies, white or black," the recording impresario John Hammond has written. "He sought the best locations, both because he enjoyed mingling with the cream of any social circle and because the money was better." Ellington himself recalled, "The Cotton Club was a classy spot. Impeccable behavior was demanded. . . . Sunday night . . . was the *night*. All the big New York stars in town, no matter where they were playing, showed up at the Cotton

Club to take bows. . . . Somebody like Sophie Tucker would stand up, and we'd play her song, 'Some of These Days,' as she made her way up the floor for a bow. It was all done in pretty grand style." Other stars who frequented the club included Helen Morgan, Bert Wheeler, Paul Whiteman, Marilyn Miller, Eddie Duchin, and George Raft. Willie (the Lion) Smith recalled that Raft "was a sharpie in those days and about the best dancer in New York," and added, "When he showed up at the Cotton, women used to ask the headwaiter to ask Raft if he would dance with them to the hot music."

The Cotton Club revues—written and produced by Harold Arlen, Dorothy Fields, Jimmy McHugh, Ted Koehler, and Lew Leslie— were as sparkling as those at Connie's Inn, and more elaborate. The club, proud of its gorgeous female entertainers, advertised "the cream of sepia talent, the greatest array of creole stars ever assembled, supported by a chorus of bronze beauties." Among the leading singers and dancers were Ethel Waters, Adelaide Hall, Leitha Hill, Carolynne Snowden, Aida Ward, Henri Wessels, Bill (Bojangles) Robinson, Anice Boyer, and George Dewey Washington. Lena Horne, who began appearing there in the early thirties, has recalled, "The shows had a primitive naked quality that was supposed to make a civilized audience lose its inhibitions. The music had an intensive, pervasive rhythm—sometimes loud and brassy, often weird and wild. The dances were eloquently provocative; and if they were occasionally stately, that stateliness served only to heighten their abandon." Mercer Ellington, in a book about his father, recalls, "The stage was set up to represent the Land of Cotton, with a plantation cabin, rows of cotton bushes. . . . The concept of the Cotton Club represented not the South of the aristocrats but the South of the Negro. The people who came there wanted what they thought was the red-hot feeling of the South as depicted by Negroes. No white acts could work there." And, as at Connie's Inn, no blacks were admitted to its tables unless they were light-skinned enough to be allowed the privilege of passing. "Only the tops of the tops in terms of names or influence could get a reservation," Cab Calloway recalled. "But even on an ordinary Sunday night it was difficult to get in. Negroes from the Harlem community would line up outside to watch the limousines drive up—Cadillacs and Rolls-Royces and Duesenbergs long enough to make you choke—and the celebrities come and go. Everybody was there. . . . Lady Mountbatten visited the Cotton Club one night and nicknamed it 'The Aristocrat of Harlem.' "

The men who, in 1929, founded the Plantation Club—farther down on Lenox Avenue, at 126th Street—doubtless wished to duplicate the Cotton Club's successful formula and compete for its customers and entertainers. That is what the Cotton Club owners assumed, according to Edward Jablonski's biography of Harold Arlen:

> The rivalry went too far when the management of the Plantation persuaded Cab Calloway to bring his orchestra from the Cotton Club to the Plantation. Calloway was one of the major attractions at the Cotton Club with his famous "Minnie the Moocher" routine. As he was an irrepressible night-club-floor personality . . . his leaving the Cotton Club was looked upon as pretty unfair competition.
>
> One night "some of the boys" dropped in on the Plantation Club . . . all the tables and chairs, reduced to splinters, shattered glasses and bottles, even the bar was deracinated and replanted at the curb. . . . When the boys finished with the Plantation Club, the street was the healthier place to be. Calloway and band, needless to say, returned to their old stand.

The "boys" who paid a visit to the Plantation Inn could only have been hired guns of the mob, for the Cotton Club, like a few other night spots in Harlem, was owned and run by gangsters. It was an open secret that the chief proprietor—though he seldom appeared on the premises—was Owney Madden, as feared a mobster and bootlegger as any operating during the twenties. He was driven around New York City in a bulletproof Duesenberg, and the Cotton Club was one outlet for the products of his illegal breweries. The writer Jim Haskins, in his book *The Cotton Club*, describes the origins of this night spot:

> About 1918 a building [called the Douglas Casino] was constructed for amusement purposes on the northeast corner of 142nd Street and Lenox Avenue. Built to compete with the very successful Renaissance Casino . . . the Douglas Casino was, like the Renaissance, a two-story building and intended as a dual operation. On the street floor was the Douglas Theatre, which featured films and occasional vaudeville acts. . . . One flight up was a huge

room, originally intended to be a dance hall. Plans to book some
of the big dances, banquets, and concerts away from the Renaissance were unsuccessful, and the dance hall remained essentially
unused until around 1920. The former heavyweight champion
Jack Johnson, who also happened to be an amateur cellist and
bull fiddler, and who was a connoisseur of Harlem night life,
rented it and turned it into an intimate supper club, the Club
Deluxe. Even reborn as a supper club, however, the place failed
to attract attention, until Owney Madden's gang came around
looking for a suitable spot for the entertainment of white down-
towners and to serve as the principal East Coast outlet for
"Madden's No. 1" beer. The Club Deluxe seated 400–500 people,
and it was just the place for which the syndicate was looking.
Madden's people made a deal with Johnson under which the
group would operate the place.

Stanley Walker, in *The Night Club Era*, his history of nineteen-
twenties cabaret life, said, "Millionaires and their ladies drank the
Madden booze in many a joint." He added this portrait of the Cotton
Club owner:

> Madden had iron in his gizzard . . . some of these friends were
> honest cops who had grown up with him on the West Side.
> Hell's Kitchen is the nursery for some of the finest policemen
> and some of the most ruthless criminals. . . .
>   His face was small. In profile its lines were like a falcon's. . . .
> The nose was a fierce beak. He had that first requisite of leader-
> ship, "a bone in the face" . . . there was something fishlike about
> the way the mouth drooped at the corners. . . . His body bore
> the scars of many bullets. . . . His hair was black and sleek. His
> eyes were . . . a very bright and piercing blue . . . usually they
> were hard, and shining, and they saw everything.

Manhattan's millionaires and their ladies not only drank down
heaps of Madden's booze, they were also fascinated by characters
like Madden himself. Reminiscing about the twenties, a writer said
in *The New Yorker* in 1940, "The smart set didn't have Elsa Maxwell
to amuse them in those days; the person they thought it would be
awfully cute to meet was Al Capone. They thrilled when Owney
Madden was pointed out to them. In spite of every discouragement,
they wore evening clothes and real jewelry to all-night madhouses

run by mobsters." Was Lady Mountbatten just as thrilled? Did she know that she was being entertained in the precincts of mobsters when, during Prohibition, she dubbed the Cotton Club "The Aristocrat of Harlem"?

In the twenties, *Variety* said, Harlem had "attained preeminence" as an "amusement center." Up there one saw "as many limousines from Park and upper Fifth Avenue parked outside its sizzling cafés, 'speaks,' night clubs, and spiritual seances as in any other high-grade white locale" in America. "Heavens," a writer recalled in *The New Yorker*, "how young everybody was! . . . Harlem was a thrill. We went there regularly well after midnight, to smoky lairs called the Drool Inn, the Clam House, and the Hot Feet. . . . Later in the morning, we snickered and leered in places which specialized in the *double-entendre* song, shouted loud. Still later, conspicuously furtive guides took us on to other *sotto-voce* cellars, where other *double-entendre* songs were sung. . . . *The New Yorker*, just as young as everybody else, solemnly pointed out that Harlem was 'not for débutantes.' "

In any case, here are some of the songs that the débutantes and everyone else were singing then: "Ain't She Sweet," "I'm the Last of the Red Hot Mamas," "Hard Hearted Hannah," "Fascinating Rhythm," "Lovin' Sam," "Somebody Stole My Gal," "You Made Me Love You," "My Blue Heaven," "Am I Blue?," "Who's Sorry Now?," "I Never Care About Tomorrow," and, of course, other songs by Cole Porter, Fats Waller, Duke Ellington, Harold Arlen, Irving Berlin, Jimmy McHugh, the Gershwins, Noble Sissle, and Eubie Blake.

Mezz Mezzrow, who had been strongly influenced by King Oliver, Louis Armstrong, and the New Orleans tradition, wrote: "The colored bands around New York had plenty of virtuoso musicians in them, but they didn't play the New Orleans music that I was crazy about; they had an entirely different pulse and flavor and I couldn't have chimed in worth a damn. . . . Even though the musicians didn't play New Orleans style, yet and still they had so much on the ball, such brilliant technique and inventive inflections to brighten up even the dullest arrangements. I just said to myself, even if it isn't my kind of music I better listen close and learn some more about this, because no matter what they're doing they do it *so good*."

The influence of Harlem musicians and their music had flowed across the Atlantic as well. "Jazz has simply taken Europe by storm," said the violinist Mischa Elman when he returned to America in 1922. "One hears it everywhere. To me, it has vast musical possibilities. Out of its wonderful rhythms will grow new ideas. It will become known as the American classical music. I think we should have a national conservatory of music at Washington so that composers of jazz and other music would be free to study and develop their art without financial disability."

Arriving in New York that same year, Darius Milhaud, the French composer, told reporters that European music was being considerably influenced by American music. "But whose music?" he was asked. "I mean jazz," Milhaud replied. The reporters, Milhaud went on to say—recalling the occasion in his autobiography—"were filled with consternation, for at that time most American musicians had not realized the importance of jazz as an art form and relegated it to the dance hall." During his visit to New York, Milhaud "never missed the slightest opportunity of visiting Harlem." The music up there "was absolutely different from anything I had ever heard before and was a revelation to me." And when he returned to Paris he "never wearied of playing, over and over on a little portable phonograph, shaped like a camera, Black Swan Records I had purchased in a little shop in Harlem." (Black Swan Records were produced in Harlem, by Harry Pace, with the help and advice of Fletcher Henderson.) More than ever, Milhaud said, "I was resolved to use jazz for a chamber work." His opportunity (though not for a chamber work) came when he was commissioned to write the music for a ballet—in collaboration with the painter Fernand Léger, who was to design the set, the choreographer Jean Börlin, and the librettist Blaise Cendrars. This turned out to be *La Création du Monde*, of which the critic Rory Guy has written, "Milhaud recognized at once the chance he had been seeking to utilize jazz elements in a composition," and constituted "his orchestra in accordance with those he had heard in Harlem, utilizing seventeen solo instruments including jazz saxophone." It was yet another of the many forms in which nineteen-twenties Harlem contributed to cosmopolitan culture and style.

But if there were many white Americans who applauded such an integration—who found the Harlem contribution an enriching component of the cultural mosaic—H. L. Mencken, of *The American Mercury*, could not be counted among them. In a 1927 editorial, he wrote, "Can it be that the Republic, emerging painfully from the Age of Rotary, comes into a Coon Age? For one, I am not above believing it. The colored brother, once so lowly, now bursts into the sunlight all along the line. In New York City he has made such astounding progress, all within a few years, that he now ranks, socially, next after English actors. . . . No dance invented by white men has been danced at any genuinely high-toned shindig in America since the far-off days of the Wilson Administration; the débutantes and their mothers now revolve their hips to coon steps and to coon steps only." It was as Menckenesque a view as had been expressed during the twenties—though, in a decade so sociable, and in a journal of reasonable civility, one might have wished for racial terminology that was not so degrading and primitive.

Bye, Bye, Blackbird

THE MOST beloved public figure in Harlem during the twenties was the petite dancer and singer Florence Mills, who lived for a time on West 133rd Street. She was an international star—was wildly celebrated by audiences in New York, London, and Paris—and Harlemites were proud to know that she lived among them. They, too, were astounded by her gifts, by the sparkle and radiance with which someone of her small build could perform. As the black poet Countee Cullen said, she was "all too slender and slight for the bright and vivacious flame of her being." Perhaps in so slight a body, her flame burned too brightly to have lasted for more than the six years she reigned as a star. But, above all, it was her neighborliness and humility that won the affections of her fellow Harlemites. One of them said, when she died: "Success never changed her. . . . When she was here she was always the same. She never wanted any special favor, any star's dressing room, even after she began to make a hit. She might have been one of the chorus if you saw her backstage. . . . She never owned an automobile, for all the money she made. She would take her nickel and walk to the subway. She didn't ride in taxicabs. And she was a fine woman."

Florence Mills' celebrity began in 1921, when, appearing in the chorus line of *Shuffle Along*—the musical comedy hit that was written by Noble Sissle and Eubie Blake—she stole the spotlight from the featured performers and became one of the leading attractions of the show. Her winning performance in *Shuffle Along* was followed by successes in such other productions as *Plantation Review, Dover Street to Dixie*, and *From Dixie to Broadway*. But it was in 1926, when she appeared in Lew Leslie's *Blackbirds*, that she scored her greatest triumph. Most of these productions were in the Broadway area, but *Blackbirds* ran for a while in Harlem, and after viewing a performance up there, George Jean Nathan wrote:

> Florence Mills is, within the limits of her field of theatrical enterprise, America's foremost feminine player. What Jolson is

among the men she is among the women. . . . There is not one of them who can sing a song so effectively as she can, though a hundred of them have voices far superior. There is not one of them who can dance as she does, try as they will to imitate her. . . . And surely there is not one of them who can so quickly, so certainly, and so electrically get an audience into her grip and keep it there. . . . Our music show theatre has never, within the present memory, known one like her.

Blackbirds, which left on a European tour in May of 1926, played in London and Paris for more than a year. At London's Pavilion Theatre, the show and its cast were toasts of the city's smart set. "They made a cult of . . . the *Blackbirds* and its black performers," Martin Green writes, in his *Children of the Sun*. Green adds that the show "was seen by the Prince of Wales twenty times."

When Florence Mills returned to New York, in September of 1927, the welcome she received at Pier 57 far outdid the one given to the city's mayor, Jimmy Walker, who had also returned on the *Ile de France*. Thousands of admirers greeted her at the pier and drove her home to Harlem in a gaily decorated motorcade. Perhaps only she knew that her triumph in *Blackbirds* might be her last, for she was then ill. Everyone who cared would know a few weeks later, when she died, after undergoing an operation. "A hundred thousand dollars' worth of flowers before the day was over," said W. A. Macdonald, of the *Boston Evening Transcript*, describing one of the days when Florence Mills lay in state, while thousands of Harlemites and white New Yorkers filed by her casket. "From all over the world that knew her," Macdonald continued, "came the flowers by cable, by telegraph, by messengers direct from those who had selected their tribute with loving care."

Harlem later gave her what is still the greatest funeral ever held in the district. This is how the *Age* reported it:

> The sun shone with fitful splendor on Sunday, November 6, as thousands of all races and ranks thronged Harlem streets and avenues to pay the last tribute of love and admiration to . . . Florence Mills.
>
> . . . [her] tiny body . . . in swathings of shimmering silk and spidery lace . . . lay in a massive casket of hand-hammered bronze, said to be a replica of the casket in which Rudolph Valentino

was laid. . . . She had been viewed by thousands, white and black, old and young, celebrities and nonentities, during the week she lay in state in the chapel of the Howell Undertaking Parlors, at 137th Street and 7th Avenue.

. . . the funeral procession was routed to pass through Seventh Avenue to 125th Street, thence through Lenox Avenue, and up that thoroughfare to 137th Street to the church [Mother A.M.E. Zion]. And both avenues were thronged with a silent host that stood in awed reverence. The number filling the streets and [windows of] houses was estimated at 150,000.

. . . A uniformed group of lodge members formed an escort, following the band, and then nine automobiles laden with the most extensive and gorgeous floral display Harlem has ever seen. An immense bleeding heart, made of deep red roses, with broad white satin ribbons fluttering from the top was the tribute sent by U. S. (Slow Kid) Thompson, the husband of Florence Mills. This filled the first of the automobiles.

Another floral offering that attracted much interest was a vast tower of red roses, four feet wide by eight feet high, which bore the simple inscription, "From a Friend." All that was known of its source was that cabled instructions came ten days ago from London for its presentation, and there was a persistent report to the effect that the Prince of Wales, who was a pronounced admirer of Florence Mills's art . . . had sent it. . . .

Behind the nine automobiles bearing flowers came the hearse. The casket was covered by a blanket of red and white roses, said to have been sent by her manager, Lew Leslie. Eighteen flower girls followed, each bearing a floral piece.

Then came the honorary pallbearers, a group of actresses including Edith Wilson, Cora Green, Evelyn Preer, Gertrude Saunders, Aida Ward, Maude Russel, Lena Wilson, and Ethel Waters. The active pallbearers were men of high rank in the musical and theatrical world: William H. Vodery, J. Flournoy Miller, Aubrey Lyles, Dewey Winglass, George Rickson, James Marshall, and Leonard Harper. . . .

The church, with a normal seating capacity of 2400, was jammed with at least 3000 people. The flower girls, following the casket as it was borne by the pallbearers, piled their floral tributes about the altar around the casket, and soon the air in the building was heavy with the perfume arising from the floral mass.

. . . An orchestra of selected musicians played the Chopin "Funeral March" as the body was borne up the aisle, the preacher intoning the scriptural passage, "I am the way and the life." As the strains of the funeral march died, the great organ, with Dr. Melville Charlton at the console, pealed forth the mournful hymn of consolation, "Come Ye Disconsolate," sung by the regular church choir. . . .

After the service, the funeral procession moved up Seventh Avenue to Woodlawn cemetery, where the body was interred. As the procession reached 142nd Street and Seventh Avenue, a low-flying aeroplane flew in slow circles overhead and released a flock of blackbirds which fluttered and flashed in the afternoon sun, recalling one of the songs made famous by Miss Mills, "Good-bye, Blackbirds."

The observer for the *Times* added this coda: "The moon came up and a cold wind shook the trees as the thousands present heaped six automobile loads of flowers over her grave. Then they went home to Harlem, talking not of Miss Mills but of Florence, as if they had known her intimately."

Florence Mills was only thirty-two when she died. No one who had enjoyed the vivaciousness of her personality and her performances could have imagined that her life would be cut off so soon. Nor, in 1927, when the twenties were as lively as ever, could anyone have guessed that the exuberance of the decade was in the early throes of death.

But What Was Harlem?

A QUESTION of community identity frequently arose during the twenties: What, indeed, was Harlem? Was it, as many people seemed to feel, mostly an "amusement center"? Or was it, as men like Fred R. Moore maintained, mostly a community of homes? It was, of course, something of both, though the opposing views were not easily reconciled. Even when the twenties were over, *Collier's* continued to describe Harlem as "a national synonym for naughtiness" and "a jungle of jazz." Jimmy McHugh and Dorothy Fields later wrote a number called "Harlem at Its Best," which Ethel Waters and others would sing:

> When you've seen gals who wail
> "Hello, baby, love for sale"
> Pound the pavements east to west
> Grabbing what they can to keep a handy man
> You've seen Harlem at its best. . . .
>
> And when you've seen them couples dance
> Like they're in a trance
> With that most primitive zest
> Rocking on the beat
> With everything but feet
> You've seen Harlem at its best.

But this view of Harlem was not the one that many residents—or a few clear-eyed visitors—held. To a resident like James Weldon Johnson, most Harlemites were "ordinary, hardworking people," who "have never seen the inside of a night club," and who were occupied with "the stern necessity of making a living, of making ends meet, of finding money to pay the rent and keep the children fed and clothed." And to a visitor like the novelist Fannie Hurst, writing some years later, "the large majority of Harlem, who lead ordered, backbone-of-the-nation lives, are seldom heard of." She was thinking of butchers, bakers, lawyers, doctors, and ordinary wage earners. Many such people went out to Lenox and Seventh Avenues only to work, to shop, to stroll, or—as Fannie Hurst noted—to visit beauticians, chiropodists, or dentists. They belonged to "the immense section of unhonored and unsung Harlem which represents decency, family unity, and social stability."

Away from the surfeit of bars, clubs, cabarets, and other jazz joints, the "unhonored and unsung Harlem" of the twenties took a small but lively interest in the serious arts. A few painters, encouraged by grants and awards from the William E. Harmon Foundation, exhibited their work at the 135th Street branch of the New York Public Library. Ernestine Rose, a white woman who headed that library (it later became nationally known as the Schomburg Center for Research in Black Culture), made her institution into one of the most hospitable gathering places for aspiring black writers and literary intellectuals. Amateur theatre groups, organized by W. E. B. Du Bois and Regina Andrews, performed regularly in its auditorium. Other groups, under other sponsorships, performed elsewhere in the community. Choruses and singing societies presented operettas and Sunday-afternoon concerts in various parts of the district. Violinists, cellists, pianists, and organists gave classical recitals in small halls and large churches. Little music schools trained many of the youngsters in the community. There was a Harlem Symphony Orchestra, led by a man named E. Gilbert Anderson. And when rising stars like Roland Hayes, Marian Anderson, Jules Bledsoe, Abbie Mitchell, and Paul Robeson were not singing downtown—at Town Hall or the Aeolian Hall—they appeared before enthusiastic audiences in Harlem.

In political and other forms of intellectual life, Harlem was the most militant community in the black world. Black nationalists, led by Marcus Garvey and his Universal Negro Improvement Association, advocated racial separatism, black pride, sovereignty, self-reliance, and a return to African modes of behavior. Black socialist radicals, led by A. Philip Randolph, Chandler Owen, and like-minded journalists and intellectuals, ridiculed the older black leadership organizations, rejected the conventional black ties to the Republicans and

Democrats, and urged the masses to join the struggles and pursue the objectives of the trade-union movement. Such radicals held the view that there could be no black progress without economic gains, a widening of employment opportunity, a democratization of labor and industry, and—as they liked to say—a complete overhauling and reconstruction of American society and the American economy. Compared with the Garvey nationalists, however, the black socialists had only a modest following. Their following might have been modest at any stage—for blacks were no great joiners of left-wing movements—but the twenties were surely an inopportune time for their message. After the war years—marked by an increase in lynchings and labor riots at home—many among the black masses had lost faith in white American movements and measures.

The black socialist radicals claimed loudly, as they had been doing since the war, to be New Negroes. Though the black nationalists, in their non-American sentiments, were probably Newer, Garvey's followers did not make much use of the term "New Negro," and since they were pessimistic concerning a future in America, the term did not properly apply to them. The black socialists who called themselves New Negroes were racial pluralists despite their radicalism. They simply insisted on a more just, progressive, and democratic form of American pluralism. Mostly, they were New Negroes in comparison with what they described as the Old Negro political and intellectual establishment—whether this establishment held the accommodationist views of Booker T. Washington or the protest ones of W. E. B. Du Bois. The *Age*, which had been a voice of Booker T. Washington even before the conservative Fred R. Moore became its editor, did not know quite what to make of these New Negroes. In 1920, after all the talk it had heard about the New Negro, the *Age* asked, What *is* this New Negro—what virtues does he have "that the Negro of yesterday, or the day before, did not possess?" Randolph's *Messenger* printed this reply:

> In politics, the New Negro, unlike the Old Negro, cannot be lulled into a false sense of security with political spoils and patronage. A job is not the price of his vote. He will not continue to accept political promissory notes from a political debtor, who has already had the power, but who had refused to satisfy his political obligations. The New Negro demands political equality. . . .

The social aims of the New Negro are decidedly different from those of the Old Negro. Here he stands for absolute and un-equivocal *"social equality."* He realizes that there cannot be any qualified equality.

. . . the methods by which the New Negro expects to realize his political aims are radical. He would repudiate and discard both of the old parties—Republican and Democratic. His knowledge of political science enables him to see that a political organization must have an economic foundation. . . .

On the economic field, the New Negro advocates that the Negro join the labor unions. Wherever white unions discriminate against the Negro worker, then the only sensible thing to do is to form independent unions. . . .

The social methods are: education and physical action in self defense. That education must constitute the basis of all action is beyond the realm of question. And to fight back in self defense should be accepted as a matter of course. No one who will not fight to protect his life is fit to live. . . .

Finally, the New Negro arrived upon the scene at the time of all other forward, progressive groups and movements—after the great world war. He is the product of the same world-wide forces that have brought into being the great liberal and radical move-ments that are now seizing the reins of political, economic and social power in all of the civilized countries of the world.

Altogether, the New Negro intellectuals of Harlem were a most ir-reverent bunch. They claimed to be more widely read than the older leadership group in Harlem, to be more sophisticated in modern ideas, and to have found the scientific key to social and economic change. They revelled in the cut and thrust of argument, whether they were discoursing on street corners, writing in the magazines they had founded to promote their beliefs, or debating one another in meeting halls and drawing rooms. The drawing-room forensics often took place on Sunday mornings, and one of the least political of the New Negroes—Theophilus Lewis, who was principally a drama critic—later likened their parlor discussions to "Samuel Johnson's arguments in the coffeehouse." George S. Schuyler—a black journal-ist and skeptical fellow-traveller—described the gatherings, often held in Randolph's apartment, as "Athenian conclaves." Nothing, he said, "escaped the group's probing minds and witty shafts." At one point, they organized themselves into a group called the Friends of Negro Freedom, and conducted a campaign to drive Marcus Garvey from his position of prominence among the black masses of Harlem.

By the mid-twenties, Garvey's U.N.I.A. had slipped into a decline that it was unable to reverse. In 1922, it had been at its most powerful, claiming a worldwide membership of four to six million. That year, its parade through the streets of Harlem was larger and more colorful than any before or after. Garvey took the salute in front of a building—on Seventh Avenue near 135th Street—that was then occupied by *The Messenger*, a magazine that had been one of Garvey's severest critics in Harlem. This was his answer to the socialist editors of that journal, who had been able to muster only a handful of followers but, as he felt, had had the temerity to ridicule the programs and objectives of his organization. His prestige had never been greater than it was then, and, as a leader—arrayed, as a writer said, like Solomon in all his glory—he had never shone more splendidly. A year later, however, Garvey was convicted of using the mails to defraud his followers—while selling shares in his ill-fated Black Star Shipping Line—and was sentenced to five years' imprisonment. Believing as much in his innocence as in his own powers of advocacy, Garvey had fired his lawyer and argued his own defense—or, as the black journalist J. A. Rogers put it, he "was so accustomed to ruling the roost that he could not stand having another speak for him." In 1925, after an unsuccessful appeal, Garvey was sent to the Atlanta Penitentiary, and in 1927, when his sentence was commuted, he was deported to his native Jamaica. From various countries, he was to try, during the next thirteen years, to restore to his movement the grand flourish it had once possessed. His efforts were unavailing, and his death, in 1940, sealed the fate of the largest organization of its kind that had ever been assembled—though in parts of Harlem, Central America, and the Caribbean remnants of it may still be seen and heard. Yet, if Garvey's great organization came to ruin, his own influence on black consciousness did not disappear. The example of his movement in Harlem was to remain an inspiring element in almost every strain of black-nationalist agitation that has since developed in the Americas. Garvey's doctrines were even to have an effect on intellectuals like Kwame Nkrumah, of Ghana, who helped during the fifties and early sixties to lead the successful struggle for

African freedom and independence—yet another sign of Harlem's importance when it was "the Negro capital of the world."

The black socialist radicals were also in disarray by the middle of the nineteen-twenties. Though many Harlemites had enjoyed reading their magazines and listening to their speeches, few had enlisted under the left-wing banner. One success of a sort had come in 1920, when Randolph, running on the Socialist Party ticket for New York State Comptroller, polled more than two hundred thousand votes— an impressive but losing performance. In Harlem, the majority of the votes he received may not even have been cast in support of his political views. He had personal qualities that made him widely admired in the public life of the community, and the votes he received may have been mostly an expression of that regard. "When you looked at Randolph, his rich voice fitted him," the musician Noble Sissle later recalled. "It went with everything about him, even his facial expression, which was one of great dignity. . . . He might use a lot of ten-cylinder words, but the layman was crazy about him, because he was so different. He had a little beat-up office up there, a raggedy desk and a few chairs. But he sat down just as the President would sit down at his desk in the White House. You'd forget about his little raggedy desk the moment you saw him sitting there. You were way off in another world. He might have sounded like a Yale or Harvard graduate with his talk, but there was a ring of sincerity to it and brotherly love to it, and you were proud to have someone like that to talk to you."

Randolph took his early political failures philosophically. Toward the end of his life (he died in 1979), he said, "Socialism and trade unionism called for rigorous social struggle—hard work and programs—and few people wanted to think about that. Against the emotional power of Garveyism, what I was preaching didn't stand a chance." He continued, "It was a dark period for us. We were in the wilderness alone. But as Negro radicals we did not work in vain. We were the very first to shape a working-class economic perspective in Negro thought." In 1925, the year Garvey was imprisoned, Randolph set out across the United States on what turned out to be the last of his many attempts to organize a trade union. This time, he succeeded, though not until 1937, after a bitter twelve-year struggle with the Pullman Company. The union he formed and led for the remainder of his active life—the Brotherhood of Sleeping Car Porters—nourished the growth of other social movements among blacks, especially during the forties, and was the base on which Randolph established himself as one of the most eloquent labor and civil-rights spokesmen in the nation's history.

PART FOUR

Life and Letters

A Tradition of the New

WHILE the black-nationalist and New Negro political organizations of Harlem were fading, an artistic movement was emerging. Called the Harlem or New Negro Renaissance, it was made up chiefly of writers, and—in the work of most of its members—represented a break with the "genteel" tendencies that had been dominant in black writing. Not all the Renaissance poets, novelists, and essayists lived in the city—though most of them did. (A few lived in Washington, D.C., where they taught or studied at Howard University.) Nor was even one of them born in Harlem. The majority had migrated there from various parts of America and the Caribbean—pulled, as one of them said, by the magnet of the black metropolis. They had also been pulled by the magnet of New York City, which, as they well realized, was the publishing capital of the nation.

Though the New Negro literary movement began to be recognized only around 1924, it began in the war years, during one of the early stages of black-militant activism in Harlem. In 1917, in the magazine *The Seven Arts*, edited by James Oppenheim and Waldo Frank, there appeared a sonnet titled "The Harlem Dancer," under the pseudonym Eli Edwards. The author, then virtually unknown, was Claude McKay, a Jamaican émigré, aged twenty-six, and the poem said, in part:

> Upon her swarthy neck black shiny curls
> Luxuriant fell; and tossing coins in praise,
> The wine-flushed, bold-eyed boys, and even the girls,
> Devoured her shape with eager, passionate gaze;
> But looking at her falsely-smiling face,
> I knew her self was not in that strange place.

Barring some of the dialect verses that Paul Laurence Dunbar wrote in the late eighteen-hundreds and early nineteen-hundreds,

McKay's sonnet represented one of the first appearances in black poetry of material that spoke boldly and affectionately about the experience of the black urban masses. Nor, earlier, had black Harlem been a subject of serious imaginative writing. In 1919, Max Eastman's magazine *The Liberator* published another of McKay's sonnets, "If We Must Die." It had been written during the "red summer" of that year, in which scores of blacks were beaten or killed, and it brought to black poetry a new spirit of race militancy. A few of its lines went:

> If we must die, let it not be like hogs
> Hunted and penned in an inglorious spot. . . .
> What though before us lies the open grave?
> Like men we'll face the murderous, cowardly pack,
> Pressed to the wall, dying, but fighting back!

The transition in black letters that McKay's early work signified is illustrated by an exchange between him and William Stanley Braithwaite, a leader of the older black literary generation. In 1918, after McKay's early work had appeared in *The Seven Arts* and in *Pearson's*—edited by Frank Harris—he submitted a number of his poems to Braithwaite, who was then a critic for the Boston *Evening Transcript*. As McKay later reported, Braithwaite, also a poet, replied that the poems "were good, but that, barring two, any reader could tell that the author was a Negro." Because of "the almost insurmountable prejudice against all things Negro," Braithwaite advised the younger man "to write and send to the magazines only such poems as did not betray" his racial identity. That sort of advice— "grim and terrible" in its sincerity—McKay was unable to accept, for, as he later added, "I felt more confidence in my own way." Besides, in the work of the great white poets he admired—Byron, Shelley, Keats, Blake, Burns, Whitman, Heine, Baudelaire, Verlaine, and Rimbaud—he could "feel their race, their class, their roots in the soil," and, he said, "likewise I could not realize myself writing without conviction."

In 1921, two other black poets, younger than McKay, attracted public attention. One was Countee Cullen, a seventeen-year-old student at De Witt Clinton High School, in Manhattan, whose "I Have a Rendezvous with Life," published in his school magazine, *The Mag-*

pie, was praised for its natural lyricism and for the precocity of its tragic feeling and insight. The other was Langston Hughes, then nineteen, who had recently graduated from Central High School in Cleveland. His "The Negro Speaks of Rivers" was published in *The Crisis* (the organ of the National Association for the Advancement of Colored People) and displayed a maturity of reflection that was considered remarkable. In 1922, McKay published his first collection of poems in America, titled *Harlem Shadows*. (Before leaving his homeland, in 1912, he had published a book of dialect verses called *Songs of Jamaica*, and in 1920, during a sojourn in London, he had published a volume there, titled *Spring in New Hampshire*.) In 1923, the decade's first major work of black fiction appeared—*Cane*, by Jean Toomer, which was a collection of finely written and poetically evocative studies of black rural life in Georgia. In 1924, Jessie Fauset, living in Manhattan, published her first novel, *There Is Confusion*, though in content and spirit—middle class and genteel—it was not representative of what New Negro fiction became. It was not until 1924, however, that all these efforts were recognized as having been portents of a new movement in black writing.

Nor, when the movement emerged fully—and was seen to take the experience of the masses more seriously than earlier black literature had done—was there any general agreement concerning the influences that had brought it into being. In tracing its development, however, certain observers were struck by the fact that the first signs of the new movement had appeared during and immediately after the war, when the spokesmen for black pride and awareness were most audible; and because of this they felt, quite plausibly, that the movement drew much of its formative energy from the upsurge of black militancy in Harlem. In their apparent break with the aesthetic and cultural attitude of their elders, most of the New Negro writers did bear a resemblance to the Harlem race radicals and nationalists, who had revolted against the established black leadership; they could be said to represent in art what the race militants had represented in politics—not an appeal to compassion and social redress but a bold assertion of self.

Though virtually all the younger writers sprang from or were educated into the middle class, they wrote very little about that group. Among the exceptions were Jessie Fauset (*There Is Confusion* and

Plum Bun) and Nella Larsen (*Quicksand* and *Passing*), whose novels called attention to the plight of a light-skinned and cultivated middle class, forced by the circumstance of race into the undifferentiated jug of black life. Jessie Fauset was a Philadelphian, a graduate of Cornell, the University of Pennsylvania, and the Sorbonne, and she worked as an assistant to W. E. B. Du Bois, the scholarly and aloof editor of *The Crisis*. Claude McKay, one of the more mass-conscious of the Harlem writers, admired her personally. She was "prim, pretty, and well-dressed, and talked fluently and intelligently," he said, but he also observed that she "belonged to that closed decorous circle of Negro society, which consists of persons who live proudly like the better class of conventional whites, except that they do so on much less money." He added, "Miss Fauset is . . . dainty as a primrose, and her novels are quite as fastidious and precious." The experience of blacks like Jessie Fauset was surely deserving of attention. Their predicament, though on a higher social plane, was not unrelated to that of most blacks, who, because of social barriers, were not free to aspire and achieve, to make of themselves whatever they were equipped by talent and imagination to be. Many among the colored elite who sought these forms of liberation did so as much from a wish to realize their own potential as from a desire to differentiate themselves from those of their race who were blacker, poorer, and less cultivated than they. But however understandable that desire was, it tended—when viewed by the masses—to inhibit sympathy for what was most human about their plight.

The novels written by and for persons of this class were really a continuation of earlier genteel black fiction, much of which used the life of ordinary blacks merely as a background against which to dramatize the claims of exceptional status or the painfulness of its denial by white society. This mode of fiction was exemplified by the short stories and novels of Charles W. Chesnutt. The novels for which he was best known were *The House Behind the Cedars*, *The Marrow of Tradition*, and *The Colonel's Dream*. All three were published between 1900 and 1905; and, in their treatment of racial material, they differed considerably from Paul Laurence Dunbar's *The Sport of the Gods*—perhaps the only novel of its period to examine the predicament of the masses themselves. Writing in 1930, the critic John Chamberlain said, "For a time people were generally unaware that the work of Chesnutt was not that of a white man. . . . The problem of the color line fascinated him. He wrote stories of the 'Blue Vein Circle of Groveland' (Cleveland?), stories of a society of Negroes of light color that sets itself up above the darker members of the race." Chesnutt wrote to Carl Van Vechten in 1926: "Between you and me, I suspect I write like a white man because by blood I am white, with a slight and imperceptible dark strain, which in any civilized country would have had no bearing whatever on my life or career, except perhaps as an interesting personal item." It was to the Chesnutt tradition of writing that *Opportunity* (the organ of the National Urban League) was referring when it said, in 1925:

> A criticism of Negro efforts at artistic expression . . . has been that the members of this group with a background of deep-toned and gorgeously colorful experience all their own have, with the characteristic self-consciousness of the parvenu, strained desperately to avoid or deny it. . . .

The magazine added:

> We expect of literature, nowadays, to reveal with some measure of faithfulness something of the life of a people; something of those subtle forces which sustain their hopes and joys, stiffens them in sorrow. A start in this direction has already been made in certain of the recently published works by Negro writers.

Those were the writers who reflected most strongly the social inclinations of the Harlem Renaissance. To judge from much of their work, they took the view that the basic truths of the black experience were to be found in the styles and conditions of ordinary life—and that these were as worthy of artistic treatment as were the qualities of middle-class living. Of course, no part of that view was shared by the prim and proper middle-class writers and most of the older black critics who championed their work. But Langston Hughes, writing in a 1926 issue of *The Nation*, declared, "We younger Negro artists who create now intend to express our individual dark-skinned selves without fear or shame. If white people are pleased, we are glad. If they are not, it doesn't matter. We know we are beautiful. And ugly too. The tom-tom cries and the tom-tom laughs. If colored people are pleased, we are glad. If they are not, their displeasure doesn't matter either." That, on the whole, was the spirit of the New Negro writing that flourished in Harlem during the twenties.

It was *Opportunity* magazine that had helped to publicize the developing New Negro literary movement. In its issue of May 1924, it reported an affair that marked "the debut of the younger school of Negro writers." This affair, a dinner held the previous month at the Civic Club in downtown Manhattan, was organized by Charles S. Johnson, editor of the magazine; and its purpose was to introduce the emerging writers to a number of white editors and critics and to what the magazine called "the passing generation" of black literati.

Among those of the passing generation who attended was W. E. B. Du Bois, the editor of *The Crisis*, a leader of the protest movement, and the nation's most prominent black scholar and intellectual. Born in Great Barrington, Massachusetts, in 1868, he had been educated at Fisk University, at Harvard, and at the University of Berlin. Among his teachers at Harvard had been Josiah Royce, George Santayana, Albert Bushnell Hart, and William James. Later, he had himself been a college professor, a historian, a sociologist, and a founding member of the N.A.A.C.P. He was also an essayist, a critic, and a novelist—though he tended to overestimate his gifts as a writer of fiction. Du Bois' greatest strengths as a literary figure lay in the areas of the racial polemic and the cultural essay—as exemplified in *The Souls of Black Folk*, a collection of such pieces that appeared in 1903, and which remains one of the most important books of its kind.

Another member of the passing generation was James Weldon Johnson. If Du Bois was the most distinguished black intellectual in the nation, then Johnson, a native of Jacksonville, Florida, was the most versatile. Born in 1871, and educated at Atlanta and Columbia Universities, he had been a schoolteacher, a song writer, a lawyer, a United States diplomat, and an editorial writer for the *Age*. Now, in 1924, he was also a poet, novelist, literary and cultural critic, and the Executive Secretary of the N.A.A.C.P. "Mr. Johnson's appearance and background didn't inspire levity," one historian has written. "He was tall, lean, and immaculate. . . . But as a host he was modest and self-effacing, always focusing attention on others." Because of this self-effacing quality, he was, among the passing generation, the friendliest toward the work of the younger writers. A genuine artist himself, he understood their need and conceded their right to affirm their own vision of black life—particularly the proletarian areas of that life, which had not played a central part in the work of the passing generation.

Master of ceremonies at the Civic Club dinner was Alain Locke, a professor of philosophy at Howard University, in Washington, D.C. He was also a critic of art and literature, and—like the editor of *Opportunity*—was one of the main interpreters and boosters of the new black writing. Locke, a Philadelphian, was educated at Harvard, the University of Berlin, and Oxford, where he was the first black American Rhodes Scholar. Among the black intellectuals of the twenties, perhaps only Du Bois was more formidably educated than Locke was. Dainty and urbane in appearance, he dressed tastefully, and a quality of fastidiousness in his eyes suggested him to be a man of fine and discriminating judgment. These looks—together with his education and his upper-middle-class background—made him an unlikely enthusiast of a movement in proletarian writing, one estranged from the sensibilities of his own class and upbringing. He was devoted to the work of this movement, however, and was to become the foremost black critic of the Harlem Renaissance.

Locke, who was born in 1886, was not exactly a member of the passing generation. In age, he stood somewhere between the generation of Du Bois and that of the younger writers, most of whom were born in the eighteen-nineties and early nineteen-hundreds. Perhaps it was his position between the old and the new—and the fact that he sometimes sought to dictate theory and method to his less educated juniors—which accounted for the strains that later developed between him and some of the younger writers. Zora Neale Hurston once complained to James Weldon Johnson that Locke was "a malicious, spiteful little snot that thinks he ought to be the leading Negro because of his degrees." She added, "So far as the young writers are concerned, he runs a mental pawnshop. He lends out his patronage and takes in ideas which he soon passes off as his own. And God help you if you get on without letting him represent you." Claude McKay wrote at one point that he doubted Locke's ability "to lead a Negro Renaissance" because of his "effete European academic quality." But Hurston and McKay were among the minority that resented or distrusted Locke's influence.

The white editors and critics who attended the début of the young black writers at the Civic Club included Carl Van Doren, of *Century* magazine; Freda Kirchway, of *The Nation*; Frederick Allen, of *Harper's*; Walter Bartlett, of *Scribner's*; Devere Allen, of *The World Tomorrow*; and Paul U. Kellog, of *The Survey Graphic*. They were apparently impressed by the significance and promise of the occasion, to judge from what Van Doren said: "I have a genuine faith in the future of imaginative writing among Negroes in the United States. What American literature decidedly needs at the moment is color, music, gusto, the free expression of gay or desperate moods." Possibly none of them was more impressed than Kellog. After what he had seen and heard at the dinner, he decided to devote an entire issue of his *Survey Graphic* to writing by blacks. This turned out to be the issue of March 1925, titled "Harlem—the Mecca of the New Negro." It was guest-edited by Locke, and included poems, stories, and essays on various facets of black life. Not all the contributors were from the younger group of writers. Some, like James Weldon Johnson, Du Bois, and the Puerto Rican-born bibliophile Arthur Schomburg, belonged to the older generation. Nor were all the contributors black, as Melville J. Herskovits and Konrad Bercovici were among them. The majority were young and black, however, and it was their contributions that were the most striking—poems and stories by Countee Cullen, Langston Hughes, Claude McKay, Rudolph Fisher, Eric Walrond, and others.

In the fall of 1925, most of *The Survey Graphic's* Harlem number appeared as a book, published by Boni & Liveright and titled *The New Negro*. It was illustrated with drawings by Weinold Reiss (son of Fritz Reiss, the Bavarian painter) and Aaron Douglas, a young black artist from Topeka, Kansas, who became the painter most closely associated with the New Negro movement. This volume and the Civic Club dinner from which it sprang are said to have officially launched the Harlem Renaissance. "Negro life is not only establishing new contacts and founding new centers," Locke said in a foreword to the book, "it is finding a new soul. We have, as the heralding sign, an unusual outburst of creative expression. There is renewed race spirit that consciously and proudly sets itself apart. Justly then, we may speak of this book, embodying these ripening forces, as culled from the first fruits of the Negro Renaissance." Of the vogue in black writing that marked the rest of the twenties, V. F. Calverton later wrote: "To be a Negro writer was to be a literary son of God. . . . A black skin, or a brown, or a pale 'yaller' was . . . like saying to a speakeasy proprietor in those days, 'I'm a friend of Robert Benchley,' or 'Carl Van Vechten'. . . . For a time it appeared as though Negro literature was the most important in the country. The Negro writer was a powerful social magnet. White writers boasted of dining with James Weldon Johnson, lunching with Burghardt Du Bois, having cocktails with Walter White."

Some Writers

WHAT were some of these writers like, and how did their work illustrate the character of the Harlem Renaissance? In 1924, *Opportunity* launched an annual literary contest, with a view to discovering new writers and to sustaining activity among the ones who were already being published. The winners of the first contest included Langston Hughes, who was then twenty-three. His winning entry, "The Weary Blues," was markedly different in style from "The Negro Speaks of Rivers"—written soon after his graduation from high school and before he arrived in Harlem—and this new style, perhaps the most individual among the New Negro poets, was the one for which he became best known. The poem said, in part:

> Droning a drowsy syncopated tune,
> Rocking back and forth to a mellow croon,
> I heard a Negro play.
> Down on Lenox Avenue the other night
> By the pale dull pallor of an old gas light
> He did a lazy sway. . . .
> He did a lazy sway. . . .
> To the tune o' those Weary Blues. . . .
>
> Thump, thump, thump, went his foot on the floor.
> He played a few chords then he sang some more—
> "I got the Weary Blues
> And I can't be satisfied. . . ."

Here, to begin with, was another example of the attention that Harlem Renaissance poetry was devoting to the urban mass experience. But, more important, "The Weary Blues" captured, as no other black poem had, both the rhythmic and the human qualities of the blues—certain moods of the big-city street scene, and the naturalness of ordinary talk. Hughes was not as inspired a lyricist or as enchanting a singer as either Countee Cullen or Claude McKay—both of whom wrote in the traditional, formal lyric modes—but if there was a poet of Harlem life, as distinguished from a poet who lived and wrote in Harlem, it was Hughes. He had no equal in the accuracy with which he recorded in poetry the spontaneities of language, thought, and feeling and the everyday sights and sounds of the black metropolis.

Hughes was born in Joplin, Missouri, in 1902, and he attended public schools in Lawrence, Kansas, and Cleveland, Ohio. In 1921, when he first came to New York, he studied at Columbia University. Something of a roamer, he also attended Lincoln University, in Pennsylvania, and by the time he became nationally recognized he had worked as a hotel waiter in Washington, D.C., and France in between jobs as a seaman. Some years after Hughes had finally settled in Harlem and had accumulated a sizable body of published work, James Weldon Johnson wrote, "Hughes is a cosmopolite and a rebel, and both of these attributes are reflected in his poetry. As a rebel, he will not be bound by poetic form and traditions. As a cosmopolite, he takes his subject matter from any level of life that interests him. His forms are for the most part free, and his subject matter is often from the lower strata. . . . He is more apt than Cullen to portray life as he sees it rather than as he feels it."

Countee Cullen was born in Manhattan in 1903, and was brought up in a Harlem parsonage—by Frederick Cullen, pastor of the Salem Methodist Episcopal Church, and his wife, who adopted him when he was eleven. He was educated at De Witt Clinton High School, New York University, and Harvard; and during the twenties he studied for a time at the Sorbonne. When his first poems began appearing in his high-school magazine, he was immediately hailed in Manhattan's poetry circles as a Harlem prodigy, and by 1925, when he graduated from N.Y.U., he was already the most widely published of the younger black poets. As his biographer, Blanche Ferguson, has written, "it seemed that no literary magazine could bear to go to press without a Countee Cullen poem." His first collection, *Color*, published in 1925, acknowledged some of the magazines in which the poems had appeared—*Vanity Fair, The Bookman, The American*

Mercury, The Crisis, Opportunity, The Messenger, The Century, Folio, Harper's, Les Continents, Poetry, Survey Graphic, and *The World Tomorrow.* In *Color,* and also in his second volume, *Copper Sun,* published in 1927, Cullen, perhaps the finest pure lyricist among the New Negro poets, displayed what the critic V. F. Calverton called an "infectious beauty of rhythm." Wallace Thurman, one of the Harlem novelists, and the stingiest with a compliment, wrote in 1928 that Cullen had "an extraordinary ear for music, a most extensive and dexterous knowledge of words and their values, and an enviable understanding of conventional poetic forms." But, Thurman added—reverting to the style of debunking, with which he felt more comfortable—Cullen was "too steeped in tradition, too influenced mentally by certain conventions and taboos." To another of the Harlem poets, Arna Bontemps, Cullen confessed that John Keats was his "god" and Edna St. Vincent Millay his "goddess." One of his poems, "To John Keats, Poet, at Springtime," goes in part:

> I cannot hold my peace, John Keats;
> There never was a spring like this;
> It is an echo, that repeats
> My last year's song and next year's bliss.
> I know, in spite of all men say
> Of Beauty, you have felt her most.
> Yea, even in your grave her way
> Is laid. Poor, troubled, lyric ghost,
> Spring never was so fair and dear
> As Beauty makes her seem this year.

Cullen, more of an aesthete than Langston Hughes or Claude McKay, was not too strongly drawn to the details of black mass experience. "I am not at all a democratic person," he said to a friend in 1923. "I believe in the aristocracy of the soul." In 1928, he married Yolande Du Bois, the only daughter of the aristocratic editor of *The Crisis.* Cullen wished to be recognized as a poet and not as a black poet. But he did not always succeed in keeping the urgencies of racial theme out of his work. "Cullen says he is interested in poetry for poetry's sake, and not for propaganda purposes," the *Age* commented in 1923—but went on to quote the poet as saying, "In spite of myself, however, I find that I am actuated by a strong sense of race consciousness . . . although I struggle against it, it colors my writing." Cullen also wrote, in a note about himself, "As a poet he is a rank conservative, loving the measured line and the skillful rhyme; but not blind to the virtues of those poets who will not be circumscribed. . . . He has said, perhaps with a reiteration sickening to some of his friends, that he wishes any merit that may be in his work to flow from it solely as the expression of a poet—with no racial considera-tion to bolster it up." However, in works like "Heritage" and "Yet Do I Marvel" Cullen showed himself to be an eloquent and engaged ironist of the black experience. Reading these poems, one cannot avoid noticing and applauding the urgent racial considerations from which they spring.

The poet and novelist Arna Bontemps was born in Louisiana in 1902, and grew up in Los Angeles. He moved to Harlem in 1924 "to become a writer," as he later said. In the "heady atmosphere" of his first literary party in Harlem, he was introduced to a number of the New Negro Renaissance figures he had been reading and hearing about on the West Coast. They included the critic Alain Locke, Jes-sie Fauset, the magazine editor Charles S. Johnson, Langston Hughes, and the short-story writer Eric Walrond. In such a group, Bontemps could not help being conscious of his own deficiency—"a hopeful newcomer, just beginning to feel comfortable in Harlem." At that time, Langston Hughes wrote later, Bontemps was "quiet and scholarly, looking like a young edition of Dr. Du Bois." It is from Bontemps—several years after the Renaissance had ended—that we get one of the more vivid reports of the attention that was lavished on the Harlem writers in the middle and late nineteen-twenties. "Within a year or two," he wrote, "we began to recognize ourselves as a 'group' and to become a little self-conscious about our 'signifi-cance.' When we were not too busy having fun, we were shown off and exhibited and presented in scores of places, to all kinds of peo-ple. And we heard their sighs of wonder, amazement, sometimes admiration when it was whispered or announced that here was one of the 'New Negroes.' Nothing could have been sweeter to young people who only a few weeks or months earlier had been regarded as anything but remarkable. . . . In Harlem we were seen in a beautiful light. We were heralds of a dawning day. We were the first-born of the dark renaissance."

Wallace Thurman was nearly incapable of writing sunnily about anything, including the Harlem Renaissance. He had few words of praise and he used them as sparingly as possible, or he concealed them within the rhetoric of his critical phrases. Cynical by temperament, strongly inclined to deprecation and complaint, he took a generally mocking and sarcastic view of things. In 1927, describing the years when black writers were so popular, he wrote, in one of his typical passages of sarcasm, "When the Negro art fad first came into being, and Negro poets, novelists, musicians, and painters became good copy, literate and semi-literate Negro America began to strut and shout. Negro newspapers reprinted every item published anywhere concerning a Negro whose work had found favor with the critics, editors, or publishers. Negro journals conducted contests to encourage embryonic geniuses. Negro ministers preached sermons, Negro lecturers made speeches, and Negro club women read papers —all about the great new Negro art. Everyone was having a grand time. The millennium was about to dawn."

Born in Salt Lake City in 1902, Thurman came to Harlem in 1925, from Los Angeles, where he had been working partly as a postal clerk and partly as a journalist. An article about him states, "Thurman is described by one who knew him as a slender young man, dark skinned, 'with hands and eyes that are never at rest.' His body was always rather fragile, probably due to his tubercular condition as well as a heavy addiction to alcohol." Theophilus Lewis, who was Harlem's leading theatre critic, wrote, in an essay on Thurman, "The man literally luxuriates in being ill. His anatomy and physiology seem to be nicely adjusted for falling out of gear from the slightest cause. Make him laugh at a joke and his jaw is likely to become dislocated. Carry a can of formaldehyde past the speakeasy where he happens to be drinking and he will immediately come down with liquor poisoning." Thurman struck Langston Hughes as "a strangely brilliant black boy, who had read everything, and whose critical mind could find something wrong with everything he read." Sometime during the twenties, Thurman wrote to a friend, "I cannot read 'Magic Mountain.' . . . It is too consciously metaphysical. . . . Anyone could tell some lugubrious German was the author." To the same friend, he said of George Gershwin's music, "The Concerto is spotty and echoes the Rhapsody. It shows a great lack of imagination. And An American in Paris is impossible. At least to me. Only the Rhapsody stands out as being something to cheer about, and there are amateurish areas through it." According to Theophilus Lewis, Thurman's "pet hates" and "abominations" were "all Negro uplift societies, Greta Garbo, Negro novelists, including himself, Negro society, New York State divorce laws, morals, religion, politics, censors, policemen, sympathetic white folks who go in for helping Negroes, and . . . every damned spot in the United States except Manhattan."

Thurman, Langston Hughes said, "wanted to be a great writer, but none of his own work ever made him happy." His first novel, *The Blacker the Berry*, published in 1929, showed his hatred for light-skinned Harlem society. It is the story of a very black girl who in the course of being rejected by Negroes of lighter complexion finds little to choose between the discrimination she encounters within her own race and that which she encounters among whites. That year, Thurman's play *Harlem* (with William Jourdan Rapp, a white writer, as co-author) had a successful run on Broadway. His royalties were substantial for a while, and enabled him to liquidate a number of his debts. He found, to his surprise, however, that there were certain other facts of life which his success as a black playwright would not alter. "A number of things happened around the theatre . . . which gave me a shock," he told Rapp soon after the play opened. "Five different times I have bought seats for myself to see 'Harlem'— including opening night—and though I asked for center aisle seats (as much as a week in advance), not yet have I succeeded in not being put on the side in a little section where any other Negro who happened to buy an orchestra seat was also placed." Members of light-skinned Harlem society would have been delighted to learn of his difficulties, for they hated his play—dealing with what Thurman liked to call the "raw" side of life—almost as passionately as he hated them. In his second novel, *Infants of the Spring*, published in 1932, Thurman turned his ire on fellow-writers and intellectuals of the Harlem Renaissance, showing them to be wanting in the talent and the attitudes that made for excellence in black art and literature. Whatever truth his indictment contained, it also expressed a sense of his own failure—for he had come by then to recognize that his literary talents were not nearly equal to the ambitions he had for himself as a novelist. Thurman, Langston Hughes said, wanted to be as great a writer as Proust, Melville, or James, but, finding that his own pages were "vastly wanting," he surrendered to despair and "contented himself by writing a great deal for money . . . drinking more and more gin, and then threatening to jump out of windows at people's parties and kill himself."

The most deft of the Harlem Renaissance fiction writers was Rudolph Fisher. His talent was not a large one—it seemed unsuited to delving into the serious issues of black experience—but he wrote excellently within the range of his gift and his essentially comic view of life. He was also a physician, and, like Countee Cullen, he had been brought up in a parsonage—partly in Washington, D.C., and partly in Providence, Rhode Island, where his father had held pastorates. A graduate of Brown University and the Howard University Medical School, he settled in Harlem around 1925. His stories appeared regularly in *The Atlantic Monthly*, *The Crisis*, *Opportunity*, and *Story*. According to one of the Harlem poets, Fisher was "the wittiest of these New Negroes," having a tongue that was "flavored with the sharpest and saltiest humor." The appeal of his writing owed much to these flavors—whether in his short stories or in his two novels, *The Walls of Jericho* (1928) and *The Conjure-Man Dies* (1932). His work was neatly written; moved swiftly, with exactitude and clarity; and used wit and humor to make penetrating observations about behavior and character. Though he does not seem to have disliked the Harlem elite as much as some of his contemporaries did, Fisher's subjects came mostly from the lower strata—especially recent and unlettered migrants from the South. In stories like "Miss Cynthie" and "The City of Refuge," he showed himself to be both amused and gently moved as he watched the newcomers in their acts of adjustment to a black metropolis that had turned out to be more impressive and complicated than they had imagined it would be. Fisher drew these people—as he also drew members of Harlem society—with a sureness of touch, a sardonic detachment, an accuracy of speech and mannerism, an implied affection for the quirks of character, and an economy of narrative style that were unique among the Harlem novelists and short-story writers.

* * *

Zora Neale Hurston was the most vivacious member of the Harlem literary set. Although she is now remembered as a novelist of considerable distinction, she wrote only a few essays and short stories during the twenties. The novels and tales on which her reputation rests—*Jonah's Gourd Vine* (1934), *Mules and Men* (1935), and *Their Eyes Were Watching God* (1937)—appeared after the Harlem Renaissance had ended. During the years of that movement, she was notable more for her lively and infectious personality—and for her contributions to black literary polemics—than for any substantial output in writing. "Spunk" and "Drenched in Light," titles of short stories she published during the twenties, may well convey the essence of her own personality.

Hurston was a native of Eatonville, Florida. Her biographer, Robert Hemenway, notes, "She was purposely inconsistent in the birth dates she dispensed during her lifetime, most of which were fictitious. . . . She claimed to be born in 1898, 1899, 1900, 1901, 1902, or 1903." But the year of her birth is thought, generally, to be 1901. Hemenway describes her as "brown skinned, big boned, with freckles and high cheekbones . . . a striking woman; her dark brown eyes were both impish and intelligent, her voice was rich and black—with the map of Florida on her tongue."

Some months after she arrived in New York, in 1925—from Washington, D.C., where she attended Howard University—Hurston won a scholarship to Barnard College, where she studied anthropology under Franz Boas. While at Barnard, she submitted stories to *Opportunity* magazine and joined the "niggerati," as she and Wallace Thurman liked to call the Harlem writers and literary intellectuals of that time. Hurston "was certainly the most amusing" member of the group, one of her colleagues later said, but she "was clever, too—a student . . . who had great scorn for all pretensions, academic or otherwise." He went on, "Almost nobody else could stop the average Harlemite on Lenox Avenue and measure his head with a strange-looking anthropological device and not get bawled out for the attempt, except Zora, who used to stop anyone whose head looked interesting, and measure it." The novelist Fannie Hurst, for whom Hurston worked as a secretary while attending Barnard, later wrote, "Regardless of race, Zora had the gift of walking into hearts."

* * *

In 1926, Langston Hughes, Wallace Thurman, and some of the other young black writers, together with the irrepressible Zora, launched a publication of their own, a magazine in which they hoped to define the position of the black literary avant-garde and, in so doing, state their aesthetic and philosophical differences with the older literary leadership. They called the journal *Fire!!*, because its mission was—in the words of one of the founding editors—"to burn up a lot of the old, dead conventional Negro-white ideas of the past." But after a spirited first issue, in November of 1926, *Fire!!* did not reappear. The financial burden of keeping it alive—printing and circulation costs—had overwhelmed the young and often insolvent rebels. The black literary patricians—men like W. E. B. Du Bois, William Stanley Braithwaite, Charles W. Chesnutt, and Benjamin Brawley—whose ideas *Fire!!* had come to destroy, can only have been moved at the magazine's death, whether "timely" or "untimely" in their eyes. This is apparent from Brawley's eulogy, written a while later, in which he made joyous and ironic use of metaphor. The flame of *Fire!!*, Brawley said, "was so intense that it burned itself up immediately." A historical footnote is even more ironic: the copies left over from the magazine's only issue were destroyed in a fire that burned through the basement of an apartment house where they had been stored.

Fittingly, the editor-in-chief of *Fire!!* had been the acerbic and self-punishing Wallace Thurman. And when he came to write *Infants of the Spring*, a roman à clef in which he savaged the Harlem "niggerati," not even the lovable Zora Neale Hurston was spared. She appears in the book as Sweetie May Car—"a short story writer, more noted for her ribald wit and personal effervescence than for any actual literary work," who was "a great favorite among those whites who went in for Negro prodigies." And if the words that Thurman puts in Sweetie May's mouth are an accurate reflection of the views she held, then she was no less cynical about the Harlem Renaissance than the author was. "Being a Negro writer these days," she says, "is a racket and I'm going to make the most of it while it lasts. . . . I don't know a tinker's damn about art. I care less about it. . . . About twice a year I manage to sell a story. It is acclaimed. I am a genius in the making. Thank God for this Negro literary renaissance! Long may it flourish!"

* * *

Among New York's white literati, no one was more friendly or help-ful to the Harlem Renaissance movement than Carl Van Vechten—some of whose work may even be said to belong to the canon of New Negro writing. In a sense, this was surprising. Aspects of Van Vechten's background made him an implausible ally of such a movement, which, whatever were its shortcomings, aimed at confer-ring the recognition of serious art on the ordinary levels and details of black life. Apparently, blacks were not unknown in Cedar Rapids, Iowa, where Van Vechten grew up. Late in his life, he was to recall having seen a "laundry woman" and a "man who cut grass." But "they were the only two Negroes in Cedar Rapids, so I couldn't become intimately acquainted with them." So blacks had not figured that much in the early shaping of Van Vechten's social and cultural attitudes.

Besides, by the early nineteen-twenties, when blacks in Manhattan began entering his life—and he began entering theirs—he had lost his interest in seriousness (possibly even in classical music, which he had once reviewed regularly for *The New York Times*), and had become a symbol of what was light, aimless, and gay in the style and spirit of the Prohibition years. Under a photograph of him, Mabel Dodge—a leader of New York's prewar well-to-do bohemia—had written, "The Conscious Despair of Irrevocable Decadence." He came to be seen as one of America's *Sonnenkinder*—the term that Martin Green, in his *Children of the Sun*, applies to the generation of English upper-class dandies who gained a certain literary and cul-tural notoriety in the years after the First World War. The English *Sonnenkinder*, Green explains, were "preoccupied with style, wor-shipped Adonis or Narcissus, were rebellious against both their fa-thers' and their mothers' modes of seriousness—were in love with ornament, splendor, high manners, and so on." Much of this has been said not only about Carl Van Vechten himself but also about some of the novels he wrote during the early twenties—*Peter Whiffle* (1922), *The Blind Bow-Boy* (1923), and *The Tattooed Countess* (1924). The last was even likened to the novels of Ronald Firbank, one of England's *Sonnenkinder*, whom Van Vechten greatly admired.

Van Vechten's narratives bristled with such pedantries as "passer-ine," "sciapodous," "oppugnancy," and "morigeration"—much to the delight of some of his readers. One of them wrote to him, "I especially love your use of erudite and unusual words, they are like caviar to the everyday English, which anybody can use, and are a compliment to the intelligence and culture of the reader. I must admit that when I read your 'Tattooed Countess,' I had to refer to a Latin dictionary to figure out the meaning of a few of them." More serious critics were not so impressed. Years later, Alfred Kazin wrote that Van Vechten not only "thrived on his own affectations" but also "meticulously detailed the perversions, the domestic eccentricities, the alcoholism, the esthetic dicta, and the social manners of ladies and gentlemen who did nothing, nothing at all." Kazin was able to find nothing kinder to say about Van Vechten than that he was "the novelist of the speakeasy intelligentsia." The judgment was not wholly unmerited. Van Vechten is himself on record as praising the "splendid drunken twenties," and in his biography, by Bruce Kellner, there is the following: "A close friend of Carl's . . . reflected in all seriousness that nobody ever completely sobered up. They moved from party to party, from club to club, drinking anything offered them. People drank all night, every night; when they slept has never been ascertained." Eslanda Goode Robeson wrote to congratulate Van Vechten for turning out "a damned good book . . . between parties." As Allen Churchill adds, in his book *The Literary Decade*, a Van Vechten party "resembled a speakeasy deluxe peopled by literary figures, stage and screen celebrities, prizefighters, dancers, elegant homosexuals, and Lorelei Lee gold diggers."

Yet this was the figure whose assistance to the growth of the Harlem Renaissance—one of the most important stages in the development of black writing—was probably greater than that of any other white American. It was Van Vechten who talked Frank Crowninshield, the editor of *Vanity Fair*, into publishing some of the first poems of Countee Cullen and Langston Hughes, and who encouraged Alfred Knopf to bring out Hughes' first collection. Among other editors and publishers of his acquaintance, he tirelessly promoted the work and the careers of the young Harlem writers. "When you say you intend helping a fellow, you don't mean maybe," Gwendolyn Bennett said to him. He wrote prefaces and reviews praising their books, and in magazine articles he upheld the seriousness of their work against the attacks of older black literary men. In appreciation, Coutee Cullen wrote, in 1927, to thank him "for so forcible a defense of my work." Such unreserved support of New Negro writing may have been possible only with the suppression of critical judgment; and Van Vechten was sometimes accused, by whites and blacks, of over-praising black writing—of recommending the good and the shoddy alike. In 1927, after Van Vechten had written introductions to two of Langston Hughes' books, Benjamin Brawley, one of the older black critics, wrote to reprove him: "From your general standing in American letters we had been led to suppose that anything that you introduced would be worthwhile. . . . There has been altogether too much emphasis on the sordid, the base, the vulgar; and all standards seem to have been thrown to the winds." The same year, Will Marion Cooke wrote to Van Vechten, "Stop exploiting the unready poets, musicians and actors of my race. It only unfits them for the supreme test." Not that black writing was the only kind to profit from his indiscriminate endorsements. In 1925, Edmund Wilson said of Van Vechten that "whatever falls in with his humor obtains the suffrage of his judgment." At any rate, a writer in the *Herald Tribune* called him "the beneficent godfather of all of sophisticated Harlem." And James Weldon Johnson, one of the more sympathetic of the older black writers and intellectuals—and a close friend of Van Vechten's—later praised his "many personal efforts in behalf of individual Negro writers and artists." No one in the country, Johnson said, "did more to forward" the Harlem literary movement.

To his famous parties, in midtown Manhattan, Van Vechten invited the cream of young Harlem writers, artists, actors, and musicians. Some of these parties, Langston Hughes recalled, "were *so* Negro that they were reported as a matter of course in the colored society columns, just as though they occurred in Harlem." But Van Vechten's invitations to the Harlem writers and entertainers were motivated as much by a love of genial gatherings as by a more serious social purpose. The journalist George S. Schuyler, who was often invited, later explained:

> The literary lights, the stars of the ballet, the kings and queens of the theatre, the painters, sculptors and editors who had attained envious preeminence frequented [Van Vechten's] salons on West 55th Street and later on at Central Park West; and to this company Van Vechten introduced their darker opposite members. Here they rubbed shoulders, sipped cocktails, nibbled *hors*

d'oeuvres, conversed, sang and danced without self-consciousness. What was at first an innovation and a novelty soon became commonplace, an institution.

Such salons in the early twenties were rare to the point of being revolutionary. At the time it was most difficult for Negroes to purchase a ticket for an orchestra seat in a theatre, even in Harlem, and it was with the greatest difficulty that a colored American in New York could get service in a downtown restaurant. Except at Coney Island, beaches were closed to Negroes and few were the other places that would tolerate their patronage. . . .

Most of the white people of Van Vechten's circle knew Negroes only as domestics and had never had them as associates. It was extremely daring for a white person to dine publicly with a Negro, and certainly to dance with one; but if those of the upper crust could be weaned over to such social acceptance, it was likely that a trend would be started which would eventually embrace the majority of those whites who shaped public opinion and set the social pace.

To this laudable endeavor Carl Van Vechten and his famous actress wife, Fania Marinoff, devoted themselves as assiduously as any sincere revolutionists could. . . . Once the idea took hold it spread in geometrical progression.

Van Vechten once gave this account of how his interest in Harlem and its writers began and developed: "Along about 1923, Knopf published a book by Walter White, called 'The Fire in the Flint.' . . . I asked Alfred to introduce Walter to me, and he sent Walter over to see me. He was working for the N.A.A.C.P. . . . Walter . . . asked me to parties, to lunches, to dinners, and so forth, and in about two weeks I knew every educated person in Harlem. I knew them by the hundreds. . . . I not only knew Negro authors, of which there were many at the time. . . . I frequented the night clubs a great deal. . . . I used to carry a silver flask with me, which held both gin and whiskey, and I was always leaving this in some bar or other. . . . My silver flask was invariably brought back to me the next day."

When, as Van Vechten added, it "became obvious to me that I would write about these people, because my feelings about them were very strong," he began making notes for a novel. No one had yet written a novel about Harlem's popular life (Fisher, Thurman, and McKay were to write theirs later); no novel had yet captured Harlem's "rich and poor, fast and slow, intellectual and ignorant"—as Van Vechten described the population to Gertrude Stein in Paris. But he must surely have heard from his associates uptown that many Harlemites—particularly the cultivated set—would not forgive him for the sort of novel he intended to write.

Van Vechten's novel appeared in the summer of 1926, bearing the title *Nigger Heaven*—for which not even the most skeptical Harlemites had been prepared. The book was a publishing sensation. As the author reported later, it sold "100,000 copies almost immediately." Not surprisingly, the title, irresistible to most white readers, accounted for a large proportion of the sales, and the contents were no more resistible. *Nigger Heaven* was an account of the romantic and professional ups and downs of an educated Harlem couple—the woman a librarian, the man an aspiring novelist. As the vagaries of this unlucky affair unfolded, readers were given a picture of Harlem in much of its variety: the life of the literate and the rich; high society, with its hostesses, dinners, balls, and parties; the strivings and frustrations of the middle class; the jealousies and resentments among different shades of society and pigment; erotic intrigues, both elegant and decadent; intellectual inquiries into the nature of race prejudice; the language and manners of the poor; numbers kings and others of dubious legal and moral standing; qualities of the "lowlife;" and the late-night excitements of cabarets, speakeasies, and dance halls.

Nigger Heaven was a hit among white readers, and did reasonably well among white critics. Among the few white commentators who disliked it intensely was D. H. Lawrence, who said in a review, "It is a false book by an author who lingers in nigger cabarets hoping to heaven to pick up something to write about, and make a sensation— and, of course, money." But in letters to Van Vechten, Gertrude Stein and F. Scott Fitzgerald praised the novel highly: Stein wrote, "You have never done anything better," and Fitzgerald said it was "a work of art." James Branch Cabell called it "an astounding and invaluable contribution to sociology," and Joseph Hergesheimer found the novel to be "a thing so rare as to be unique."

Most Harlemites who bought novels—or who bought this one— convicted *Nigger Heaven* on the evidence of its title alone. (Apparently, many among the masses—whose interests did not, as a rule, run to literature—bought *Nigger Heaven* as well. Charles W. Chesnutt wrote to Van Vechten at the time, "I note what you say . . . about 'Nigger Heaven' being read by the Negro masses. I agree with you that if that is true it is the first time such a thing has occurred. Up until now the colored people have not been extensive book buyers.") Langston Hughes wrote, "Negroes did not read it to get mad. They got mad as soon as they heard of it. And after that many of them never did read it at all. Or if they did, they put a paper cover over it and read it surreptitiously, as though it were a dirty book." Ethel Waters, who was a friend of Van Vechten's, recalled, "I'd heard of his book, 'Nigger Heaven,' and had condemned it because of its obnoxious title—without reading it. Later I read this novel and thought it a sympathetic study of the way Negroes were forced to live in Harlem." Writing, during the controversy, to his friend James Weldon Johnson, Van Vechten quoted a Harlem newspaper as saying, "anyone who would call a book Nigger Heaven would call a Negro nigger." Charles S. Johnson, the editor of *Opportunity*, said to Van Vechten in a letter, "I might make a stir about your title and be a good 'race man,' but fundamentally I too am anxious to have the sting of the term extracted in the fashion that such employment promises to do. . . . My supreme tribute to the book is that I wish a Negro had written it." Van Vechten's father, out in Cedar Rapids, had not liked the title, either. Before the book came out, he had written to his son, "I have myself never spoken of a colored man as a 'nigger.' If you are trying to help the race, as I am assured you are, I think every word you write should be a respectful one towards the black." But, as the younger Van Vechten later explained, he himself never used the word.

It was to be said in his behalf that on an early page of *Nigger Heaven* Van Vechten had supplied a footnote: "While this informal epithet is freely used by Negroes among themselves, not only as a term of opprobrium, but also actually as a term of endearment, its employment by a white person is always fiercely resented." It was also clear that the novel—ironically or not—had taken its title from remarks made by one of its main characters:

> Nigger Heaven! That's what Harlem is. We sit in our places in
> the gallery of this New York theatre and watch the white world

sitting down below in the good seats in the orchestra. Occasionally, they turn their faces up towards us, their hard, cruel faces, to laugh or sneer, but they never beckon. It never seems to occur to them that Nigger Heaven is crowded, that there isn't another seat, that something has to be done.

Van Vechten could well have heard similar statements from blacks of his acquaintance, for the term Nigger Heaven had been in common use in Harlem ever since the white theatres along Seventh Avenue had, in deciding to admit blacks during the war, confined them to the balcony. Nevertheless, as one of Van Vechten's black friends told him, he had, in the title of his book, aired certain "family" matters and should therefore not have been surprised by the black reaction.

The bitterest attack on *Nigger Heaven* was written by W. E. B. Du Bois, who had warned Van Vechten earlier what cultivated Harlem's response to the book was likely to be. Reviewing it in *The Crisis*, Du Bois said:

> "Nigger Heaven" is a blow in the face . . . an affront to the hospitality of black folk and to the intelligence of white. . . . the phrase "Nigger Heaven," as applied to Harlem is a misnomer. "Nigger Heaven" does not mean . . . a haven for Negroes—a city of refuge for dark and tired souls; it means in common parlance, a nasty, sordid corner into which black folk are herded, and yet a place which they in crass ignorance are fools enough to enjoy. Harlem is no such place as that. . . .
>
> But after all, a title is only a title, and a book must be judged eventually by its fidelity to truth and its artistic merit. I find this novel neither truthful nor artistic. . . . It is a caricature. It is worse than untruth because it is a mass of half-truths. . . .
>
> I read "Nigger Heaven" . . . because I had to. But I advise others who are impelled by a sense of duty or curiosity to drop the book gently in the grate and try the *Police Gazette*.

James Weldon Johnson and Langston Hughes, close friends of Van Vechten's, were among the few blacks who wrote in praise of *Nigger Heaven*. In a review in *Opportunity*, Johnson called the novel "an absorbing story" and went on to say, "Mr. Van Vechten is . . . the only white novelist I can think of who has not viewed the Negro as a type, who has not treated the race as a unit, either good or bad. . . .

The story comprehends nearly every phase of life in the Negro metropolis. It draws on the components of that life, from the dregs to the froth." Some time later, Hughes maintained that Van Vechten had written "sympathetically and amusingly and well about a whole rainbow of life above 110th Street that had never before been put into the color of words." In 1928, when Du Bois' novel *Dark Princess* appeared, Van Vechten launched an attack of his own. Writing to James Weldon Johnson, he said, "I do not like Mr. Du Bois's book. . . . He writes well, but so much of it is utterly assinine. It is the first book by a Negro of which I would say it were better for the Negroes that it had not been written."

Claude McKay, the earliest voice of the Harlem Renaissance, was born in a mountain village of Jamaica and migrated to the United States in 1912, at the age of twenty-two. He had been a police constable in his homeland, had won a small reputation as a local poet, and had come to America to study scientific farming. He soon lost this ambition, however. After about two years at Tuskegee Institute, in Alabama, and at an agricultural college in Kansas, he dropped his studies and headed for New York. As he explained later, he had been seized by the "vagabond" spirit, gripped by "the lust to wander and wonder." This was his way of saying that he had decided to become a poet in his adopted country—"to achieve something new, something in the spirit and accent of America." In and around New York City, he worked during the next few years as a longshoreman, a bartender, a porter in clubs and hotels, and a dining-car waiter on the Pennsylvania Railroad; and during this time he was writing some of the best of his early American poems—notably "Harlem Shadows," published in 1917, and "The Harlem Dancer" and "If We Must Die," both published in 1919. When the last of these appeared, in *The Liberator*, the magazine observed that McKay "seems to have a greater and more simple and strong gift of poetry than any other of his race has had." Max Eastman, editor of *The Liberator*, and a friend and mentor of McKay's, said he "resembled a portrait of King Christopher of Haiti," that "his eyebrows arched high up and never came down," and that "his finely modelled features wore in consequence a fixed expression of ironical and rather mischievous skepticism."

In 1919, McKay, again yielding to wanderlust, sailed for London, where he lived for about a year; wrote articles for Sylvia Pankhurst's radical newspaper, the *Worker's Dreadnought*; and published his collection *Spring in New Hampshire*. Returning to New York, he worked briefly as an associate editor of *The Liberator* and published *Harlem Shadows*. This appeared in 1922, and, reviewing it for the *Age*, James Weldon Johnson wrote, "No Negro poet has sung more beautifully of his own race than McKay, and no Negro poet has equalled the power with which he expresses the bitterness that so often rises in the heart of the race."

Later in 1922, McKay took off again—this time for Russia. He had become something of a Communist sympathizer, and wished, as he later said, to "go and see" what and how the Bolsheviks were doing. He also wished to "escape from the . . . hot syncopated fascination of Harlem" and "the suffocating ghetto of color consciousness." He was not to return for more than a decade. From Russia, where the Bolsheviks lionized him—as much for the strangeness of his color as for the interest he took in their revolution—he moved on to Western Europe and then to North Africa, where he lived and roamed until 1934.

He was therefore not in Harlem during the high period of the New Negro Renaissance—a movement with which his name was closely linked, and which his early poems had helped to bring about. But then, as he heard through the transatlantic grapevine, the younger black writers were in no hurry to welcome him back to the Harlem scene. They held his brief Russian fling against him, and feared that his return might be politically harmful to the growing New Negro literary movement. Moreover, as McKay said some years later, "I was an older man and not regarded as a member of the renaissance, but more as a forerunner." Though his feelings must have been hurt, he did have this consolation: "I had done my best Harlem stuff when I was abroad, seeing it from a long perspective."

Some of that work had been appearing in New York publications, and at one point James Weldon Johnson began writing to McKay, in Paris, urging him to return home. "You ought to be here to take full advantage of the great wave of opportunity that Negro literary and other artists are enjoying," Johnson said. "In addition, we need you to give more strength and solidity to the movement." But McKay was not so sure that he wished to return to America then. He later wrote:

> The Johnson letter set me thinking hard about returning to Harlem. All the reports stressed the great changes that had occurred there since my exile, pictured a Harlem spreading west and south, with splendid new blocks of houses opened up for the colored people. The reports described the bohemian interest in and patronage of Harlem, the many successful colored shows on Broadway, the florescence of Negro literature and art, with many promising aspirants receiving scholarships from foundations and patronage from individuals. Newspapers and magazines brought me exciting impressions of a more glamorous Harlem. . . .
> But . . .

McKay's "but" signified the state of feeling that then—in 1928—existed between him and the Harlem middle-class intelligentsia. His novel *Home to Harlem*, written during his years abroad—and drawing heavily on memories of his life in the community—had recently been published in New York, and, like Van Vechten's novel two years earlier, it had been denounced by the Harlem elite. In the eyes of these critics, *Home to Harlem* was no less a libel against respectable blacks than *Nigger Heaven* had been. There were similarities, to be sure. McKay's novel was, like Van Vechten's, a best-seller. Critical response was just as mixed, most whites praising it and most cultivated blacks condemning it. But whereas *Nigger Heaven* had traversed a wide social and cultural landscape, *Home to Harlem* remained pretty much within the warm and lusty precincts of proletarian living. Black condemnation of his book, McKay said, "was so general, bitter and violent that I was hesitant about returning to the great Black Belt." From Harlemites, including some who were visiting Paris, he heard that his novel was "obscene," that it "exploited Negroes" and "betrayed the race," that it showed "contempt for the Negro bourgeoisie," and that it had been written merely to exploit the commercial success of *Nigger Heaven*.

Back in New York, W. E. B. Du Bois, who had led the attack on Van Vechten's novel, assaulted McKay's similarly. He wrote in *The Crisis*, " 'Home to Harlem' for the most part nauseates me, and after the dirtier parts of its filth I feel distinctly like taking a bath. . . . McKay has set out to cater to that prurient demand on the part of white folk for a portrayal in Negroes of that utter licentiousness which convention holds white folk back from enjoying. . . . He has used every art and emphasis to paint drunkenness, fighting, lascivious sexual promiscuity and utter absence of restraint in as bold and as bright colors as he can." The reviewer for the *Times*, who read the novel somewhat differently, found it to contain "the rhythm of life that is a jazz rhythm." McKay, he added, "has pitched his novel to the rhythm of the man who runs the elevator or to the racial movement of the poems and blues of Langston Hughes . . . it is the real stuff, the lowdown on Harlem, the dope from the inside." The dope from the inside was precisely what bourgeois black critics did not wish to be exposed; for—regarding their class as the exemplary black group—they feared that white readers would take McKay's dope to represent the total life of Harlem.

In two letters that McKay wrote from Europe, he both defended and explained himself. One was to Du Bois: ". . . nowhere in your writings do you reveal any comprehension of esthetics, and therefore you are not competent to pass judgment upon any work of art. . . . Certainly I sympathize with and even pity you for not understanding my motive, because you have been forced from a normal career to enter a special field of racial propaganda and, honorable though that field may be, it has precluded you from contact with real life." The other, to the more sympathetic James Weldon Johnson, said, "I have not deviated in any way from my intellectual and artistic ideas of life. I consider the book a real proletarian novel, but I don't expect the nice radicals to see that it is, because they know little about proletarian life. . . . I cannot agree with their dislike of the artistic exploitation of low-class Negro life. We must leave the real appreciation of what we are doing to the emancipated Negro intelligentsia of the future."

McKay's remarks to Du Bois and Johnson were a reemphasis of what most of the younger Harlem writers were attempting: in effect, to widen the class boundaries of black poetry and fiction, to make literature mirror and acknowledge the experience and style of the masses, the way the majority of blacks lived. Many among the genteel leadership of black writing regarded such material as racially embarrassing, supportive of the belittling opinion whites held about black life, and rife with details that did not merit a central place in serious literature. But, as Langston Hughes said several years later, in recalling what he—as one of the younger insurgents—had set out to do, "I felt that the masses of our people had as much in their lives to put into books as did those more fortunate ones who had been born with some means."

What is most significant in the record of such writers may not lie so much in the quality of their work—parts of it good and lasting, parts of it poor and forgettable—as in their disengagement from the middle-class outlook and attitude that had influenced the bulk of the black writing that preceded theirs. For in doing this, they helped to set black literature—along with American writing as a whole—upon a course that has since become broader, more democratic in sensibility, and more searching in method and thought. Assessing this outcome, in his book *The Negro Novel in America*, the literary historian Robert Bone has written: "The Harlem school writers found Negro literature in the grip of narrow class prejudice and moral melodrama; they liberated it by a combination of literary realism and local color. However unscrupulously they may have exploited the fad, they established the Negro novelists' right to distinctive cultural material, and they provided Negro literature with an indispensable transition to the modern age."

A'Lelia Walker

THE SOCIAL SIDE of the Renaissance in Harlem was best typified by A'Lelia Walker, known for her wealth, her geniality, and her cosmopolitan circle of friends. What Carl Van Vechten's parties were downtown—interracial gatherings of poets, novelists, journalists, critics, musicians, actors, and dandies of café society—A'Lelia's were in Harlem. Her guest lists, someone said, "read like a blue book of the seven arts." A regular guest at these uptown affairs was Van Vechten himself—or Carlo, as his acquaintances in Harlem called him—for he was probably as close a white friend as A'Lelia Walker had. The only offspring of Madame C. J. Walker—the cosmetics millionairess, who died in 1919—she had inherited the major portion of her mother's fortune, and was easily the wealthiest woman in Harlem. Her expensively catered parties were held either at Villa Lewaro, the mansion her mother had built in Westchester County; at her main Harlem residence, on West 136th Street; or at a smaller and more intimate apartment, on Edgecombe Avenue.

Not everyone in Harlem society was impressed by A'Lelia's glamour and money or by her connections among artists and intellectuals. There was an old upper crust that positively despised her. "Quite often, when the matter of her social leadership was mentioned among certain people," the *Amsterdam News* said in 1931, "there were those who smiled scornfully; and one knew that they were thinking of other women whose brilliantly intellectual qualities, highly polished and superficial culture, so-called background, or supposedly great family inheritance perhaps better qualified them to be society leaders." Part of what such people smiled scornfully at were her social origins—the daughter of a woman who had started out in life washing clothes for a living. They had to admit that A'Lelia's wealth was greater than theirs, but its sources in hair dressing marked her in their eyes as parvenu. Unlike many of them, she was not a college graduate, and therefore did not share their associations with the many sororities and Greek-letter societies of Harlem. Compared with the parties they gave, they saw A'Lelia's as the frivolous gatherings of a black-and-tan Bohemia.

This was not wholly correct. Her guests were by no means all bohemians. According to the *Amsterdam News*, they included "prominent individuals in both European and American society." And, as the paper went on to say—though it overstated the point, somewhat—"One had to have the most correct and formal introduction to enter" her parties. Not being an artist or an intellectual, A'Lelia did not herself possess bohemian qualities or credentials. She was mainly a gregarious clubwoman who enjoyed the company of artists and intellectuals, as they, apparently, enjoyed hers. She was drawn to other sorts as well. Van Vechten wrote that at her parties black poets and numbers bankers mingled with downtown racketeers and visiting celebrities. Altogether, hers was a lively and sociable spirit; she made no attempt to suppress it, and was certainly backed up by the extroverted tenor of the twenties.

Far from bohemian, A'Lelia was as conspicuous and as extravagant a consumer as any in the Harlem bourgeoisie—perhaps more so, since she was richer than the rest of them. Who else in Harlem could afford the upkeep of the three residences she owned? She wore the most expensive clothing and jewelry, acquired from the fashionable shops of New York and Paris. With the socialites and clubwomen of her circle, she spent many evenings over bridge and poker; and with others of her friends she sometimes took in the after-hours cabarets, or dined out at Craig's, one of Harlem's better restaurants. In his novel *Nigger Heaven*—where A'Lelia appears as Adora Boniface—Van Vechten gave this description of one of her Harlem apartments: "Most of the furniture . . . was representative of the Louis XIV epoch. . . . The walls were in a pale lavendar satin, and adorned, here and there, with pictures, Fragonard and Boucher sketches, or something very like them. On the tea table a Sèvres service, in turquoise and amethyst paste, was laid out. The carpet was Aubusson. On the mantelpiece, between a clock and two candlesticks, also Sèvres, stood a few photographs framed in silver."

In December of 1924, the *Age* described a "brilliant affair" at A'Lelia's "palatial residence." It was a pre-Christmas Sunday-evening party, and dancing went on "until early Monday morning," when "a buffet breakfast" was served. When she died in 1931, at the age of forty-six, a writer in Harlem said, "There will be no more gay weekly Thursday afternoons at 80 Edgecombe Avenue with her laughter and vivaciousness. Those Thursday afternoons with her were looked forward to with eagerness; for one could forget the cares and worries of the day while listening to the piano music of Carrol Boyd and Joey Coleman; watching Al Moiret and Freddie Washington dance beautifully through her charming rooms; hear Alberta Hunter sing in her most intimate manner, and listen to the incomparable singing of such ladies and gentlemen of the theatre as Adelaide Hall, Maude Russell, Paul Bass, George McLean, Broadway Jones, and Jimmy Daniels."

A'Lelia would not have been called beautiful, at least not in the twenties. She was unmistakably black, and in those days—except among the more racially proud, or in the eyes of the mass-conscious writers of the Harlem Renaissance—black was not as beautiful as it later became. Nor, in other features, would A'Lelia have passed the tests for beauty that then prevailed. Whatever was subtly attractive in her eyes and plain-looking face passed unseen by those who were unable or unready to recognize the appeal of features that were too Negroid or too African. She also stood, as her mother had, about six feet tall, which—since her other proportions were voluptuous— merely caused her detractors to describe her as an Amazon. Despite the conventional judgment of her looks, she was a strikingly handsome woman. The more insightful men, of whatever race, found her hard to resist, though—male imagination being what it is—her wealth and social position may have added considerably to the ways in which she appealed to them. A'Lelia looked "like an Ethiopian princess," a journalist in Harlem said. And in *Nigger Heaven*, this is how Van Vechten described her: "She was undeniably warm-hearted, amusing, in her outspoken way, and even beautiful, in a queenly African manner that set her apart from the other beauties of her race whose loveliness was more frequently of a Latin than an Ethiopian character. . . . She *was* beautiful . . . beautiful and regal. Her skin was almost black; her nose broad, her lips thick. Her ears were set well on her head; her head was well set on her shoulders."

She was not, however, too lucky in love, each of her three marriages having ended in divorce. The first had ended around 1914, before she moved to Harlem, from Indianapolis, as A'Lelia Walker Robinson. In June of 1919, on her thirty-fourth birthday—and three days after her mother's funeral—she took a second husband, Dr. Wiley Wilson, a physician. This marriage was dissolved four years later, and in May of 1926 she became the wife of Dr. J. A. Kennedy, also a physician. But, as the *Age* said, the couple "never lived together," and were divorced in April of 1931, a few months before she died.

A'Lelia had no children of her own, but adored an adopted daughter from her first marriage. None of her own three weddings approached the splendor of the one she gave for this daughter, Mae Walker Robinson, in November of 1923. Harlem, no stranger to magnificent weddings, had seen nothing to match the occasion on which Mae married Dr. Gordon Henry Jackson, a physician from Chicago. According to the *Age*, it was "the most elaborate social function ever occurring among the colored citizens of New York City." The paper went on to give this account of the event, which began at St. Philip's Protestant Episcopal Church:

> 134th Street, from 7th to 8th Avenues, was jammed with thousands of people, colored and white. . . . hundreds of automobiles of every type and description. . . . Admission to the church was entirely by card, and so great was the interest, it is reported that many not having invitations expressed a willingness to pay $50 if one could be obtained.
>
> . . . The wedding party was whisked away to Villa Lewaro, at Irvington-on-the-Hudson, the palatial $250,000 mansion built by the bride's grandmother, where the wedding reception was held.
>
> Hundreds of guests wended their way to the suburban home by auto and by train, and the spacious edifice was thronged from top to bottom. The automobiles that conveyed the people . . . composed a line that stretched from Irvington to Tarrytown. A musical program was played . . . on the fine pipe organ built into the music room. There were also pianoforte numbers and harp numbers, as well as vocal solos.
>
> . . . The wedding in all its appointments, including the prenuptial affairs, marked the apex of elegant sumptuousness.

Though "everything was in perfect taste," there was "an elaborate display of wealth," and the mother of the bride was said to have paid $62,000 in wedding expenses.

By 1930, A'Lelia Walker's interest in the Villa Lewaro mansion had declined to the point where she began advertising it for sale. Her preference as a buyer was her friend Van Vechten, to whom she wrote: "I have been holding on to this place through sentiment (my mother), but I've arrived at the conclusion it is foolish of me to maintain such a large and expensive home with no family ties and I spend all my time in New York City. It is assessed at $190,000. I'll let it go for $150,000. . . . there isn't a person I'd rather have Villa Lewaro than you." But Van Vechten lacked either the means or the desire to acquire such a house, and it remained unsold for some time.

In December of 1930, the furnishings were auctioned off, at prices well below their real worth. According to Bessye Bearden—mother of the artist Romare Bearden, and a member of A'Lelia's social circle —"a few of us who had once enjoyed the hospitalities" of the mansion "stood with wet eyes and looked on." She continued, in a report to the Chicago *Defender*: "One of the highest prices paid for any article was $1,500 for an Aubusson tapestry. . . . A purchaser . . . paid $1,000 for a 10-piece Hepplewhite mahogany dining room suite. . . .

"The library of more than 600 volumes, many of which have never been opened, went for about $1,800. The prize of the library was a set of 10 volumes of great operas, with an introduction by Guiseppe Verdi . . . a limited edition for which the original subscription price was $15,000. Hand-colored plates, full Morocco binding, and an inlaid cabinet built for the volumes . . . brought $300.

"Another rare set of works were the 14 volumes of the Bible, bound in half wood and half pigskin and printed on imperishable paper by Updike of the Merrymount Press. . . . These went for $6 per volume.

"The library included the complete works of Rabelais, Balzac, Rousseau, Casanova, the Decameron of Boccaccio, Plato, and Marcus Aurelius.

". . . the Flemish oak billiard table went for $225. The ten high-backed armchairs in the same wood brought but $175, and the rugs in that room brought from $25 to $100, less than one third of their original value.

"Sofa cushions were sold at $1.50 each. Any number of footstools covered with lace, went for $8 to $10 each. Armchairs brought $25, $35, and $50. A red lacquered cabinet was sold for $42, lamps at $11 and $12 each, small Persian rugs brought between $25 and $50, and larger Persian rugs were sold for $75 and $250.

"The sale included the enormous oil paintings, such as 'Aurora,' by Victor DeCollangue; red brocaded seats and window chairs; phonograph chairs that looked like solid gold; costly lamps of Chinese jade, both green and white; several silver services; whole sets of china, tea sets of silver with Chinese dragons swallowing the sun; great red velvet sofas, armchairs, a statuette of Romeo and Juliet in marble; one of Lucretia Borgia in ivory and bronze, and a Japanese prayer rug, for which Madame Walker paid $10,000, and countless pieces of ivory."

On an evening in August of 1931, A'Lelia, who had given some of the biggest parties in Harlem, attended a smaller affair in Long Branch, New Jersey, to celebrate the birthday of a friend. It was to be her last party. She collapsed during the evening, and died some hours after. Hers was another of the great funerals of Harlem—as her mother's (1919), Bert Williams' (1922), and Florence Mills' (1927) had been, and as Fats Waller's (1943) and Bill (Bojangles) Robinson's (1949) were to be. The first four hundred mourners who viewed her remains—lying in state at Howell's Funeral Parlor, on Seventh Avenue—were admitted by invitation only. Later, some ten thousand ordinary Harlemites filed by her $5,000-silver-bronze casket. According to the *Amsterdam News*, "she wore a gown of beige and gold lace over lavender satin, with apple green satin slippers, an imported necklace of genuine amber Chinese prayer beads. . . . a ring of old silver, with large setting of French amber was on a finger of her left hand, as she had always worn it in life." As mourners filed by her bier, "a lone airplane" circled overhead, piloted by Colonel Hubert Julian, a celebrated black aviator of the day.

The Rev. Adam Clayton Powell, Sr., of the Abyssinian Baptist Church, delivered the eulogy, and, as Langston Hughes later wrote, "a night club quartette that had often performed at A'Lelia's parties arose and sang for her. They sang Noel Coward's 'I'll See You Again,' and they swung it slightly, as she might have liked it. It was a grand funeral and very much like a party." A poem, "To A'Lelia," that Hughes had written specially for the occasion was also read. At Woodlawn cemetery, in the Bronx, where the burial took place, many mourners had hoped to catch a glimpse of A'Lelia's friend and honorary Harlemite Carl Van Vechten. But Carlo wasn't there. "Mr. Van Vechten was absent from the city," a Harlem newspaper reported, "and in a lengthy telegram . . . said he would be unable to return for the funeral, which he regretted very much." A'Lelia's obsequies were silent—there were no ceremonies over the grave. As her remains were interred, Colonel Julian's plane, which had maintained its vigil over the proceedings, descended "noiselessly from the heavens," according to the *Amsterdam News*, and "dropped a final floral tribute to the memory of the dead heiress."

When A'Lelia Walker died, the young writers and artists of the Harlem Renaissance lost one of their steadfast admirers and benefactors. Not only had she always invited them to her parties, but in the late twenties she had converted a ground-floor section of her townhouse on West 136th Street into a meeting place for them. She named it the Dark Tower Tea Club, after a monthly column, The Dark Tower, that the poet Countee Cullen wrote for *Opportunity* magazine. The walls of the room were inscribed with poems by Cullen and Hughes, and hung with the work of the painter Aaron Douglas. Writers, artists, and their friends in music and theatre regularly gathered there.

With A'Lelia's death, life at the Dark Tower also expired, heralding the collapse of the Harlem Renaissance movement itself. Her death, Langston Hughes later recalled, "was really the end of the gay times of the New Negro era in Harlem." He continued, "That Spring [1931] for me (and, I guess, all of us) was the end of the Harlem Renaissance. We were no longer in vogue, anyway, we Negroes. Sophisticated New Yorkers turned to Noel Coward. Colored actors began to go hungry, publishers politely rejected new manuscripts, and patrons found other uses for their money. . . . The generous 1920's were over." They were indeed. The decline of the Harlem Renaissance had coincided with the rise and spread of the Great Depression.

PART FIVE

Hard Times

The Beat Goes On

WHEN Wall Street fell, on the last Tuesday of October 1929, there was far less alarm in Harlem than in the more prosperous neighborhoods of the city. Harlem did not abound in holders of stocks, bonds, and other securities. There was no distance in American life greater than the few miles from the center of wealth and possibility downtown to the black district in uptown Manhattan—which people were already calling a ghetto, and where the majority of the residents were poor. So to most Harlemites what the newspapers were calling Black Tuesday looked to be very much a white occasion. The looks were deceiving, to be sure—as Harlemites were to realize when the aftermath of Black Tuesday began to be felt—for Harlem was to be more badly hit by the Depression than any other section of New York City.

The effects of the Depression in Harlem were not immediately evident, however—at least not in all areas of life in the community. Here and there, the high spirits of the twenties still prevailed, as though certain circles remained oblivious of the curtailments of style and consumption the Depression demanded. Many of the night spots and the theatres were as crowded as they had been during the twenties. There were more Saturday-night rent parties than ever—though that was surely because they were more necessary than ever. People still danced all night in the great ballrooms on Seventh and Lenox Avenues. According to Cab Calloway, whose band opened at the Savoy Ballroom a month after the Wall Street crash, jazz was "swinging" then; night clubs, speakeasies, and jazz joints "were packed every night." In February of 1931, a reporter from a downtown newspaper drew this picture of late-night Harlem: "Lighthearted throngs . . . shouting flip greetings at friend and stranger with equal abandon . . . the clink of glass and bottle. The agonizing wail of muted trumpet and sax. The throaty shout of 'hot' blues singers. Music! Lights! Night clubs!" Attending an affair at the Rockland

Palace Ballroom in May of 1934, one guest—well aware of how hard the times actually were—was stunned by the "abundance" of food and drink, the "gorgeous" evening gowns, the "prosperity" of the atmosphere. In May of 1932, the Renaissance cinema was the scene of a "glittering" occasion—the première of a film starring Bill (Bojangles) Robinson. It was called *Harlem Is Heaven*. And in March of 1933, Vere Johns, a Jamaican-born writer for the weekly *Age*, observed that while theatres in certain areas of Manhattan had "closed like windows," those in Harlem "managed to struggle along and keep their doors open." This showed, he said, that "Harlemites will not allow hard times to make hermits of them."

Until 1934, when there was a change of management, the Lafayette Theatre, on Seventh Avenue at 132nd Street, had been Harlem's most popular musical stage. Called the cradle of stars, it also presented such established ones as Bessie Smith, Mamie Smith, the Mills Brothers, Maxine Sullivan, Ethel Waters, Lil Hardin, Jackie (Moms) Mabley, Stepin Fetchit, Bill Robinson, Huddie (Leadbelly) Ledbetter, Duke Ellington, Bennie Moten, Jimmie Lunceford, Fletcher Henderson, Claude Hopkins, and Earl Hines. Nancy Cunard, the mutinous daughter of an upper-class English family, who became enamored of Harlem life during the thirties, described the Lafayette as "a sympathetic old hall." Perhaps she was thinking mainly of the faded elegance of the place, with its air of a small Edwardian music hall. A sympathetic spirit did not always prevail among the patrons of the Lafayette—certainly not when they were required to judge the quality of amateur performances. Miss Cunard herself noticed that the audiences could be "merciless" to new and untried talent of a sort that "would have passed with honor anywhere out of America."

The Lafayette's manager in those days was Frank Schiffman, one of the major impresarios in the history of popular entertainment in Harlem. Born on Manhattan's lower East Side and educated at the City College of New York (where he was a classmate of Edward G. Robinson), Schiffman spent all but the first few years of his career at the managerial end of Harlem show business. He ran the Lafayette in partnership with Leo Brecher, an Austrian-born entrepreneur, who owned other theatres in Harlem and in the Broadway area as well. One of the four notable periods in the history of the Lafayette ended in 1934, when Schiffman and Brecher disposed of it and acquired another theatre, on 125th Street.

The racial character of 125th Street had changed almost completely by then. It was no longer the all-white thoroughfare it had been in the earlier decades of the century. The black population, which had been spreading steadily from the environs of 135th Street, had reached the neighborhood of 125th Street, and was soon to cover most of Harlem, down to 110th Street, the southern border of the district. Increasing numbers of blacks were now shopping in the department stores of the area (though they were still fighting to be hired as salesclerks) and showing up at its many places of amusement. The three major theatres on 125th Street between Seventh and Eighth Avenues were Loew's Victoria, the Harlem Opera House, and Hurtig & Seamon's Music Hall. It was the last of these (which had been renamed the Apollo) that Schiffman and Brecher acquired when they relinquished control of the Lafayette. They continued running it as the Apollo, and under their management the theatre became one of the most popular and important institutions in the history of black American entertainment.

When Schiffman and Brecher took it over, in January of 1934, they promised, in a newspaper advertisement, that the Apollo would "mark a revolutionary step in the presentation of stage shows," that its extravaganzas would be "lavish and colorful," that it would be the "finest theatre in Harlem" and "a resort for the better people." As events were to show, one half of that promise militated against the other half. The Apollo did take its revolutionary step in the presentation of stage shows and extravaganzas, but in doing so, quite successfully, it became a resort not for "the better people" but chiefly for the masses—and since those two classes were deeply at odds in matters of cultural style and taste, it remained a matter of dispute whether the Apollo had indeed become the finest theatre in Harlem. But these differences of cultural opinion did not appear immediately. For instance, the Apollo's first presentation under the Schiffman-Brecher regime—featuring "gorgeous steppers" and "jazz à la carte," with Ralph Cooper, Aida Ward, and Benny Carter's orchestra—does not seem to have displeased either of Harlem's major social factions. If the masses complained, reports of the event contain no evidence of it. And, on the other side, the reviewer for the *Age*—which shared the standards of "the better people"—applauded at least two aspects of the program: one was "the entire absence of sensuous dancing, salacious jokes, and hokum," and the other was "the decent attiring of the chorus or, I should say, the ladies of the ensemble." There were very few evenings in the future, however, when the representative of the *Age* found himself pleased with what he saw and heard at the Apollo.

In the thirties and early forties—to speak only of those periods—the Apollo presented almost every notable black singer, dancer, and comedian in America, and virtually all the major jazz bands, black and white. Harlem recognized almost no popular entertainer until he or she had appeared and excelled at the Apollo. The audiences were not only demanding and discriminating judges of black performance; they could also be more merciless—to professionals and amateurs alike—than the ones at the Lafayette had been. On occasion, even as celebrated an orchestra as Louis Armstrong's was treated with less than proper deference at the Apollo. It wasn't that the audiences were indifferent to Satchmo's lyrical and melodic genius—who could have been? It was just that Armstrong may have come into the Apollo on a night when sounds and reminders of Dixieland were the last things that the hardened metropolitan sensibilities of the Harlem masses wished to entertain.

Two of the great favorites at the Apollo—one of whom may have helped to drive "the better people" away—were the comedians Jackie (Moms) Mabley and Pigmeat Markham. "The better people" may have found in Mabley, who was garrulously naughty but seldom coarse, a redeeming comic value of some sort. Not in Markham, however—a virtuoso of the bawdy and the low-down. Abram Hill, a writer in Harlem, described Markham's work:

> His main attraction is his gags, capers, and burlesque of the people who crowd the Apollo from top to bottom to see him render his version of their doings. He gathers his material from the saloons, house-rent parties, street scenes, domestic rifts, and anything that isn't too subtle for his followers to grasp.
> . . . anything for a laugh. He will halt in the middle of a number, rush offstage and dash back in a bathing suit or a woman's corset and a wig. This brings the laugh he is working for; and he slips out of the corset. Then he threatens to remove the balance of his

clothes, britches and all. A cop rushes out and Pigmeat flees. The audience howls.

In one of his sketches—presented at the Apollo in June of 1934—Markham, escorting a pretty soubrette, enters a small neighborhood hotel and requests a room for the night. Oh, no, the manageress replies; her accommodations are not for unmarried couples. Well, then, Markham says, send for a preacher. The preacher arrives and unites the couple in matrimony, and the newlyweds retire to their room. But a police officer bursts into the premises and apprehends the preacher on his way out. It appears that he is not a clergyman, after all, but a racketeer in collar and gown. Appalled by the disclosure, the manageress summons Markham and his bride:

> MANAGERESS: You two have to get your clothes and get outa here. You are not married.
> MARKHAM: Not married? But didn't the Reverend just marry us?
> MANAGERESS: He was no Reverend. . . . The cop just took him away . . . you've got to get out.
> MARKHAM: It's too damn late now. C'mon, gal.

To the reviewer for the *Age* who had seen an earlier version of the sketch at the Alhambra, on Seventh Avenue, Markham's work was "repulsive." The sketch had "smelled to high heaven" when the reviewer first saw it, "and it stinks worse now." Continuing, he called on comedians like Markham to "wash their faces and rely on their natural talent—minus the filth." Such performers, he added, would do well to emulate the "clever" comic routines of men like George Jessel, Ted Healy, Joe Penner, Jack Benny, Charlie Ruggles, Jack Oakie, Stuart Erwin, and Joe E. Brown. These were brilliant comic artists, to be sure, but would their styles have gone over at the Apollo? It is doubtful. For what the proletarian crowds at the Apollo recognized and applauded in the work of comedians like Pigmeat Markham were facets of their own style and experience. When they howled at what Markham said and did, they were howling at wonderful comic dramatizations of themselves or of certain blacks they happened to know.

Ella Fitzgerald and Billie Holiday, two of the jazz singers who gained fame during the Depression, served part of their early ap-

prenticeship at the Apollo. In 1934, soon after Fitzgerald, then sixteen, had won an amateur-night contest at the Harlem Opera House,
next door, Frank Schiffman signed her for an engagement. It was
during this engagement at the Apollo that she was discovered by the
gifted drummer Chick Webb, who adopted her—she was born in
Virginia, and orphaned—and later groomed her as the vocalist for his
band. Webb's band was then a favorite at the Savoy Ballroom, farther uptown. Not long after, she became nationally and internation-
ally known, as the voice that popularized "A Tisket, a Tasket." Like
Ella Fitzgerald, Billie Holiday was not a native of Harlem; she had
moved there as a teen-ager from Baltimore, her home town. Unlike
Ella, Billie was discovered not at the Apollo or any of the other
theatres on 125th Street but at one of the night clubs in Jungle Alley,
as a block of Harlem's 133rd Street was called. That was in 1933,
when Billie—the daughter of Clarence Holiday, a guitarist in Fletcher
Henderson's band—was seventeen. John Hammond, the recording
impresario, who takes credit for discovering her, has recalled in his
autobiography:

> Early in 1933 . . . I dropped in at Monette Moore's place on 133rd
> Street, a stop on my Harlem rounds. I was expecting to hear
> Monette, a fine blues singer. Instead, a young girl named Billie
> Holiday was substituting. . . . Billie's accompanist was Dot Hill,
> and among the first songs she sang was "Wouldja for a Big Red
> Apple?" . . . the second song Johnny Mercer ever wrote lyrics
> for. Billie had come to New York from Baltimore two years
> before, aged fifteen. . . . She was not a blues singer, but she sang
> popular songs in a manner that made them completely her own.
> She had an uncanny ear, an excellent memory for lyrics, and she
> sang with an exquisite sense of phrasing. . . . I decided that night
> that she was the best jazz singer I had ever heard.

Soon after that, Billie made her first appearance at the Apollo, and
of her début there she later said, "There's nothing like an audience at
the Apollo. . . . They didn't ask me what my style was, who I was,
how I had evolved, where I'd come from, who influenced me, or
anything. They just broke the house up."

According to Ruth L. Saul, who visited Harlem in the late twenties
and early thirties, "not all white people came to the clubs in expensive autos to listen to good music, to dance, and to watch the

dancers. My husband and I had no car. We would come uptown by bus or subway and go home the same way. . . . I had Canadian friends visiting whose first request was to go to the Apollo amateur night." And recalling other lively moods of Harlem during the Depression, the artist Romare Bearden has said, "A group of us moved together at the time. Three nights a week, we were at the Savoy Ballroom. Charlie Buchanan, who ran the place, liked artists to come to the Savoy. The best dancing in the world was there, and the best music. When we left the Savoy, we'd go to the after-hours spots, where we'd see people like Clifton Webb and Danielle Darrieux. The artists would talk to these people. Sometimes Peter Arno, of *The New Yorker*, would come up to join us. They called us the Dawn Patrol. We moved till dawn, from one after-hours spot to another. One of the places we went to was Mom Young's, on 131st Street. She had been in what you call the sporting life. You brought in one-pound coffee cans, and for a quarter you could have them filled with beer. Each night, Mom Young would cook up a different thing— gumbo, chili, and so forth. Then, late at night, the chorus girls would all come out. Mom Young had a special room, just for the artists and writers, some of them from downtown. Then the gangsters came up, too. There was a woman who ran a big house on 116th Street, and Dutch Schultz would always be there. When he arrived, he would close up this woman's place. He would say to her, 'I don't want any more people in.' He always had thousands of dollars on him, and he would say to this woman, 'Now, how much would you make for two days' business?' When she told him, he'd give her three times that much. Then the girls had to go out, take all their clothes off, and put on black stockings and high-heel shoes. All this for Dutch. It didn't necessarily mean he wanted to sleep with the girls. He liked to sit and talk with this woman, and tell her all his business. He'd say to her, 'Let's talk and have a drink.' Then as they talked, the girls would be parading around for him. That's how he wanted it. And here were we, the young artists, looking on at all of this. I'd say that we young artists had the same kind of ambience that Toulouse-Lautrec had. It was a very interesting time. You'd want to be either in Harlem then or in Paris. These were the two places where things were happening."

Sunny Gets Blue

IT WAS only when one looked away from the theatres, the ball-rooms, and the night spots that one saw the mounting wreckage of the Depression. One would surely have wished to be in Paris then. The *Herald Tribune* reported in February of 1930 that the stock-market collapse had "produced five times as much unemployment in Harlem as in other parts of the city." In the summer of 1934, more than 19,000 Harlem families were on home relief. Out-of-work actors and musicians, among other jobless, gathered around the Tree of Hope—near the Lafayette Theatre—and touched its trunk for luck. There was a continuing inflow of poor migrants from the South, causing many tenements to become run-down and overcrowded. The New York Urban League estimated in 1932 that there were more than two hundred thousand blacks in Harlem—or, according to the League, more than the entire population of Syracuse. (According to other estimates, the population of Harlem in 1930 was 204,000, and that of Syracuse, 209,000.) Nowhere in Manhattan could there have been worse tenement conditions than those described by Warren J. Halliburton and Ernest Kaiser in their book *A History of Broken Dreams*. They write:

> The stock market crash of 1929 had marked the beginning of a new era....
>
> In twenty-five years Harlem's population had increased more than 600 per cent. Two and three families were living in apartments meant for one family. Properties became badly run down from overuse and neglect, and the tenants grew sullen. Men, women, and children combed the streets and searched in garbage cans for food....
>
> Many families were reduced to occupying quarters below street level. More than ten thousand lived in cellars and basements....
>
> There were boardinghouses in which beds were rented by the

week, day, night, or hour. Brownstones were turned into rooming houses, private residences into tenements, and apartments into one-room flats. Space once renting by the month for forty dollars now brought in one hundred to one hundred and twenty-five dollars. The higher the rents, the greater the number of people needed to pay for the shelter.

By 1930 Harlem contained some 200,000 people. Half of them depended upon unemployment relief.

Government aid failed to meet the needs of all the hungry, the homeless, and the jobless. In 1931, John D. Rockefeller, Jr., gave fifteen thousand dollars to the Harlem Coöperating Committee on Relief and Unemployment—a group organized by residents of the community. From a donor with Rockefeller's resources, a more sizable sum might have been expected, but during the Depression the demands on his generosity were nationwide, and, in any event, no other individual gift to the sufferers of Harlem was nearly as large as his. Major churches, like Abyssinian Baptist and St. Philip's Protestant Episcopal, ran employment agencies, shelters, and soup kitchens for the needy. In the first three months of 1931, the Abyssinian Baptist Relief Bureau served 28,500 free meals and distributed 525 food baskets, 17,928 pieces of clothing, and 2,564 pairs of shoes. Night clubs staged special programs and gave the proceeds to agencies aiding the poor. On Christmas Eve of 1934, the Cotton Club handed out three thousand food baskets, each containing a five-pound chicken; five pounds of potatoes; a head of cabbage; three pounds of carrots; a dozen apples; six oranges; cans of tomato soup, evaporated milk, and pork and beans; a pound of sugar; a package each of rice and tea; and two loaves of bread. By such charity, Owney Madden, the gangster who ran the Cotton Club, caused Harlemites to feel that he was not such a bad sort after all—despite his club's policy of barring all blacks from its tables.

Small restaurants carried signs in their windows reading, "All You Can Eat for 40 Cents—Soup, Entree, Dessert," or "All You Can Eat for 35 Cents—Choice of Fine Meats, Desserts, Coffee, Tea, or Milk." A man who lived in Harlem during the thirties recalls, "At lunchtime, the bars had free cheese, free salami, free crackers. So if you were down and out but had ten cents to buy a couple of beers you could also have your lunch." In 1933, when housewives complained of price gouging in the food stores, the *Age* printed a price schedule, supplied by the Commissioner of Public Markets:

Butter (lb. tub)	28 cents
Eggs (B grade, per doz.)	22 cents
Sirloin steak (per lb.)	35 cents
Smoked Ham (per lb.)	19 cents
Leg of Lamb (per lb.)	24 cents
Chickens (frying, per lb.)	26 cents
Lettuce (Iceberg, per head)	9 cents
Spinach (per lb.)	7 cents
Oranges (per doz.)	27 cents

On block after block, tenants, with their belongings, were put out on the street for nonpayment of rent. In 1931, from ten to twenty evictions a day were reported to the Urban League. It was at this time that, according to Nancy Cunard, "the Communists . . . put up a strong and determined defense." She went on, "Black and white comrades together go where the evictions are taking place and move the things back. Police and riot squads come with bludgeons and tear bombs; fights and imprisonments, and deaths too, occur." (Ralph Ellison's novel *Invisible Man*, published some years later, was to contain riveting accounts of such incidents.) In 1933, the Brotherhood of Sleeping Car Porters—along with its office furniture and records—was thrown out of its national headquarters, a four-story brownstone on 136th Street. This was during the worst year of the Depression and at the lowest point of the Brotherhood's twelve-year struggle to win recognition from the Pullman Company as the legitimate bargaining agent of the porters. Members had lost hope; the majority had stopped paying dues; and the union, with little or no income, was on the verge of collapse. But its officers were a tenacious bunch. Though A. Philip Randolph, the president, provided unwavering moral leadership, the union might not have survived—or triumphed, as it did four years later—without resourceful organizers like Benjamin McLaurin. Later, McLaurin described what he did when the Brotherhood was evicted from its headquarters: "I picked up the pieces and moved into an apartment on 140th Street. There were five rooms in this apartment and we used the two front rooms for offices. . . . I promoted a weekly rent party, to get money to pay rent. It was the only income we had. . . . We used to go from house to house holding rent parties. . . . Saturday mornings I spent preparing food and most of the day cooking. I cooked chitterlings and pigs feet. . . . I used to cook a hundred pounds of chitterlings, plenty of stew and potato salad. . . . I cooked so much of that stuff that it nauseates me now. I don't want to be around if anybody is cooking it. . . . It was on this income, for two years at least, that we kept the headquarters together. We couldn't hire stenographers. Everybody had to do his own typing. . . . There were many days when we didn't know where the next mouthful was coming from. But it wasn't important. We could live on a bottle of milk and a loaf of bread."

Few could have been surprised when a riot broke out in Harlem on an afternoon in March of 1935, for it was fed by emotions that had been smoldering beneath the hardships of the Depression. A rumor had spread through sections of the community that a black teen-ager had been beaten to death in a department store on 125th Street, where he had been caught stealing a ten-cent pocketknife. Only the latter part of the story was true, but the crowd that began milling in front of the store did not know this until most of the damage had been done. Struggling to break from the grasp of two salesmen who had caught him, the boy had bitten one of them on the thumb and the other on the wrist. What followed was recounted by Hamilton Basso in *The New Republic*:

> The man who was bitten on the thumb began to bleed. He shouted: "I'm going to take you down to the basement and beat the hell out of you." [The boy was not beaten, however. He was released in the basement, and, taking a rear exit, ran home.] . . .
> Meanwhile in the store the anger and resentment of the crowd had mounted. A woman screamed that they were beating the boy to death. . . . Threats of violence began to be heard. A speaker started to address the crowd. Policemen reached the scene and tried to break up the gathering. The people refused to move. The speaker continued his harangue. . . . The crowd waited for the boy to reappear. . . . Men in the crowd suggested that they go and free the boy. Women became hysterical. . . .
> Then, its siren shrieking through the streets, an ambulance stopped before the store. It had been called for by the man whose

finger had been bitten, but the crowd . . . thought that it had come to take the boy to the hospital. It began to surge into the store. Three other speakers had joined the first orator and one of them had mounted a ladder. A policeman started toward the man on the ladder and the first fighting began. . . . It was now well out of hand and the policeman sent in a call for reinforcements. A brick crashed through a window . . . a hearse appeared. Now it was believed that the boy had been killed. The crowd, yelling with rage, poured into the store.

Mobs rampaged along 125th Street, stoning the police, smashing shopwindows, and looting the major stores. At least four of the rioters died, and scores were hospitalized. Businesses suffered losses and damages in the hundreds of thousands of dollars. Hamilton Basso saw the outburst as springing from long-standing "anger and resentment." So did Mayor Fiorello LaGuardia's Commission of Inquiry, which was made up of prominent New Yorkers, black and white. The Commission said, in a preliminary finding, "This sudden breach of the public order was the result of a highly emotional situation among the colored people of Harlem, due in large part to the nervous strain of years of unemployment and insecurity." It was the first major riot in the history of black Harlem, and it would not be the last.

The Lord Will Provide

THE CHURCHES of Harlem can hardly have been thankful for the Depression, but at no previous time had there been so many of them, and in no earlier decade had they been so well attended. It was the storefront churches that had multiplied the fastest. "There are something like one hundred and sixty colored churches in Harlem," James Weldon Johnson wrote in 1930. "A hundred of these could be closed and there would be left a sufficient number to supply the religious needs of the community." The hundred that Johnson had in mind were the storefront churches. People of his class were adherents of the major denominations—of churches that were, in his words, "regularly organized and systematically administered." The storefront gatherings—which another writer described as "a thick underbrush of ephemeral and ever-changing cults and sects"—were housed in former candy stores, groceries, and shoe-repair shops, or in basements, lofts, and the back rooms of tenements. They were furnished with camp chairs and cheap-looking benches; preaching was done from rough-hewn platforms; and music was provided on an upright piano or on a bass drum and cymbals. The preachers were generally self-trained or self-called; and while many of them were honest men, genuinely devoted to the ethics and duties of their calling, others were, in Johnson's words, "parasitical fakers, even downright scoundrels." A leader of one of the major churches had said as early as 1926, "No, we haven't too many churches in Harlem. We do have too many house churches. Somebody wants to be a leader, deacon, or preacher, and if the church doesn't give it to him he will establish a little church of his own where he can be seen. Selfishness is really the cause of so many of these churches."

Selfishness was not the only cause. Nor was it true that the major churches were sufficient to supply the religious needs of the community. There was a genuine demand in Harlem for the storefront congregations and their preachers. People who worshipped in these places were among the poorest and least educated, and their religious needs were of a sort, or of a style, that the major churches did not or could not supply. The decorum of traditional liturgy was of no interest or use to storefront worshippers. They desired, above all, an atmosphere conducive to emotional spontaneity, to the informalities and improvisations of religious expression. The civil-rights spokesman Bayard Rustin—who lived in Harlem during the thirties—has said, "The big churches were too calm. Here were these people coming in from the South. They were used to screaming and yelling at services, rolling in the aisles, and speaking in tongues. But the middle classes which supported the big churches were now beyond all these things." Besides freedom of expression, storefront worshippers looked to their ministers to provide solace or answers to their social and economic problems—of which there could hardly have been more than there were during the Depression. According to the *Age*, any storefront preacher "with a panacea" was "listened to and hailed as a leader."

During the thirties, the great cult leaders of Harlem—the superstars of grass-roots religion—were the evangelists George W. Becton and Father Divine. The average storefront church seldom had a membership of more than fifty. Becton and Divine, whose religious kingdoms spread beyond the bounds of Harlem and of New York, had followers in the thousands. Nor did they conduct their meetings in humble storefronts. Becton, who preferred to be known as the Reverend Dr. Becton, was the only grass-roots evangelist who sometimes spoke from the pulpits of the major churches—bringing a bit of swagger and liveliness, even sexiness, to the usually staid proceedings of those bodies. Divine's "heavens" and "peace missions" were housed in brownstones, which he either owned or rented. When he was not presiding in his own missions, over his own "angels," only the large ballrooms of Harlem were able to hold the crowds that turned out to hear him. Becton and Divine were colorful and dramatic figures, vastly influential among their followers, and—thanks to the revenues of their ministry—almost as vastly rich.

Becton settled in Harlem during the twenties, some years before Divine. The writer Claude McKay called him "the first of the great cult leaders to excite the imagination and stir the enthusiasm of the entire Harlem community." He was tall, handsome, and well built, and his clothes were expensively tailored. Nancy Cunard, who remarked on his pearl-gray suit, top hat, cane, and ivory gloves, was also struck by his "exquisite smartness," his "youthful look," his physical "sparkle," and his "lovely figure." His style on the platform ("his terrific physical activity") caused him to be nicknamed the Dancing Evangelist. In his more important public appearances, he was accompanied by his own singing group and his own jazz band. And when he preached, McKay said, women "swayed like reeds" in response to his "well-modulated voice" and "agile movements." To Miss Cunard, Becton's performances had "nothing to do with God." She saw him as "a poet in speech," the "personification of expressionism," and "a great dramatic actor."

Becton called his religious movement the World's Gospel Feast. Its quarterly publication, the *Menu*, offered "A Square Deal for God." He urged sexual abstinence on his followers, though there was little in his manner to discourage them from secretly cultivating him in their sexual imaginations. He was proud of his fine suits ("If Jesus were alive, he would dress like me"), and made no apology for the size of his income ("God ain't broke"). Somewhat as the first John D. Rockefeller had once sought to soften public resentment of his fortune by distributing dimes to the poor, Becton became wealthy by taking from the poor no coin that was larger than a dime. Langston Hughes explained the gimmick: "Dr. Becton had an envelope system, called 'The Consecrated Dime—A Dime a Day for God.' And every Sunday he would give out his envelopes. And every Sunday he would collect hundreds of them . . . each with seventy cents therein. . . . Every package of dimes was consecrated to God—but given to the Reverend Dr. Becton." With the proceeds, he was able to acquire extensive real-estate holdings, placing some at the service of his church and retaining others for his personal use. There may not have been a more brilliantly furnished apartment in Harlem than Becton's. In the streets, people talked about his "golden slippers and golden bed"; a golden gate that led from his music and reception room to his "Holy Chambers"; the "white-and-gold bathroom," resembling "an Oriental bazaar"; and a bathtub that was "concealed in casements." Becton died under mysterious circumstances. He disappeared one

night in 1933 while he was visiting a branch of his church in Philadelphia. His body, riddled with bullets, was later found in one of the
less frequented streets of that city. Earlier, the radical Miss Cunard
had had an audience with Becton: "During our talk he leant forward
earnestly: 'In what manner do *you* think will come the freeing of my
race?' 'Only by organized and militant struggle for their *full* rights,
side by side with Communism.' He smiled. 'And in what way do
you think?' I asked him. 'I think it will be by prayer,' he murmured. I
wanted to shout at him. . . . But now, one year after I saw him,
Becton is dead. 'Bumped off' suddenly and brutally by some gangsters, shot in a car."

When Father Divine settled in Harlem, in 1933—though he had
been going there to preach from time to time—his followers had
already come to accept him as "the living God." Since 1919, his
ministry had been based in Sayville, on Long Island, but he had been
forced to abandon Sayville when his white neighbors had him arrested on a charge of disturbing the peace. They had found his
nightly meetings too noisy and had disliked the fact that his angels
were both black and white. Divine was tried in Mineola, found
guilty, and sentenced to a year in jail; but he had hardly begun
serving his sentence when Supreme Court Justice Lewis J. Smith,
who had passed sentence, died of a heart attack. This act of God was
deemed by his followers to be an act of Father Divine himself—final
proof that he was indeed the Omnipotent. "I hated to do it," Divine
was heard to say when news of the judge's death reached him in his
prison cell. He was released on bail after serving thirty-three days of
his sentence (which was later reversed by the Appellate Court). He
then moved his headquarters to Harlem, where, on making a tri-
umphal entry, he was hailed as the greatest black messiah since
Marcus Garvey.

Father Divine began life as George Baker somewhere in the South.
In the first stages of his ministry—especially after he first moved to
New York, in the early years of the century—he went by such names
as the Messenger, Major J. Devine, and the Reverend J. Divine. Very
little was known about his origins and his early priesthood, except by
a few of his followers, and when he emerged as the preeminent black
cult leader of his time neither he nor his angels wished to cooperate

with any inquiry into his past. But in 1936 St. Clair McKelway and A. J. Liebling, of *The New Yorker*, were able to uncover these details of his background:

> He is around sixty now, and the earliest records of his life are obscure. People who knew him when he was in his twenties think he came from Georgia, or Florida, or Virginia. They are not sure which. But in 1899, beyond all question, he was a man named George Baker and was earning an honest living in Baltimore, mostly by clipping hedges and mowing lawns. . . . He was frugal, and when winter came he had usually saved up enough money to loaf for a while. If his store of coins began to get too low, he would find odd jobs on the docks. He did not seem to be very ambitious.
>
> On Sundays he taught . . . Sunday school. . . . He was a serious-minded young fellow and worried a lot about God. He didn't feel, or claim to be, closer to God than any . . . other.

After migrating to Manhattan, Divine ministered in one of the black neighborhoods of the old Tenderloin. From there, he moved to Brooklyn, and from Brooklyn to Sayville, where he became Father Divine, God, the King of Glory. "I teach now as of 1900 years ago," he later told a gathering of his followers in Harlem. "I came to comfort you, bless you, give you homes for your bodies, rest for your souls, relief from all sorrow, for I am the written word." One reporter described the "written word" as "a thin little man, less than five feet tall." He was bald, and wore double-breasted suits, tan shoes, bright neckties, and shirts "with the kind of collar known as 'Barrymore.'" His voice was "high and soft in ordinary conversation, but capable of great power and emotion."

Even before moving to Harlem, Divine had been a splendid provider for his followers. He had found jobs for them, given them lodgings in his Sayville headquarters, and invited them regularly to sit at his magnificently laid banquet tables—free jobs, free housing, and free food. "The Messenger didn't work and yet he was never in want," McKelway and Liebling wrote. "It seemed miraculous to his disciples. There was a fine dinner every evening, and the Messenger always had a roll of bills in his pocket. When the disciples wondered at these things, and asked the Messenger to explain them, he would say, 'God will provide,' and smile on them from the head of the table."

HARD TIMES

In 1932, when Divine made a special appearance in Harlem after his release from prison, thousands jammed the Rockland Palace Ballroom to celebrate his arrival. "At this moment, the entire world needs a savior," said a writer for the *Age*. "And Harlem . . . is no exception." In his sermons, Divine called on his followers to eschew smoking, drinking, crime, violence, race hatred, profane language, hair-straightening, installment-buying, and sex. His organization ran grocery stores, lodging houses, shoeshine stands, barber shops, dry-cleaning establishments, newsstands, and little food shops that served fifteen-cent dinners. Such dinners were, of course, humble repasts compared with the splendid banquets that Divine gave in his headquarters, or "Heaven." A Harlem writer who managed to gain admittance to one of these affairs made this report:

> And there sat "God": striped shirt, striped tie, plain gray suit, and a bald head. . . .
> And the food! . . . I have never seen better food at any banquet anywhere in the world, and I have never seen as much of it and as freely given. . . . The Father sits at the center of the head table, and there are two long tables reaching out from it . . . to the far end of the hall. All the food, every dish and every cup of it, passed by him; he touches the dishes with his hands, thus blessing the food, and sends one dish to the right and another to the left. Each diner serves himself and passes a great platter on. . . .
> First the vegetables: rice, mashed potatoes (with much butter on them), stewed carrots, steamed cabbage, hominy, stewed corn, etc.
> Then the meats: . . . stuffed sausage, tenderized ham, halves of chickens (young and tender), great inch-thick steaks, from the tenderest of beef, breaded veal, and so on.
> Then the drinks: . . . iced coffee, iced tea, then hot coffee, hot tea, then postum. . . .
> Then bread: egg-yellow cornbread squares, followed by white bread, then cracked wheat, then whole wheat, then rye, then doughnuts (sugared), then crackers.
> Then came great bowls of gelatins in different colors and kinds, and some apple sauce. . . . later came plates with great slices of cake . . . followed by great tub-like bowls of ice cream. . . .
> And this food, all of it, was the best food that can be had anywhere on earth . . . the diners and angels [were] at least 1000

times as happy as any group I have ever seen anywhere in my life....

[Divine] said things like this: "For the first time we have the true gospel on earth. I have left the world of Imagination, I have entered the world of Recognition, I have come into the world of Realization." What shouts of approval greeted that pronouncement.

This man, up to now . . . has beat the New Deal a mile in the solution of the economic problems of his constituents.

At the dinner table, Father Divine had also beaten the major churches of Harlem: not even the wealthiest of them were able to feed the poor as regularly and as bountifully as he did. "Father Divine is going to close all the church doors," one of his satisfied disciples said. "He will win; no one can stop him. You have no right paying for God. He is free."

Though this prophecy was not fulfilled, it helped to arouse the major churches in opposition to Divine and his works. Addressing a group of his fellow-clergymen, R. C. Lawson denounced the Father's claim to divinity as "a sham and a delusion"—an ingenious device to distract his followers "from the worship of the true and living God." In the early nineteen-forties, Father Divine, harassed by his enemies and by lawsuits over his real-estate holdings, moved his headquarters to Philadelphia. The vacuum he left in Harlem was soon filled by such other superstar evangelists—some of whom had been unsuccessfully competing with him—as Elder Lightfoot Michaux, Mother Horn, and Sweet Daddy Grace.

For members of the established churches—who were paying heavily for the acquisition and upkeep of their great stone edifices—God was certainly not free. Worship of "the true and living God" could hardly have been more expensive anywhere or at any time than it was in Harlem during the Depression. Between 1900 and the nineteen-twenties, when most of these churches moved to Harlem from midtown Manhattan, they had committed themselves to large financial outlays, either to erect new buildings or to buy existing ones that whites were getting ready to abandon. James Weldon Johnson wrote in 1930, "Some critics of the Negro—especially Negro critics—say that religion costs him too much; that he has too many churches, and that many of them are magnificent beyond his means; that church mortgages and salaries and upkeep consume the greater part of the financial margin of the race and keep its economic nose to the grindstone. All of which is, in the main, true."

In 1911, St. Philip's Protestant Episcopal Church completed a new building, on West 134th Street, at a cost of more than $200,000. In 1914, St. James Presbyterian Church began erecting a home on 137th Street, which cost $83,000; years later, it moved into a larger structure, on West 141st Street, which it had bought for $248,000. In 1918, the Metropolitan Baptist Church paid $87,000 for a building that had been occupied by a white congregation. In 1923, Grace Congregational Church paid $55,000 for its new headquarters, on West 139th Street. That year, the Abyssinian Baptist Church moved into a brand-new $300,000 edifice, on West 138th Street. And during the same year, Salem Methodist paid $258,000 for a new chapel at Seventh Avenue and 129th Street. One of the costliest buildings, that of Mt. Olivet Baptist, at 120th Street and Lenox Avenue, was bought in 1924, for $450,000. And in 1926 St. Mark's Methodist acquired a $600,000 structure, near the intersection of St. Nicholas and Edgecombe Avenues. Bethel African Methodist Episcopal, Mother A.M.E. Zion, and Union Baptist were among the other major churches that moved into costly buildings during those years. Harlemites had indeed "invested more money in church property than in any other institution," as the writer Wallace Thurman stated in 1927.

In 1930, a study by the Greater New York Federation of Churches revealed that forty-one of the major Harlem churches owned property valued at $6,698,550, and that thirty-one of them had outstanding debts of $1,763,800. Among the ones that had liquidated their debts was Abyssinian Baptist. In 1928, five years after the building was completed, its pastor, Adam Clayton Powell, Sr., staged a public bonfire, at which members of the congregation witnessed the burning of the church's mortgage notes. But among the churches with debts still outstanding were: Mt. Olivet Baptist ($217,000), Union Baptist ($130,050), Mt. Calvary Methodist ($118,000), St. Mark's Methodist ($275,000), St. James Presbyterian ($95,000), and Mother A. M. E. Zion ($165,000).

Even before the Depression, ministers of such churches had been severely criticized for their "extravagant" investments in church property. Commenting in 1923 on one of the larger mortgages, the *Age* said, "The burden . . . is entirely beyond the ability of the members to carry. . . . This is an example of wild financing, brought on by the ambition of the pastor to have a big church . . . he plunged his trusting membership into a sea of debt, which bids fair to overwhelm them." Later, in 1931, a reader of the *Amsterdam News* said in a letter to the editor, "The wealth drawn from the Negro race by the Negro clergymen, if directed into industrial channels, would build up the downtrodden economic conditions and develop a greater field of opportunity for Negro youth, and thus bring about a greater degree of respect for the race from other races." John E. Nail, an early Harlem real-estate dealer, complained in 1925 that the "magnificent" church buildings were straining their congregations "to the point of suffocation," but he probably exempted his own church, the wealthy St. Philip's Protestant Episcopal, for which he was a business agent.

Black clergymen strongly defended their policy of erecting or acquiring expensive and impressive edifices. Rejecting the idea that the churches would render a more useful service by investing in economic development, William P. Hayes, the pastor of Mt. Olivet Baptist, argued, "The church has never been authorized to engage in commercial pursuits. . . . It destroys the character and violates the fundamental purpose of the church to subordinate its major interests to a sordid quest of mammon." Powell, of Abyssinian Baptist, was all in favor of "vanity and value in building"—the title of a sermon he preached in 1922, at a ground-breaking ceremony for his three-hundred-thousand-dollar edifice. And the Greater New York Federation of Churches concurred fully with preachers like Powell. Harlem, the Federation stated in 1930, was "the greatest Protestant center in New York City," and, as such, its church buildings ought not to be "plain" and "without ornamentation"; by their design, they should "speak of the worth, dignity and beauty of the Christian life."

The ministers of the nineteen-twenties and thirties were among the great clergymen in the history of black Harlem. They included Hutchens C. Bishop (and his son Shelton), of St. Philip's Protestant Episcopal; Adam Clayton Powell (and his son Adam, Jr.), of Abyssinian Baptist; J. W. Brown, of Mother A. M. E. Zion; William P. Hayes, of Mt. Olivet Baptist; Frederick A. Cullen, of Salem Methodist; W. W. Brown, of Metropolitan Baptist; William Lloyd Imes, of St. James Presbyterian; George Sims, of Union Baptist; Charles Martin, of the Fourth Moravian; John W. Johnson, of St. Martin's Protestant Episcopal; and Ethelred Brown, of Harlem Community. As the *Herald Tribune* described them in 1930, they were men of great "magnetism," of "extraordinary" personalities, and of "unusual native eloquence." Some were more than just spiritual guides and counsellors. They took a keen interest in public issues, and often influenced the political choices and judgments that their members made. Hayes, a staunch Republican, used his pulpit to rail against all forms of racism and discrimination, North and South, and to advocate a continuance of the historic relationship between blacks and the Republican Party. Imes was a fierce partisan of the trade-union movement —especially of those branches of it in which black workers were organized. Ethelred Brown was a socialist—a fact that was often evident in his sermons. And, in a pragmatic, nonideological fashion, the senior Adam Clayton Powell was probably the most militantly mass-conscious of the older ministers.

Until Powell retired, in the late nineteen-thirties, he was the best-known clergyman in Harlem, and his church the most famous. Of a visit to Abyssinian Baptist in the twenties, a white journalist wrote:

> The pastor, a tall, colored man, with a thunderous voice and big curly head of hair, looks very much like the picture of Alexandre Dumas. . . . I am yet to listen to a better choir. . . . I am yet to listen to a better church organist. . . . This church, like most other Negro churches, is really more than a church. It is a social center. At a service on a Sunday, the pastor comments upon the political events that have taken place during the week, and sways the audience to his view by his thunderous oratory. He speaks as much of earthly events as he praises the Lord. Not a thing that has happened in the world escapes him; and he is not afraid to denounce the things he does not agree with.

As a preacher, Powell leaned toward what he called the social gospel, and on a Sunday in December of 1930 his congregaton heard him at, or near, his most inspiring. In his sermon, "A Hungry God," Powell, aroused by the plight of many Harlemites during the Depression, declared, "We clothe God by clothing men and women. . . .

When you give men and women coats, shoes, and dresses, you are giving clothes to God." He was "ashamed," he said, to be seen alighting from his handsome Packard at the front door of his church when he had just passed so many suffering people in the streets of Harlem. And such people, he continued, needed "more than sympathy and prayers." They needed food and clothing. Hence, he was going to "give one thousand dollars of my salary during the next three months to help relieve this terrible unemployment situation." But that was not all, he told his listeners. He was also calling on them to pledge five per cent of their income for the next four months to the same cause. Momentarily stunned by their minister's dramatic announcement, Abyssinian members rushed forward with thousands of dollars in cash and pledges. Powell said later that it was the most impressive climax to a sermon he had ever witnessed.

Soon after, Powell put his fellow-clergymen on the spot by demanding that they, too, donate part of their income to the poor. Apparently, they were either not inclined to comply or not in a position to do so. William Hayes, of Mt. Olivet, came the closest to matching Powell's gesture. Turning down a yearly salary increase of four hundred dollars, he cited "the stringency of the times and the heavy indebtedness of the church." To the *Age*, George Sims, of Union Baptist, made a lengthy plea of his own financial plight. "Pastor Sims states that Dr. Powell is fortunate in that he is pastor of one of the richest congregations in this country," the paper reported. "The majority of the preachers were less fortunate than Dr. Powell. . . . If these men would give one-fourth of their salaries, as was suggested by Dr. Powell, their families would have to join the bread lines at once. . . . As for second-hand cars, nearly all Negro preachers are using second-hand machines. Rev. Sims's car is a 1926 model . . . made new by a coat of paint."

In 1937, after serving for twenty-nine years, the senior Powell retired from the ministry of Abyssinian Baptist. He was then seventy-two, and pleaded that his advancing years were making it harder and harder for him to continue in harness. He had tendered his resignation two years earlier, but his parishioners had refused to accept it. Doubtless they felt that he merely wished to abdicate in favor of his son, or perhaps they were reminding him that some time earlier they had elected him minister for life. In any event, it must have been difficult for them to imagine what their church would be like without him. The younger members could not remember a time when Powell had not been their minister, and older members knew of no prouder chapter in the history of their church than the one that began in 1908, when Powell arrived from New Haven to become their leader. He had led them from midtown Manhattan to Harlem, where he put up the fine building in which they had been worshipping since 1923. In the nearly three decades of his New York ministry, the church, whose membership was now fourteen thousand, had become the largest black congregation in America—perhaps in the world. And Abyssinian Baptist had identified itself so closely with the religious and economic needs of the community that, in the minds of blacks, it, too, had come to be a synonym for Harlem. "Under Adam Clayton Powell, the Abyssinian Church became a symbol of service and a voice of intelligent protest for the Harlem community," a commentator on Harlem's religious life said later. "For him, the neighborhood was his parish and all the people his charges."

When the old man retired, the junior Adam Clayton Powell inherited his father's pulpit. Born in New Haven in 1908, he was six months old when the family moved to Manhattan. From Townsend Harris High School, he went on to the City College of New York, where his career was short and undistinguished. Over six feet tall and built like an athlete, he was handsome and gregarious, and was light-skinned enough to pass for white, if he had wanted to. Archer Winsten, of the *Post*, once described Powell's complexion as "whiter than yours." So white did he look that, in the late nineteen-twenties and early thirties, he may have been one of the few "blacks" admitted to the tables of the Cotton Club. According to one of Powell's contemporaries, he was "a killer with the girls . . . so handsome, he could go out with any girl he wanted." That might have been mostly what he did at City College, and he dropped out in his sophomore year.

Powell did not then aspire to a career in the ministry. His ambition was to become a physician, and at Colgate University, to which he was admitted after leaving City College, he registered for a program of premedical studies. It was soon afterward, as a classmate of his later disclosed, that he received his "call" to the clerical life. "One day before we returned to school, his father said he wanted to talk with me. He explained how he had built the church up . . . and how he wanted Adam, his only son, to follow in his footsteps. He asked me if I could influence Adam to switch to theology. I talked it over with Adam on the way back. And he made up his mind then and there that he'd switch. He realized that it was all set up for him, and all he had to do was to walk in and take over." Powell was ordained in 1931 and became an assistant to his father.

As a young minister, Powell was not only free in his personal behavior but also outspoken and provocative from the pulpit. It was an open secret that he frequented night clubs, liked good Scotch whisky, and was as much attracted to the women of café society as they were to him. He himself remarked later that when he preached his first trial sermon at Abyssinian Baptist—on the night of Good Friday of 1929—several pretty showgirls from the Cotton Club had seats in the front pews. As far as is known, the senior Powell— himself a remarkably handsome and attractive man—did not achieve a similar accolade from female admirers. He did, however, carry on a certain discreet affair of his own, as his son ultimately found out. "My father was always preaching against whiskey," he later recalled. "He and Teddy Roosevelt helped organize the Anti-Saloon League in New York. One of my earliest memories is of attending a meeting and sitting between Roosevelt and my father. . . . [Once] I came home for Christmas holidays. My only dress shirt was dirty so I decided to borrow one from my father—boiled shirts, he called them. As I was rummaging around his drawer I came across three empty gin bottles. I was aghast. Immediately I went to him and said, 'Father, father, you're always preaching against whiskey. How can this be?' 'You've heard me preach against whiskey,' he said, 'but I've never said a word against gin.' "

Writing a year after he retired from the pulpit, the older Powell claimed that "there was not a dissenting voice" to his son's election as minister of Abyssinian Baptist. The transition was "fine and harmonious," he said, and he added, "I did not ask anybody to vote for him." Powell made this claim in his autobiography, *Against the Tide*, which is a generally sunny and self-congratulatory record of his career. In its tone and its selection of material, it reflects a preference for what William Dean Howells once called "the smiling aspects of life," or what others, of a post-Victorian, post-Edwardian disposition, might call the suppression of unpleasant detail. At any rate, Powell's account of how his son came to be elected seems to be a lavish retouching of the real story—quite at variance with a more believable account given by one of the younger man's biographers:

> Abyssinian's membership divided neatly between the younger liberals and the older conservatives. The *Amsterdam News* took notice of the crisis: "The elders . . . are even more determined that the young Mr. Powell will never become their pastor."
>
> But Adam Powell, Sr., with his consummate powers of conciliation managed to keep the rift from widening in public view. He met with the elders privately and argued that his son's clamorous liberalism was little more than youthful high spirits and would in no way impinge upon his administration of the church's affairs. Gradually, the rumors of dissension in Harlem's most populous . . . congregation faded.

Under the senior Powell's leadership, Abyssinian Baptist—despite conservative tendencies among its membership—had been nothing if not liberal and progressive, so it must have been a problem greater than liberalism that accounted for the church's reluctance to elect the young Powell as its minister. The "clamorous liberalism" that his opponents found troubling might well have been a reference to the vociferous support that young Powell sometimes gave to the Communist movement in Harlem, though he himself was never a member. For instance, what were his opponents in the church to think when they read this report in the *Age?*

> Rev: Adam Clayton Powell, Jr. . . . told an audience . . . that he will talk communism . . . and use everything he has to advance communism. He said the doors of his church are open to them, and "You can come there and say anything you want to say. . . . The day when you can no longer come there and meet and protest and demonstrate in a peaceful manner, that is the day I walk out with you."

Another example of his conduct that elements within the church found troubling was his marriage, in 1933, to Isabel Washington, a divorcée and a showgirl at the Cotton Club. To the conservative members of Abyssinian Baptist, she seemed a most inappropriate and unconventional choice for a clergyman's wife. But all such objections were overruled by Powell's supporters in the church and, apparently, by his father's unceasing efforts at conciliation.

"He may be counted on to carry on the Powell tradition," one of the older Harlem clergymen said when young Adam assumed the Abyssinian pulpit. Not only did he carry on that tradition, he added to it dimensions of his own. As he later said, his father had been "a radical and a prophet," and *he* was "a radical and a fighter." On another occasion, he recalled, "My father said he built the church and I would interpret it. This I made up my mind to do. I intended to fashion that church into a mighty weapon, keen-edged and sharp-pointed. I intended to move the people out of the church where God was—along the avenues and byways where hundreds of thousands were languishing in hopeless squalor."

LEFT: The Apollo, on West 12[
Street

BELOW: Tenants (surrounded by
lookers) sit with their belongings
a Harlem street, after being evic
during the Depression, for nonp
ment of rent

RIGHT: A Harlem wedding party,
1932

BOTTOM, RIGHT: The Rev. George
Becton, at home

RIGHT: Mother A. M. E. Zion Church
OPPOSITE, TOP: Abyssinian Baptist Church
BELOW: Father Divine's "angels" on parade
OPPOSITE, BOTTOM: At a Sunday service during the nineteen-thirties

LEFT: The Rev. Adam Clayton Powell, Sr.
RIGHT: The Rev. Adam Clayton Powell, Jr., addressing a Harlem rally during World War II
BELOW: The Rev. Adam Clayton Powell, Sr., and an Abyssinian Baptist Sunday School group

LEFT: Joe Louis and his bride, Marva Trotter, stroll down a Harlem boulevard in 1935. It was the day after his victory over Max Baer
BOTTOM, LEFT: The Lafayette Theatre. Opening night of "Voodoo Macbeth" in 1936
BELOW: A street scene during the late nineteen-thirties

RIGHT: Paul Robeson after service at Mother A. M. E. Zion Church, where his brother was pastor
BELOW: A street scene during the late nineteen-thirties
OPPOSITE, TOP: God and Marx on Lenox Avenue. On the top floor of this building at 131st Street is the headquarters of the Harlem branch of the Communist Party. Competing business is transacted below
OPPOSITE, BOTTOM: Augusta Savage

The Depression and the Arts

DURING the Depression, Harlem helped to produce one of the more important groups of black painters and sculptors that have yet emerged in America. Because they were not equally successful, they were not to become equally well known. Some—like Romare Bearden, Richmond Barthé, Robert Blackburn, Ernest Critchlow, Elton Fax, Norman Lewis, and Jacob Lawrence—have been recognized as being among the major American artists of the Depression and post-Depression eras. Others—like William Artis, Henry Bannarn, Selma Burke, Vertis Hayes, and Gwendolyn Knight (the wife of Jacob Lawrence) —were to be known chiefly within the circle of their colleagues and to ardent partisans of black painting and sculpture. As was true of the New Negro writers of the nineteen-twenties, none of the thirties artists were born in Harlem. A number of them, like Barthé and Fax, had attended art schools elsewhere before settling in New York. A few, like Critchlow and Lewis, lived in Brooklyn. Gwendolyn Knight was a native of the West Indies. Others had either grown up in Harlem (Bearden and Lawrence, for instance, came there to live when they were quite young) or migrated there as adults, from different parts of the country. For all of them, however, Harlem was at the center of their social and creative influence.

Much of this influence was supplied by such older painters and sculptors as Aaron Douglas, E. Simms Campbell, Charles Alston, and Augusta Savage. Douglas, one of the few painters associated with the Harlem Renaissance movement, had been living and working in the community since the mid-twenties, when he arrived there from Kansas. His paintings and murals were among the first works by black American artists to reflect a serious interest in African moods and motifs. Campbell, who was from St. Louis, had also been associated with the Harlem Renaissance; he was mainly a cartoonist, whose drawings had appeared in *Esquire* and *The New Yorker*. Alston, a

North Carolinian, was close enough in age to the younger artists to be called a member of their generation, but he had begun painting earlier than they did—in 1930, while he was completing a degree at Columbia—and so had become one of their mentors.

The most influential of the older artists was the sculptress Augusta Savage. Born in Florida, she was one of five natives of that state who made notable contributions to the cultural and intellectual life of black Harlem—the others being James Weldon Johnson, J. Rosamond Johnson, A. Philip Randolph, and Zora Neale Hurston. At her studio, Savage often put her own work aside to teach and encourage the ambitious young people who came in off the streets—Romare Bearden, William Artis, Jacob Lawrence, Norman Lewis, and Gwendolyn Knight among them. "She sacrificed herself and a lot of her art in trying to help the young artists," Bearden has said. "She set up—on 142nd Street and later on 135th Street—a kind of studio in storefronts. I would pass by there, or Norman Lewis would, and we would see this woman sculpting and modelling. While you were wondering what was going on, she looked out and saw you, and beckoned to you, 'Come on in.' You went in thinking she was going to show you how to sculpt and draw right away. Instead, she gave you a broom. You had to learn to clean up first." Praising her on another occasion, Bearden said that Augusta Savage "attracted the gifted children in Harlem like a magnet," that she "poured out warmth and enthusiasm," and that what "astonished and delighted" the young people was that "this talented woman artist, who had studied in Europe, had come back to Harlem and was freely available to them."

Not all the ambitious young people she attracted became artists. Some, like Kenneth B. Clark, the social psychologist, forsook their early training to pursue other careers. Clark, a native of Panama who moved to Harlem, with his parents, at an early age, was defeated by his own belief in excellence—a belief that contributed to his later achievements as a distinguished social scientist. Recalling his days at Augusta Savage's studio, Clark said, "I knew from my early dabbling in art that I did not have the sort of gift that would have developed into something more than mediocrity. I was not able to communicate in the way I saw some of my colleagues doing. I remain envious of all artists. They seem to me to communicate something about the human predicament with a reality and a depth that are beyond words. It was Augusta Savage who implanted in me the respect and envy I feel for artists, and I thank her for lighting that spark." Clark also recalled an example of the lengths to which Savage would go in order to instruct her young students: "I felt more comfortable working with clay than with paint, but perhaps I was less comfortable than I felt. Once I was doing this nude, and was having trouble with the breasts. Gwendolyn Knight was sitting next to me, and I kept looking at her, to see whether I could make a breast that looked like a breast. Gwen knew what I was doing, but she would not help me. Augusta came along and said, 'Kenneth, you're having trouble with that breast,' and I said, 'Yes, I am.' And she simply opened her blouse and showed me her breast."

Of her deceptively plain appearance and the significance of her own work as a sculptress, Bayard Rustin has said, "She was dark, a little on the hefty side, very dynamic. She reminded me of Mary McLeod Bethune, in that if you passed her in the street you would say that she wasn't attractive. But when she walked into a room, she became more attractive than the most beautiful woman in the room —because she brought a light and a fire. She did marvellous studies in black ethnic types, which ended up in a Chicago museum. In terms of appreciating and portraying the physical beauty of black Americans in sculpture, she preceded everybody else. She was temperamental, as all artists are. She helped great numbers of young and struggling artists to get on their feet."

None of the young artists she helped to train and inspire became more successful, or portrayed Harlem life more faithfully and imaginatively, than Jacob Lawrence. Speaking of Lawrence's early work, one critic has said that he was "a new voice with its own pitch and a distinct black resonance," and that "his subject was Harlem, which he saw freshly . . . with empathy and a mordant folk wit." Without Savage's aid, first as a tutor and later as a sponsor—when Lawrence sought the assistance of the Federal Arts Project, designed by the Works Progress Administration—he might well have transferred his interest and talent to a different realm of art. A modest, amiable, soft-spoken man, Lawrence has said, "If I weren't painting, I'd probably like to be in music. I like the idea of solving problems on some of the instruments."

Of what she was striving to accomplish with the young black artists of the thirties, Savage, mixing generosity with modesty, said at one point, "I have created nothing really beautiful, really lasting. But if I can inspire these youngsters to develop the talent I know they possess, then my monument will be in their work."

At no other time have there been as many theatre groups in Harlem as there were during the nineteen-twenties. The Lafayette Players, the Harlem Experimental Theatre, the Krigwa Players, the Negro Art Theatre, the Utopia Players, the Dunbar Garden Players, and the Harlem Community Players were just a few. Small and mostly amateur groups—producing either the classics or tame melodramas of middle-class life—they did not represent what could be called legit-imate black theatre. Hardly any of the plays they produced had been written by blacks or dealt seriously or in depth with black experience. The fault was not wholly theirs, however, for there were then almost no producible dramas that had been written by blacks. The three plays of the twenties that, in authorship and material, came closest to meeting the criteria for black theatre were *Appearances*, by Garland Anderson; *Harlem*, by Wallace Thurman and William Jourdan Rapp; and *Lulu Belle*, by Edward Sheldon and Charles MacArthur—and even the last two of those were the fruit of black and white collab-oration and all-white authorship, respectively. In any case, they were hardly the sort of work that the bourgeois theatre groups of Harlem cared to produce. *Harlem* and *Lulu Belle* were plays about the mass experience, presenting slices of popular life that—in the minds of culturally refined blacks—pandered to a faddish nineteen-twenties curiosity about the tawdry and more colorful aspects of life in Har-lem. Both were produced on Broadway and were well received. Virtually all the other serious plays about blacks then in existence had been written by whites. Ridgely Torrence's trilogy (*Granny Maumee*, *The Rider of Dreams*, and *Simon the Cyrenian*) had been staged during the First World War. And between 1920 and 1930 plays like *The Emperor Jones* and *All God's Chillun Got Wings*, by Eugene O'Neill; *In Abraham's Bosom*, by Paul Green; *Porgy*, by DuBose Heyward; and *Green Pastures*, by Marc Connelly were pro-duced in theatres downtown.

Most of Harlem's little-theatre companies failed during the De-pression. Broadway itself fell on hard times, and the majority of the black actors and actresses, whether they had appeared uptown or downtown, were thrown out of work. Indeed, the problem was nationwide, as a historian of the period has pointed out:

> Of all the artists to experience the effects of the Depression, the worst off were the show people. Unable to compete with the motion picture industry, actors, stagehands, technicians, musicians, and vaudeville performers found themselves displaced by technology even before the Crash. Sound films replaced the orchestra; mechanical music replaced musicians; actors were eclipsed by the Hollywood star system; and stagehands and stage mechanics were no longer needed. . . . Professional theatre people were stranded without work in major cities all over the country.

In 1935, Hallie Flanagan, the director of the Federal Theatre Project—one of the New Deal programs for subsidizing the arts— invited the European-born John Houseman, who was then in his early thirties, to organize and run a unit of the project in Harlem. Miss Flanagan's first choice had been Rose McClendon, the leading lady of the Harlem stage. Beyond Miss McClendon's prestige as an actress, Miss Flanagan had probably been impressed by a letter she had written to the *Times*. Calling for the establishment of a permanent black theatre—along the lines of the Abbey Theatre, in Dublin —Miss McClendon had said, "Such a theatre could . . . create a tradition that would equal the tradition of any national group," developing "not an isolated Paul Robeson, or an occasional Bledsoe, or Gilpin, but a long line of first-rate actors." But Miss McClendon was in ill health—she died soon after—when Hallie Flanagan invited her to begin such a task, under the auspices of the Federal Theatre. As Miss Flanagan later reported, Miss McClendon had an additional reason for declining the invitation: "At the first meeting in Miss McClendon's house, I asked whether it would not be advisable to have the direction and designing of their project by members of their own race; Miss McClendon felt that since Negroes had always been performers and had had no previous opportunity of learning direction and design, they would prefer to start under more experienced direction." John Houseman, who was suggested by Miss McClendon, accepted the assignment, and set up headquarters in the old Lafayette Theatre.

After restoring the Lafayette to "some semblance of respectability and warmth," as he later said, Houseman assembled a company of some seven hundred actors, singers, dancers, and technicians—the largest number of Harlem theatre people that had ever been at work in any one place. "The Negro Theatre will do plays about Negro life in all its phases, preferably by Negroes," he explained to a reporter in Harlem. "They will produce any play on any subject and of any social and political [orientation], provided it is by a Negro and of competent workmanship." This, it seemed, would surely be the beginning of the black theatre that had never truly existed in Harlem and that Miss McClendon had proposed.

But there was the old problem—one that Houseman was not then familiar with. When he began looking around for plays to produce, he could find few that had been written by blacks. And of those hardly any met his standards of "competent workmanship." How was there to be the black theatre that he and Rose McClendon envisioned if there was neither authentic black material nor black writing of an acceptable quality? Miss McClendon had noted in her letter to the *Times*, "What makes a Negro Theatre is . . . the selection of plays that deal with Negroes, with Negro problems, with phases of Negro life, faithfully presented and accurately delineated. Any other attempt is doomed to failure."

Relaxing his standards somewhat, Houseman turned up a handful of performable black scripts, and with one of these—*Walk Together Chillun*, by Frank Wilson—he inaugurated the Harlem theatre program in February of 1936. His next presentation was *The Conjure Man Dies*, a comic adaptation of the novel by the Harlem Renaissance writer Rudolph Fisher. Yet another of the black plays Houseman presented at the Lafayette was *Haiti*, by William Du Bois, a melodrama based on the lives of Toussaint L'Ouverture and Henri Christophe, who, along with Jean Jacques Dessalines, were the greatest leaders in Haitian history. But despite the program for black theatre that he had earlier outlined, Houseman also believed that there was a place in any theatre company—whatever its ethnic or cultural identity—for "those classical and modern masterpieces that are the common heritage of the English-speaking people." Hence, in later months he also presented Shaw's *Androcles and the Lion*, O'Neill's *S.S. Glencairn*, and an adaptation of *Macbeth*.

Macbeth—"Voodoo Macbeth," people in Harlem called it—was as imaginative and sensational a production as there is in the annals of New York theatre. In Houseman's words, it was "the first full-scale professional Negro Shakespearean production in theatrical history." The author of this extraordinary transformation of the Shakespeare classic was the precocious Orson Welles, then twenty years old. When Houseman invited him to adapt and direct the play for a Harlem audience, Welles responded with the idea of shifting the action from Scotland to the jungles of Haiti during the reign of the black King Christophe. *Macbeth*, of all the Shakespearean dramas, had seemed the most adaptable to the black stage. Welles told Bosley Crowther, of the *Times*, "The stormy career of Christophe, who became 'The Negro King of Haiti,' and ended by killing himself when his cruelty led to a revolt, forms a striking parallel to the history of Macbeth. The costumes and settings are therefore in the period of Haiti's grimmest turbulence. Place names have been altered with particular care to retain the rhythm to Shakespeare's lines. Malcolm and Donalbain don't flee to England but to 'the Coast.'" For his historic all-black dramatis personae, Welles cast Jack Carter as Macbeth, Edna Thomas as Lady Macbeth, Maurice Ellis and Marie Young as the Macduffs, J. Louis Johnson as the Porter, Canada Lee as Banquo, and Eric Burroughs as Hecate. "Our supernatural department was very strong," Houseman recalled several years later, going on to explain, "In addition to the witches and sundry apparitions called for by the Bard, we had a troupe of African drummers. . . . Their first act, after they had been cast . . . was to file a formal requisition for five live black goats. These were brought into the theatre by night and sacrificed, hugger-mugger, according to approved tribal ritual."

Opening night—April 14, 1936—was as impressive as any that Harlem had seen. Marching bands entertained the thousands who gathered in front of the Lafayette to witness the arrival of black and white celebrities. Newsreel and still cameras recorded the scene. According to a Harlem reporter, the first-nighters were "bejewelled, ermined, and top-hatted"—as "smart as any seen at a Gilbert Miller opening." For Houseman and Welles, the next morning's reviews were "a joy to read"—especially the *Times*'s, which said, "As an experiment in Afro-American showmanship, 'Macbeth' merited the excitement that fairly rocked the Lafayette Theatre last night." The play ran for ten weeks in Harlem and eight weeks at the Adelphi Theatre, downtown. It was then taken on the road for extended runs at other W.P.A.-sponsored theatres, in Bridgeport, Hartford, Chicago, Indianapolis, Detroit, Cleveland, and Dallas.

"Voodoo Macbeth" was among the last of Houseman's productions at the Lafayette, and not long after he resigned from the Harlem program; in 1939, the entire Federal Theatre Project came to an end. "As the Great Depression lifted and the economy began to pick up under the stimulus of an approaching war, the Federal Arts projects became superfluous and politically embarrassing," Houseman said later. "The Federal Theatre was liquidated, buried, and largely forgotten in the new excitement of World War II." The legacy of the Federal Theatre Project was not as enriching to theatrical life in Harlem as many participants in the program had hoped. Certainly it did not bring about the national black theatre that had been Rose McClendon's dream. The hundreds of actors, actresses, and other theatre personnel who had found employment at the Lafayette were given few opportunities, in Harlem or elsewhere, to further their careers or develop their talents. This, at any rate, was John Houseman's conclusion when, in his autobiography, he looked back on the results of his work in Harlem:

> Viewed in the perspective of years, my accomplishments with the Negro Theatre seem far from impressive. Theatrically, their final effects were almost nil: Negro playwriting was not appreciably encouraged by our efforts, and Negro actors (with a few notable exceptions) were held, for another twenty years, within the galling bounds of stereotyped roles. The theatre technicians . . . (being excluded from every professional union theatre in America except as cleaners or janitors) went back into other trades. No Negro company came into existence for thirty years after the dissolution of the Federal Theatre and no Negro audience clamored for a continuation of the entertainment they had apparently enjoyed under the auspices of the W.P.A.

Houseman was not entirely correct. At least one important black theatre group came into existence soon after the federal project ended. This was the American Negro Theatre, founded in Harlem in 1940 by the playwright Abram Hill and the actor Frederick O'Neal. Though small and poorly financed, the A.N.T., some of whose performances were staged in the auditorium of the library on West 135th Street, was one of the most distinguished companies ever organized in Harlem. It lasted for eleven years, during which, according to Hill, it "trained over two hundred people," presented "fifteen major and five studio productions," and "attracted some fifty thousand patrons to witness 325 performances." Among its major productions were Hill's *Strivers Row*—satirizing a certain set within Harlem society—and Philip Yordan's *Anna Lucasta*.

The A.N.T.'s importance lies in one of the main objectives it pursued: to destroy the remaining vestiges of minstrelsy and stereotype in black acting, and demonstrate that blacks were capable of portraying human character in all its diversity and complexity. It was quite a task for one small group to accomplish, but the extent to which the A.N.T. achieved its purpose may be judged by the subsequent careers of some of the actors and actresses it helped to discover and develop—such notable additions to the American stage as Frederick O'Neal, Sidney Poitier, Hilda Simms, Harry Belafonte, Earle Hyman, Alice Childress, and Ruby Dee.

Of all the art forms in Harlem, poetry and fiction were the hardest hit by the Depression. By the mid-nineteen-thirties, the lively Harlem Renaissance literary movement of the previous decade had virtually expired—its voices exhausted, dispersed, or fallen into various degrees of silence. About the only member of that movement who remained as active as he had ever been—oblivious of the decline in black literary fortune and celebrity—was Langston Hughes. *The* survivor of the Harlem Renaissance, Hughes went on living and writing in Harlem until his death, in 1967. Rudolph Fisher and Wallace Thurman died in 1934. Nella Larsen resorted to nursing, and disappeared into the obscure expanses of Brooklyn. Jean Toomer, who had not lived in Harlem for any length of time, lapsed into religious mysticism, becoming a follower of Gurdjieff. Eric Walrond—after publishing his impressive book of short fiction *Tropic Death* in 1926 —devoted himself to writing articles and to managing black magazines. Zora Neale Hurston left Harlem for her native South, where— as a novelist and as a cultural anthropologist—she did her best work. Countee Cullen, Arna Bontemps, and Jessie Fauset turned predominantly to teaching, in high schools and colleges. W. E. B. Du Bois

and Alain Locke, the elite critics of the Harlem Renaissance, continued to deliver high cultural judgments, but—perhaps because there
was so much less to judge—with declining authority and influence.
James Weldon Johnson, Walter White, and Claude McKay wrote
mostly autobiography and social history—aging creative men, falling
back, in a dry season, on the gleanings of memory.

The most important young writers in Harlem during the late
thirties—though their best work did not appear until the forties and
fifties—were Richard Wright and Ralph Ellison. (In 1946, Ann
Petry, not as well known, published *The Street*, a novel of Harlem
life.) Wright and Ellison arrived in Harlem toward the end of the
Depression and, for a time, supported themselves by doing research
and writing for the Federal Writers Project. As Jerre Mangione, a
historian of the project, later wrote, "The emergence of Richard
Wright as a top rank novelist, while still a member of the Project,
was the clearest testimony of how the Project could provide a young
writer with the economic means and the psychic stamina he needed
to test his talent. Less known was the Project's contribution to the
literary development of Ralph Ellison, who was a friend of Wright."

When Wright arrived in Harlem, in 1937, he was already a published writer. He had been living in Chicago since 1927, after moving
there from Memphis, where he grew up. He was nineteen when he
came to Chicago, and had taught himself to write by reading, among
other works, Mencken's *A Book of Prefaces*. Wright had begun writing poetry and fiction while working with the Illinois unit of the
Federal Writers Project, and his work had appeared in *Left Front*,
Anvil, and the *New Masses*—periodicals sympathetic to the Communist movement, which he joined in 1932. Upon his arrival in
Harlem, Wright joined the New York unit of the Federal Writers
Project and—at the invitation of James Ford and Benjamin Davis,
two of the city's leading black Communists—became the Harlem
editor of the *Daily Worker*.

One of his first Harlem pieces for the *Worker*—an account of a
Communist Party branch meeting—now stands as a rare snapshot of
Communist activity in Harlem during the thirties:

> Leaving the blare and glare of Lenox Avenue you walk up one
> flight of stairs and enter an obscure room whose walls are covered
> with murals depicting the historical struggles of the Negro in

America. This is the Nat Turner Branch of the Harlem Division of the Communist Party. It was so named in honor of a black slave who died struggling for freedom.

Before you have time to sit down your eyes are drawn to a huge black placard.

IN MEMORY OF OUR BELOVED BROTHER ALONZO WATSON, WHO DIED FIGHTING FOR DEMOCRACY IN SPAIN.

So you know, even before the meeting starts and you hear them talk, that there are people here who will give their lives for what they believe. This Nat Turner Branch has a membership of about 20; and of that 20, 16 were present. . . . 9 women and 7 men. Of the 7 men 2 were white. The Negro men and women were of the working class and manner, accent, and deportment. . . .

As the meeting gets underway you notice that there are no abstractions, no splitting of intellectual hairs. Every word is simple and straight to the point. They are not concerned about whether the world exists or what reality is. They meet here to devise ways and means of changing that world into a more human one. . . .

. . . you learn that two delegates from this branch are to attend a conference on Harlem housing conditions; there are announcements urging members to attend classes to learn public speaking; and there is a call and response for two comrades to picket a department store where a strike is in progress.

Then a startling discussion arises over the American Labor Party. There is no desire here to "grab" the A.L.P. Members are urged to join to help build that organization. . . .

. . . Next they decide to give a lawn party to raise funds to send a comrade to the Workers School.

The comrades are urged to buy and sell tickets to aid the National Hunger March to Washington. . . . "We must support," says the organizer. "We in Harlem know what hunger is."

Petitions demanding of Congress and the state of Alabama the freedom of five remaining Scottsboro Boys are passed around. . . . The meeting is going fast now; they want to get through as soon as they can in order to listen to an educational report on the situation in China.

An open-air meeting is planned on neighborhood problems. . . .

The weakest spot in the entire meeting is the discussion regarding the *Daily* and *Sunday Workers*. The comrade who had been delegated to obtain the *Daily* and deliver it to members of his branch had failed. He tried desperately to shunt his responsibility on to the shoulders of someone else. Hot words flew to and fro. He was finally made to realize that it was his fault and that next time he had to get those papers and deliver them!

A reception for the mothers of the Scottsboro Boys was planned next. From high political issues they went without a change in the tone of the discussion down to ice cream, fried chicken, how to bake a cake, and how to make good punch, etc. A committee was elected to arrange this reception. A "man" comrade refused to serve on this committee on the grounds that it was a "woman's affair," and a "woman" comrade bawled him out with strong words. "What's good for one Communist is good for any Communist," she said.

Party recruiting came next. One member was introduced, a Negro woman worker. She was welcomed unanimously and voted in.

Business over, a white comrade, a student, rose to give a talk on the international scene, with an emphasis on China. . . .

While Wright was turning out reports for the *Worker*, he wrote for himself as well. His first book, *Uncle Tom's Children*—a collection of short fiction, most of it written in Chicago—appeared in 1938. That year, commenting on a five-hundred-dollar prize he had won from the magazine *Story*, he told a reporter in Harlem that he hoped the money would last "until I get my second book completed." It was, he said, "about Chicago—Negro life there," and "it's got to be good, because I want to show that 'Uncle Tom's Children' was no accident." The novel he was completing was the highly acclaimed *Native Son*, which indeed proved that his first book had not been a fluke.

Soon after moving to Harlem, Wright became a friend and something of a mentor to Ellison, his junior by six years. Ellison, a native of Oklahoma City, had been living in New York since the summer of 1936. He had come—as a music major studying the trumpet and classical composition at Tuskegee Institute, in Alabama—to earn tuition and board for the fall term. Failing to earn the required amount, he decided to drop out of school and remain in New York. "At the time, I still thought of myself as a musician," Ellison said later, but since he did not "have enough money to join a union," he turned to other forms of work to support himself. Through Langston Hughes, Ellison was introduced to Wright—having requested the meeting after reading a few of Wright's early poems. "I had been reading lots of modern poetry and works on its technique," Ellison has explained, "and this was the first time *I* had found the spirit and techniques of modern poetry present in a Negro writer." During the friendship that developed, Ellison impressed Wright as being "terribly curious about art, the meaning of experience, and especially Negro experience." In their talks about literature and technique, Wright suggested certain major novels that the younger man might read to see how the great writers achieved their effects. Partly as a result of this relationship, Ellison's first published writing appeared in *New Challenge*, a short-lived literary magazine that Wright found time to edit. By the seriousness with which both men inquired into the problems of literary art and craft, they represented a new and more sophisticated tendency in black writing. They were interested in doing something more than presenting the vigor, the color, and the vicissitudes of black life—the aim of most of their immediate black predecessors. They inclined strongly toward the serious investigation and the studious literary rendering of black American life. And in the early stages of their relationship Wright may have been as inspiring a literary influence on Ellison as any that later entered Ellison's life. *Native Son*, Wright's major work—parts of which Ellison had read in manuscript—was published in 1940. No black novel of a similar stature appeared until 1952, when Ellison published his justly praised *Invisible Man* (much of it set in Harlem), a less militant exploration of its subject but one that was even more thoughtful and searching than *Native Son* had attempted to be.

In the Ring with Joe

To HARLEMITES in the middle and late thirties, Joe Louis was easily the most heroic figure in America. Naturally, this had much to do with the fact of his color. He was the best black heavyweight boxer to have come upon the scene since the days of Jack Johnson; indeed, he was the outstanding prizefighter, black or white, of his generation. Still, Louis's effect upon the imagination of Harlemites would not have been as inspiring as it was if the rising arc of his career and fame—his succession of triumphs in the ring, each more important than the previous one—had not coincided with a low point in the fortunes of black Americans. That low point was, of course, simultaneous with the Great Depression. During those years, neither Father Divine, with his free banquets for blacks, nor Franklin D. Roosevelt, with his New Deal, managed to lift the spirits of suffering Harlemites as much as Joe Louis did. Louis's achievements in the ring did not, of course, shorten the bread lines of Harlem or bring an end to blacks' social and economic miseries. They did, however, make those miseries easier to bear. As the most conspicuously successful member of his race during those hard times, Louis was adopted as a champion of his people's cause—a representative of their aspirations and a reassuring example of their potentialities in American life.

This is not to say that Joe Louis belonged to Harlemites alone. He did not even live in the community. But Harlem was where he usually stayed when he came to New York for one of his fights or on one of his social visits, and Harlem, the Negro capital of the world, was doubtless the urban community in which he gained the strongest sense of what he meant to blacks as a whole. This sense, however, never became a source of conceit. Though he was mobbed whenever he appeared in Harlem—whether he was out for a leisurely stroll or was attending some important public event—he seemed far less conscious of his celebrity than his admirers were. But from the patience with which he surrendered himself to their attention it was evident that he well understood their emotional and psychological need to make something special of his example. He was twenty-one in 1935—gloriously young, broodingly handsome, and tantalizingly inarticulate and taciturn. Women, of whatever social class, found him irresistible—regardless of the fact that he was already linked to a long train of steady lady friends. "For the benefit of some Harlem lovelies," a newspaper up there announced at one point, "Joe Louis is due in Harlem next week." He "is magnetic and disturbing," a Harlem society columnist declared to her female readers. She added, "He upsets your apple cart of what the socially trained gentleman should do. But you like it.... Joe Louis gets in your hair."

He was just as inspiring to prominent public figures in Harlem whose lives and careers showed little or no sign of being hurt by the Depression. The 15,000 blacks who showed up at Yankee Stadium for Louis's fight with Primo Carnera, in June of 1935 included such Harlem notables as Dr. C. B. Powell, the co-publisher of the *Amsterdam News*; Ferdinand Q. Morton, a New York Municipal Civil Service Commissioner; Hubert Delaney, the New York City Tax Commissioner; Harry Bragg, the Assistant Attorney General of New York; Walter White, the Secretary of the N.A.A.C.P.; William T. Andrews, a State Assemblyman; Dr. Louis T. Wright, a surgeon to the New York City Police Department; Adam Clayton Powell, Jr., assistant pastor of the Abyssinian Baptist Church; and Duke Ellington and Claude Hopkins, bandleaders. That night, when Louis, who had then had twenty-two fights as a professional and had won them all, knocked out Carnera, a giant of a man who had once held the heavyweight championship of the world, Harlem was more jubilant than it had been over any previous public event. The community was jubilant again when, a few months later, he quickly disposed of Max Baer—also a former heavyweight champion—at Yankee Stadium. But there were to be fluctuations in this kind of emotion, for Louis did not win every time he fought, and did not always dispatch his opponents with the swiftness and power that his black following had come to expect and demand. For instance, Harlemites were both stunned and crushed when, in June of 1936, at Yankee Stadium, Louis was knocked out by Max Schmeling, of Germany—his first loss as a professional. The thought that he might be vincible had simply never entered their minds. A couple of months later, in a letter to the editor of the *Age*—which was then the leading newspaper in Harlem —a resident of the community recalled "that fateful night when millions of . . . shocked listeners heard the unbelievable words in the fourth round, 'Louis is down for the first time in his fistic career,' and then in the twelfth, 'Max Schmeling, winner.' " The writer continued, "For a moment, I was paralyzed. Then I suddenly rose and rushed from the room to keep from bursting into tears. When I reached my bedroom, I was weak, and my eyes were blurred. It was a terrible nightmare." Of that nightmare, a black sports columnist wrote, "Yes, sir, all Harlem is mourning." How could Joe have lost, have let his black supporters down? In exploring that question, the columnist took note of a rumor then sweeping Harlem—that Joe, who had recently married the lovely Marva Trotter, had, to the detriment of his training, spent too much time in the company of his new bride. But the columnist dismissed the rumor as a "cruel attack upon Mrs. Louis." Whatever the reasons for his poor performance against Schmeling, Louis atoned for it two months later, when he knocked out Jack Sharkey, at Yankee Stadium. "Joe Louis is king again," a newspaper in Harlem proclaimed.

In June of 1937, Louis scored his most important victory: by knocking out Jim Braddock, at Comiskey Park, in Chicago, he became the heavyweight champion of the world. Switching off their radios, some hundred thousand Harlemites poured into the streets in celebration—beating drums, blowing horns, ringing cowbells, drinking and partying far into the next morning. In Harlem, perhaps only Jack Johnson was not so deeply impressed. Johnson may have envied the growing popularity of the younger man; in any event, he never had much good to say about Louis's ability as a boxer. In 1908, Johnson had become the first member of his race to win the heavyweight championship of the world; and, at what was then a relatively primitive stage of American race relations—another time when Negroes desperately needed victories of any sort—Johnson had been an idol of blacks. Now that Louis had joined him in the history books, Johnson was believed not only to envy the new champion but to resent him as well.

However, in August of 1937, at Yankee Stadium, Louis, in narrowly outpointing Tommy Farr, barely looked like the heavyweight champion he was supposed to be. This was another letdown for his supporters in Harlem, since the only victories of his that thrilled them—the only ones that justified the emotional investment they had made in him—were those he scored by a knockout. Again looking around for a scapegoat, they settled this time upon Louis's trainers, and accused them of tampering with Joe's natural flair for aggressive boxing in an attempt to convert the Brown Bomber into a defensive fighter. "A clever defense requires fast thinking, and this Joe cannot do," one writer in Harlem said. A punch that had been aimed at Louis's handlers had landed on Joe instead. But all that was soon forgotten.

Louis's return bout with Max Schmeling, in June of 1938, was a racial and political incident of international significance. War clouds were then gathering in Europe, and, over here, the German challenger—viewed as a representative of the Nazi regime—was linked to Hitler's doctrines of anti-Semitism and Aryan supremacy. Upon Joe Louis fell the task of upholding the American experience and the democratic way of life. There were ironies in this, to be sure. On a visit to the White House during the closing years of the Depression —in which blacks had suffered greater hardships than any other group in the nation—Louis was reminded by President Roosevelt, "Joe, we're depending on those muscles for America." And, as Louis later recalled, almost all Americans were pulling for him "to K.O. Germany"—even those who "still were lynching black people in the South." At all events, in the fight, at Yankee Stadium, Louis swiftly vindicated all the hopes that the nation had reposed in him, by knocking out Schmeling a little more than two minutes into the first round. If white Americans breathed a sign of relief—feeling that what was best in their values had been successfully defended— blacks did not hesitate to take full credit for the achievement. Joe Louis "has conquered the world," a writer in Harlem commented, and this victory was celebrated still more wildly up there than any of the previous ones had been. While there was the usual high-spirited revelry in the bars and night clubs, emotions in the streets boiled over into a near-riot. Scuffles broke out, stones and other missiles were thrown, buses and private vehicles were attacked. Of all this, the police took as lenient a view as possible. They made few arrests, their commissioner having instructed them to let Harlem have a good time. But the old-fashioned and upstanding gentlemen who ran the *Age* were not so lenient. Severely embarrassed by the disorderly display, the paper said in an editorial, "Joe Louis not only represents his race, but, as world champion, represents the United States. . . . Those of his own race can harm him with their overenthusiasm."

In any case, Louis suffered other hurts as well, not all of which were caused by the overenthusiasm of his race—and hardly any of which showed through his invincible combination of reticence and nobility. One instance occurred in 1942, when the champion who had quickened the pride of his nation reported to Camp Upton, New York, for his induction into the Army. All recognition of his exceptional status ended as soon as he stepped from the chauffeur-driven limousine that had taken him to the induction center. He himself, with characteristic dispassion, put it this way: "They gave me my uniform and sent me over to the colored section." There were no reports in the Harlem papers of how Louis was treated when he arrived at Camp Upton, but hardly any black American would have been surprised to learn of his reception. It was one of the traditional ceremonies of an Army that would soon be fighting abroad in the name, once more, of democracy and human dignity. During what remained of his life, however—as in much of what had gone before—Louis showed by his conduct that his spirit was not confined to "the colored section" but inhabited those broader areas of American experience which were shared by all men and women of civility and good will.

Another War, Another Time

As THE First World War had done, the Second confronted blacks with one of the historic problems of their citizenship—whether and how to fight abroad in defense of freedoms that were denied them at home. And, not surprisingly, there were in the early forties many Harlemites who wanted little or nothing to do with military service. Many of those who enlisted would fight in the cause of the "Double V"—victory abroad and victory at home. Still, there was considerably less resistance to this war effort than there had been to the one in 1917, when an organized movement of young Harlem intellectuals campaigned fiercely and openly against black enlistment of any sort. *Life* found in 1942 that there was "no place in the nation where civil defense is now a more burning topic than in Harlem." At least a quarter of the Harlem residents were "doing some kind of war work," it said, with some fifteen thousand enrolled as air-raid wardens, and thousands of women "learning first aid, knitting sweaters, serving in canteens, studying internal-combustion engines." *Life* also noted that even prostitutes had been seen wearing the white arm bands of air-raid wardens; but that the police—uncertain which cause the ladies were truly serving—had soon put a stop to that.

Of the Harlemites who wanted litttle or nothing to do with the war, the black playwright Loften Mitchell wrote, "Irritated black people argued that when colored Ethiopia was attacked, Uncle Sam hadn't raced to her defense, but when white Europe was in trouble, Uncle was right there." He added, "Others declared openly they were not going to fight for colonial England, colonial France, and jim crow America." A 1943 article in *The Nation* said of Harlem, "The people there have asked the question, 'What will the war bring us?' The answer, as most of them see it, is 'Nothing.' They still want the United States to win but only casually. They are for the United

Nations [the Allied forces] as a matter of form but their hearts aren't in it."

There were at least two other reasons that such Harlemites were cool toward the war effort, and one of them was the survival of racial segregation in the armed forces. In 1942, the *Age* printed this letter from a twenty-four-year-old solider:

> Hope with me that I shall see, before another 24 years, a second Emancipation Proclamation from prejudice; from prejudice by these part-time Americans who . . . are tearing to tatters and ripping to rags the American flag's meaning of equality. . . .
>
> I wish this was a mixed Army. Then we Americans could actually be fighting side by side, shoulder to shoulder, skin for skin. Then I could easily glare at the Japs and grit: this is my country, my native land . . .

The other reason was the exclusion of black workers from the munitions industry, at least until late 1941, although for a while before America entered the war the nation's defense plants had been busy building ships, tanks, planes, and guns for the European Allies. More than twenty years later, the magazine *American Labor* reported:

> It had been announced that 250,000 workers would be absorbed in supplying defense needs, but there was little place for Negro workers, regardless of training. The president of North American Aviation set forth the industry's thinking in a press interview, declaring that "regardless of training, we will not employ Negroes in the North American plant. It is against company policy." Standard Steel Corporation told the Kansas City Urban League: "We have not had a Negro worker in twenty-five years, and do not plan to start now."

That policy began to change, however slightly, only after A. Philip Randolph, of the Brotherhood of Sleeping Car Porters, used the Harlem headquarters of his union to mobilize more than a hundred thousand blacks, with a view to leading them on a protest march to Washington. Alarmed by the possible effects of such a gathering in the nation's capital, President Roosevelt made the demonstration unnecessary. After a meeting with Randolph and other black figures at the White House, he issued one of his more historic executive orders, declaring that as a matter of national policy "there shall be no discrimination in the employment of workers in defense industries." The barriers to black workers in defense plants did not suddenly or wholly collapse, but an important breaching of those barriers had occurred. Nor was it until 1948, following another of Randolph's publicized confrontations with the White House, that the President, then Harry Truman, ordered that the armed forces end their policy of racial segregation.

One result of Randolph's March-on-Washington campaign during the early forties was that he joined Adam Clayton Powell, Jr., as one of the two most popular political figures in Harlem. Each had a wide following and a distinct type of mass appeal. Randolph's appeal sprang from a recognition of his personal integrity and from his long association—in Harlem and at the national level—with working-class and civil-rights causes. "Randolph more nearly fills the bill of being the Negro's national leader than anyone else in recent years," a Harlem newspaper columnist wrote in 1944. Powell's appeal stemmed chiefly from his colorful and scrappy personality, his position as the leader of a major black church, and his own achievements as an activist in behalf of the Harlem masses. His characteristic style undoubtedly won him as much admiration as did any other aspect of his life or conduct. Some years later, the *Post* described him as "the matinee idol of the pulpit," going on to say that Powell dressed, talked, and acted "like a Broadway dandy," displayed "his joy in creature comforts," and loved "sleek sports cars . . . beautiful clothes, good Bordeaux wines, and, of course, *haute cuisine*." He lost none of his popular appeal when, in November of 1944, the *Age* published this item about him:

> Charging that a nightclub performer had superseded her in her husband's affections, Mrs. Isabel Washington Powell filed suit in Supreme Court on Monday for separation from Rev. Adam Clayton Powell, Jr. . . . The suit put at rest a series of rumors that had been bruited about Harlem and café society for some time that the Rev. Powell had tired of his wife, who left the stage eleven years ago to become his mate, and was asking her to grant him a divorce so that he could marry Hazel Scott, 23-year-old swing pianist and torch singer. . . .
> Mrs. Powell asserted . . . that Rev. Powell . . . had accused her

of being unsympathetic to his political ambitions and had asked her . . . to divorce him. . . . "He stated that my actions toward him had driven him to the arms of another woman and that he could no longer live with me. . . . Only recently did I learn why he tossed me aside. It was because of his infatuation for this nightclub performer. . . ."

Reporters who saw Hazel Scott at the Cafe Society Uptown quoted her as identifying herself as the woman in the case. She said that "if the day comes that he is free, I think that I'll be an extremely lucky girl to be his wife."

Months later, when Powell took the jazz pianist as his bride, his supporters thought nothing of it—not even of the fact that he, a native-born American, had married a West Indian.

Powell's popularity had been growing since 1931, when, as his father's assistant, he administered the Depression-relief program at the Abyssinian Baptist Church. That year, by leading a protest march on City Hall, he brought about the reinstatement of five black doctors who had been fired from Harlem Hospital. In 1932, he was an active member of one of many committees formed to support the defense of the Scottsboro Boys—nine black youths in Alabama who had been sentenced to death on a charge of raping two white girls on a freight train. In 1934, Powell—along with John Johnson, the pastor of St. Martin's Episcopal Church, and Sufi Hamid, a radical labor agitator —led a boycott against department stores along 125th Street ("Don't Buy Where You Can't Work") which forced these stores to end their policy of refusing to hire black salesmen and saleswomen. In the late nineteen-thirties, Powell headed a group called the Greater New York Coordinating Committee, which won jobs for blacks in Consolidated Edison, the New York Telephone Company, and a number of bottling and pharmaceutical enterprises. Such deeds and accomplishments left no doubt that he had extended the ministry of the Abyssinian Baptist Church further into the realm of social action than his father had done. In summary, as the journalist Roi Ottley was to write of him, Powell was "an incredible combination of showman, black parson, and Tammany Hall . . . a salvationist and a politician, an economic messiah and a super-opportunist, an important mass leader and a lighthearted playboy . . . the new and different kind of leader that the Negro church has produced."

In 1941, Powell was swept into office, as Harlem's first black member of the City Council since that body was called the Board of Aldermen. In 1943, Benjamin Davis succeeded him in the office when Powell declined to seek reelection. The lines of New York's Twenty-second Congressional District had recently been redrawn, making it virtually certain that in 1944 a black candidate would be elected to the House of Representatives, and Powell wanted very much to become the first black congressman from Harlem.

For that office, Harlem had only two serious candidates in mind—Powell and Randolph. Powell, a registered Democrat, was backed by the Tammany Hall machine as well as by his large mass following in Harlem. Randolph, who turned fifty-five in 1944, (he was Powell's senior by nineteen years), had no regular party affiliation—if anything, he was still a Norman Thomas Socialist—but was favored by a large nonpartisan coalition that wished to draft him into the campaign. Besides, as a Harlem journal reported, the Republicans and "the strong anti-Powell bloc in the Democratic ranks" were prepared to throw their support to Randolph "the minute he consents to become the candidate." After giving the matter some thought, however—and consulting officers of his union, some of whom disliked the idea of his candidacy—Randolph decided against running. He did not "wish to become involved in the entanglements of politics," he announced to his supporters, adding, "While I've been assured that I would have no partisan alliances that would tie my hands, I am constrained to believe that the law of compensation demands and requires that there be a payoff somewhere down the road in some form or another." To those who had organized vigorously in his behalf, this came as a shock, almost a betrayal of their cause and of their faith in him. "By preferring to remain as Randolph the idealist," one of his supporters wrote in the Harlem press, "Randolph has done himself no good . . . and even his best friends agree with his enemies, who are now pointing the finger at him and saying: 'Randolph let us down.'" Powell was elected, and remained Harlem's only black congressman for nearly a quarter of a century. The year after his son's election, the senior Powell wrote of Randolph, "Financially, he will doubtlessly die a poor man but he will be immeasurably rich in all the attributes that make genuine manhood." The prediction was as accurate as the tribute was generous.

Harlem Explodes

ON THE evening of August 1, 1943, Harlem erupted into the worst disturbance that had ever occurred in the community. It was a Sunday, and the afternoon had been sunny and tranquil. The day—as a visiting writer observed—had been marked by music and laughter. Neighbors and friends had conversed amiably on front stoops. Mothers had gently steered baby carriages along the sidewalks. And young lovers, arm in arm, had strolled contentedly up and down the avenues. It was, the visitor later said, "a reassuring picture."

At around seven that evening, James Collins, a white policeman, was stationed in the lobby of the Hotel Braddock, on 126th Street near Eighth Avenue. Not surprisingly—for the Braddock was known to be a haunt of unruly elements—his attention was called to a dispute between the hotel management and a female guest. She had registered there a short time earlier but had found the accommodations unsatisfactory and had decided to leave. Having spent scarcely any time there, she approached the managment to say that she was entitled to a refund of all payments she had made; when her demand was refused, she exploded loudly and lengthily into profanity. At this point, Patrolman Collins told her that she was disturbing the peace, and ordered her to desist. She refused to comply, he attempted to place her under arrest, and, in the struggle that followed, Robert Bandy—a black soldier who was visiting the hotel—intervened in her behalf. Wresting away Collins' nightstick, Bandy struck him over the head with it, wounding him, and ran from the hotel. The policeman fired his revolver at Bandy, hitting him in the left shoulder. He then took Bandy into custody and, with a crowd following, marched him to Sydenham Hospital, not far away.

While both men were having their wounds attended to, the crowd in front of the hospital grew steadily larger and angrier—augmented by passersby who were told that a white cop had shot a black soldier.

A sullen crowd on a hot summer's evening made for as ominous a chemistry as can exist in Harlem, and it was not long before the reaction began. When no word came from the hospital concerning the state of the wounded men, someone in the crowd imagined the worst and shouted that the soldier was probably dead. At this, a bottle was sent crashing against a wall of the hospital, unleashing a stampede of emotions.

The people dispersed through the streets and avenues, breaking store windows and spreading word that a white cop had shot and killed a black soldier, and thousands of other Harlemites poured out of their homes and joined the uprising. Business places were sacked, cars were overturned and set on fire, and policemen and firemen were stoned. During the rampage, Mayor Fiorello LaGuardia toured the streets in a sound truck, appealing for an end to the disorder, but scarcely anyone listened to him, even though in Harlem at that time he was the most respected and admired white New York political figure. Important black leaders came out to join in the appeal for calm, with no more success. One of them, Walter White, the executive secretary of the National Association for the Advancement of Colored People, said later that their pleas "were greeted with raucous shouts of disbelief, frequently couched in language as violent as the action of the window-smashers."

The disorder raged through the night, till sunrise on Monday. Very little then remained in most business places. Millions of dollars' worth of merchandise—furniture, rugs, bed linen, food, liquor, jewelry, clothing, cosmetics: almost everything that the looters were able to move—had been cleaned out and carried away. According to the *Post*, "clothes, dirty wash, canned goods, milk bottles, loaves of bread, and smashed liquor bottles littered the streets." Several hundred people were arrested—including youths who were strutting about in the top hats and tails they had stolen. Hundreds more were wounded—victims of police clubbing or shooting, or of lacerations they had suffered in forcing themselves through jagged openings in show windows. At least six deaths were reported. Adam Clayton Powell, Sr., said later that the riot was "the hottest hell ever created in Harlem."

August 2, 1943, the morning after the riot, was the nineteenth birthday of James Baldwin. Of all the well-known writers that black

Harlem had helped to produce, he was the first one born and raised in the community. *Go Tell It on the Mountain,* a novel he published ten years later, remains the best fictional account of storefront religion uptown. And in other forms of writing he evoked qualities of Harlem life with a vexed eloquence that the community had inspired in no previous writer. His father, a preacher from the South, had migrated to the North after 1919, the year some of the bloodiest race riots in the nation's history broke out in Washington, D.C.; Charleston, South Carolina; and other major cities—riots in which black soldiers, recently returned from fighting in France, were attacked with no regard for the uniforms they wore. A proud and sternly uncompromising man, the elder Baldwin had not found much relief in Harlem from the social and racial pains he had suffered in the South. He continued to harbor a deep rage against the conditions of American life that denied him the status he knew to be his right. By his acquaintances and by James, his eldest son, he was remembered as being "ingrown, like a toenail." Yet, for all his refusal to surrender the vision he held of himself, he was by no means sympathetic to what his oldest son wished to become—a writer instead of a minister. He died on July 29, 1943—the day the last of his children was born, three days before the worst outbreak of rioting that Harlem had yet seen, and four days before the nineteenth birthday of the son whose choice of a career he had disputed but whose best work, a brilliant fusion of writing and sermonizing, soon earned for the family name a distinguished place in the literature of moral protest.

"On the morning of the 3rd of August," James Baldwin later wrote in one of his major essays, "we drove my father to the graveyard through a wilderness of smashed plate glass. . . . As we drove . . . the spoils of injustice, anarchy, discontent, and hatred were all around us. It seemed to me that God himself had devised, to mark my father's end, the most sustained and brutally dissonant of codas." Surveying the remains of that coda, Baldwin went on to say:

> I truly had not realized that Harlem *had* so many stores until I saw them all smashed open; the first time the word *wealth* ever entered my mind in relation to Harlem was when I saw it scattered in the streets. But one's first, incongruous impression of plenty was countered immediately by an impression of waste. None of this was doing anybody any good. It would have been better

to have left the plate glass as it had been and the goods lying in the stores.

It would have been better, but it would also have been intolerable, for Harlem had needed something to smash.

Notwithstanding the poetry and irony surrounding the rage that Baldwin describes, a question remained: Why had Harlem needed something to smash? At the time, there were almost as many answers as there were experts. Some argued that it was in the very nature of ghetto dwellers to smash. Others blamed the uprising on the legacy of the Depression, on social and racial oppression, on commercial exploitation, on the unskilled and unlettered migrants from the rural South who were unable to meet the demands of urban living, or on common thieves and criminals. Roy Wilkins, of the N.A.A.C.P., confined his answer to the incident that had sparked the riot—an incident that, in his view, reawakened indignation over the treatment of black American soldiers during wartime. He wrote in the magazine *The Crisis*:

> A soldier in uniform was shot by a policeman in Harlem. . . .
> Negro soldiers have been shot down by civilian police in Alexandria, La., in Little Rock, Ark., in Baltimore, Md., in Beaumont, Texas, and in a half dozen other places. They have been humiliated, manhandled, and beaten in countless instances.

Wilkins concluded, "The Harlem mob knew all this. It hated all this. It could not reach the Arkansas cop who fired a full magazine of his revolver into the prone body of a Negro sergeant, or any of the others, so it tore up Harlem."

The West Indians

IN THE nineteen-thirties, more than twenty per cent of Harlem's black population were people from the West Indies. They were a vocal and assertive minority, and came from such islands as Anguilla, Antigua, the Bahamas, Bermuda, British Guiana (not an island, but one of the northern territories of South America), Dominica, Grenada, Haiti (which shared an island with the Dominican Republic), Jamaica, Martinique, Montserrat, Nevis, St. Croix, St. Kitts, St. Lucia, St. Thomas, St. Vincent, Trinidad, and Tobago. Some of these were French, Dutch, and Scandinavian territories, but the majority were British. Though the West Indians were predominantly black, they were not always united as an immigrant group. They clung to the regional and insular attitudes of their particular backgrounds, and there were almost as many rivalries among them as there were between them and the majority of black Americans in Harlem—who viewed the West Indians with a mixture of reserve and resentment. It was chiefly on this occasion—when the West Indians were bunched together by American blacks and attacked as foreigners and outsiders—that they tended to close ranks, especially the ones who, despite their insular differences, realized that they were all products of British colonial experience.

It is not surprising that black Americans in Harlem should have viewed West Indians in the manner that they did. As a writer for the *Herald Tribune* observed in 1930, the native-born black was "a distinctly American product," and shared "the white American's scorn for foreigners of any kind." And, according to *The Saturday Evening Post*, in 1925, West Indians were "notably lacking in the Southern Negro's diplomacy," made "lots of noise about their rights," and were "very quick to go to court—the last place on earth the Southern Negro seeks." In some other ways, West Indians also behaved like the aliens black Americans saw them to be. "West Indian Harlem,"

Langston Hughes once said, was "warm, rambunctious, sassy . . . little pockets of tropical dreams in alien tongues." West Indians did not readily defer to the native-born blacks among whom they lived. In fact, they often carried on as if they considered themselves superior to their black American brothers and sisters—though the latter, especially when they listened to some of the "thick" and singsong West Indian accents, did not hesitate to reciprocate feelings of superiority.

In Harlem, many West Indians from the British territories still flew Union Jacks from their business places and apartment windows. Some of the men (dressed in white boots, cream flannels, and schoolboy caps) went every summer afternoon up to Van Cortlandt Park to play their games of cricket—as white and as alien a game as black Americans could imagine. And how were native-born blacks to feel about the following example of West Indian behavior? On a Wednesday night of May 1937, some five thousand West Indians in Harlem turned out for a ball to celebrate the coronation of King George VI. Ticket prices for the affair had been advertised in English currency—12s/6d (twelve shillings and sixpence) and 8s/4d. Part of the ball took the form of a pageant, in which the coronation ceremony—held earlier in London—was reenacted, and a reporter from *The New Yorker* wrote this account:

> Dr. Murcot Wilshire, lay reader at St. Ambrose [acted] as the Archbishop of Canterbury. The prettiest and best-dressed lady present, Miss Ulrica Baird, was chosen as Queen. The King was Gordon Ward, much darker than his consort. . . . He wore red knee breeches and a close-fitting scarlet coat, while she was dressed from head to foot in white satin, with a flowing train. Everybody sang "God Save the King" and "Rule Britannia," after which Dr. Wilshire solemnly administered the oath. Then the couple were crowned, the Queen receiving a smaller but no less glittering crown than the King.

While the majority of black American churchgoers in Harlem were Methodists, Baptists, and storefront evangelicals, most West Indians (like Dr. Wilshire, of St. Ambrose) were Episcopalians—though some were Methodists and Baptists as well, and others were Catholics and Moravians. Nor, as the Greater New York Federation of Churches reported in 1930, were West Indians "averse to having a white pastor," since they had been "accustomed to it in the islands from which they came." Like most immigrants, West Indians in Harlem remained fond of their native cuisine, and many of the foods they cooked were obtained from markets that imported such provisions from the different islands.

And though certain West Indian traits were grudgingly admired, they still raised resentful questions among many black Americans. Why, for instance, were the West Indians so ambitious and enterprising? Why did they seem to seek employment in areas where many black Americans did not? Why didn't they seem to realize they were taking jobs away from native-born blacks? And why were so many of them in business, in the skilled trades, and in the professions? Perhaps only a West Indian could answer these questions, as W. A. Domingo, a Jamaican-born journalist, did during the twenties:

> Coming to the United States from countries in which they had experienced no legalised social or occupational disabilities, West Indians very naturally have found it difficult to adapt themselves to the tasks that are, by custom, reserved for Negroes in the North. Skilled at various trades and having a contempt for body service and menial work, many of the immigrants apply for positions that the average American Negro has been schooled to regard as restricted to white men only, with the result that through their persistence and doggedness in fighting white labor, West Indians have in many cases been pioneers and shock troops to open the way for Negroes into new fields of employment. . . .
>
> It is safe to say that West Indian representation in the skilled trades is relatively large; this is also true of the professions, especially medicine and dentistry.

"Black Jews" was one of the epithets frequently used to describe West Indians in Harlem. Even *The Saturday Evening Post* had had occasion to observe that West Indians took to business "as though it were a racial genius." And even W. A. Domingo had had to admit that his fellow West Indians were, "like the Jew . . . forever launching out in business." As he went on to say, "such retail businesses as are in the hands of Negroes in Harlem are largely in the control of the foreign born." *Largely* may have been an exaggeration, however. West Indians were, after all, in the minority, and only a small percentage of them could have been entrepreneurs. Though, for their numbers, West Indians were heavily represented in Harlem business ventures, it is likely that black Americans, being the large majority, were more heavily represented. But it is true that West Indians ran many of the black-owned drugstores and grocery stores. In the nineteen-thirties, the Antillean Realty Company—headed by A. A. Austin, from Antigua—was the biggest company of its kind in Harlem. "In no other land that we know of," the *Age* later said of Austin, "could an immigrant and a Negro have achieved such success." Howard A. Howell, from Barbados, owned one of Harlem's more prestigious funeral parlors, and was perhaps the leading mortician for the well-to-do. P. M. H. Savory, a physician from British Guiana, was a co-publisher of the *Amsterdam News* (along with Dr. C. B. Powell, a black American), a partner in the Victory Mutual Life Insurance Company, and head of the Community Financial Corporation—all based in Harlem. Casper Holstein, from the Virgin Islands, was Harlem's most prosperous numbers banker during the twenties—before Dutch Schultz and other white mobsters took control of the policy racket uptown. And several other West Indians were prominent in one form of business or another.

In the thirties and forties, about a third of all professional men and women in Harlem were either West Indians or of West Indian parentage. In 1931, James S. Watson, a Jamaican, became New York's first black municipal judge. Claude McKay (from Jamaica) and Eric Walrond (from British Guiana) had been leading writers during the Harlem Renaissance. During the First World War and the early twenties, West Indians—Hubert Harrison and Cyril Briggs, from the Virgin Islands; Richard B. Moore, from Barbados; W. A. Domingo and Marcus Garvey, from Jamaica—had been among the main forces behind the growth of left-wing and black nationalist agitation in Harlem. Ashley Totten and Frank Crosswaith, from the Virgin Islands, and T. Thomas Patterson, from Jamaica, worked closely with A. Philip Randolph in his struggle to organize and win recognition for the Brotherhood of Sleeping Car Porters—the most significant black trade union that had yet been formed in the United States; working from within the A.F.L.–C.I.O., it did more than any other group to reduce discrimination against blacks in the organized-labor movement. Though W. E. B. Du Bois and James Weldon Johnson were not West Indians, they claimed West Indian parentage.

And in 1827, long before blacks thought of moving to Harlem, John B. Russwurm, a Jamaican living in New York, founded *Freedom's Journal*, the first important black newspaper published in the United States. The black American historian Carter G. Woodson must have been thinking of some of these West Indian examples—in Harlem and elsewhere—when he wrote in 1931: "In proportion to their numbers in this country, the West Indians have made a much larger contribution to the higher striving of the race here than native Negroes of the United States."

Among most Harlemites, this fact, if it was generally known, did not appreciably soften the feelings about West Indians as pushy foreigners and outsiders. According to Adam Clayton Powell, Jr., West Indians "forged ahead faster than the rest" and were regarded with "envious scorn." Powell also said, "The same feeling the average white bigot has when a Catholic marries a Jew was the experience of Harlem Town when a West Indian married an American black." In 1931, a graduate student at Columbia observed that "West Indian Negroes are likened to the Jews." He continued, "Thrifty, ambitious, and consistent, the 'monkey chasers' [as some native-born blacks called West Indians] became competitors of the Southern Negroes in the professions, businesses, trades, and other vocations. The Southern Negroes regard these alien rivals with distrust. On jobs where Southern Negroes have control, every effort is made to keep out the too aggressive British West Indian Negroes." And, addressing a gathering in Harlem in 1934, the journalist Robert L. Vann declared, "If you West Indians don't like how we do things in this country you should go back where you came from; we Americans won't tolerate your butting into our affairs. We are good and tired of you. . . . there should be a law deporting the whole lot of you; failing that, you should be run out of Harlem." Vann's fury was doubtless aroused by a tendency among West Indians to feel that, in matters of race relations, they were either more militant or more enlightened than black Americans. This was hard to accept from a group which—no matter how noisy they were about black pride and black political rights—were in no hurry to surrender their West Indian citizenship. The view among their critics in Harlem was that while they enjoyed the privileges of residency they were content to shirk the burdens and responsibilities of American citizenship. Some had indeed become citizens, but others preferred to ally themselves with the many West Indian organizations in Harlem that worked to preserve their cultural and regional identities.

Not all of Harlem's West Indians and black Americans were in conflict, however. Many of them made and maintained friendships, socialized joyously, or waged political struggles together. And some West Indians scolded their fellow islanders for clinging to their native organizations and attitudes, or for being critical of a country to which they had all come in search of economic betterment.

As any number of people in Harlem realized, the jealousies and animosities between West Indians and black Americans were absurd, especially since they shared common problems as a non-white group. According to Nancy Cunard, they were always "falling out about empty 'superiorities' and 'inferiorities,' forgetting the white enemy." And it was the silliness of all this that had caused a West Indian journalist to write: "West Indian Negroes, you are oppressed. American Negroes, you are equally oppressed. West Indians, you are black. Americans, you are black. It is your color upon which white men pass judgment, not your merits, nor the geographical line between you. Stretch hands across the seas."

PART SIX

Style, Class, and Beyond

At the Savoy

THE Savoy Ballroom, on Lenox Avenue, was the largest dance hall in Harlem, and one of its great centers of popular style. It was opened in 1926, and occupied the second floor of a building that took up the entire block front from 140th Street to 141st. Saturday nights and Sunday nights were the liveliest of the week. On those nights, the dance floor was shared by all and sundry, including white stars of stage and screen from downtown. One of them, Lana Turner, is said to have nicknamed the Savoy the Home of the Happy Feet—a name that stuck, and that circulated far and wide. To most Harlemites, however—especially the ones who danced there every night of the week—the Savoy was the Track, the home of the Lindy Hop.

The ballroom was not open on August 1, 1943, the Sunday night when the rioters tore up Harlem. Some time earlier, the police, ill at ease with the Savoy's interracial gatherings, had closed it down temporarily. This act was assigned an excessive influence when certain social workers began their study of why the riot had occurred—a number of them concluding that the disturbance might not have taken place if the Savoy had been open. In other words, the Harlemites involved would, in all likelihood, have been out dancing instead. Silly as such a conclusion was, it did underscore the importance and popularity of the Savoy as a social institution in Harlem.

The Savoy was by no means the only well-attended dance hall uptown. But it was the greatest of them all—Harlem's shrine of the public dance, where the best of the big and swinging bands of the late twenties, the thirties, and the forties were to be heard. *Ebony* reported in 1946 that the Savoy cost about half a million dollars a year to operate, that it took in around a million dollars a year, and that in the twenty years of its existence "28 million feet stomped" there.

The Savoy was owned by Moe Gale, a white impresario, and managed by Charles Buchanan, a black Harlem businessman. *The Savoy Story*, a booklet commemorating the ballroom's twenty-fifth anniversary, records that it was "the booming business at Broadway's famous Roseland and Arcadia ballrooms" that inspired Moe Gale to launch "a similar 'million dollar' *palais de danse*" in Harlem. What to call the block-long building that he put up on Lenox Avenue was a problem that faced Gale and his business associate, Charles Buchanan. They considered and rejected names like Paradise, Avalon, Trianon, Palladium, Cinderella, and Dreamland. None of those seemed appropriate to a dance hall that they hoped "would outrival the splendor" of Broadway's Roseland and Arcadia. The name they found most appealing was the Savoy, for it "exemplified all the elegant splendor of fabled old-world palaces." Just before it opened, in March of 1926, the *Age* ran this description of it:

> When one enters the building he finds himself in a spacious lobby set off by marble staircase and cut glass chandelier. The hall itself is decorated in a color scheme of orange and blue. One half of the floor is heavily carpeted. There are tables, settees, etc., where guests may rest between dances. There is a soda fountain at one end of the hall. . . .
>
> The dance floor is about 200 feet long and about 50 feet wide. It is made of the best quality maple flooring, polished to the highest degree. Two bandstands and a disappearing stage are in the rear. Above are vari-colored spotlights. The Savoy will be open every evening. Admission: 50 cents, week nights; 75 cents, Sundays and holidays.

According to *The Savoy Story*, "The gay and festive opening night was attended by city, state and federal government celebrities, church dignitaries, social leaders, sports and newspaper world personalities, representatives of Harlem's outstanding fraternal organizations, sororities, civic, cultural, welfare and education groups, and a long list of famous Broadway and Hollywood stage and screen stars, as well as musicians, many of whom are now world renowned. . . . those fortunate to be present were overawed with pulsating excitement as they viewed the eye-filling sumptuousness of the widely heralded edifice. . . . there was no other place of such magnificence in Harlem, or on the Broadways of the world, for that matter. They glided and whirled on the sleek and springy unobstructed dance floor! They jumped with ecstatic joy to the music of . . . two of the 'best bands in the land,' the Savoy Bearcats, directed by personable Leon Abbey, and high-hatted, clarinet-playing Fess Williams and his Royal Flush Orchestra. Few first-nighters will ever forget the dynamic Fess, whose eye-catching trade mark was a shimmering, glittering diamond-studded suit, and whose showmanship eventually catapulted him to national fame from the newly born Savoy's number one bandstand."

The hall admitted all the classes and conditions of Harlem, from top professionals to truck drivers, shoeshine boys, and domestic servants (known in the self-mocking euphemisms of Harlem as "pot wrestlers" and "kitchen mechanics"). According to *Ebony*, "Royalty from Europe and other foreign lands make the Savoy . . . a must on their lists when visiting New York," and celebrities, "a dime a dozen," included the Roosevelts, the former Prince of Wales, Marlene Dietrich, Carl Van Vechten, Lana Turner, Greta Garbo, Alice Faye, and "millionaire playboys from Park Avenue." And in 1941 Maurice Zolotow, writing for *The Saturday Evening Post*, reported:

> Sober white citizens . . . are welcome at the Savoy, and since Benny Goodman's playing of "Stompin' at the Savoy" spread its fame abroad in 1936, the Savoy has become a favorite of the tourists, along with Radio City and the Empire State Building. When Greta Garbo visits Manhattan, she spends most of her evenings at the Savoy. She has found, from experience, that it is an ideal place to go when you want to be alone.
>
> Another characteristic of the Savoyards that endears them to Hollywood stars in search of obscurity is the fact that they don't chase celebrities or hunt for autographs. To them, dancing is a serious business.

A former dancer at the Savoy has recalled, "There were maybe ten or twelve bouncers, all very nice, gentle, soft-spoken. But they were usually ex-prizefighters. . . . There were two bandstands, two bands, and never any pause in the music. As one band was leaving, the second band would pick up the beat. They had hostesses in long gowns. . . . *Café au lait* most of them, and they were from Sugar Hill. Very haughty. They wouldn't talk to the average person. . . . To the right of the bandstand was a spot about ten feet square, called the Cats' Corner, and it had an invisible rope around it. . . . The King would dance in that spot, and then it would be left empty. They'd say, 'He left the floor too hot to follow.' "

Music was just as serious a business at the Savoy. Only the best bands could hold their own there or were invited back. They included those of Jimmy Lunceford, Benny Goodman, Tommy Dorsey, Tiny Bradshaw, Lucky Millinder, Duke Ellington, Bennie Moten, Earl Hines, Louis Armstrong, Chick Webb, Count Basie, Cab Calloway, Fletcher Henderson, Fess Williams, Claude Hopkins, Teddy Hill, Charlie Barnet, Lionel Hampton, and Erskine Hawkins. "The best band is the one that keeps the floor filled," Charlie Buchanan once said, and no band kept the floor filled unless it could swing. According to the trombonist Dicky Wells, "if you didn't swing, you weren't there long." In 1929, Cab Calloway and his band, newly arrived in New York, flunked their first test at the Savoy. They just didn't swing, and Buchanan was on the verge of handing them their walking papers. "I was furious with the guys in the band," Calloway later said. " 'Dammit,' I hollered, 'I tried to tell you this jive music wouldn't make it in New York. This ain't Toledo or Mendota, this is New York. You've got to come into New York swinging!' " Luckily, they were given another chance, and managed to redeem themselves.

Swinging though the better New York bands were, there began coming into the Savoy in the early thirties a group of musicians from the Southwest—especially Kansas City and Oklahoma City—who were in no way awed by what the boys in Harlem were doing. They regarded themselves as the original and authentic exponents of swing. (This, despite the fact that in New York Fletcher Henderson was seen by many as the father of swing music.) They played with such ease, such natural drive, that their music seemed to be generated not within themselves but by the spontaneous verve of the dancers for whom they were playing—as though their styles owed less to imagination and mastered technique than to the tradition and inspiration of small-town Saturday-night dancing. That may have been why Ralph Ellison, who grew up in the Southwest, said later, "We didn't give a damn about what kind of jazz they were playing in the East, because we had swing—what we called 'stomp music.' " The jazz historian Marshall Stearns seems to agree. "The Southwestern style grew up in direct response to the everyday needs of an audience of dancers from the countryside of the deep South," he writes. "They wanted their music hot and strong." Among the musicians who brought this Southwestern style and drive into the Savoy were Bennie Moten, Walter Page, Count Basie (though he was a native of Red Bank, New Jersey), Andy Kirk, Ben Webster, Lester Young, Hot Lips Page, Mary Lou Williams, and the blues singer Jimmy Rushing.

There was at least one orchestra in Harlem that swung as "hot" and as "strong as the Southwesterners did. That was Chick Webb's—by far the most popular of all the bands that played at the Savoy. "The only time we were bothered was when we played opposite a little guy named Chick Webb," Count Basie said in recalling his early appearances at the Savoy. Webb's group played what came to be called "the Savoy tempo." In its relationship to what the dancers did on the floor, it bore a resemblance to the bands of the Southwest. Duke Ellington later remarked that Webb's "command of his audiences" sprang from his "communication with the dancers"—with what their feet were doing.

As a result, in the big-band battles that were regularly staged at the Savoy, Webb and his boys were almost always unbeatable. "Chick Webb would just lay for other bands to come there," Dicky Wells said. "And he'd rather they came on Fridays, Saturdays, or Sundays, because then the place would be packed with dancers, and they'd say, 'Play that number you played last Tuesday, Chick. We can dance by that.' He'd play it and the house would start rocking. Lots of times the dancers more or less dictated what the bands played. Chick used to sit back looking out the window while his band played early in the evening, but when the visiting band would get rough—here he would come, and that was it!" Mary Lou Williams recalled that Webb was "the acknowledged King" of the Savoy. "Any visiting band could depend on catching hell from little Chick, for he was a crazy drummer and shrewd to boot," she said. "Chick would wait until the opposition had blown its hottest numbers and then—during a so-so set—would unexpectedly bring his band fresh to the stand and wham into a fine arrangement, like Benny Carter's 'Liza,' that was hard to beat. Few visiting bands could stand up to this." Sam Woodyard, who later played the drums in Ellington's orchestra, has said of Webb, "He was the first drummer who made sense in a big band. . . . He knew how to shade and color, and how to bring a band up and keep it there." Gene Krupa, himself an illustrious drummer, once described Webb as "the most luminous of all drum stars, the master." In 1937, Krupa was a member of the Benny Goodman band that took on Chick Webb's in one of the greatest battles ever staged at the Savoy. According to the *Age*, some five thousand dancers were in the ballroom, and outside another five thousand "battled mounted cops and patrolmen for places near enough to the Savoy to hear the music of these two great orchestras." The report continued, "It was the first time that Harlem would get an opportunity to see the Goodman aggregation which includes two Negroes [Teddy Wilson and Lionel Hampton] as featured musicians in action." Samuel Charters and Leonard Kunstadt, two historians of the New York jazz scene, gave this account of the Webb–Goodman encounter: "Benny came into the Savoy with his greatest band, but the Savoy was jammed with Chick's loyal fans. The Goodman band played at their best, but they couldn't win the crowd away from little Chick. He finished the session with a drum solo, winning a thunderous ovation, while Goodman and his drummer, Gene Krupa, just stood there shaking their heads."

There was little in Webb's physical appearance to suggest the force and drive he generated in his orchestra. He was short, frail of build, and partly crippled—"a sickly hunchback," someone called him. According to Ella Fitzgerald, who was his vocalist for several years (and who inherited the leadership of the band when Webb died, in 1939), he was "always in pain" but "no one ever knew it"— for "there was so much music in that man."

Reminiscing about the Savoy several years later, Charles Buchanan said: "Half the bands that developed in the twenties and thirties did so because of the Savoy. They had a place to start, a place to perfect their arrangements. I would hire them for a couple of weeks and then Frank Schiffman at the Lafayette and later at the Apollo would take them. In this way we kept them working. As long as you kept them working, the better they became. Ella Fitzgerald developed at the Savoy. I knew her very well—young, simple, an orphan. She won an opportunity contest at one of the theatres near the Apollo. Chick Webb saw her at the Apollo soon after and brought her up to the Savoy. We had no money, but we had the budget. So I said to Chick, 'I'll put ten dollars and you put ten dollars.' We pooled the twenty dollars and hired Ella. The second week we paid her fifty dollars. The third week we dressed her up. Now, Ella has done a lot since then. But if there had not been a Savoy and an Apollo she might never have gotten started.

"We hired two bands every night of the week, so even if we had only five hundred people on the floor we still had to pay for two bands. Chick Webb's band was the best. It had the beat. That's why the dancers loved him so. There were also the Savoy Sultans, and they were good. But everybody loved Chick. What made me feel a band was good for the Savoy? I had a tin ear for music, but I knew a good beat, a good rhythm. Webb's band had it. Guy Lombardo's band had it too. His band was a favorite of mine and one of the first white bands to play at the Savoy. Cab Calloway came in with a band by the name of the Missourians. Believe me, it was the finest band in personal demeanor. But they didn't have the jive. However, I kept them for about four weeks. While playing at the Savoy, Cab developed a good band. I used to let Benny Goodman come up and rehearse at the Savoy. He wanted to get that rhythm of Chick Webb. (Webb would say to him, 'You'll never get my rhythm.') So Benny said to me at one point, 'Charlie, give me a night at the Savoy.' I said, 'Sure,' because the band was good. Benny said, 'How much are you going to pay?' I said, 'Union scale—ten dollars a man and twenty for leaders.' Benny said, 'Oh, you can't do that.' I said, 'Look, Benny, until you prove to me that you can bring 'em in that's what I'm going to pay you.' The next time I hired Benny, I had to pay him $3,300 for one night.

"A key to the success of the Savoy was that we maintained such a standard of order that girls were not afraid to come. Outside of the music, if you can't get girls to come you have nothing. The girls came because we guaranteed the best behavior. We had burly fellows, dressed in tuxedos, who threw any trouble-maker out.

"To a certain group of young people the Savoy was their life. That's all they had. We used to see the same kids come there every day. Some of them had holes in their shoes. But if you took pity on one of them and bought him a new pair of shoes, all of a sudden he couldn't dance. He wasn't accustomed to good shoes. At one stage about half the people at the Savoy were white and half colored. The cops used to hate it. They closed us down for three months in 1943.

But we used that period to redecorate. We were friends with Mayor LaGuardia, so we knew we wouldn't stay closed permanently.

"The Savoy closed in 1958. It closed for one of the same reasons that Frank Schiffman had, eventually, to give up the Apollo. For instance, take Ella Fitzgerald. I'd ask Ella to play a night for me. But much as I knew Ella, her manager would say, 'You know, I'm sending her on a college date. She's getting three thousand dollars a night.' We could no longer afford to hire such attractions. Then in 1958 the whole trend of disorder started. If you put a kid out, he'd throw a brick and break your window. When we closed, the Savoy building was torn down to make way for an urban renewal housing project."

"Cool Deal, McNeil"

In THE late thirties and early forties, the term "jitterbug" referred not only to a popular dance form but to the dancer as well and to almost anyone whose speech and manner of dress identified him as a "hep cat." One could have been called a jitterbug whether one was dancing the Lindy Hop, the Big Apple, the Suzie-Q, the Hucklebuck, the Shorty George, the Camel Walk, the boogie-woogie, or the jitterbug. Many jitterbugs were musicians or well-known members of the marijuana culture. And almost anyone was accepted as a jitterbug or hep cat if he talked "jive"—an in-group language that hardly any "square" could make sense of.

The language was so esoteric that outsiders could appropriate it only by consulting textbooks like Cab Calloway's *Hepster's Dictionary*. There one found definitions like these:

AIN'T COMING ON THAT TAB: won't accept the proposition.
APPLE: the big town, the main stem, Harlem.
BLEW THEIR WIGS: excited with enthusiasm.
BUSH: weed, reefers, marijuana.
DILLINGER: a killer-diller, too hot to handle.
DIME NOTE: ten-dollar bill.
DRACULA: something in a class by itself.
EARLY BLACK: evening.
FAUST: an ugly girl, a hag.
FINE DINNER: a good-looking girl.
GLIMS: the eyes.
KILL ME: show me a good time.
LAY YOUR RACKET: to jive, to sell an idea.
LEAD SHEET: a top coat.
MAIN ON THE HITCH: husband.
OFF THE COB: corny, out of date.
SLIDE YOUR JIB: to talk freely.

STYLE, CLASS, AND BEYOND

TOGGED TO THE BRICKS: dressed to kill.

TWISTER TO THE SLAMMER: the key to the door.

Another of the major jive linguists of Harlem was Dan Burley, a columnist for the *Amsterdam News* and, later, for the *Age*. His *Original Handbook of Harlem Jive* may have been a more authoritative compilation than Calloway's, since it appears to have circulated more widely. Burley's column in the *Age*, Back Door Stuff, often read like pure gibberish, though not to any hep cat who was in the habit of reading. Here is a sampling from one of his columns:

> And what's on the rail for the snail? Let's get some cash and talk some trash and get all set for the crash. Feeling sorta hip. I'm strictly for the vaunce and those for the vout can nix-nay the play and do without. It's a cool deal, McNeil, when you play a stray and dig the bray of those not gay picking up clay that you're righteous that way. And I'm Jap from the flap and don't need a slap for me to backcap any cat on the tap. . . . How does that sound, clown?

Serious magazines attempted lengthy explications of Harlem jive, as *Esquire* did in 1944:

> True jive is not the stereotyped jargon affected by the high school ice cream parlor crowd and brain-fagged comedians. Jive has etymology, formal rules, a constantly expanding vocabulary currently estimated at over a thousand words and an infinite number of phrase combinations. Burley calls it "language in motion," and though he often discusses it in the most scholarly terms, he claims you can't understand the idiom unless you understand the people who use it. Jive, he says, is the Negro's defense mechanism.

Among the whites who mastered Harlem jive was the jazz clarinetist-saxophonist Milt Mezzrow. A Chicagoan, Mezzrow became so nicely integrated into Harlem's hep-cat culture that the jitterbugs regarded him as one of their own. In Cab Calloway's *Dictionary*, the term "Mezz" stood for "anything supreme, genuine"; and Burley's *Handbook* defined "Mezz" as "tops, sincere." The terms "mezzroll" and "the mighty mezz" also came to stand for the best in marijuana—quantities of which Mezzrow was able to supply his friends in Harlem. He later wrote his own explanation of hep-cat talk: "This jive is a private affair, a secret inner-circle code cooked up partly to mystify the outsiders, while it brings those in the know closer together, because they alone have the key to the puzzle. The hipster's lingo is a private kind of folk poetry, meant for the ears of the brethren alone."

Many jitterbugs and hep cats dressed as sensationally as they spoke. Their usual mode of attire was the zoot suit, which received this description from *The New Yorker* in 1941:

> We herewith submit a preview of men's Easter fashions from the world's least inhibited fashion centre, Harlem. Trousers will be deeply pleated, with waistband just under the armpits, thirty-inch knees, and fifteen-inch cuffs. A popular suit jacket is one that measures thirty-six inches down the back seam and has a fly front, shoulders padded out three and a half inches on each side, two breast pockets, and slashed side pockets. This may be worn with a white doeskin waistcoat. Shoes are pointed, the most popular leathers being light-tan calfskin and colored suede. Hats may be worn in the porkpie shape or with crowns six inches high. Colors, as always, are limited only by spectrum.

The New Yorker left out one important accessory of the zoot suit—a long watch chain, hitched to the waist of the trousers, which looped down to the ankles.

Cab Calloway's zoot suits were probably the most spectacular and expensive in Harlem, and he may also have owned more of them than anyone else up there. Writing for the *Post* in 1943, Earl Wilson reported that Calloway, who sometimes changed into twelve outfits a night, hadn't a thing to wear—"Only 40 suits and 40 pairs of shoes to match." They could not all have been zoot suits, but Wilson went on to say that one of Cab's brown outfits had cost $225; a white one, $187; and the rest were "just some old things" that he had picked up for $150 each. Only in color and in cut were ordinary jitterbugs able to replicate Calloway's stuff. They would have been unable to do so, in quality and price. While Calloway paid $150 for his cheapest suit, the common jitterbug-in-the-street paid an average of $33.50.

Older and squarer Harlemites were partly amused and partly appalled by how the jitterbugs looked and talked. One of them wrote to the local press that the hep cats used "more grease in their hair than you use on your car," that their shoes resembled "canoes," and that their suits made them seem like "chimpanzees."

When Malcolm Little (the future Malcolm X) moved to Harlem in 1941, he had recently turned sixteen, and had arrived in the black metropolis at a high point of the zoot-suit craze. In Boston, where he had been living, he had owned a zoot suit, but it was nothing like the one he bought as soon as he got to Harlem—"a sharkskin gray 'Cab Calloway' " model, as he described it many years later. To go along with his new outfit, the young Malcolm also bought himself a pair of "the ghetto's Cadillac of shoes in those days"—knob-toed, orange-colored, kick-up Florsheims. But when, years later, he looked back on this youthful version of himself—after he had become the serious and militantly censorious Malcolm X—he was unable to avoid a self-mocking grin. He then recalled the astonished look of a grandmother when, draped in full zoot attire, he appeared at her front door to escort one of her offspring out for an evening. "What could she have thought of me in my zoot and conk and orange shoes?" he mused in his autobiography. "She'd have done us all a favor if she had run screaming for the police. If something looking as I did then ever came knocking at my door today, asking to see one of my four daughters, I know I would explode."

In those days, however, the daughters did not mind—or, at any rate, not all of them did. It was a thrill to be called for by a hep cat, who was togged to the bricks, and taken to the Savoy, where both would blow their wigs boogieing, Lindying, and trucking.

Seventh Avenue:
The Great Black Way

SEVENTH Avenue was the most handsome of the boulevards running through Harlem. It was bisected into an uptown and a downtown
drive by a narrow strip of park, planted with trees and flowers. Despite the renown and importance of 125th Street—the district's main
commercial artery—it was Seventh Avenue that deserved to be called
the main street of Harlem. It reflected almost every form of life
uptown—with its stores, churches, beauty parlors, doctors' offices,
theatres, night clubs, nice-looking apartment buildings, and private
brownstones. The novelist Wallace Thurman referred to it as Harlem's "most representative" avenue, "a grand thoroughfare into which
every element of the Harlem population ventures either for reasons of
pleasure or of business." From 125th Street to 145th Street, he added,
Seventh Avenue was "majestic yet warm," and reflected "both the
sordid chaos and the rhythmic splendor of Harlem."

In the twenties, Seventh Avenue was the headquarters of Harry
Pace's Black Swan phonograph company, which produced some of
the earliest recordings of jazz and the blues. On the avenue, there
were the Renaissance ballroom and such fine theatres as the Roosevelt,
the Alhambra, and the Lafayette. Among the churches there, Salem
Methodist was perhaps the largest, and among the cabarets, the most
famous were Connie's Inn and Smalls' Paradise. During the thirties,
James Van Der Zee, Harlem's best-known photographer, had his
studio on the avenue. Of Van Der Zee, a sympathetic and inde-
fatigable recorder of Harlem life, Cecil Beaton wrote in 1938: "In
Harlem he is called upon to capture the tragedy as well as the hap-
piness in life, turning his camera on death and marriage with the
same detachment." Several of the left-wing ideologues who harangued
crowds at the corner of Lenox Avenue and 135th Street edited their
little magazines from offices on Seventh. The Blyden Bookstore and
the National Bookstore, virtual academies of black consciousness,

were on the avenue. Owned by Dr. Willis Huggins and Lewis Michaux, respectively, their stocks leaned heavily to volumes on African and Afro-American history. "If we couldn't find a book anywhere else," a customer of the National Bookstore later said, "we always knew that Michaux had a copy on hand; but perhaps more important than the availability of books was the kind of books he had—books on Africa now out of print; books on the history of *us*." At the corner of Seventh and 125th Street—across the way from Michaux's bookstore—was Harlem's best hotel, the Theresa. It was not until around 1940, however, that the Theresa began admitting blacks, at which point, according to *Ebony*, it became "the social headquarters for Negro America, just as the Waldorf is the home for the white elite. The magazine added: "To its famous registration desk flock the most famous Negroes in America. It is the temporary home of practically every outstanding Negro who comes to New York. . . . Joe Louis stays there, along with every big-time Negro fighter. So does Rochester and the Hollywood contingent, all the top bandleaders who haven't the good fortune to have their own apartments in town, Negro educators, colored writers, and the Liberian and Haitian diplomatic representatives. Big men in the business world jostle top labor leaders in the flowered, mirrored lobby."

To many in Harlem, Seventh Avenue, a boulevard of high style, was "the Great Black Way." One requirement of a grand funeral procession in Harlem was that it make its way up or down Seventh Avenue at some point. Father Divine's religious marches and Marcus Garvey's black nationalist parades—resplendent with colorful banners and uniforms—achieved a special swagger only when, from other streets and thoroughfares, they swung into Seventh Avenue. When the great black fraternal organizations (the Elks, the Odd Fellows, the Monarchs, the Masons, or the Pythians) came to Harlem for an annual convention, a high point of their gathering was an extravaganza of march and music that they staged on Seventh. Perhaps none of these shows was more attractive than the one in 1927, when some thirty thousand lodge brothers and sisters, stepping to the accompaniment of twenty-five marching bands, cakewalked and Charlestoned down the avenue to tunes like "Me and My Shadow" and "Ain't She Sweet."

But Seventh Avenue presented no finer spectacle than its Easter

Parades and its Sunday-afternoon promenades, when the high and low of Harlem—in their best clothes or wearing the latest in fashion —strolled leisurely up and down the avenue. Here is what a writer for *The New Yorker* observed on a Sunday in 1926:

> Now that Fifth Avenue is no longer a promenade, only a fashionable procession of shoppers . . . we have been seeking elsewhere for a street which still retains the loafing stroll as a tempo. . . . Seventh Avenue between 127th and 134th Streets . . . is still the real thing in promenades. . . . Here the elite of colored New York stroll almost any evening in a true Sunday-afternoon-in-the-park manner. Here the young men in evening clothes and jaunty derbies or in more sporting outfits of spats, colored shirts, trick canes, loiter on the corners or in front of the theatres and laugh. . . . dusky young school girls go arm in arm, sometimes four or five abreast. Here old women waddle along, leading their favorite hound or poodle; and a group of mammies, exchanging gossip as though in a small-town back yard, mingle with flashy young flappers. . . . Prosperous old men with heavy gold watch chains slung ponderously over wide bellies stroll. . . . Harlem takes its ease on one of the widest and more lovely avenues in the city.

On other Sunday afternoons, male strollers were to be seen in silk toppers, homburgs, cutaways, velvet-collared Chesterfields, boutonnieres, monocles, lorgnettes, gaiters, frock coats, and white gloves. Women carried Yankee sand pocketbooks, and wore high-cuffed peek-a-toe slippers, wide-brimmed hats (decorated with flower bouquets), and veils in chartreuse, lime, pink, blue, black, and white. In 1932, a journal in Harlem reported that many women were wearing "sleek black carouls" with "silver fox and sable trimmings" and "white satin or velvet evening frocks, with draped bodies." Waistlines were "anywhere from the hip top to a high empire line." Dresses were trimmed with fur, "kolinsky fur, the preference." Popular that year was a Paris-designed beret, with "a perky feather" shooting skyward. Shoes were generally suede, in various shades of gray. And almost all the women of fashion showed signs of having had an "oatmeal facial."

Of course, not all the strollers on Seventh Avenue were *that* smart-looking. And not all belonged to the better classes. It was not so hard to spot the prostitutes. Accustomed to their own style of street walking, they could not quite conceal the habitual rhythms of their gait or suppress the erotic insolence of their derrieres. Prosperous pimps and racketeers—at the wheels of expensive automobiles—cruised up and down the avenue, trolling for the attention of the young, the pretty, and the innocent. Men dressed as exquisitely as Adolphe Menjou—the "dicty's," as such classy types in Harlem were called—shared the stroll with day laborers, elevator operators, and shoeshine boys, whose humbler duds were probably what the cut-rate economies of Delancey Street permitted. Servants of rich Park and Fifth Avenue families wore the hand-me-downs of their employers, striving, with amusing result, to look the part of what they had on. A number of women were out in ensembles that, as any knowing eye could tell, had been put together on their own sewing machines. It is also plausible to surmise that more than a few of the strollers were attired in "hot" merchandise, since Harlem was a major marketplace for stolen apparel.

Surveying all this from the sidewalks, sharp-tongued Harlemites, who came out to judge the show, made wicked remarks about some of the styles on parade. Rudolph Fisher recorded similar remarks in his novel *The Walls of Jericho*:

> "My Gawd—did you see that hat?"
> "Hot you, baby——!"
> "——co'se it's a home-made dress—can't you see that crooked hem?"
> "What is these young folks comin' to—dat gal's dress ain' nothin' but a sash!"
> "Now you know a man that black ain' got no business in no white linen suit—"

The *Age* was surely correct when it said, of a promenade in 1934, that "the creme de la creme" mingled with the "has beens," the "would-be's," the "four flushers," the "shallow fops," and the "humble."

But it was the relaxed and neighborly air of the stroll that mattered the most, and James Weldon Johnson captured it memorably, when he wrote, in 1930:

> One puts on one's best clothes and fares forth to pass the time pleasantly with friends and acquaintances and, most important of all, the strangers he is sure of meeting. One saunters along, he

hails this one, exchanges a word or two with that one, stops for a short chat with the other one. He comes to a laughing chattering group, in which he may have only one friend or acquaintance, but that gives him the privilege of joining in. He does join in and takes part in the joking, the small talk and gossip, and makes new acquaintances. He passes on and arrives in front of one of the theatres, studies the bill for a while, undecided about going in. He finally moves on a few steps farther and joins another group and is introduced to two or three pretty girls who have just come to Harlem, perhaps only for a visit; and finds reason to be glad that he postponed going into the theatre. The hours of a summer evening run by rapidly. This is not simply going out for a walk; it is like going out for an adventure.

No other resident of Harlem has described so vividly the charm, the sweetness, of those bygone Sunday afternoons on Seventh Avenue.

LEFT: An aerial view of Seventh Avenue, as it looked in the nineteen-thirties and forties
ABOVE: The Hotel Theresa (Harlem's Waldorf-Astoria) is the background of a 1946 parade in honor of Joe Louis

LEFT: James Van Der Zee
ABOVE: Interior of James Van Der Zee's photo studio

Dancing at the Savoy

The Social Event of the Holiday Season

BARN DANCE
THE GOOSE HANGS HIGH OVER HARLEM

THANKSGIVING
Day and Night

RURAL RHYTHMS
Erskine Hawkins

Thurs. Nov. 21
MATINEE 3 P. M.

WORLD'S FINEST BALLROOM **SAVOY** 140 STREET on LENOX AVE.

THIS SUN. MAY 19
MATINEE 3 P.M.
3 BANDS - ALL DAY - ALL NIGHT

SAVOY — SAVOY

World's Finest Ballroom
140th Street on Lenox Ave.

ELLA FITZGERALD

GALE Inc present
THE FIRST LADY OF SWING
ELLA Fitzgerald
AND HER 8 famous.. ORCH.
Featuring TAFT JORDAN

RING OUT...

New Years EVE CELEBRATION

A HISTORY MAKING NIGHT AT THE WORLD'S FINEST BALLROOM

SAVOY

The Thrill of a Life Time

HARVEST MOON BALL
ALL-AMERICAN DANCE CLASSIC

Friday August 9

WORLD'S FINEST BALLROOM **SAVOY** 140 St. on LENOX AVE.

The WORLD'S FINEST BALLROOM **SAVOY** Presents THE KING OF THE SAXOPHONE

SUNDAY JAN. 14
Charlie BARNET and his ORCHESTRA

Ella FITZGERALD and her ORCHESTRA

Erskine HAWKINS

Come Early Matinee 3

2 GREAT BANDS

FRIDAY SEPT. 2 ND

SAVOY HAY STATION

BARN DANCE

Come IN YOUR
OVERALLS · SLACKS
PAJAMAS · GINGHAMS
DUNGAREES
SHIRT SLEEVES OR
What Have You

PRIZES to the MOST UNIQUE COSTUMES

SAVOY
WORLD'S FINEST BALLROOM
LENOX AVE. 140TH ST.

Starts **THIS SAT. & SUN.** ONE WEEK ONLY
THE COUNT · THE HAWK IN A MUSICAL FREE FOR ALL

COUNT BASIE
"BATTLE of RHYTHM" vs.
★ ERSKINE ★ HAWKINS

Next Thurs. Dec. 5 - Special BASIE-HAWKINS Swing Session

COUNT BASIE
WORLD'S FINEST BALLROOM

SAVOY

ERSKINE HAWKINS
140 St. on LENOX AVE.

THIS SUN. MAY 12
ONE DAY ONLY
MAT. 3 P.M. 2 A.M.

THE 4 INK SPOTS
AND SUNSET ROYAL ENTERTAINERS

THE WORLD'S FINEST BALLROOM **SAVOY** 140 STREET on LENOX AVE.

THE FOUR INK SPOTS

Thur JAN 18 th
The WORLD'S FINEST BALLROOM **SAVOY**

LADIES · FREE

Jack Teagarden

THE WORLD'S No 1 SWING TROMBONIST "PAUL WHITEMAN ALL STAR MAN..."

& his ORCHESTRA

plus

ELLA FITZGERALD & HER ORCHESTRA

AL COOPER'S Savoy SULTANS & their "Jump Rhythm"

BELOW: Elks at their headquarters
RIGHT: Fess Williams's Royal Flush Orchestra, which
played at the opening of the Savoy Ballroom in 1926
BOTTOM, RIGHT: Elks on Seventh Avenue

TOP, LEFT: 409 Edgecombe Avenue
LEFT: A view of Strivers Row
ABOVE: Bill (Bojangles) Robinson's funeral procession passes along
Seventh Avenue in 1949

Society

Up UNTIL the end of the nineteen-forties, at least, Harlem's "society," or social elite, was made up of two branches, an old and a new. Members of the old branch would just as soon have ignored the existence of the new, but they felt that if it had to be recognized the comparison would be no threat to them, for they considered themselves to be superior by far, the true representatives of society in Harlem. Among them were descendants of successful old New York families, while others sprang from an educated class in the South—the one that W. E. B. Du Bois described as the Talented Tenth, and to whom he assigned the task of providing enlightened black social and political leadership. Predominantly fair-skinned, they were refined in their manners and conservative in their cultural interests, and were among the first black professionals—lawyers, doctors, journalists, teachers, and seminary-trained clergymen—to settle in Harlem. But some time after they became greatly outnumbered by the black masses in Harlem, the old elite found their social influence eroding and their cultural position being challenged by a new set of achievers.

It was the distinction between themselves and the new achievers that they sought to take advantage of. In 1937, a publication sympathetic to their position—*The Vanguard*, which called itself a "Register of Those in Front"—carried a list of Harlem families that it described as "the Elite of African Descent." Included were persons of "fixed domiciles of long standing," those with a "reputation for good moral character," and those who had "achieved a measure of economic success and intellectual development." In 1926, the *Age*—whose editor, Fred R. Moore, was a member of the old branch—had used terms like "Harlem's best society" and "the real society" to describe the group it recognized as the true elite. Such a group, the paper said, was "composed of clean living and clean thinking people, some with brains and a capacity for hard work as well as for play in its proper place." They were "content to enjoy the relaxation of social intercourse," but only in the company of "their own wives," for they were not "chasers after strange women." The unmarried among them "may change their partners in the social whirl," but not after they have "settled in the choice of a partner for life."

Among those whom the *Age*, then and later, would have placed in "Harlem's best society" were Charles W. Anderson, the city's leading black Republican, who had once been the Collector of Internal Revenue for the Third District of New York; Charles H. Roberts, E. P. Roberts, Peyton F. Anderson, James Granady, and Louis T. Wright, prominent physicians; Gertrude Elise Ayer, New York's first black public-school principal; Roscoe Conkling Bruce, son of Blanche K. Bruce, a former United States Senator from Mississippi; John E. Nail, a successful real-estate broker, and his father, John B. Nail; James Weldon Johnson and his wife, Grace, who was a daughter of John B. Nail; Edward A. Johnson, a lawyer, and the first black elected to the New York State Assembly; Hutchens C. Bishop, the rector of St. Philip's Protestant Episcopal Church; Adam Clayton Powell, Sr., the pastor of the Abyssinian Baptist Church; Ruth Logan Roberts, the wife of Dr. E. P. Roberts, and a daughter of Warren Logan, who had been a treasurer of Tuskegee Institute; Myra Logan and Arthur Logan, young physicians; Roy Wilkins, William Pickens, Walter White, and W. E. B. Du Bois, of the N.A.A.C.P.; and James Watson (a West Indian), Hubert Delaney, and Charles Toney, prominent judges. In 1941, when several of them attended a social affair in honor of Dr. E. P. Roberts, the *Age* described the gathering as representing "Harlem society in its full meaning."

In the eyes of such people, the younger branch of society was merely the smart or fast set—social celebrities and hostesses, members of café society. Its members were dismissed as fun-lovers, party-givers, fancy dressers, and conspicuous consumers, who owned and displayed themselves in expensive automobiles. Though they were not without their lawyers and doctors, few of them were thought to have serious intellectual interests. They were seen as avid sports fans, who much preferred discussing baseball statistics to reading good books. Of this group—in other cities as well as in Harlem—the black sociologist E. Franklin Frazier wrote, "Even if they did not act like 'gentlemen,' they were able to imitate white 'society' in their standards of consumption and entertainment. In fact, they tended to ridicule the so-called 'culture' and exclusiveness of the older Negro 'society.' "

This group practiced its own forms of snobbery. As Nancy Cunard observed, "There are near-white cliques, mulatto groups, dark-skinned sets who will not invite each other to their houses; some would not let a white cross their thresholds. . . . The snobbery around skin color is terrifying." Nor was there any general agreement among them concerning who did or did not belong to their society—though income was at least one qualification on which almost everybody agreed. To some members, a racketeer was perfectly acceptable as long as he lived stylishly and expensively. To others, that kind of tolerance was unthinkable. One subject of such a disagreement was the West Indian Casper Holstein, who during the nineteen-twenties was Harlem's richest numbers banker. His critics in society held the source of his income against him. His boosters thought only of how much money he had and of some of the causes and charities he financed. *The American Mercury* said of Holstein, in 1947, "He was a dignified and extraordinarily taciturn man who donated large sums to Negro causes and provided annual grants for exceptional Negro writers and artists." In literary contests that the magazine *Opportunity* sponsored during the Harlem Renaissance, one of the top prizes won annually by young black poets and story writers was the Casper Holstein Award. There was also the case of A'Lelia Walker, the cosmetics heiress. Those who rejected her claims to membership in society cited her background—she was, it was pointed out, the daughter of a former washerwoman. Others could not overlook her wealth and the glamour that surrounded her. At all events, it mattered little to her what anyone thought, for she was rich and attractive enough to lead a society of her own. According to an article in *Fortune*, in 1939, while Cab Calloway belonged to Harlem society—having been "sponsored by a Harvard-bred doctor"—Duke Ellington did not. This was odd, in view of Ellington's personal elegance, brilliant gifts, and outstanding contributions to American music. Odd, indeed; unless it was a case of everyone, in an unusual example of consensus, agreeing that Ellington constituted an aristocracy in himself—"beyond category," as he said of some of the music he wrote and played. Bojangles was another who posed a problem for the new Harlem socialites. "Bill Robinson," *The New Yorker* reported in 1934, "has not been accepted by the intellectuals or by the exclusive society people of Harlem to the extent, for instance, that Fred Astaire has been accepted in corresponding circles further downtown, but on the other hand he has never sought such recognition and would not consider it in any way significant if it were offered to him."

In his 1926 novel *Nigger Heaven*, Carl Van Vechten wrote, "The Negro fast set does everything the Long Island fast set does, plays bridge, keeps the bootlegger busy, drives around in Rolls-Royces, and commits adultery, but it is vastly more amusing than the Long Island set for the simple reason that it is *amused*." Members of this set turned up frequently at fashion shows, wore Paris styles, went to Reno or Mexico for their divorces, and presented their daughters at formal débutante cotillions. They were regular guests at grand costume balls and elaborate weddings. Some were light-skinned enough to pass for white, and, on occasion, did not hesitate to do so. According to Romare Bearden, "They didn't buy paintings." And E. Franklin Frazier wrote, "Although they may pretend to appreciate 'cultural' things, this class as a whole has no real appreciation of art, literature, or music. . . . The black bourgeoisie, especially the section which forms Negro 'society,' scarcely ever read books for recreation." In 1953, *Ebony* delivered an even harsher judgment. The "only bond" that united the "freshman society crowd," the magazine said, was "a profound dislike for each other and a profound respect for money, clothes, and position."

To the Harlem Renaissance novelist Wallace Thurman, who had no detectable affection for black society at any level, the old and new branches of Harlem society were indistinguishable. In the late twenties, he wrote:

> [They are] the more successful and more socially inclined professional folk—lawyers, doctors, dentists, druggists, politicians, beauty-parlor proprietors, and real-estate dealers. They are for the most part mulattoes of light brown skin and have succeeded in absorbing all the social mannerisms of the white American middle class. . . . They are both stupid and snobbish as is their class in any race. Their most compelling if sometimes unconscious ambition is to be as near white as possible, and their greatest

expenditure of energy is concentrated on eradicating any trait or characteristic commonly known as negroid.

Their homes are expensively appointed and comfortable. Most of them are furnished in good taste, thanks to the interior decorator who was hired to do the job. Their existence is one of smug complacence. They are well satisfied with themselves and their class. They are without a doubt the basic element from which the Negro aristocracy of the future will evolve. They are also good illustrations, mentally, sartorially, and socially, of what the American standardizing machine can do to susceptible material.

These people have a social life of their own. They attend formal dinners and dances, resplendent in chic and expensive replicas of Fifth Avenue finery. They arrange suitable intercoterie weddings, preside luxuriously at announcement dinners, pre-nuptial showers, wedding breakfasts, and the like. They attend church socials, fraternity dances, and sorority gatherings. They frequent the downtown theaters, and occasionally, quite occasionally, drop into one of the Harlem nightclubs which certain of their lower-caste brethren frequent and white downtown excursionists make wealthy.

On Strivers Row and Sugar Hill

IN HARLEM, the old and the new branches of the black elite shared certain residential enclaves. Some lived in privately owned brownstones or in such exclusive apartment buildings as Graham Court, the Carolyn, the Dunbar, and the Dorrance Brooks. But the heaviest concentrations of them were to be found on what had come to be known as Strivers Row and Sugar Hill. Strivers Row is the name that poorer Harlemites gave to the tree-lined blocks of 138th and 139th Streets between Seventh and Eighth Avenues. On those blocks were some of the finest town houses in Harlem. Designed by Stanford White, among other architects, for the developer David H. King, Jr., they had been built in 1891 as homes for Harlem's white well-to-do. In 1918, when the black invasion of Harlem began to send whites fleeing from 138th and 139th Streets, the houses were taken over by the Equitable Life Insurance Company. For a while, the company kept the brownstones vacant, considering them to be too good for black occupancy. By 1919, however, it had relented, and blacks began buying or renting the buildings. They were then called the Kingscourt Houses—a name so redolent of exclusiveness that the new black residents made every effort to live up to it. A Kingscourt Block Association was formed, and all owners and tenants were required to obey its written regulations.

It was around then that poorer Harlemites, watching how strenuously the black bourgeoisie tried to emulate the residential style of well-to-do whites, began using the term "Strivers Row." Thurman wrote that "the leading Babbits . . . of Harlem" lived on Strivers Row. Babbits or not, some of Harlem's top professional people did live there. They included the architect Vertner Tandy (he had designed St. Philip's Protestant Episcopal chapel and Madame C. J. Walker's mansion, Villa Lewaro); such prominent physicians as Louis T. Wright, Charles H. Roberts, and Wiley Wilson (a former husband of

A'Lelia Walker); William Pickens; and the musicians Noble Sissle and Fletcher Henderson. Adam Clayton Powell, Jr., wrote in 1945:

> Concentrated in "Strivers Row" . . . were the dowagers of Harlem's society. These queenly, sometimes portly, and nearly always light-skinned Czarinas presided over the Harlem upper class. Their protocol was more rigid than that of the Court of St. James. There was an open door for all who were light-skinned and for most of those of the professional group. The entire pattern of this society was white. Social functions were particularly successful if one or more of the guests were white. If invited Harlemites brought with them their darker-skinned friends, they were shunned and sometimes pointedly asked to leave.

Strivers Row may indeed have had its light-skinned "dowagers" and "Czarinas." But several of its residents—like the prizefighter Harry Wills, the comedian Stepin Fetchit, and the jazz pianist Eubie Blake—were self-made black-skinned people who sprang from humble roots. It is hard to imagine a man like Blake, who learned to play ragtime in some of the most infamous brothels of Baltimore, observing the protocol that Powell described.

The area called Sugar Hill (associated with the sweet and expensive life) sloped north from 145th Street to 155th Street, and lay roughly between Amsterdam Avenue, to the west, and Edgecombe Avenue, to the east. Originally part of Washington Heights, it was named Sugar Hill after certain well-to-do blacks began living there. From the top of the Hill, at 155th Street and Edgecombe, one looked down—literally and socially—on most of the Valley, as central Harlem was called. Nearly all the poorer Harlemites lived in the Valley. And nearly all the crime, overcrowding, and other social problems were down there. This is not to say that the Valley held nothing but crime and deprivation. The Valley was Harlem in all its diversity, the center of its culture. It had most of the churches, schools, community centers, night clubs, theatres, dance halls, bookstores, editorial offices, libraries, art studios, and business places. Many of Harlem's fashionable apartment houses were down there, and so, of course, was Strivers Row. The Valley also had all the funeral parlors; it was where Sugar Hillites went—or returned to—when they died.

The Hill was special. According to the writer Frank Hercules, a former resident, "Class divisions defined themselves, became manifest, when the A train pulled into 125th Street. At that point, the lower-class Negroes got off. The middle-class Negroes stayed on. Their stop was 145th or 155th." The people up there lived in splendid brownstones and high-rent apartment houses. Langston Hughes, who once lived in the area, said Sugar Hillites were "acquainted personally . . . with liberals like Pearl Buck and John Haynes Holmes," went to "civic banquets at the Astor," and lunched "with emancipated movie stars at Sardi's."

Sugar Hill became a black neighborhood some years after Strivers Row did. When blacks began settling there, during the late nineteen-twenties, Washington Heights was occupied chiefly by upper-middle-class Jewish, German, and Irish families. As the blacks moved in, these families fled, either to the suburbs or to the great apartment buildings along West End Avenue and Riverside Drive. Perhaps the Jews fled later than the rest, for as Bayard Rustin, another former resident of the Hill, has said, "Jews tend not to run as quickly from blacks as ordinary whites do." In any case, by the late nineteen-thirties Sugar Hill had become Harlem's smartest residential area.

Celebrities of all sorts—the moneyed, the talented, the socially prominent, the intellectually distinguished, the fast crowd—lived along the streets and avenues of the section. "The most exciting facet of living on Sugar Hill is knowing the big names which would stud its mailboxes and doorbells if Hill buildings only had such earthy things as mailboxes and doorbells," *Ebony* noted in 1946. "Harlem's most talked-about men and women in law, sports, civil liberties, music, medicine, painting, business and literature live on Sugar Hill." They had their exclusive tennis club, the Metropolitan, on Convent Avenue, whose members included Lester Granger, a leader of the National Urban League, and William J. Trent, an executive of the Negro College Fund. Now and then, tennis greats like Alice Marble dropped by and gave pointers to promising black youngsters, one of whom was Althea Gibson, a future Wimbledon singles champion. Restaurants like Craig's Colony Club, on St. Nicholas Place, appealed to the discriminating palates of the area. Fat Man's Bar-and-Grill, on 155th Street, attracted such celebrities, black and white, as Cab Calloway, Artie Shaw, Jimmy Dorsey, Duke Ellington, Jack Teagarden, Katharine Cornell, Tallulah Bankhead, Paul Robeson, and Maxine Sullivan. A black visitor from the Valley in 1940 found that Sugar Hillites walked at a more leisurely pace than folks in lower Harlem; that their children "romped with more restraint"; that their doormen were uniformed in colors to match the canopies under which they served; that the "housewives parading up and down Edgecombe Avenue spoke in sharp Yankee accents to their pups"; and that the streets were lined with "rows of white-stoned private dwellings." The idea "fixed itself firmly" in the mind of the visitor that "this was truly the community of better than average Negroes in New York." Adam Clayton Powell, Jr., wrote in 1935, "On Sugar Hill . . . Harlem's would-be 'sassiety' goes to town. 'Midst paneled walls, parquet floors, electric refrigeration, colored tile baths, luxurious lobbies, elevators and doormen resplendent in uniforms, they cavort and disport themselves in what is called the best *ofay* manner."

Surprising as it may sound, not all the black residents of Sugar Hill were members of Harlem "sassiety." Hundreds of working-class strivers slipped into the neighborhood in order to be seen as residents of a swanky area. Sugar Hill rents were surely beyond their means, and to pay the landlord on time many of them did up there what they were used to doing in the Valley: they took in roomers and boarders or threw Saturday-night rent parties. In some of the more expensive apartment buildings, pimps and racketeers mingled with the upper crust—though only in the inescapable democracy of the lobbies and elevators. In January of 1930, a Harlem newspaper carried this item: "Mme. Stephanie St. Clair . . . of 409 Edgecombe Avenue was arrested on Monday morning. . . . She was charged with possessing a quantity of numbers slips. . . . Her house was raided over a year ago on suspicion of her playing the policy game." No. 409 Edgecombe was the choicest address on Sugar Hill—more prestigious than No. 555 Edgecombe, known then as the Roger Morris Apartments. In August of 1934, the police raided the fashionable Park Lincoln building, on Edgecombe Avenue, looking for stolen property. In Apartment 3-P, they recovered the loot—a man's suit, a brown briefcase, a yellow locket, a string of white beads, gold coins and rings, gold earrings and breast pins, a gold necklace, and a pair of crystal earrings. Two burglars' jimmies and two handguns were also found.

It was not such tenants, however, but the people of means and solid status who set the social tone of Sugar Hill. Over the years, distinguished Sugar Hillites included George S. Schuyler (journalist); Henry and Mollie Moon (journalist and social worker); Hale Woodruff (painter); Isabel Washington (a former wife of Adam Clayton Powell, Jr.); Ralph Ellison; Dan Burley (journalist); the Clifford Alexanders (whose son Clifford Alexander, Jr., became Secretary of the Army in the Carter Administration); Ferdinand Smith (a West Indian-born labor leader); Langston Hughes; Dean Dixon (conductor); Billy Strayhorn (conductor and arranger); Luckey Roberts and Teddy Wilson (jazz pianists); A'Lelia Walker; Duke Ellington and his sister, Ruth; Dr. George E. Haynes (sociologist); Myra Logan (physician); Jane Bolin and Charles Toney (judges); Kenneth and Mamie Clark (psychologists); Canada Lee, Paul Robeson, Abbie Mitchell, and Jules Bledsoe.

During the thirties and forties, the tenants of 409 Edgecombe Avenue included W. E. B. Du Bois; William Stanley Braithwaite (poet and critic); William T. Andrews (State Assemblyman); Roy Wilkins and Walter White (officials of the N.A.A.C.P.); Charles Toney; Aaron Douglas (painter); Pearl Fisher and Ivy Fisher (sister and widow, respectively, of the novelist Rudolph Fisher); Josh White (folk singer); Thurgood Marshall; William Melvin Kelly, Sr. (a former editor of the *Amsterdam News*); Mercer Ellington (musician); and Elmer Carter and Ellen Tarry (journalists). At fourteen stories high, 409 was also the tallest building on the Hill; and Walter White's apartment, on the thirteenth floor, was known as the White House of Harlem, because of the many notables from the worlds of politics, literature, and theatre who were entertained there.

Many years later, at her home in Greenwich Village, the actress Jane White—a daughter of Walter White and a graduate of Smith College —reminisced about 409 Edgecombe Avenue and about life among Harlemites of her class in the days before Harlem and Sugar Hill declined in status and lost the grand hold they once had on the popular imagination. "We lived in a wonderful apartment, with five enormous rooms," she said. "Some time ago, I was given a book about George Gershwin, and when I looked at the apartments he lived in I was put in mind of so many of the apartments at 409. The style of decoration was the same, uptown and downtown—spare, full of wonderful art work, with all kinds of Mexican serapes and the like. There were wonderful floors in our building, hard floors. There were mold-ings and panels on the walls. Really sensational. I used to enjoy going with my parents down the hall to see Judge Charles Toney and his wife, Lilly. They had a great, dark apartment with massive mahog-any furniture and heavy draperies. I loved to sit back in an enormous armchair and just hear them droning on. It gave me a great feeling of security. It was an enormously safe and comfortable kind of exis-tence. And I remember a Jewish contemporary of mine telling me that her family had lived in that building when it was Jewish."

Miss White went on to say, "I began my career in the theatre while living up there. 'Strange Fruit' was my first play, and that was in 1945. My name was recommended to José Ferrer by Paul Robeson. Robeson told Ferrer that Walter White had a daughter who was comely and of the right color—because they needed a fair-skinned black girl, of sufficient dignity and whatnot. So I got the part, and always thought of it as a fluke. Through the forties and fifties, I was commuting back and forth. I did a number of Broadway and Off Broadway plays at the time. At one in the morning I would be taking the Eighth Avenue subway up, getting off at the top of the Hill. I had no fears whatsoever. It was a benign community—a gentle, warm community, where people cared about each other, with great good will and politeness.

"The parties in Daddy's and Mother's apartment were formidable. The kinds of people who were there included Wendell Willkie, Wil-liam Robeson (the CBS executive), Carl Van Vechten, Clarence Darrow, and so on. We had a full-sized grand piano at one time, because almost everybody had a piano at one time. . . . George Gershwin played 'Rhapsody in Blue' on our piano soon after he wrote it. He loved to play his own things. You couldn't stop him. Another person who was there, at some of our parties, was Sergei Eisenstein, the great Russian director. He was heard to say that my mother was one of the most beautiful women he had ever seen. I saw Claude McKay, Langston Hughes, Countee Cullen, Harold Jackman coming to our parties.

"It was only by hindsight that I realized I was moving in Harlem society. Henry and Mollie Moon, the Hubert Delaneys—I knew them well. Louis T. Wright was our family physician. People like Judge Charles Toney and Thurgood Marshall were always part of our circle. It turns out that those were some of the members of Harlem society then, but I was not aware of that. They were just people we knew, people who were just friends of ours. I grew up with Franklin Williams, who is now head of the Phelps-Stokes Fund. He lived in Brooklyn, but he was part of my crowd. Marjorie Costa, who was Carmen McRae's road manager, is now going into some kind of social-work position. There was Marion Bruce, who married Dr. Arthur Logan. She is actually a distant cousin, through my mother's side. I recently got a telephone call from the sister of a girl who shall be nameless. It was a moving telephone call, because she said, 'Shirley has been passing all these years.' It was strange to hear the term 'passing.' I hadn't heard it for so many years. I didn't think people *did* that anymore. It was like out of another century. It was silly, I suppose, for me to have been so astounded, because people have always 'passed' and will do it forever."

Miss White continued, "The Polo Grounds"—home of the former New York Giants baseball team—"was in operation when I was growing up on Edgecombe Avenue. It was nearby. From some of the apartments on Edgecombe, you could look across and down on the Polo Grounds. I remember crisp fall afternoons when I was madly in love with three good-looking fellows, baseball fans, who used to park their cars near 409. I used to tingle all over when I walked by that parking lot. I was not a baseball fan, or a sports fan of any kind, but I remember you could always hear the loudspeaker from the Polo Grounds. I would hear the loudspeaker say, 'Alvin Dark, shortstop.' That was all I knew about baseball.

"James Weldon Johnson was a close friend of my parents. One thing I shall always remember about James Weldon is going up to Great Barrington to spend a summer weekend with him and his wife, Grace—in this exquisite house that has always remained as my idea of what a country house should be. It was a converted barn to which they had added a wing. It was exquisitely appointed, and off across a little stream and across a sweep of green lawn was a little cabin that Johnson did his writing in. There was a beautiful desk, with a little pot of flowers and a bowl of beautiful apples. It was just *so* elegant. In those days, I was, I suppose, on my way to a career in the theatre, so I was *terribly* pushy, and a *great* showoff. I had, you know, to be paid attention to. But Johnson was so generous, so giving a human being. There were a lot of people of his renown and position who would have said, 'Yes, little girl, well, that's interesting.' But I would make dress designs for my paper dolls and cut them all out, and I would have *stacks* of them. And he would always be willing to take me on his knee and pore over these dress designs. And I'm sure it was just *killing* for him, poor thing. But he just endured it, and with such grace. To me, that was a real fellow there—to be able to put up with this annoying little girl and her cutouts.

"I knew Langston Hughes more than any of the other young writers of the Harlem Renaissance. He was such a gay, living human being. I *loved* him. He was so marvellous, with a twinkle in his eyes. It was wonderful to have lived among people then. Sometimes you wonder, How was it possible? Because things were not ungrim then. Some of the years we are talking about were during the Depression. *I* never got any sense of diminished enthusiasm, diminished vigor, diminished hope. Of course, it's entirely possible that some of those lives, when I was not conscious of them, or after I knew them, came to bad ends. But I'm talking about a period when I was just an onlooker."

She summed up: "There was a wonderful vivacity and excitement. I do think that those of us who were growing up then held that view of life in the United States. There was a sense that *if* you kept your nose clean, and if you *went* to school, and you *held* a good job, and you *made* a little money, and you washed and ironed your clothes— that it was all going to turn out all right. This turned out to be a fallacy. And I think that is why a good many of us, and I don't exclude myself, have subsequently been through rather bitter times. During such times, we felt bitter about what we thought was a true investment in a wonderful future for this country—where we *would* all get along together, and allow each other breathing space. It came as a shock to me that there were barriers against my becoming one of the great stars of all time. Because I thought I'd done all the things right. But it's not that simple, is it? I'm harking back to a time before the truth became known—when there was a self-esteem, an enormous self-assuredness, an enormous optimism."

The Thrill Is Gone

IF BLACK Harlem was once a heaven, or was seen to be one by the migrants and the commentators of the nineteen-twenties, it had ceased to be that by the beginning of the nineteen-fifties. When the early optimism had been exhausted, there remained, among the majority of the population, almost all the racial and social hardships that many had hoped would be nonexistent in the finest urban community that blacks had ever occupied in the United States.

Added to this circumstance was the fact that by 1950 many of those who helped to make Harlem the most brilliant black city in the world had died—depleting the reservoir of idealism and exemplary achievement that had nourished the community's positive sense of itself. Among those who died were Bob Cole, of the Cole and Johnson musical team (1911); George Walker, Bert Williams's stage partner (1911); Ada Overton Walker, one of New York's first black female stars (1914); Philip A. Payton, Jr., "the father of black Harlem" (1917); Scott Joplin (1917); James Reese Europe, pioneering jazz musician in New York (1919); Madame C. J. Walker (1919); Bert Williams (1922); Florence Mills, a blithe spirit of the musical stage (1927); Charles S. Gilpin, the first major black American actor of this century (1930); A'Lelia Walker (1931); Rudolph Fisher and Wallace Thurman (1934); Richard B. Harrison, who starred as "De Lawd" in Marc Connelly's *Green Pastures* (1935); Rose McClendon (1936); Hutchens C. Bishop, the rector of St. Philip's Protestant Episcopal Church (1937); Charles W. Anderson, Harlem's leading Republican politician, and James Weldon Johnson (1938); Arthur Schomburg, whose book collection became the foundation of the Schomburg Center for Research in Black History (1938); Ida L. Moore, co-owner of the *Age* and the wife of its editor (1939); Chick Webb (1939); Marcus Garvey, the ancestor of Harlem's black-nationalist movement (1940, while living in London); Fats Waller, the first of the outstanding jazz musicians to have been raised in Harlem (1943); Jules Bledsoe, the actor and concert singer (1943); Fred R. Moore, the editor of the *Age* (1943); Edward A. Johnson, the first black elected to the New York State Assembly (1944); Will Marion Cook, the pioneering ragtime and jazz composer (1944); Peyton F. Anderson, one of the earliest black physicians to settle in Harlem (1945); Mattie Fletcher Powell, the wife of Adam Clayton Powell, Sr. (1945); Frederick A. Cullen, the minister of the Salem Methodist Church (1946); Countee Cullen, the foster son of Frederick Cullen, and a leading poet of the Harlem Renaissance (1946); Jack Johnson, the first black heavyweight champion of the world (1946); John E. Nail, one of the rental agents who helped open up Harlem to black residency (1947); Jimmie Lunceford (1947); Claude McKay (1948); and Bill (Bojangles) Robinson, Harlem's great tap-dancer (1949).

By 1950, many notable residents had moved out of the community. "In the twenties, thirties, and forties, there was a concentration," Kenneth B. Clark has said. "But in the late forties and early fifties, dispersal began. As the black middle class progressed and moved away, the community lost certain kinds of stimulating people and energy." According to the historian John Henrik Clarke, who became a resident of Harlem in the early thirties, "In the years after the Second World War, Harlem became a community in decline. Many old residents, now successful enough to afford a better neighborhood, moved to Westchester, Long Island, or Connecticut." When the poet Arna Bontemps, who had lived in Harlem during the twenties, returned on a visit about twenty years later, he found it to be "another place." People he had known, some of whom had helped to bring Harlem its fame, "did not live there anymore." A national black magazine reported in 1951 that St. Albans, in Queens, was becoming the "suburban Sugar Hill." The publication ran photographs of the expensive houses that Harlem celebrities—including Count Basie, Mercer Ellington, Billie Holiday, and Ella Fitzgerald—had bought out there.

Not much remained of Harlem's once glamorous cabaret life. Since the end of Prohibition, in 1933, the district had been losing its appeal as Manhattan's late-night playground. After the riot of 1935, whites found a new reason to curtail their visits to Harlem. And following the bigger riot of 1943 only the more dauntless and devoted among them ventured uptown after dark. The Cotton Club—"The Aristocrat of Harlem"—moved downtown, to Broadway and Forty-eighth Street, in 1936. Several popular night clubs of the nineteen-twenties and thirties went out of business, though a few, like Smalls' Paradise, remained open. Stage shows were as lively and crowded as ever at the Apollo—perhaps the only place of its kind in Harlem on which stardust would continue to fall for years to come. The big bands still swung at the Savoy, but not as many as in the past, and not as spiritedly as they had in the thirties and early forties. Innovative bebop stylists like Dizzy Gillespie, Charlie Parker, Thelonious Monk, and Kenny Clarke, who had been experimenting with their new sounds—their subversive revolts against the swing tradition—at Minton's Playhouse, in Harlem, began appearing more frequently downtown, especially at the jazz clubs along West Fifty-second Street. "The heyday of Negro entertainment is long gone," a Harlem newspaper columnist wrote in 1949. "Nobody comes to Harlem anymore. Nobody seems to care. . . . Only a few places offer anything approaching a show, and even so it's nothing like the days when 'Harlem jumped.' "

There remained, of course, the majority of those who had been living there for decades—those who were unable to move elsewhere, and those who, because they liked it where they were, had no desire to. Above all—the clearest sign that black Harlem, despite its decline, was not about to disappear—all the major churches were still there. In 1950, while observing Harlem's fiftieth year as a black community, the *Age* asked this question of a few residents: "Why do you live in Harlem?" A telephone operator replied, "You feel at home here. It certainly isn't the worst place in the world to live in." An ice vender said, "I know everybody in my block and I don't think I want to go anywhere else to live until I go to heaven." A waiter said, "I live in Harlem because I know of no other place to go." And an unemployed man said, "What a question! I can't find anywhere else to live, and if I could I don't think I'd want to live there. I'm originally from Daytona, Florida, but I've been in Harlem for seventeen years. I wouldn't know how I'd feel living any place else. There's something in Harlem that gets in one's blood. It gets there and stays—it never leaves."

The place may indeed have got into the blood, even into the bones, of some who went on living there, yet Harlem was no longer the social and cultural magnet it had once been. It had ceased to be the exciting metropolis to which almost all blacks once dreamed of coming—in search of refuge, opportunity, gaiety, a wider freedom, and a brighter future. The hearts of new arrivals no longer missed a beat just at being there—as when the young Duke Ellington, on seeing Harlem for the first time, likened it to scenes from *The Arabian Nights*. In the South, if there were still boats that were "leaving soon for New York," not so many of the passengers were headed for Harlem. Not so many blacks down there felt—as their elders had in the buoyant and optimistic twenties—that Harlem was where they belonged.

Notes

While this work rests upon the aid of all its sources, I should like to make special mention of a few of them. Anyone who attempts today a reconstruction of Harlem's cultural history—especially the earlier stages of it—will find, gratefully, that a path to the subject has already been charted by such pioneering works as James Weldon Johnson's *Black Manhattan*, Seth. M. Scheiner's *Negro Mecca*, Gilbert Osofsky's *Harlem: The Making of a Ghetto*, and Claude McKay's *Harlem: Negro Metropolis*. And since the origins of black Harlem cannot be fully understood without some knowledge of how and where its inhabitants lived previously, the contemporary investigator will be equally indebted to the following, for their descriptions and accounts of the black experience in mid- and lower Manhattan in the late nineteenth and early twentieth centuries: Johnson's autobiography *Along This Way* and his novel *The Autobiography of an Ex-Colored Man*; Mary White Ovington's *Half a Man* and *The Walls Came Tumbling Down*; Paul Laurence Dunbar's novel *The Sport of the Gods*; Adam Clayton Powell, Sr.'s autobiography *Against the Tide*; and the files of the now defunct New York *Age*, which, for the greater part of its existence, was the major black newspaper in the city. Research papers prepared during the thirties by the Harlem branch of the W.P.A. Writers Program also cast much light upon aspects of black life in Manhattan, before the migration to Harlem began. All the material mentioned thus far— and much more that is contained in black newspapers and magazines, clippings, books, manuscript collections, recordings, and photographs is to be found at the Schomburg Center for Research in Black Culture, than which there is no more valuable resource of its kind in the country.

Occupying an important place in Harlem's cultural history is the literary movement it helped to energize during the twenties and thirties. The fiction and poetry of this movement—which contain much material that can be used in a historical narrative of Harlem life—are generally available; but it is chiefly at the James Weldon Johnson Memorial Collection at Yale that one may examine the voluminous correspondence that passed among these writers and their sponsors, correspondence which illuminates not only the literary and social climate of what was called the Harlem Renaissance but also the personalities of the men and women who were at its center. But despite the wealth of material in the Johnson Memorial Collection, the modern researcher will also have to rely heavily on the files of *Opportunity* and *The Crisis*—black periodicals that helped to stimulate the Harlem Renaissance—and upon Langston Hughes' *The Big Sea*, which is the best autobiographical record of the years when Harlem represented the most animating literary voice in the black world.

"Forgotten Streets"

Origins and growth of black population of Manhattan: James Weldon Johnson, *Black Manhattan* (New York: Atheneum, Studies in American Negro Life, 1968; originally published in 1930), p. 4; and Gilbert Osofsky, *Harlem: The Making of a Ghetto* (Harper Torchbooks, 1966), p. 83. New York Presbytery debates decision of St. James Presbyterian to move to Harlem: "White Landlords Make Objection to Church," *Age*, June 11, 1914. "there is no good and no bad Negro section": Mary Rankin Cranston, "The Housing of the Negro in New York City," *Southern Workman*, June 1902. "their difficulty in procuring a place": Mary White Ovington, "The Negro Home in New York," *Charities*, Oct. 7, 1905. "college graduates and cutthroats": G. L. Collin, "The City within a City," *Outlook*, Sept. 29, 1906.

"The ambitious Negro has moved": Mary White Ovington, *Half a Man* (New York: Hill and Wang, American Century Series, 1969), p. 19. "the red would be seen overrunning": Bayrd Still, *Mirror for Gotham* (New York: New York U. Press, 1956), p. 240. "It is the southwestern corner": "The Negro Quarter," *Tribune*, Oct. 13, 1895. "Amid scenes of indescribable": "The New Ghetto," *Harper's Weekly*, Jan. 9, 1897. "country bred" migrants from the South: W. E. B. Du Bois, "The Black North," *N.Y. Times*, Nov. 17, 1901. They "had heard of New York": Paul Laurence Dunbar, *The Sport of the Gods* (New York: Collier-Macmillan, 1970; originally published in 1902 by Dodd, Mead), p. 68.

Occupations among blacks in Manhattan: Helen Tucker, "The Negro Craftsman in New York," *Southern Workman*, Oct. 1907, Jan. 1908, Feb. 1908, and March 1908; George E. Haynes, *The Negro at Work in New York City* (New York: Columbia U. Press, 1912), pp. 58–59, 68–75, 80–81, 98–103. "The Negroes have something over": Du Bois, "The Black North," *N.Y. Times*, Nov. 17, 1901. "natural antipathy to the negroes": J. G. Speed, "The Negro in New York," *Harper's Weekly*, Dec. 22, 1900; reprinted in *Harlem on My Mind*, Allon Schoener, ed. (New York: Random House, 1968), pp. 19–22. "Negro, Italian, and Jew": Jacob Riis, *The Battle with the Slum* (New York: Macmillan, 1902), p. 110. Findings by graduate student at Columbia: John P. Clyde, "The Negro in New York," M.A. thesis, Columbia U., 1899.

"Property is not rented to": Speed, *Harper's Weekly*, Dec. 22, 1900. "a certain style" and "an atmosphere of refinement": Mary White Ovington, "Mission Sketches," *Charities*, Oct. 7, 1905. "The poorest negro": Jacob Riis, *How the Other Half Lives* (New York: Scribner, 1890), pp. 115–16. "sadly cluttered" but "not bare and ugly": Ovington, "The Negro Home in New York," *Charities*, Oct. 7, 1905.

Black Bohemia

"a city of crime and gaiety": Samuel Hopkins Adams, *Tenderloin* (New York: Random House, 1959), pp. 9–10. Charles Parkhurst's sermon and its aftermath: M. R. Werner, "Dr. Parkhurst's Crusade," *New Yorker*, Nov. 19, 1955. "Saloons kept open": Adams, *Tenderloin*, pp. 9–10. "Many of the worst dives": Herbert Asbury, *The Gangs of New York* (New York: Alfred A. Knopf,

1927), p. 177. "conducted with the quietness": "New York's Rich Negroes," *Sun*, Jan. 18, 1903. Other sources for the boxers, jockeys, and saloons of Black Bohemia are: Johnson, *Black Manhattan*, p. 61; Richard Latimer, "History of Negro Saloons," a research paper for the W.P.A. Writers Program, at the Schomburg Center for Research in Black Culture; Floyd G. Snelson, "Harlem," *Age*, Feb. 28, 1939. "a cabaret over a stable": interview with Eubie Blake.

"From the stories the boys tell": Noble Sissle, "Show Business," *Age*, Oct. 23, 1948. "It drew its pupils from": Dunbar, *The Sport of the Gods*, pp. 94–95, 117. "The 'spread' was truly": *Globe* (which later became the *Age*), Feb. 17, 1883. "The floor of the parlor" and "The stout man at the piano" and "originated in the questionable resorts": James Weldon Johnson, *The Autobiography of an Ex-Colored Man*, in *Three Negro Classics* (Avon Library, 1965), pp. 447, 450–52. "Take that ragtime out": interview with Blake. "Many of them are unfit": Ann Charters, ed., *The Ragtime Songbook* (New York: Oak Publications, 1965), p. 26.

"human derelicts . . . valley of Baca": Reverdy C. Ransom, *The Pilgrimage of Harriet Ransom's Son* (Nashville: Sunday School Union, undated), p. 228. In the evenings after parliament adjourned: J. H. Plumb, *The Light of History* (New York: Delta Books, 1972), pp. 234–35. "En route to the Mission": Ransom, *The Pilgrimage*, pp. 232–33. "the most notorious red light district": Adam Clayton Powell, Sr., *Against the Tide* (New York: Richmond R. Smith, 1938), pp. 49–57.

Social Leadership

"the Southern type of revival": Clyde's M.A. thesis, "The Negro in New York." "Strangers who visit": Ovington, *Half a Man*, p. 67. "What kind of Negroes do the American people want": quoted in Benjamin Brawley, *The Negro Genius* (New York: Dodd, Mead, 1937), p. 194 (Apollo Editions). "utterances were sensational": "The Black Man's Burden," *Tribune*, April 14, 1899. "most of these people came": Ransom, *The Pilgrimage*, p. 207. Early biographical material on Adam Clayton Powell, Sr., and references to the growth of the Abyssinian Baptist Church may be found in: "The Rev. A. C. Powell Tells about First Negro Mayor of Ohio," *Age*, Feb. 23, 1929; "The World's Richest Negro Baptist Church," *Age*, April 17, 1913; "A Great Churchman," *Age*, Dec. 10, 1938.

St. Philip's drew "some of the most": *The Anniversary Book of St. Philip's Church* (New York, 1943), pp. 9, 26. "When he talked of Christ": Mary White Ovington, *The Walls Came Tumbling Down* (New York, Schocken, Paperback Series, 1970), pp. 40–41. William H. Brooks as "the most influential": "St. Mark's Methodist Episcopal Church," *The Colored American*, June 1906.

"the principal place of resort": Ransom, *The Pilgrimage*, p. 202. "there was scarcely a decent restaurant": James Weldon Johnson, *Along This Way* (Viking Compass Edition, 1968), p. 171. Fifty-third Street "is to the Negro colonies": "Sports and Amusements of Negro New York," W.P.A. Writers Program research paper at the Schomburg Center. Descriptions and accounts of Theodore Drury and his opera company: Johnson, *Along This Way*, pp. 172–74; *Black Manhattan*, pp. 116–17; "The Drury Opera Company in Verdi's 'Aida,' " *The Colored American*, Aug. 1903.

"the ambition of every respectable": "The Sons of New York," *Tribune*, March 20, 1892. "The taint of slavery": Ovington, *Half a Man*, p. 96. "It will be news to many": "Wealthy Negro Citizens," *Times*, July 14, 1895. "I must have the wrong number": "Well-to-Do Negroes in and around New York," *Tribune*, Feb. 22, 1903. "You must remember": "New York's Rich Negroes," *Sun*, Jan. 18, 1903.

Music and Comedy

"The neighborhood is full": "New York's Rich Negroes," *Sun*, Jan. 18, 1903. "hordes of the newly rich": Snelson, "Harlem," *Age*, Feb. 28, 1939. "the manner and means" and "the radiant point": Johnson, *Along This Way*, pp. 172–73, 177. Virginia Cunningham in her *Paul Laurence Dunbar and His Song* (New York: Dodd, Mead, p. 179) states that "the very air" of the Marshall hotel "was more intoxicating than the liquor."

"Black-faced white comedians": George Walker, "The Real 'Coon' on the American Stage," *Theatre Magazine*, Aug. 1906. In his *Blacking Up* (New York: Oxford U. Press, 1974, p. 51), Robert C. Toll speaks of minstrelsy as "the first example of the way American popular culture would exploit and manipulate Afro-Americans and their culture to please and benefit white Americans." "At no time have colored stage folk": Lester A. Walton, "The Future of the Negro on the Stage," *The Colored American*, Oct. 1905. "Rosamond Johnson's songs set a new": Jack Burton, *The Blue Book of Tin Pan Alley* (Watkins Glen: Century House, 1950), p. 107. Will Marion Cook as "the most original genius": Johnson, *Along This Way*, p. 173. "I know why the caged bird": Paul Laurence Dunbar, *The Complete Poems* (New York: Dodd, Mead, Apollo Editions, undated), pp. 102–3. "I am told that Mr. Cook": Ovington, *Half a Man*, p. 174. William Dean Howells' introduction to Dunbar's *Lyrics of a Lowly Life* is reprinted in *The Complete Poems*. Acquaintances rushed up . . . but "it did not appear": Johnson, *Along This Way*, p. 152.

"In those days": Walker, "The Real 'Coon' on the American Stage." Dressed "always a point": Johnson, *Along This Way*, p. 177. Walker "greatly preferred" and "As a friend said": Ann Charters, *Nobody* (New York: Collier-Macmillan, 1970), pp. 34, 89. "highly intelligent": Johnson, *Along This Way*, p. 176. "The way we've aimed": Charters, *Nobody*, p. 71. They had "vindicated their right" and "Williams is the": "The Drama," *Tribune*, Feb. 19, 1903. The lyrics to "I'm a Jonah Man" are quoted from Charters, *The Ragtime Songbook*, p. 71. "He would tell his audiences": Lawrence W. Levine, *Black Culture and Black Consciousness* (New York: Oxford U. Press, paper, 1977), pp. 360–61. "There were a lot of": "Cake Walk Champ Returns," *Age*, Sept 1, 1934. "the funniest man I ever saw": Charters, *Nobody*, p. 132. Bert Williams reflected upon his own life and career in "The Comic Side of Trouble," which he wrote for the Jan. 1918 *The American Magazine*.

Departures and Arrivals

"With the advent": This report, which appeared in the *Tribune* in 1903, is reprinted in Grace M. Meyer, *Once Upon a City* (New York: Macmillan, 1958), pp. 285–86. "With the coming of the Civil War": Richard O'Connor, *The Roaring Days of New York's West Side* (Phila.: Lippincott, 1958), pp.

11–13. "On August 12": Frank Moss, *Story of the Riot* (New York: Citizens Protective League), pp. 1–2. "These assaults": "A New York Riot," *Tribune* (editorial), Aug. 18, 1900. "I heard many native Americans": Speed, "The Negro in New York," *Harper's Weekly*, Dec. 22, 1900. "Let every Negro get a permit": J. A. Rogers, "The Race Riot of 1900," W.P.A. Writers Program research paper at the Schomburg Center. "This is a conservative": "Negro Pastor Defies Police to Answer," *N.Y. Times*, Aug. 27, 1900. Brooks's letter to Mayor Van Wyck ("We ask for no money") was reprinted in Moss' *Story of the Riot*. "An investigation was held": Johnson, *Black Manhattan*, pp. 129–30. "every day was moving day": Ovington, *The Walls Came Tumbling Down*, p. 33.

"tiptoeing up some of the": Frederick Bermingham, *It Was Good While It Lasted* (Phila.: Lippincott, 1960), pp. 41–42. "The people attracted to": Osofsky, *Harlem: The Making of a Ghetto*, p. 79. "impeccably respectable": Lloyd Morris, *Incredible New York* (New York: Random House, 1951), pp. 201–2. The *Harlem Home News* reported on "the 'nigger' dance" on Sept. 8, 1911.

A Struggle for Harlem

The *Herald* took note of an "untoward circumstance" in its issue of Dec. 24, 1905; the report, headed "Negroes Move into Harlem," is reprinted in Schoener, *Harlem on My Mind*, p. 23. "Speculators who intend to make": Osofsky, *Harlem: The Making of a Ghetto*, pp. 87–89. "The great subway proposition": "White Landlords Make Objections to Church," *Age*, June 11, 1914. "The hardships I suffered": "Payton Closes Harlem Realty Deal," *Age*, July 12, 1917. "to get even": "Local Realty Men Doing Big Business," *Age*, Dec. 5, 1912. "With offices rivalling": "To Use Race Prejudice," *Tribune*, July 26, 1904. (Other informative reports on Philip A. Payton and his business associates are: "Afro-American Realty Company," *The Colored American*, Nov. 1904; "Growth of the Afro-American Realty Company," *The Colored American*, Feb. 1906; Roscoe Conklin Simmons, "The Afro-American Realty Company," *The Colored American*, May 1905. Payton's partners in the Afro-American Realty Company included such prominent black New Yorkers of the time as James C. Thomas, an undertaker; James C. Garner, a house-cleaning and renovating-business man; Wilford H. Smith, a lawyer; Fred R. Moore, journalist; William H. Brooks, clergyman; and Charles W. Anderson, the city's leading black Republican politician. See also "Charles J. Crowder vs. Afro-American Realty Company and Philip A. Payton, Jr.", Oct. 25, 1906, County Clerk's Office, New York City.)

"In the eyes of the whites": Johnson, *Black Manhattan*, p. 150. "The Negro invasion": "Heart of Harlem Now to Be Invaded by Negroes," *Harlem Home News*, July 28, 1911. Negroes "should buy large tracts": "Loans for White Renegades Who Back Negroes Cut Off." *Harlem Home News*, April 7, 1911. "signed an agreement" and "The document": Osofsky, *Harlem: The Making of a Ghetto*, pp. 106–7; "Loans for White Renegades . . . Cut Off," *Harlem Home News*. The case of Caroline Morolath and Rafael Greenbaum: "White Property Owners Quarrel," *Age*, Aug. 14, 1913.

"The deal pulled off": "Pull Off Big Deal," *Age*, March 30, 1911. (See also "Doors of New Church Opened" and "Becoming a Colored Residential Section," *Age*, March 30, 1911, and Jan. 19, 1911, respectively; "Whites Ousted by Blacks from More Harlem Homes," *Harlem Home News*, March 31, 1911.) Negroes would "not stay long": "Loans for White Renegades . . . Cut Off," *Harlem Home News*. "Can nothing be done": letter to the *N.Y. Times* reprinted in *Age*, "The Negro in Harlem" (editorial), July 11, 1912. "Are you aware of the fact": "White Landlords Make Objections to Church," *Age*, June 11, 1914.

"The Promised Land"

Designated boundaries of Harlem: Osofsky, *Harlem: The Making of a Ghetto*, p. 221. "The old Harlem was dead": Konrad Bercovici, "The Black Blocks of Manhattan," *Harper's*, Oct. 1924; reprinted in Bercovici, *Around the World in New York* (New York: Century, 1924), pp. 211–48. "I can remember": Arthur Gerald Goldberg, "A New York Childhood," *New Yorker*, Nov. 9, 1929.

Harlem "became a symbol of liberty": Powell, *Against the Tide*, pp. 70–71. "Harlem . . . draws immigrants": Chester T. Crowell, "The World's Largest Negro City," *Saturday Evening Post*, Aug. 8, 1925. "Only Negroes *belong*": Eslanda Goode Robeson, *Paul Robeson: Negro* (London: Gollancz, 1930), pp. 47–48. "The most populous city block": A. J. Liebling, *Back Where I Came From* (New York: Sheridan House, 1938), p. 147. "the natural boundaries of Harlem": "Millions of Dollars in Harlem Realty," *Age*, July 31, 1920. Ralph Ellison's testimony before the Senate Sub-Committee on Executive Reorganization (1966) is reprinted in *Crisis of the Cities*, a booklet published by the A. Philip Randolph Institute, New York City, 1968.

"Negroes lived in some 1,100 houses": Osofsky, *Harlem: The Making of a Ghetto*, p. 122. "In one district": E. F. Dykoff, "A Negro City in New York," *Outlook*, Dec. 23, 1914. The *Age* is "mortified" at aspects of black conduct: "Dragging the Race Down" (editorial), *Age*, June 9, 1910. "The New York *Age* . . . finds men of value": letter to the editor quoted in *Age* editorial ("The Age Sifts the Chaff from the Wheat"), Oct. 3, 1912. "The *Age* has always believed": "Brief History of the Growth and Development of the New York *Age*," *Age*, Dec. 29, 1923. Blacks must "learn to value money": quoted in Seth M. Scheiner, *The Negro Mecca* (New York: New York U. Press, 1965), p. 70.

Powell urged members to "go into business": "$4,500,000 Is Spent Annually in Harlem," *Age*, Oct. 3, 1912. The *Outlook* article reporting on Harlem's business development in 1914 is Dykoff's "A Negro City in New York." For percentage and kinds of black-owned businesses in the early years, see the *Age*, March 12, 1921 ("Lenox Avenue Perfumery Company . . ."); April 9, 1921 ("Business on 135th Street Is Booming"); Aug. 21, 1920 ("Three Unusual Business Enterprises in Harlem"). "Many of the white businessmen": "Opportune Time for Racial Business Growth in Harlem," *Age*, Sept. 30, 1923.

Every nationality "making money out of Negroes": James Weldon Johnson, "On Harlem," *Age*, Dec. 24, 1914. Complaints by president of the Colored Men's Business Association ("One great handicap") and response of black customers ("In patronizing the Negro merchant"): "Influential Trade Body," *Age*, April 13, 1916. The two *Age* editorials titled "Clean 'Em Out" appeared in the issues of April 6 and 13, 1911. "Harlem is evidently": "Harlem Wants Crooks Lynched to Stop Crimes," *Harlem Home News*, March 10, 1911. Harlem street gangs: "20,000 Negroes Live in Harlem," *Age*, May 11, 1911. Baseball game ends in disorder: "The Shortstop Used a Big 'Mitt' and It Nearly Caused a Riot," *Harlem Home News*, April 28, 1911.

Harlem "infested" with saloons: "Too Many Saloons in Harlem," *Age*, Oct. 1, 1914. Eugene Kinckle Jones' estimate of the number of saloons and liquor stores in Harlem appeared as a letter to the editor of the *Outlook* ("A Negro City in New York"), March 10, 1915. "If those who drink liquor": "Raise Cry of Persecution," *Age*, March 8, 1916. John W. Connor introduced afternoon teas: "Afternoon Teas Now the Rage in Harlem," *Age*, April 16, 1914.

Style in Ragtime

"Some of the dances were pretty wild": Willie (the Lion) Smith and George Hoefer, *Music on My Mind* (New York: Da Capo, 1975), p. 32. The turkey trot is described on p. 96 of Marshall and Jean Stearns's *Jazz Dance* (New York: Macmillan, 1968). The Texas Tommy described: Caroline and Charles Faffin, *Dancing and Dancers Today* (New York: Dodd, Mead, 1912), pp. 269–71. The Texas Tommy "*was* like the Lindy": Stearns, *Jazz Dance*, p. 129. "In a cabaret, little tables": Morris, *Incredible New York*, pp. 318–19. "drew space, headlines, and cartoons": Johnson, *Black Manhattan*, p. 174. "I'd 'ball the jack'": Stearns, *Jazz Dance*, p. 125. "The Negro race is dancing": "Race Is Dancing Itself to Death," *Age*, Jan. 8, 1914. Women entertainers "extremely careless": "The Cabaret as Seen in Harlem," *Age*, June 1, 1916.

Vernon and Irene Castle "transformed the dance craze": Morris, *Incredible New York*, pp. 321-22. "was the only music that completely" and "a very commanding figure": Irene Castle McLaughlin, "Jim Europe—A Reminiscence," *Opportunity*, March 1930. Europe was "the Duke Ellington of his time": interview with Noble Sissle. "one of the most remarkable men": "Negro Place in Music," *Evening Post*, March 13, 1914; reprinted in Robert Kimball and William Bolcom, *Reminiscing with Sissle and Blake* (New York: Viking, 1973), p. 60.

"were wonderful musicians and singers": interview with Sissle. "a musical associan . . . who could not read notes": "Deacon Jones and the Clef Club," *Age*, June 7, 1917. "Never has such a large": Lester A. Walton, "The Clef Club Concert," *Age*, June 2, 1910. Flyer advertising second Clef Club concert: reprinted in Kimball and Bolcom, *Reminiscing with Sissle and Blake*, p. 57. "Few white people had ever heard": *Craftsman*, March 1913. "After the turn of the century": interview with Sissle. "Later, when Europe formed": Sissle, "Show Business," *Age*, Sept. 24, 1948.

"there never was any such music": "Theater Comment," *Age*, April 3, 1909. "I have often sat": Lester A. Walton, "Theatrical Comment," *Age*, April 3, 1913. "I am a composer of ragtime": Walton, "Theatrical Jottings," *Age*, Aug. 14, 1913. "From ragtime to grand opera": *Age*, March 5, 1908; quoted in Samuel B. Charters and Leonard Kunstadt, *Jazz: A History of the New York Scene* (New York: Doubleday, 1962), p. 43.

Joplin "created an entirely new phase": *The American Musician*, June 24,

1911; quoted in Charters and Kunstadt, *Jazz*, p. 49. "A single performance": Rudi Blesh and Harriet Janis, *They All Played Ragtime* (New York: Grove Press, Evergreen Books, 1959), p. 249. Joplin did not recover "from the blow": Blesh and Janis, *They All Played Ragtime*, p. 249. Vera Brodsky Lawrence praises *Treemonisha*: Vera Brodsky Lawrence, "Scott Joplin and Treemonisha," in libretto notes to Deutsche Grammophon recording of *Treemonisha* (stereo 2707083), pp. 10–12.

The Beauty Business

Powell denounces the smoking of cigarettes by women: "They Smoked Cigarettes," *Age*, March 17, 1910. "Prominent white women": "New York Society," *Age*, Jan. 14, 1909. "In the columns of our contemporary": "A Lack of Race Pride," *N.Y. Times*, Aug. 8, 1909. On "the lastest fad": "Now the Men Straighten Hair," *Age*, Feb. 9, 1911. James P. Johnson recalls early form of conking: Martin P. Williams, *Jazz Panorama* (New York: Crowell-Collier, 1962), pp. 58–59.

Beauticians, early beauty schools, and systems: "Negro Beauty Parlors in New York," W.P.A. Writers Program research paper at the Schomburg Center. The Walker System as "a passport to prosperity": advertisement in the *Age*, Aug. 14, 1913. Walker System "became essential": Claude McKay: *Harlem: Negro Metropolis* (Harcourt Brace Jovanovich, Harvest Books, 1940), p. 98. Madame Walker explains size of annual income: "Over 10,000 in Her Employ," *Age*, March 2, 1916; "Wealthiest Negro Woman's Suburban Mansion," *N.Y. Times*, Nov. 4, 1917. (It was also in the latter article that the *N.Y. Times* described Madame Walker's mansion at Irvington, in Westchester county. For a description of Madame Walker's apartment on West 136th Street in Harlem, see also "Queen of Gotham's Colored 400," *Literary Digest*, Oct. 13, 1917.) Madame Walker's two accounts of how she developed her hair-growing formula and business are contained in the foregoing *N.Y. Times* and *Literary Digest* articles.

Harlem at Sixteen

This chapter is a summary of one of the earliest magazine articles to give a detailed insider's view of black life in Harlem: Charles Martin, "The Harlem Negro," A.M.E. Zion *Quarterly Review*, Oct.–Nov.–Dec. 1916.

Democracy and the Flag

The soldiers made a "splendid showing": James Weldon Johnson, "Negro Loyalty in the Present Crisis," *Age*, March 29, 1917. The men "would walk out of their way": Arthur Little, *From Harlem to the Rhine* (New York: Covici-Friede, 1936), p. 14. "It was amusing to see": "Biographical Sketch of J. C. Thomas," W.P.A. Writers Program research paper at the Schomburg Center. "these darkies playing soldiers": "Negro Organizations in New York," W.P.A. Writers Program research paper at the Schomburg Center.

The Wilson Administration's "generally indifferent . . . regard for blacks": David M. Kennedy, *Over Here*: The First World War and American Society

(New York: Oxford U. Press, 1980), p. 281. "One colored man came into": Johnson, *Black Manhattan*, p. 233. Sermon of F. M. Hyden at St. James Presbyterian Church: "Pastor Preached Loyalty to the Nation," *Age*, March 29, 1917. Adam Clayton Powell, Sr., on "This is the proper time": "Tells Negroes to Wage Bloodless War for Their Constitutional Rights," *Age*, March 29, 1917. "The cup overflowed": Johnson, *Black Manhattan*, p. 238. Silent protest parade down Fifth Avenue: "Negroes in Protest March in Fifth Avenue," *N.Y. Times*, July 29, 1917; "A Negro March with Muffled Drums," *Survey*, Aug. 4, 1917. "Let us not hesitate": "Close Ranks," *Crisis*, July 1918. Hubert Harrison's reply to the "Close Ranks" editorial was titled "The Descent of Du Bois" and was published in his periodical *The Voice* on July 25, 1918; it was later re-printed in Harrison's collection of writings *When Africa Awakes* (New York: Poro Press, 1920). "Since when has the subject race": quoted in Jervis Anderson, *A. Philip Randolph: A Biographical Portrait* (New York: Harcourt Brace Jovanovich, 1973), p. 101. "loud-lunged orators": "Soap Box Orators," *Age*, June 28, 1919.

The letter of Hamilton Fish, Jr., to his family was published in the *Age*, May 11, 1918, under the heading "15th is the Most Envied American Regiment Abroad." "I seem to feel": wartime diary of James W. Johnson. "I have seen many of your papers" and the *Age*'s acknowledgment of its error: "Return of Our Fighters," *Age*, Feb. 15, 1919.

Toward a Black Theatre

"Aside from the Lincoln and Lafayette": George S. Schuyler, *Black and Conservative* (New Rochelle, N.Y.: Arlington House, 1966), p. 139. "prominent Negroes" barred at the Lafayette: "Drawing Color Line is Resented," *Age*, Nov. 14, 1912. *Darkydom* called "the biggest and best": "Miller and Lyles Score a Big Hit," *Age*, Oct. 28, 1915. Lafayette Players "a boon to the Negro public": Schuyler, *Black and Conservative*, p. 124. "The Negro performer in New York": Johnson, *Black Manhattan*, pp. 171–72. Theophilus Lewis criticizes Lafayette Players: Theodore Kornweibel, Jr., *No Crystal Stair* (Westport, Conn.: Greenwood Press, 1975), pp. 112, 116. The *Globe* and the *Evening Post* reviews of Ridgely Torrence's three one-acters were later quoted in *Current Opinion* ("First Steps Towards a National Negro Theatre"), May, 1917. *The New Republic* comments on the same event appeared in its issue of April 14, 1917, under the heading "After the Play."

O'Neill's *The Dreamy Kid* as an "apprentice work": Louis Sheaffer, *O'Neill: Son and Playwright* (Boston: Little, Brown, 1968), p. 469. "Are you Charles Gilpin": Louis Sheaffer, *O'Neill: Son and Artist* (Boston: Little, Brown, 1973), p. 33. Heywood Broun's praise of Gilpin is quoted in Sheaffer, *O'Neill: Son and Artist*, p. 33. "It has remained for Charles Gilpin": "For a Negro Theatre," *New Republic*, Nov. 16, 1921. If Gilpin had "not been a Negro": Moss Hart, *Act One* (New York: Random House, 1959), p. 87. "I can honestly say": Sheaffer, *O'Neill: Son and Artist*, p. 37. "I'd be afraid to risk him": Sheaffer, *O'Neill: Son and Artist*, pp. 35, 37.

Robeson "soon became Harlem's special favorite": Eslanda Goode Robeson, *Paul Robeson: Negro*, pp. 68–69. George Jean Nathan's and Lawrence Stallings' comments on Paul Robeson (in *The American Mercury* and the

World, respectively) are quoted in Eslanda Goode Robeson's biography of her husband, pp. 76–77. "My experience as author with actor": O'Neill's statement appeared in *The Messenger* magazine, July 1925.

"Here Comes My Daddy Now"

"Harlem had a complete life": Eslanda Goode Robeson, *Paul Robeson: Negro*, p. 67. "The Harlem of 1919": Schuyler, *Black and Conservative*, p. 97. "There was a certain standard": quoted in Anderson, *A. Philip Randolph*, p. 57. "The negro soldiers were astonished": "Fifth Avenue Cheers Negro Veterans," *N.Y. Times*, Feb. 18, 1919. "The multitude of fellow citizens": Little, *From Harlem to the Rhine*, p. 361. "The Hellfighters marched between": "Old Fifteenth Given Rousing Reception," *Age*, Feb. 22, 1919. "Mothers, and wives, and sisters": Little, *From Harlem to the Rhine*, pp. 357–62. "We wonder how many people": "Under the Victory Arch," *Age*, Feb. 22, 1919. "under a canopy of blue": "Old Fifteenth . . . ," *Age*, Feb. 22, 1919.

"Eight months after the armistice": Johnson, *Black Manhattan*, p. 246. "The experience of victory": Arthur M. Schlesinger, Jr., *Crisis of the Old Order* (Boston: Houghton Mifflin, 1957), p. 11. "by long odds the most dangerous": "Radicalism and Sedition Among Negroes as Reflected in Their Publications: The Investigating Activities of the Department of Justice, Exhibit 10," *Senate Documents*, 66th Congress, 1st sess., 1919, vol. 12, p. 172.

Garvey: "Poet and Romancer"

There "recurred the feeling": Schuyler, *Black and Conservative*, p. 121. Blacks "ready for any program": David Cronon, *Black Moses* (U. of Wisconsin Press, paper, 1955), p. 36. "I was on a soapbox": Anderson, *A. Philip Randolph*, p. 122. "skeptical Harlemites": Cronon, *Black Moses*, p. 40. Many of Hubert Harrison's views on race consciousness and class consciousness were published in his magazine *The Voice* and are collected in his *When Africa Awakes* and *The Negro and the Nation* (New York: Cosmo-Advocate Press, 1917). Bringing his "magnetic personality": Johnson, *Black Manhattan*, p. 253. "We are striking homeward": quoted in Johnson, *Black Manhattan*, p. 254.

"Such opponents held": J. A. Rogers, *World's Great Men of Color*, Vol. 2 (New York: Collier-Macmillan, 1947), p. 422. The terms "jackass," "ignoramus," "pig," "buffoon," and "ugly" were used in anti-Garvey articles in *The Messenger* and *The Crisis* magazines, between 1920 and 1925. "The massive head": Lucien White, "Marcus Garvey: The Man . . . ," *Age*, Oct. 21, 1922. Herbert Seligman's portrait of Garvey was published originally in the *World* Sunday Magazine (Dec. 4, 1921) and was later reprinted by the *Age* on Dec. 10, 1921. "a supremely audacious move": Cronon, *Black Moses*, p. 51.

"low-roofed, hot": Rogers, *World's Great Men of Color*, p. 419. "upon the arrival of": "Garvey Holds Court," *Age*, Aug. 19, 1922. "Though he was opposing": Rogers, *World's Great Men of Color*, p. 419. "in raiment that": Rogers, *World's Great Men of Color*, p. 427.

From Ragtime to Jazz

"the sophisticates": Ethel Waters with Charles Samuels, *His Eye Is on the Sparrow* (New York: Doubleday, 1951), p. 124. "After you worked there":

His Eye Is on the Sparrow, pp. 124–25. The stride piano style "was created": James Lincoln Collier, *The Making of Jazz* (Boston: Houghton Mifflin, 1978), pp. 198–99. "New York pianists tried": Smith and Hoefer, *Music on My Mind*, p. 85; "To the Harlem cabaret owners": p. 92 of *Music on My Mind*. "I was learning a lot": Waters and Samuels, *His Eye Is on the Sparrow*, p. 145. "the greatest influence": Duke Ellington's prefatory remarks in Smith's and Hoefer's *Music on My Mind*. Description of Mamie Smith: Charters and Kunstadt, *Jazz*, p. 89. See also, "Quality Corporation Books Mamie Smith," *Age*, Nov. 13, 1920. Discussion of the origins and development of the Pace & Handy Music Company is based on W. C. Handy, *Father of the Blues* (New York: Macmillan, paper, 1941), p. 186. Ethel Waters' account of her experiences with Harry Pace and Black Swan Records: *His Eye Is on the Sparrow*, pp. 138, 141–42. "By 1919": Smith and Hoefer, *Music on My Mind*, p. 112.

"What a City!"

They were "pleased with the conditions": Crowell, "The World's Largest Negro City," *Saturday Evening Post*, Aug. 8, 1925. "pullulation of energy": John Chamberlain, "The Negro as Writer," *Bookman*, Sept. 1930. "Men and women dressed in the height of fashion": Floyd G. Snelson, "When Harlem Started Fun," *Age*, Oct. 29, 1949. "And we'll get drunker and drunker": Carl Van Vechten, *Parties* (New York: Bard/Avon Books, originally published by Alfred A. Knopf, 1930), p. 79. "The swarming, prosperous crowds": Morris, *Incredible New York*, p. 333. Covarrubias in Harlem: "Negro Drawings," *American Mercury*, Nov. 1927. Stanley Walker recalled white New Yorkers' attraction to Harlem night life in his *The Night Club Era* (New York: Frederick A. Stokes, 1933), pp. 249, 255. "One could visit these places": Archie Seale, "The Rise of Harlem as an Amusement Center," *Age*, Nov. 2, 1935. "Ten years ago": editorial, *American Mercury*, Oct. 1927.

"He is a seedy, collarless" and "Strutting the streets": "When Rural Negro Reaches Crucible," *N.Y. Times*, April 17, 1927; reprinted in *Harlem on My Mind*, pp. 70–71. Arna Bontemps recalled his first impressions of Harlem ("a foretaste of paradise") in his article "The Two Harlems," *American Scholar*, Spring 1945. Cab Calloway "awestruck by the whole scene": Calloway with Bryant Rollins, *Minnie the Moocher* (New York: Crowell, 1976), p. 68. "Why, it is just like the Arabian Nights": Duke Ellington quoted in "The Sound of Harlem" (an illustrated booklet), Jazz Odyssey, Vol. III; produced by Frank Driggs for Columbia Records, 1964.

"Oh, to be in Harlem again": Claude McKay, *Home to Harlem* (Harper, 1928), p. 15. "This is it": Rudolph Fisher, "Miss Cynthie," in *The Negro Caravan*, Sterling Brown et al, eds. (Citadel Press, 1941), pp. 54–65. "Fifth Avenue begins prosperously": Wallace Thurman, "Negro Life in New York's Harlem," *Haldeman-Julius Quarterly*, 1928.

"There Won't Be Any More Liquor"

"Christy, are they . . . going to enforce it?": Walker, *The Night Club Era*, p. 2. M. C. Strachan denounces movie houses as "nurseries of vice": "Harlem Church Votes Expulsion . . . of Any Member Given to Attending Movies or the

Theater," *Age*, Feb. 19, 1927. Movies playing in Harlem in 1927: advertisements in the *Age*. "Harlem's greatest danger": "Mother Zion Pastor Preaches Powerful Sermon . . . ," *Age*, Dec. 3, 1921. Turning Harlem into a Sunday School: "Is Harlem to Become a Chinatown?", *Age*, Oct. 27, 1923. "a wide-open town": "A Wide Open Harlem," *Age*, Sept. 2, 1922. Hooch-selling "drugstores" and the effects of bad whiskey upon Harlemites: See (among several *Age* articles on those subjects) "Harlem, the Hooch Seller's Paradise . . . ," April 21, 1923; and "Poison Hooch Claims Holiday Victims . . . ," Jan. 5, 1924. Fred R. Moore's open letter to church leaders: "Harlem Pastors Are Called upon to Take Position . . . ," *Age*, Oct. 13, 1923. Powell pledges "hearty cooperation": "Ministers of Harlem Are Showing Cooperation," *Age*, Oct. 20, 1923. *Age* prints rumors about clergymen: "Bold Bootlegger Activity in Harlem Causes Thought That Officials Must Profit," Sept. 22, 1923; "Why Are Harlem Ministers Silent on Bootlegging," Sept. 29, 1923. Moore prints threatening letter from bootleggers: "The Bootlegger's Ring Sends Death Threat to Editor . . . ," *Age*, Sept. 23, 1924. "Washtubs and basements": Seale, "The Rise of Harlem as an Amusement Center," *Age*, Nov. 2, 1935.

Streets of Dreams

"Harlem's grafters alone": Crowell, "The World's Largest Negro City." Numbers bankers denounced as "plutocrats": "Clearing House Numbers Gambling Has Invaded All Ranks . . . ," *Age*, May 10, 1924. "Now, here's a number that might come out": "Harlem Church Pastor Tells Members to Play Number of Hymn Announced," *Age*, Nov. 20, 1926. Numbers money in the collection plate: "Clearing House Numbers Gambling Has Invaded All Ranks . . ."

The Saturday Night Function

"Saturday night was a gay time": Bill Chase, "House Rent Parties Were an Institution," *Age*, Oct. 29, 1949. "For many years": Ira De A. Reid, "Mrs. Bailey Pays Her Rent," in *The New Negro Renaissance*, Arthur P. Davis and Michael W. Peplow, eds. (New York: Holt, Rhinehart and Winston, 1975), pp. 164–72. "They would crowd a hundred or more": Smith and Hoefer, *Music on My Mind*, p. 156. "garish extroverts": Maurice Waller and Anthony Calabrese, *Fats Waller* (New York: Collier-Macmillan, 1977), p. 31. Basie became a "daily customer": Nat Shapiro and Nat Hentoff, eds., *Hear Me Talkin' To Ya* (Penguin, 1955), p. 249. "Right after James P.": Shapiro and Hentoff, *Hear Me Talkin' To Ya*, p. 249. "Piano players called": Smith and Hoefer, *Music on My Mind*, pp. 154, 157. "Up in Harlem ev'ry Saturday night": Chris Albertson and Gunther Schuller, *Bessie Smith: Empress of the Blues* (New York: Schirmer Books, 1975), p. 134.

Around Midnight

The Negro was "in the ascendancy": Carl Van Vechten, "Negro Blues Singers," *Vanity Fair*, March 1926. "First, there is the impulse": George Tichenor, "Colored Lines," *Theatre Arts Monthly*, June 1930. "Here the crowd is usually": "Harlem Breakfast Caps Gotham Night," *Daily News*, Oct. 31, 1929; reprinted in *Harlem on My Mind*, p. 81. "*the* place to see 'high Harlem' ": Thurman, "Negro Life in New York's Harlem," *Haldeman-Julius Quarterly*, 1928. Bentley "used to draw the celebrities": Chase, "House Rent Parties Were an Institution," *Age*, Oct. 29, 1949. Romare Bearden recalled Gladys Bentley in an interview. Elmira sings "Stop It, Joe": Charles G. Shaw, *Night Life* (New York: John Day, 1931), p. 79. "the customers . . . varied from tush hogs": Smith and Hoefer, *Music on My Mind*, pp. 166–73. Mexico's proprietor "ran the hottest": Shapiro and Hentoff, *Hear Me Talkin' To Ya*, pp. 228–29. Mezzrow recalls after-hours cutting contests: Milton Mezzrow and Bernard Wolfe, *Really the Blues* (New York: Random House, 1946), p. 231.

"There ain't enough cars": Dicky Wells, *The Night Club People* (Boston: Crescendo Pub. Co., 1971), p. 18. "People would come in": Duke Ellington, *Music Is My Mistress* (New York: Da Capo paperback, 1973), p. 64. "Only members are admitted": Bercovici, "The Black Blocks of Manhattan," *Harper's*, Oct. 1924. Wilkins as "a power" in Harlem: "Barron W. Wilkins Slain," *N.Y. Times*, May 25, 1924; reprinted in *Harlem on My Mind*, pp. 59–60. Connie's Inn "for *whites*": Nancy Cunard, "Harlem Reviewed," in *Negro: An Anthology*, Cunard, ed. (New York: Frederick Ungar, 1970; first published in 1934), p. 50. The *Age* criticizes Connie's Inn for racial policy: "Harvest of Hooch Crimes in Harlem Keep Policemen Busy," Jan. 12, 1924. Connie's patrons included "the piquant": "Socialites Mix in Harlem Club," *Daily News*, Nov. 1, 1929; reprinted in *Harlem on My Mind*, p. 83. "the swankiest of all": Jimmy Durante and Jack Kofoed, *Night Clubs* (New York: Alfred A. Knopf, 1931), p. 115.

Cotton Club as "the hangout for the Mink Set": Edward Jablonski, *Harold Arlen: Happy with the Blues* (New York: Doubleday, 1961), p. 57. "Duke loved the highest of societies": John Hammond, *On Record* (New York: Ridge Press, Summit Books, 1977), p. 137. "The Cotton Club was a classy spot": Ellington, *Music Is My Mistress*, p. 80. Raft "was a sharpie": Smith and Hoefer, *Music on My Mind*, p. 172. "the cream of sepia talent": Jablonski, *Harold Arlen*, p. 54. "The shows had a primitive": Lena Horne (as told to Helen Arstein), *In Person: Lena Horne* (New York: Greenberg Press, 1950), p. 42. "The stage was set up to represent": Mercer Ellington, *Duke Ellington in Person* (Boston: Houghton Mifflin, 1978), p. 44. "Only the tops": Calloway with Rollins, *Minnie the Moocher*, p. 90. "The rivalry went too far": Jablonski, *Harold Arlen*, p. 52. Origins of the Cotton Club: Jim Haskins, *The Cotton Club* (New York: Random House, 1977), pp. 29–30.

"The smart set didn't have Elsa Maxwell": "That Was New York," *New Yorker*, Feb. 17, 1940. Harlem had "attained preeminence": "Is This Really Harlem?" *Harlem on My Mind*, p. 80; reprinted from the *Amsterdam News*, Oct. 23, 1929. "Heavens, how young": "That Was New York," *New Yorker*, Feb. 17, 1940. (Two other useful articles about Harlem's entertainment in its heyday are: Eric Waldrond, "Charleston, Hey! Hey!" *Vanity Fair*, April 1926; and Rudolph Fisher, "The Caucasian Storms Harlem," *American Mercury*, Aug. 1927.)

"The colored bands around New York": Mezzrow and Wolfe, *Really the Blues*, pp. 239–40. "Jazz has really taken Europe": James Weldon Johnson (quoting Mischa Elman), "Views and Reviews," *Age*, July 22, 1922. Darius Milhaud's comments on jazz and music in Harlem are quoted from his autobiography, *Notes without Music* (New York: Alfred A. Knopf, 1953), pp. 135–37. "Milhaud recognized at once": liner notes by Rory Guy for Angel recording S-37442. "Can it be that the Republic": editorial, *American Mercury*, Oct. 1927.

Bye, Bye, Blackbird

"all too slender and slight": Countee Cullen in *Opportunity*, Dec. 1927. "Success never changed her": W. A. Macdonald, "Baby, You've Come Home to Die," Boston *Evening Transcript*, Nov. 7, 1927; reprinted in *A Treasury of Great Reporting*, Louis L. Snyder and Richard B. Morris, eds. (New York: Simon and Schuster, 1949), pp. 461–64. (See also "Rise of Florence Mills," *Age*, Oct. 27, 1923.) "Florence Mills is, within": "George Jean Nathan Pays Tribute to Florence Mills," *Age*, April 17, 1926; reprinted from the *Morning Telegraph*—no date given. "They made a cult of": Martin Green, *Children of the Sun* (New York: Basic Books, 1976), p. 209.

Return from Europe: "Hundreds Throng Dock to Welcome Florence Mills," *Age*, Oct. 1, 1927. "A hundred thousand dollars' worth of flowers": Macdonald, "Baby, You've Come Home to Die." The *Age*'s report of Florence Mills' funeral appeared on Nov. 12, 1927, under the heading "150,000 Throng Harlem to Pay Last Tribute and Honor to Dainty Star Florence Mills." The *N.Y. Times* report, "Scores Collapse at Mills Funeral," appeared on Nov. 7, 1927.

But What Was Harlem?

"a national synonymn for naughtiness": John B. Kennedy, "So This Is Harlem," *Collier's*, Oct. 28, 1933. Most Harlemites as "ordinary, hardworking": Johnson, *Black Manhattan*, p. 161. "the large majority of": Fannie Hurst, "The Other and Unknown Harlem," *N.Y. Times* Sunday Magazine, Aug. 4, 1946.

"What *is* this New Negro?": "New Negro—What Is He?" *Age*, Jan. 24, 1920. *The Messenger* printed a reply, "The New Negro What Is He," in its Aug. 1920 issue. "Samuel Johnson's arguments": interview with Theophilus Lewis. "Athenian conclaves": Schuyler, *Black and Conservative*, p. 144.

Garvey "was so accustomed": Rogers, *World's Great Men of Color*, p. 424. For Randolph's total vote as the Socialist Party's candidate for New York State Comptroller, see *New York State Legislative Manual* (Albany, 1920), p. 154. "When you looked at Randolph": interview with Noble Sissle. "Socialism and trade unionism called for": interview with Randolph.

A Tradition of the New

As McKay later reported: Claude McKay, *A Long Way from Home* (New York: Arno Press, 1969), p. 27. She was "prim, pretty": McKay, *A Long Way from Home*, p. 112. "For a time people were": Chamberlain, "The Negro As Writer," *Bookman*, Sept. 1930. "Between you and me": Chesnutt to Van

Vechten, James Weldon Johnson Memorial Collection at Yale. "A criticism of Negro efforts": "Out of the Shadow," *Opportunity*, May 1925. "We younger Negro artists": Langston Hughes, "The Negro Artist and the Racial Mountain," *Nation*, June 1926. The affair marking "the debut of the younger . . . Negro writers" was reported in *Opportunity* of May 1924, titled "The Debut of the Younger Negro School of Writers." "Mr. Johnson's appearance and background": Blanche Ferguson, *Countee Cullen and the Negro Renaissance* (New York: Dodd, Mead, 1966), p. 86. "a malicious, spiteful": Zora Neale Hurston to James Weldon Johnson, Johnson Memorial Collection at Yale. Locke's ability "to lead a Negro Renaissance" questioned: McKay, *A Long Way from Home*, p. 313.

"I have a genuine faith": Arna Bontemps, ed., *The Harlem Renaissance Remembered* (New York: Dodd, Mead, 1972), pp. 12–14. "Negro life is not only": Alain Locke, ed., *The New Negro* (New York: Atheneum, paper, 1968; first published by Albert and Charles Boni, New York, 1925), p. xvii. "To be a Negro writer was to be": V. F. Calverton, "The Negro and American Culture," *Saturday Review*, Sept. 21, 1940. Among other sources for this chapter are: W. E. B. Du Bois and Alain Locke, "The Younger Literary Movement," *Crisis*, Vol. 27, 1924; Amritjit Singh, *The Novels of the Harlem Renaissance* (Penn. State U. Press, 1976); Benjamin Brawley, *The Negro Genius*; Aaron Douglas, "The Harlem Renaissance as Seen by the Artist," *The Pursuit of a Culture and Human Dignity* (Dillard U., 1970–71); and "High Points of Achievement," *Age*, Jan. 9, 1926.

Some Writers

"Hughes is a cosmopolite": James Weldon Johnson, ed., *The Book of American Negro Poetry* (Harbrace Paperbound Library, 1959), pp. 232–34. "it seemed that no literary magazine": Ferguson, *Countee Cullen and the Negro Renaissance*, p. 41. "infectious beauty" of Cullen's poetry: V. F. Calverton, "The Negro's New Belligerent Attitude," *Current History*, Sept. 1929. Cullen had "an extraordinary ear": Wallace Thurman, "Negro Poets and Their Poetry," *Bookman*, July 1928. John Keats was his "god": Bontemps, *The Harlem Renaissance Remembered*, p. 18. "I am not . . . a democratic person": Cullen to Harold Jackman, Johnson Memorial Collection at Yale. "Cullen says he is interested": "Countee Cullen Wins Second Prize in Poetry Contest . . . ," *Age*, Dec. 8, 1923. Cullen called himself a "rank conservative" in an autobiographical note he wrote for Johnson's *Book of American Negro Poetry*, pp. 219–21. (See also "The Negro as Revealed in His Poetry," *Opportunity*, April 1927; and Harry Alan Potamkin, "Race and a Poet," *New Republic*, Oct. 12, 1927.)

Moved to Harlem "to become a writer": Bontemps, *The Harlem Renaissance Remembered*, pp. 18–19. Bontemps "quiet and scholarly": Langston Hughes, *The Big Sea* (New York: Hill and Wang, American Century Series, 1940), p. 248. "Within a year or two": Bontemps, "The Two Harlems," *American Scholar*, Spring 1945.

"When the Negro art fad": Wallace Thurman, "Negro Artists and the Negro," *New Republic*, Aug. 31, 1927. "Thurman is described": *The Harlem Renaissance Remembered*, pp. 148–49. "The man literally luxuriates": Theophilus Lewis, "Wallace Thurman Is Model Harlemite," *Amsterdam News*, March 4, 1931. "a strangely brilliant": Hughes, *The Big Sea*, p. 234. "I cannot read 'Magic Mountain'" and "The Concerto is spotty": Thurman to Harold Jackman, Johnson Memorial Collection at Yale. Thurman's "pet hates": Lewis, "Wallace Thurman Is Model Harlemite." "wanted to be a great writer": Hughes, *The Big Sea*, p. 234. "A number of things happened": Thurman to William Jourdan Rapp, Johnson Memorial Collection. Thurman's pages "vastly wanting": *The Big Sea*, p. 235.

Fisher the "wittiest of these New Negroes": *The Big Sea*, p. 240. "She was purposely inconsistent": Robert Hemenway, *Zora Neale Hurston* (U. of Illinois Press, 1977), pp. 9, 13. Hurston "was certainly the most amusing": *The Big Sea*, pp. 238–40. "Regardless of race": Fannie Hurst, "Zora Neale Hurston: A Personality Sketch," *Yale University Gazette*, July 1960. "to burn up a lot": *The Big Sea*, pp. 235–36. The flame . . . "was so intense": Brawley, *The Negro Genius*, p. 264. Hurston fictionalized as Sweetie May Car: Wallace Thurman, *Infants of the Spring* (New York: Macaulay, 1932), pp. 229–30.

A "laundry woman": "The Reminiscences of Carl Van Vechten," Oral History Collection, Columbia U. "The Conscious Despair of": Bruce Kellner, *Carl Van Vechten and the Irreverent Decades* (U. of Oklahoma Press, 1968), p. 42. "preoccupied with style": Green, *Children of the Sun*, p. 6. "I especially love your use": Chesnutt to Van Vechten, Johnson Memorial Collection. Kazin's comments on Van Vechten: his *On Native Grounds* (New York: Reynal & Hitchcock), p. 245. The "splendid drunken twenties" and "A close friend of Carl's": Kellner, *The Irreverent Decades*, pp. 3, 219. "a damned good book": Eslanda Goode Robeson to Van Vechten, Johnson Memorial Collection. "resembled a speakeasy": Allen Churchill, *The Literary Decade* (Englewood Cliffs, N.J.: Prentice Hall, 1971), p. 235.

"When you say you intend": Gwendolyn Bennett to Van Vechten, Johnson Memorial Collection. "for so forcible a defense": Cullen to Van Vechten, Johnson Memorial Collection. Benjamin Brawley's and Will Marion Cook's letters to Van Vechten are also at the Johnson Memorial Collection. "whatever falls in with his humor": Edmund Wilson, "A Letter to Elinor Wylie," in *The Shores of Light* (New York: Noonday Press, 1952), p. 260. "the beneficent godfather": Donald Tilden, "This Young Spade," *Herald Tribune*, Oct. 13, 1925. James Weldon Johnson praised Van Vechten's efforts in his *Along This Way*, p. 382.

"were *so* Negro": *The Big Sea*, p. 251. Schuyler recalled Van Vechten's parties in his article, "The Van Vechten Revolution," *Phylon*, Fourth Quarter, 1950. "Along about 1923": "The Reminiscences of Carl Van Vechten," Columbia U. Van Vechten's letter to Gertrude Stein is quoted in Kellner, *The Irreverent Decades*, p. 208.

Sold "100,000 copies": "Reminiscences of Carl Van Vechten." "It is a false book": Diana Trilling, ed., *The Portable D. H. Lawrence* (Viking, 1946), pp. 638–39. "You have never done anything better": Gertrude Stein quoted in *The Irreverent Decades*, p. 221. "a work of art": Fitzgerald to Van Vechten, *The Letters of F. Scott Fitzgerald*, Andrew Turnbull, ed. (New York: Bantam, 1963), p. 496. "an astounding and invaluable": quoted in *The Irreverent Decades*, p. 222. "a thing so rare": Edward Leuders, *Carl Van Vechten and the Twenties* (U. of New Mexico Press, 1955), p. 86.

"I note what you say": Johnson Memorial Collection. "Negroes did not read it": *The Big Sea*, pp. 270–71. "I'd heard of his book": Waters and Samuels, *His Eye Is on the Sparrow*, p. 194. Van Vechten to James Weldon Johnson and Charles Johnson to Van Vechten, Johnson Memorial Collection. "I have myself never spoken": *The Irreverent Decades*, pp. 210–11. He himself never used the word: "Reminiscences of Carl Van Vechten."

"While this informal epithet": Van Vechten, *Nigger Heaven* (New York: Grosset & Dunlap/Alfred A. Knopf, 1926), p. 26. "Nigger Heaven! That's what Harlem is": *Nigger Heaven*, p. 149. W. E. B. Du Bois' attack on Van Vechten's novel appeared in *The Crisis*, Dec. 1926, in a column titled "Books." "an absorbing story": James Weldon Johnson, "Romance and Tragedy in Harlem," *Opportunity*, Oct. 1926. "sympathetically and amusingly": *The Big Sea*, pp. 270–71. "I do not like Mr. Du Bois's book": Johnson Memorial Collection.

Seized by the "vagabond" spirit, etc.: McKay, *A Long Way from Home*, p. 4. McKay "seems to have a greater": "Claude McKay," *Liberator*, July 1919. He "resembled a portrait of": Claude McKay, *Selected Poems* (New York: Harcourt Brace Jovanovich, Harvest Book, 1953), p. 7. "No Negro poet has sung more": James Weldon Johnson, "A Real Poet," *Age*, May 20, 1922. McKay explained his reasons for visiting Russia: *A Long Way from Home*, pp. 321–22. "You ought to be here": Johnson Memorial Collection. "The Johnson letter": *A Long Way from Home*, pp. 306–7. "was so general" and "exploited Negroes": *A Long Way from Home*, pp. 307, 315–19. Du Bois' scathing review of McKay's novel appeared in the June 1928 issue of *The Crisis*, headed "The Browsing Reader." To contain "the rhythm of life": John Chamberlain, "When Spring Comes to Harlem," Sunday *N.Y. Times*, March 11, 1928. "nowhere in your writings": Herbert Aptheker, ed., *The Correspondence of W. E. B. Du Bois*, Vol. 1. (U. of Mass. Press, 1973), p. 375. "I have not deviated": Johnson Memorial Collection. "I felt that the masses": *The Big Sea*, p. 267. "The Harlem school writers": Robert Bone, *The Negro Novel in America* (New Haven: Yale U. Press, paper, 1958), p. 107.

A'Lelia Walker

"read like a blue book": "Royalty and Blue-Blooded Gentry Entertained by A'Lelia Walker . . . ," *Amsterdam News*, Aug. 26, 1931. "Quite often, when the matter" and "prominent individuals": "Royalty and Blue-Blooded Gentry Entertained by A'Lelia Walker . . ." "Most of the furniture": Van Vechten, *Nigger Heaven*, p. 79. "a brilliant affair": "Mme. A'Lelia Walker Entertains Friends," *Age*, Dec. 20, 1924. "There will be no more" and "looked like an Ethiopian princess": "Royalty and Blue-Blooded Gentry Entertained by A'Lelia Walker . . ." "She was undeniably warmhearted": *Nigger Heaven*, pp. 27–28.

A'Lelia Walker's marriages: "Weds Three Days after Burial of Her Mother," *Age*, June 14, 1919; "A'Lelia Walker's Third Husband Gets Divorce," *Age*, April 25, 1931. Wedding of Mae Walker Robinson: "Marriage of New York Heiress to Chicago Physician," *Age*, Dec. 1, 1923. "I have been holding on to": Johnson Memorial Collection. Villa Lewaro's furnishings sold at auction: Bessye Bearden, "Valuables Bought by Those Who Opposed Mansion on Hudson," Chicago *Defender*, Dec. 6, 1930. (See also "Throngs Attend Auction Sale . . . in Mme. Walker Villa Lewaro," *Age*, Dec. 6, 1930; "Villa Lewaro . . . Sold at Last," *Age*, March 5, 1932.)

Funeral of A'Lelia Walker: "Huge Throng Mills about While Plane Hovers over Scene," *Amsterdam News*, Aug. 26, 1931; Hughes, *The Big Sea*, pp. 245–47. Her death "was really the end" and "That Spring": *The Big Sea*, pp. 247, 334.

The Beat Goes On

According to Cab Calloway: Calloway with Rollins, *Minnie the Moocher*, pp. 71–72. "Lighthearted throngs": article in an unidentified newspaper, quoted in *Age* (editorial), Feb. 28, 1931. Stunned by the "abundance": "Attention Harlem Women," *Age*, May 12, 1934. A "glittering" occasion: Vere Johns, "New Colored Picture with Bill Bojangles Robinson," *Age*, May 28, 1932; "Colored Stars Make Good in New Picture," *Age*, June 4, 1932; " 'Harlem Is Heaven' Has Brilliant World Premiere . . . ," *Age*, June 4, 1932.

"a sympathetic old hall": Nancy Cunard, "Harlem Reviewed," in *Negro*, p. 49. Frank Schiffman and Leo Brecher as Harlem theatre owners: Jack Schiffman, *Uptown: The Story of Harlem's Apollo Theatre* (New York: Cowles, 1971), early chapters. "mark a revolutionary step": advertisement in *Age*, Jan. 27, 1934. "the entire absence of": Vere Johns, "In the Name of Art," *Age*, Feb. 3, 1934. "His main attraction is his gags": Abram Hill, "The Comedian 'Pigmeat' Markham," W.P.A. Writers Program research paper at the Schomburg Center. Markham's hotel sketch and critical reaction: Vere Johns, "In the Name of Art," *Age*, June 2, 1934. Ella Fitzgerald adopted by Chick Webb: Schiffman, *Uptown*, p. 173. Billie Holiday discovered: Hammond, *On Record*, p. 92. "not all white people came": Ruth L. Saul, letter to the author. "A group of us moved together": interview with Romare Bearden.

Sunny Gets Blue

"produced five times as much unemployment": Beverly Smith, "Harlem's Distress Intensified . . . ," *Herald Tribune*, Feb. 10, 1930. Families on Home Relief: "19,000 Harlem Families Were on Home Relief during Month of June . . . ," *Age*, Aug. 18, 1934. The New York Urban League estimated: quoted in "Picturing Harlem," *Age*, March 1932. "The stock market crash": Warren J. Halliburton and Ernest Kaiser, *Harlem: A History of Broken Dreams* (New York: Doubleday, Zenith Books, 1974), pp. 54–56. Abyssinian Baptist Bureau served: Powell, *Against the Tide*, p. 199; "More Than 600 Find Employment Through Abyssinian Relief Bureau," *Age*, Jan. 17, 1931.

Night clubs aid the jobless: "Edwin Smalls Presents 'Cabaret Night' to Aid Unemployed," *Age*, March 7, 1931; "Harlem Outdoes Itself," *Age*, Dec. 29, 1934. Small restaurants carried signs: "Depression Brings Harlem Better Food . . . ," *Amsterdam News*, Nov. 4, 1931. "At lunchtime, the bars had": interview with Bayard Rustin. Food price list: quoted in "The Forgotten Housewife," *Age*, July 22, 1933. (See also "Food Rackets in Harlem . . . ," *Age*, May 12, 1934.)

From ten to twenty evictions: James Hubert, "Harlem Faces Unemployment," *Opportunity*, Feb. 1931. "the Communists . . . put up": Cunard,

"Harlem Reviewed," *Negro*, p. 54. Brotherhood of Sleeping Car Porters evicted: "Porters Brotherhood Dispossessed . . . ," *Age*, Sept. 16, 1933; "The Reminiscences of Benjamin McLaurin," Oral History Collection, Columbia U. Outbreak of 1935 rioting ("The man who was bitten"): Hamilton Basso, "The Riot in Harlem," *New Republic*, April 3, 1935.

The Lord Will Provide

"There are something like": Johnson, *Black Manhattan*, p. 163. "a thick underbrush": Robert A. Parker, *The Incredible Messiah* (Boston: Little, Brown, 1937), p. 50. "No, we haven't too many churches": quoted in Ira De A. Reid, "Let Us Prey," *Opportunity*, Sept. 1926. "The big churches were too calm": interview with Rustin. Any storefront preacher "with a panacea": "Job Campaign Drives," *Age*, May 7, 1938.

"the first of the great cult leaders": Claude McKay, *Harlem*, p. 83. "exquisite smartness" (and other descriptions of Becton by Nancy Cunard), "Harlem Reviewed," in *Negro*, pp. 50–52. Women "swayed like reeds": McKay, *Harlem*, p. 84. "Dr. Becton had an envelope system": Hughes, *The Big Sea*, p. 277. His "golden slippers", etc., McKay, *Harlem*, p. 84. McKay also refers to Becton's death on p. 85 of *Harlem*.

Father Divine's trial and imprisonment: Sara Harris, *Father Divine* (New York: Collier Books, paper, 1971), pp. 40–41. "He is around sixty now": St. Clair McKelway and A. J. Liebling, "Who Is the King of Glory," *New Yorker*, June 13, 1936. "I teach now as of": "10,000 Crowd Rockland Palace to Hear Father Major Divine . . . ," *Age*, Dec. 26, 1931. "At this moment": "Observations Made on a First Visit to Father Divine's Meetings," *Age*, April 9, 1932. "And there sat 'God' ": William Pickens, "Whatever Happens in the Future . . . God's Gone to Town," *Age*, June 1, 1940. "Father Divine is going to close": quoted in "10,000 Crowd Rockland Palace . . . ," *Age*, Dec. 26, 1931. "a sham and a delusion": "Bishop Lawson Denounces Divine," *Age*, Jan. 30, 1931. See also "Father Divine Says He's Leaving Harlem," *Age*, July 25, 1942.

"Some critics of the Negro": Johnson, *Black Manhattan*, p. 163. The purchase prices and building costs of expensive Harlem church buildings appeared regularly in the *Age* between 1910 and 1930. Study by the Greater New York Federation of Churches: *Negro Churches of Manhattan*, 1930, pp. 10–28. "The burden is entirely": "Graft among the Preachers," *Age*, March 24, 1923. "The wealth drawn from": "The Church Should Aid in Making Opportunities," *Amsterdam News* (letter to the editor), Nov. 4, 1931. "to the point of suffocation": "Buildings Erected by New York's Negro Congregations Too Costly," *Age*, April 25, 1925. "The church has never been": "Mt. Olivet Defends Building Fine Structures . . . ," *Age*, May 9, 1925. "vanity and value": "Cornerstone Laid for New Abyssinian Church House," Age, July 1, 1922. "the greatest Protestant center": *Negro Churches of Manhattan*, p. 10.

Men of great "magnetism": Beverly Smith, "Harlem—the Negro City." *Herald Tribune*, Feb. 11, 1930. (See also William L. Welty, "Black Shepherds: A Study of the Leading Negro Clergymen in New York City, 1900–1940," Ph.D. dissertation, N.Y.U., 1969.) "The pastor, a tall": Bercovici. "The Black Blocks of Manhattan." Adam Clayton Powell, Sr., and the social gospel: He wrote during the thirties ("The Church in Social Work," *Opportunity*, Jan. 1923): "The church which will grip and hold men in the future will be the church that vitally relates itself to every problem of the masses." "A Hungry God": quoted in Powell, *Against the Tide*, p. 198; "Dr. A. Clayton Powell Starts Drive among Abyssinian Church Members to Relieve Unemployment Situation." *Age*, Dec. 6, 1930. "the stringency of the times": "Rev. William P. Hayes Refuses Raise in Salary," *Age*, Jan. 24, 1931. "Pastor Sims states": "Rev. George Sims Takes Issue with Rev. A. Clayton Powell with Regard to Charges Made against Clergy," *Age*, Jan. 3, 1931. "Under Adam Clayton Powell": Ben Richardson, "Adam Clayton Powell, Sr.," in *Great American Negroes* (New York: Crowell, 1956), p. 209.

"a killer with the girls": Neil Hickey and Ed Edwin, *Adam Clayton Powell and the Politics of Race* (New York: Fleet, 1965). "My father was always": Claude Lewis, *Adam Clayton Powell* (Greenwich, Conn.: Gold Medal Books/Fawcett, 1963), p. 14. Powell's defiant remarks about Communists and their reception at Abyssinian Baptist Church: "Rev. A. Clayton Powell, Jr., Declares Himself On Communism; Will Quit If His Church Debars Radicals," *Age*, June 3, 1933. "there was not a dissenting voice": Powell, *Against the Tide*, pp. 286–87. "Abyssinian membership divided": Hickey and Edwin, *Adam Clayton Powell and the Politics of Race*, p. 49. "He may be counted on": *Against the Tide*, p. viii. "My father said": Adam Clayton Powell, Jr., *Marching Blacks* (New York: Dial, 1945), p. 92.

The Depression and the Arts

"She sacrificed herself": interview with Romare Bearden. "attracted the gifted children": Romare Bearden and Harry Henderson, *Six Black Masters of American Art* (New York: Doubleday, Zenith Books, 1972), pp. 93–94. Kenneth B. Clark's recollections of Augusta Savage: interview. "She was dark": interview with Rustin. "a new voice": Milton W. Brown, "Jacob Lawrence," in *Jacob Lawrence* (New York: Dodd, Mead, 1974), p. 10. "If I weren't painting": interview with Jacob Lawrence. "I have created nothing": *Six Black Masters of American Art*, p. 96.

A discussion of black playwrights and their work in the twenties and thirties is contained in Doris E. Abramson, *Negro Playwrights in the American Theatre*: 1925–1959 (New York: Columbia U. Press, 1967). "Of all the artists": John O'Connor and Larraine Brown, eds., *Free, Adult, Uncensored: The Living History of the Federal Project* (Wash., D.C.: New Republic Books, 1978), p. 1. "Such a theatre could": Rose McClendon, "As to a Negro Theatre" (letter to the editor), *N.Y. Times*, Sec. 10, June 30, 1935. "At the first meeting": Hallie Flanagan, *Arena: The History of the Federal Theatre* (New York: Benjamin Bloom, 1940), p. 63. Flanagan's appointment of John Houseman is also recalled in the latter's autobiography, *Run Through* (New York: Curtis Books, paper, 1972), p. 175. "some semblance of respectability": *Run Through*, p. 182. "The Negro Theatre will do": "Federal Aid for Negro Theatre in Harlem is Assured . . . ," *Age*, Nov. 30, 1935. "those classical and modern masterpieces": "Federal Aid for Negro Theatre in Harlem is Assured . . ." "the first full-scale": *Run Through*, p. 190. Welles told Bosley Crowther of the *N.Y. Times: Run Through*, pp. 197–98. "Our supernatural department": *Run Through*, p. 189. Opening-night comments by a Harlem reporter and a review in the *N.Y. Times* are quoted in *Run Through*, pp. 198–200. "As the Great Depression lifted": *Free, Adult, Uncensored*, p. x.

"Viewed in the perspective": Run Through, pp. 209–10. American Negro Theatre "trained over two hundred": Loften Mitchell, ed., *Voices of the Black Theatre* (New Jersey: James T. White, 1975), p. 118.

"The emergence of Richard Wright": Jerre Mangione, *The Dream and the Deal* (Boston: Little, Brown, 1972), pp. 255–56. "Leaving the blare and glare": Richard Wright, "What Happens at a Communist Party Branch Meeting in the Harlem Section," *Daily Worker*, Aug. 16, 1937. "until I get my second": "Negro W.P.A. Writer Sees Prize Winning Book Placed on Sale," *Age*, May 14, 1938. "At the time": Ellison, "The Crisis of Optimism," in *The City in Crisis* (A. Philip Randolph Institute, 1968). "I had been reading lots": Constance Webb, *Richard Wright: A Biography* (New York: Putnam, 1968), p. 405. "terribly curious about": Webb, *Richard Wright*, pp. 145–46.

In the Ring with Joe

"magnetic and disturbing": Geraldyn Dismond, "Joe Louis Doesn't Play/ Emily Post Games," *Age*, July 6, 1935. Prominent Harlemites at Louis' fight with Carnera: "Louis-Carnera Bout Draws 15,000 Negroes, 1,300 Police," *Herald Tribune*, June 23, 1935; reprinted in *Harlem on My Mind*, pp. 139–40. For various Harlem reactions to Louis' fights during the thirties, see the following items in the *Age*: "The Sport Dial," June 27, 1936; "Joe Louis Is King Again," Aug. 22, 1936; "Suspense" (letter to the editor), Sept. 5, 1936; "Say Joe Fought under Orders," Sept. 4, 1937; "Is Joe Slipping?" Sept. 11, 1937; "Joe Louis, Wife Going to Europe," July 2, 1938; "The Digest," June 11, 1938; "Too Much Enthusiasm" (editorial), July 2, 1938; "An Inspiration to Youth" (editorial), June 25, 1938. See also "100,000 Celebrate Louis Victory over Braddock," *N.Y. Times*, June 22, 1937; reprinted in *Harlem on My Mind*, p. 144. Louis visits President Roosevelt, comments upon the support of Southern lynchers, is inducted into the Army: Edna and Art Rust, *Joe Louis: My Life* (New York: Harcourt Brace Jovanovich: 1978), pp. 137, 172.

Another War, Another Time

"no place in the nation": "Harlem Buzzes wth Civilian Defense Tasks," *Life*, June 15, 1942. "Irritated black people": Loften Mitchell, *Black Drama* (New York: Hawthorne Books, 1967), p. 112. "The people there have asked": Charles Williams, "Harlem at War," *Nation*, Jan. 16, 1943. "Hope with me": "In Which Archie Waters Writes of His Enlistment in the Army" (letter to the editor), *Age*, Aug. 8, 1942. "It had been announced": *American Labor*, Aug. 1968.

"Randolph more nearly": Ludlow Werner, "Across the Desk," *Age*, April 29, 1944. "the matinee idol of the pulpit": Irwin Ross, "Adam Clayton Powell, Jr.," *N.Y. Post*, March 26, 1956. "Charging that a nightclub": "Rev. Powell's Wife Sues for Separation . . . ," *Age*, Nov. 25, 1944. Months later: "Hazel Scott Weds Adam Powell . . . ," *Age*, Aug. 11, 1945. "an incredible combination": Roi Ottley, *New World A-Coming* (New York: Arno Press, 1969), pp. 220–21. "the strong anti-Powell bloc": "To Draft Randolph for Congress," *Age*, April 15, 1944. Did not "wish to become involved": "Randolph Turns Down Congress," *Age*, April 22, 1944. "By preferring to remain": Ludlow Werner, "Across the Desk," *Age*, April 29, 1944. "Financially, he will": Adam

Clayton Powell, Sr., *Riots and Ruins* (New York: Richmond K. Smith, 1945), p. 134.

Harlem Explodes

"a reassuring picture": from an article by Evelyn Seely in *PM*, Aug. 3, 1943; quoted in Dominic J. Capeci, *The Harlem Riot of 1934* (Phila.: Temple U. Press, 1977), p. 98. "were greeted with raucous shouts": Walter White, *A Man Called White* (Indiana U. Press, paper, 1948), p. 237. "the hottest hell ever": Powell, *Riots and Ruins*, pp. 43–56. (See also "Riot Rocks Harlem," *Age*, Aug. 7, 1943; an editorial in the same issue; Margaret Marshall, "Some Notes on Harlem," *Nation*, Aug. 21, 1943; Kenneth B. Clark and James Barker, "The Zoot Effect in Personality: A Race Riot Participant," *Journal of Abnormal and Social Psychology*, April 1945.)

"ingrown toenail," "On the morning of the 3rd," and "I truly had not realized": James Baldwin, title essay in *Notes of a Native Son* (Boston: Beacon Press, paper, 1955), pp. 85–114. "A soldier in uniform": *Riots and Ruins*, p. 45, quoting Roy Wilkins' article in *The Crisis*, Sept. 1943.

The West Indians

"a distinctly American product": "West Indian and Southern Negroes Adjust to Rivalries," *Herald Tribune*, Feb. 14, 1930; reprinted in *Harlem on My Mind*, pp. 128–29. West Indians "notably lacking": Crowell, "The World's Largest Negro City." "Dr. Murcot Wilshire": "Coronation Ball," *New Yorker*, May 22, 1937. West Indians not "averse to having a white pastor": *The Negro Churches of Manhattan*, p. 7.

"Coming to the United States": W. A. Domingo, "Gift of the Tropics," in *The New Negro*, pp. 344–45. "as though it were a racial genius": Crowell, "The World's Largest Negro City." Were "like the Jew": Domingo, "Gift of the Tropics." "In no other land": "Success Story" (editorial), *Age*, May 16, 1942. West Indians comprising a third of the professionals in Harlem: "Well Caught, Mr. Holder," *New Yorker*, Sept. 25, 1954.

"In proportion to their numbers": Carter G. Woodson, "The Contribution of the West Indian to America . . . ," *Age*, Oct. 31, 1931. "forged ahead faster": Powell, *Marching Blacks*, pp. 80–81. "likened to the Jews": "Factors in the Cultural Background of the American Southern Negro and the British West Indian Negro That Condition Their Adjustment in Harlem," M.A. Thesis, Columbia U., 1936. "If you West Indians don't like": "West Indians Protest Speech by Courier Editor," *Age*, March 17, 1934. Some West Indians scolded their fellow islanders: Vere Johns, "Through My Spectacles," *Age*, Oct. 21, 1933. Were always "falling out about": Cunard, "Harlem Reviewed," *Negro*, p. 48. "West Indian Negroes, you are oppressed": quoted in Ira De A. Reid, *The Negro Immigrant* (New York: Columbia U. Press, 1939), p. 123.

At the Savoy

"28 million feet": "The Home of the Happy Feet," *Ebony*, Oct. 1946. *The Savoy Story* is a commemorative booklet produced by the ballroom's management in 1951. "When one enters": "Fletcher Henderson . . . at the Savoy," *Age*, March 6, 1926. "Royalty from Europe": *Ebony*, Oct. 1946. "Sober white citizens": Maurice Zolotow, "Harlem's Great White Father," *Saturday Evening*

Post, Sept. 27, 1941. "There were maybe ten or twelve": "Laying Down Some Leather," *New Yorker*, Feb. 15, 1969.

"The best band" and "if you didn't swing": Wells, *Night People*, p. 59. "I was furious with the guys": Calloway with Rollins, *Minnie the Moocher*, pp. 72–73. "We didn't give a damn": Jervis Anderson, "Going to the Territory," *New Yorker*, Nov. 22, 1976. "The Southwestern style": Marshall Stearns, *The Story of Jazz* (New York: Oxford U. Press, 1956), p. 189. "The only time we were bothered": *The Story of Jazz*, p. 204. Webb's command of his audiences: Ellington, *Music Is My Mistress*, p. 99. (See also Otis Ferguson, "Breakfast Dance in Harlem," *New Republic*, Feb. 12, 1936.)

"Chick Webb would just lay": Wells, *Night People*, pp. 34–35. "the acknowledged King": Shapiro and Hentoff, *Hear Me Talkin' To Ya*, p. 194. "He was the first drummer who": Stanley Dance, ed., *The World of Duke Ellington* (New York: Scribner's, 1970), p. 196. "the most luminous": *Hear Me Talkin' To Ya*, p. 195. "battled mounted cops": "A Great Spectacle" (editorial), *Age*, May 21, 1937. Charters and Kunstadt describe the Goodman-Webb battle royal in their *Jazz*, p. 259. "a sickly hunchback": Charters and Kunstadt, *Jazz* p. 254. He was "always in pain": Ted Yates, "Ella Fitzgerald Found Her 'Yellow Basket' ", *Age*, Oct. 2, 1943. Recollections of Charles Buchanan: interview.

"Cool Deal, McNeil"

Rare copies of Cab Calloway's *Hepster's Dictionary* and Dan Burley's *Original Handbook of Jive* may be found at the Schomburg Center in Harlem. "And what's on the rail": Burley, "Back Door Stuff," *Age*, March 5, 1949. "True jive is not the stereotyped": Stanley Frank, "The Jive Is On," *Negro Digest*, July 1944; condensed from an article in *Esquire*, no date given. "This jive is a private affair": Mezzrow and Wolfe, *Really the Blues*, p. 215. *The New Yorker* describes the zoot suit: "Down to the Bricks," April 12, 1941.

"Only 40 suits": Earl Wilson, "Cab's Haberdashery," *Negro Digest*, Oct. 1943; condensed from the N.Y. *Post*, no date given. In August 1943, an article in *Negro Digest* reported that most zoot suits were then selling for $33.50 ("Origin of the Zoot Suit"). "more grease in their hair than": Archie Seale, "New York Town," *Age*, Feb. 8, 1947. "a shark-skin gray" and "the ghetto's Cadillac": *The Autobiography of Malcolm X* (New York: Grove Press, paper, 1964), pp. 78, 79. "What could she have thought": *Autobiography of Malcolm X*, p. 65.

Seventh Avenue: The Great Black Way

Harlem's "most representative" avenue: Thurman, "Negro Life in New York's Harlem." "In Harlem he is called": Cecil Beaton, *Portrait of New York* (London: B. T. Batsford, 1938), p. 104. "If we couldn't find a book": Daniel H. Watts, "Rockefeller's Negroes," *Liberator*, June 1967. *Ebony*'s articles on the Theresa hotel ("The Waldorf of Harlem") appeared on April 1, 1946. For a report on one of Father Divine's marches, see "Father Divine's Followers Stage Colorful Easter Parade," *Age*, April 7, 1934. The Elks on Seventh Avenue: "30,000 Negro Elks Parade," *N.Y. Times*, Aug. 24, 1927; reprinted in *Harlem on My Mind*, p. 71.

"Now that Fifth Avenue": "Color", *New Yorker*, Oct. 9, 1926. "sleek black carouls," etc.: Ardenne Duane, "Style Chats," *Age*, Dec. 31, 1932. "My Gawd—did you see that hat?": Rudolph Fisher, *The Walls of Jericho* (New York: Arno Press, 1969), pp. 188–90. "the creme de la creme": "Father Divine's Followers . . . ," *Age*, April 7, 1934. "One puts on one's best": Johnson, *Black Manhattan*, p. 163.

Society

"Harlem's best society": "Libeling Harlem Society" (editorial), *Age*, Jan. 30, 1926. "Harlem society in its full meaning": "Dr. E. P. Roberts . . . Given Reception by Family," *Age*, July 1, 1941. "Even if they did not act": E. Franklin Frazier, *Black Bourgeoisie* (New York: Collier Books, 1962), p. 165. "There are near-white cliques": Cunard, "Harlem Reviewed," *Negro*, p. 53. "He was a dignified": Will Chasan, "Harlem's Aristocracy," *American Mercury*, June 1947. Calloway in society, but not Ellington: "Harlem," *Fortune*, July 1939. "Bill Robinson": "Bojangles," *New Yorker*, Oct. 6, 1934.

"The Negro fast set": Van Vechten, *Nigger Heaven*, p. 226. "They didn't buy paintings": interview with Romare Bearden. "Although they may pretend": Frazier, *Black Bourgeoisie*, p. 172. The "only bond": "Is Negro Society Phony?" *Ebony*, Sept. 1953. "[They are] the more successful": Thurman, "Negro Life in New York's Harlem."

On Strivers Row and Sugar Hill

For origins of Strivers Row, see "St. Nicholas Historic District . . . ," Landmarks Preservation Commission, New York, March 16, 1967. "Concentrated in 'Strivers Row' ": Powell, *Marching Blacks*, p. 81. "Class divisions defined": Frank Hercules, "The Decline and Fall of Sugar Hill," *Herald Tribune*, Feb. 28, 1965. "acquainted personally": Langston Hughes, "Down Under in Harlem," *Negro Digest*, June 1944; condensed from *The New Republic*, no date given. "Jews tend not to run": interview with Bayard Rustin.

"The most exciting facet": "Sugar Hill," *Ebony*, Nov. 1946. A black visitor . . . found: Abram Hill, "Sugar Hill," W.P.A. Writers Program research paper at the Schomburg Center. "Harlem's would-be 'sassiety' ": Adam Clayton Powell, Jr., "Harlem Declares Its Rent Too High," *Post*, March 28, 1935. "Mme. Stephanie St. Clair": "Mme. Stephanie St. Clair Held in $2500 Bail . . . ," *Age*, Jan. 4, 1930. Police raid fashionable Park Lincoln: "Theatrical Entertainer Admits Burglarizing . . . ," *Age*, Aug. 18, 1934. "We lived in a wonderful apartment": interview with Jane White. (See also "The White House," *Ebony*, April 1946.)

The Thrill Is Gone

"In the twenties": interview with Kenneth B. Clark. "In the years after": John Henrik Clarke, ed., *Harlem U.S.A.* (New York: Seven Seas Books, 1964), p. 14. He found it to be "another place": Bontemps, "The Two Harlems." The "suburban Sugar Hill": "Celebrities Seek Quiet Rest and Privacy in St. Alban's," *Ebony*, Sept. 1951. "The heyday of Negro entertainment": Bill Chase, "What's Wrong with Our Show Business," *Age*, Aug. 1949. "Why Do You Live in Harlem?": Camera Quiz, *Age*, April 29, 1950.

Acknowledgments

In addition to sources cited in the Notes, several individuals and institutions contributed indispensably to the completion of this work.

For correspondence, interviews, and helpful suggestions, I wish to thank Clifford Alexander, Sr., Ada Bastian, Romare Bearden, Howard Bennett, Eubie Blake, Charles Buchanan, Philip Butcher, Dr. Kenneth B. Clark, Stanley Dance, Charles C. Hart, John Hewett, Brenda Huggins, Nathan Irving Huggins, Ruth Jett, James W. Johnson, Madison Jones, June Kelly, Jacob Lawrence, Theophilus Lewis, Margaret Magie, Harry Roberson, Bayard Rustin, Ruth L. Saul, George S. Schuyler, Louis Sheaffer, Bobby Short, Noble Sissle, William J. Sowder, and Jane White (Mrs. Alfred Viazzi).

My search for documentary and illustrative material relied heavily on the resources of the Schomburg Center for Research in Black Culture, based in Harlem. I am especially grateful to those of its staff members—among them Betty Gubert, Jean Blackwell Hutson, Ernest Kaiser, Yvette LeRoy, Valerie Sandoval, and Deborah Willis-Thomas—who gave me more of their time than their formal duties required. I am also indebted to the main branch of the New York Public Library; the late Donald C. Gallup, curator of the James Weldon Johnson Memorial Collection at the Beinecke Rare Book Library, Yale University; the Special Collection and the Oral History Collection of the Butler Library, Columbia University; the Bobst Library of New York University; Mary Horowitz, who often interrupted her studies at the NYU Law School to assist me with the research; Hazel Hertzberg of Teachers College, Columbia University; John C. Broderick of the Manuscript Division of the Library of Congress; Dorothy Gilliam of *The Washington Post*; C. Gerald Fraser of *The New York Times*; Helen Stark, librarian at *The New Yorker*; Una Mulzac of the Liberation Bookstore in Harlem; Laura Lane Masters of the American Heritage Publishing Company; the Presbyterian Historical Society in Philadelphia; Nick Caruso of the New York County Clerk's Office; Dan Dawson and Cheryl Shackleton of the Studio Museum in Harlem; the New-York Historical Society and the Museum of the City of New York; Maria Zini of the Carnegie Library, Pittsburgh; Clifton H. Johnson of the Amistad Research Center, Dillard University; Ann Allen Shockley of the Fisk University Library; Carolyn Davis of the George Arent Research Library, Syracuse University; and Nancy Goeschel of the New York City Landmarks Preservation Commission.

I thank Paul Brodeur of *The New Yorker* for suggesting that I attempt this work. I would not, however, have been able to undertake or complete it without the approval, guidance, and support of William Shawn, the editor of *The New Yorker*. Nor would it have been easy for me to accomplish the task without the generous assistance of the Simon Guggenheim Memorial Foundation, which granted me a Fellowship in 1978. Here I must also record my gratitude to Whitney Balliett, Joseph Epstein, Ved Mehta, Richard Rovere, and Bayard Rustin for recommending me highly to the Guggenheim Foundation.

Ronald Sanders and Beverly Sanders helped to sustain my enthusiasm by constantly sharing with me their special excitement for aspects of New York's and Harlem's social history. The manuscript also benefited from their criticisms.

As a year-round resident of Manhattan, I am grateful to the late Dr. Robert P. Kemble and his widow, Luella, who frequently extended me the gracious, spacious, and tranquil appointments of their home in South Hadley, Massachusetts, where I wrote large portions of the manuscript.

The factual accuracies of this work owe much to the rigorous investigative and corrective skills of Richard Sacks and David Thigpen of *The New Yorker*'s fact-checking department. Its text bears, secretly, the improvements of Charles Patrick Crow, my editor at *The New Yorker*, and Patricia Strachan, my editor at Farrar, Straus and Giroux. And its appearance as a book is deeply indebted to my agent, Robert Lescher, who—in his deft and deceptively easy fashion—ran more interferences in its behalf than I am able to thank him for.

J.A.

Index